The Sting of Life

Modern Asian Literature Series

The Sting of Life

Four Contemporary Japanese Novelists

Van C. Gessel

Columbia University Press New York

COLUMBIA UNIVERSITY PRESS
NEW YORK OXFORD

The Press acknowledges a grant from the University of California
toward the cost of publishing this volume.

LIBRARY OF CONGRESS CATALOGING-IN-PUBLICATION DATA

Gessel, Van C.
The sting of life: four contemporary Japanese novelists /
by Van C. Gessel.
p. cm. —(Modern Asian literature series)
Bibliography: p.
Includes index.
ISBN 0-231-06850-6
1. Japanese fiction—20th century—History and criticism.
I. Title. II. Series.
PL747.65.G47 1989
895.6'35'09—dc19 88–36598
CIP

Photographs in the text have been graciously provided by:
Shimao Miho, Endō Shūsaku, Yasuoka Shōtarō and Kōdansha Publishing Company.

Book design by Charles Hames

Printed in the United States of America

Casebound editions of Columbia University Press books are Smyth-sewn
and printed on permanent and durable acid-free paper

For Elizabeth

Contents

Preface
ix

One
Demobilization of the Literary Self
1

Two
Collapse of the Literary Group
33

Three
The Loss of Home: Yasuoka Shōtarō
75

Four
The Eternal War: Shimao Toshio
125

Five
Human Handicapped: Kojima Nobuo
181

Six
Salvation of the Weak: Endō Shūsaku
231

Afterword:
An All-But-Lost Generation
283

Notes
289

Bibliography
305

Index
315

Preface

FROM THE outset of my studies of modern Japanese literature, I have been interested in the kinds of narrative structures that various authors employ in their attempts to describe Japan's experience of war, defeat, and foreign occupation. This problem of form has many dimensions, but in recent years I have been most intrigued by the stubborn survival of the *shi-shōsetsu,* the semi-autobiographical fiction often translated as the "I-novel." Its reappearance in the postwar period is controversial, since many voices after the defeat made it abundantly clear that they regarded the form, with its traditional disregard of social issues and its narrow focus on private experience, utterly useless to describe the demise of individual will and prerogative which the war and its aftermath so abundantly demonstrated. The authors who began writing immediately after the war (who will be discussed below as the "Sengoha," or the postwar generation) insisted from a Marxist orientation that the chief mandate of a new postwar literature had to be the depiction of individuals subject to and manipulated by historical and social forces larger than any personal concerns.

Despite all this discussion, however, the *shi-shōsetsu* underwent a revival, and literary responses to the war and defeat began to take the form of minimalist stories that described confused, awkward people who seemed to lack the ability to think about Japan's recent traumas; they could only live through them on the emotional—or, perhaps more accurately, physiological—level. Stories of this nature began to appear with increasing frequency, interestingly enough, right around the time that the American Occupation came to an end in 1952.

The challenge of interpreting stories of this nature and, more importantly for me, the problem of trying to determine why the autobiographical narrative was resuscitated have been the focus of my studies for the past decade. I commenced with the naive assumption that an I-novel is an I-novel; that the postwar version, though drawing from very different materials, would still largely concentrate on the straightforward presentation of the narrator/author's subjective experience; and that this would largely remain uncluttered by the attempt to provide perspective on that experience.

As I read the fiction of several authors, however, my sense of what was being conducted in the new *shi-shōsetsu* changed radically. Writers such as Yasuoka Shōtarō, Shimao Toshio, Kojima Nobuo, and Endō Shūsaku—each of whom is discussed in detail in this book—have injected something entirely new into a rather tired literary form. They have brought to the *shi-shōsetsu* a vigorous sense of irony—or, if you will, a split perspective which allows them to describe and simultaneously to undercut their personal experiences. This subtle but tremendously important shift in technique allows them to create quiet, unruffled surfaces to their narratives, while intimating the anxieties that flow just beneath. The "I" of their autobiographical fictions is displaced and disoriented, and the realignment of characters and focuses creates something original and artistically exciting in contemporary Japanese literature. The erection of an old form—one associated with the days of tranquillity and individual free will—by builders who have no confidence in its foundation, the moral strength of the protagonist, produces a tension and a potential for expression that is new to twentieth-century Japanese fiction. I do not think it any coincidence that this ironic fictional form was created just as the Japanese set out to create their "economic miracle," attaining unprecedented material success at what some feel is the cost of tremendous spiritual erosion.

A study of contemporary literature must always be a work in progress, and for this book I have set a cut-off date of 1980: anything that can be classified as a work of fiction published after that date has been excluded from my study, primarily to allow me some critical perspective in my review of the literature. It was tempting to try to include Kojima Nobuo's lengthy *Wakareru riyū* (Reasons for Parting, 1982), Yasuoka Shōtarō's *Ryūritan* (Tales of Wanderers, 1981), Endō Shūsaku's *Sukyandaru* (Scandal, 1986; trans. 1988), and several story collections by Shimao Toshio. But since three of the four novelists considered here persist in writing fiction and essays in prodigious quantities, I knew I had to stop somewhere. That conviction was strengthened when, in the course of my final revisions of this manuscript, Shimao Toshio passed away. Although at some future date I hope to come back to the post-1980 writings of these four, I want to present my findings on the significant contributions they made in the three decades between 1950 and 1980.

The initial research which I did in Japan for this book was supported by grants from the Fulbright Commission and the Social Science Research Council, and I express my gratitude to both. I have profited during my studies from the advice and encouragmeent of many. I have, to echo the words of Endō Shūsaku when he received the Akutagawa Prize, been blessed with a wealth of excellent *sempai*. My sincere thanks go to Professor Donald Keene, who provided me with a variety of insights that would never have occurred to me without his help. Later revisions benefited greatly from new directions suggested by Professors Cyril Birch, William H. McCullough, and Irwin Scheiner, who read and commented at length upon my manuscript; special thanks go to Professor Mary Elizabeth Berry, who helped me clarify for myself just what I was doing. I have, in addition, been aided by Professors Kathryn Sparling and Saeki Shōichi; by friends and colleagues at Columbia University, Notre Dame, and Berkeley, and by a remarkable group of students who participated with me in a graduate seminar on these four authors at Berkeley. Their ideas have greatly expanded my own perspectives on this group.

In Japan, I had the opportunity to meet and work closely with Endō Shūsaku, who performed the role of patron and friend affably and with unmatched generosity. I was also able to meet with Kojima Nobuo, who has remained extraordinarily helpful throughout our subsequent correspondence. Regretfully, I never had the chance to meet Shimao before his death in 1986; I retain some hope of contacting Yasuoka.

I also wish to thank Dr. Carol Christ, Dean of Humanities at Berkeley, for a generous grant to assist in publication of this book. Oyama Shizu of the Japan PEN Club was very helpful in obtaining the photographs of the four authors. At Columbia University Press, Jennifer Crewe's faith in my work has helped me overcome many frustrations, and Karen Mitchell has tightened and smoothed it out through kind and careful editing. Finally an expression of the deepest, most personal kind of gratitude to my wife Elizabeth, who has remained patient with me through the emotional rollercoaster rides that have attended the preparation of the manuscript for publication.

The Sting of Life

I

Demobilization of the Literary Self

In any list of casualties of the Pacific War, on the Japanese side one would have to include the steadfast literary construct of self that had been forged by the prewar "I" novelists. Whatever the shortcomings of their individual works, these practitioners of the semi-autobiographical fictions called *shi-shōsetsu* managed to put into place a solid tradition of ego-centered narratives that came to form the mainstream of prose writings in the 1920s and 1930s. Convinced that the refining of the individual self was the ultimate end of art, these writers represented much of both the virtue and the vice of their age—the age of Meiji in which a modernized national identity was established, and the age of Taishō in which Japan began to test its newfound international strength.

In the prewar period, Shiga Naoya (1883–1971), known to his contemporaries as the "god of literature," was perhaps the most successful of the I-novelists in transforming faith in himself into literary form. Of himself he wrote: "I have come truly to love myself. I now find my face truly beautiful. And I believe there are few men who have possessed the greatness that I have within me."[1] And one of Shiga's chief fictional alter egos, Kensaku of *An'ya kōro* (A Dark Night's Passing, 1921–37; trans. 1976), asserts:

> In the process of trying to avoid someone because I don't like him, I come to hate him. It's a terrible habit, I know. I always begin by liking or disliking someone immediately, and if I like a person, I assume he's good, and if I dislike him, I assume he's bad. But you know, I'm hardly ever wrong in my judgment. . . . I really don't make many mistakes about people. It's not only people either; I'm usually right in my discernment of a particular situation too. When I sense something is wrong, I usually find out later that there was good cause for me to feel that way.[2]

Writing those words in 1937, Shiga was confident in the validity of his own perceptions, and the faith he had in the efficacy of his personal judgments gives strength to his quasi-fictional characters. Only a decade later—but a decade of war and defeat for Japan—Dazai Osamu's literary alter ego Yōzō says:

> I still have no understanding of what makes human beings tick. My apprehension on discovering that my concept of happiness seemed to be completely at variance with that of everyone else was so great as to make me toss sleeplessly and groan night after night in my bed. It drove me indeed to the brink of lunacy. . . . Again, I never once answered back anything said to me by my family. The least word of reproof struck me with the force of a thunderbolt and drove me almost out of my head. Answer back! Far from it, I felt convinced that their reprimands were without doubt voices of human truth speaking to me from eternities past; I was obsessed with the idea that since I lacked the strength to act in accordance with this truth, I might already have been disqualified from living among human beings.[3]

A process of self-dismantlement, with an accompanying demolition of the literary self, is beginning here with Dazai. But the transformation was apparently more painful than he could endure: joining his artistic creations who saw themselves as "victims of a transitional period of morality,"[4] Dazai committed suicide. It was left to a generation of authors who had passed through the defeat as younger men to take up where Dazai left off, and to complete the demobilization of the literary self.

Those who carried out this act of dismantlement belong to what contemporary historians call the *senchū-ha,* the "war generation."

This generation is composed of men and women born in the decade bracketing 1920, whose youthful experiences therefore coincided with the years of mounting intellectual repression and military expansion in Japan. Both as participants in and as chroniclers of those difficult years, the war generation survived—at least physically—the devastations of World War II. But that taxing dual role foisted upon them severed the self as experiential participant from the self as detached observer. The result, when they finally sat down to write about their experiences, would be an inevitable layer of irony between author and quasi-autobiographical protagonist, a layer that was largely lacking in the I-novels of the self-confident prewar generation.

The chief mutual characteristic of the senchū-ha, according to one of their number, is a feeling of "chronic weariness," a stupor both physical and spiritual.[5] The senchū-ha generation has produced a wealth of talented novelists, poets, playwrights, and critics, many of whom occupy central positions in the Japanese literary world today. The present book will confine itself to four of those novelists—not because their experiences or writings are necessarily "representative" of their contemporaries, but because they embody the variety of the age and typify in several ways the widespread sense of deprivation and spiritual malaise that characterize the senchū-ha. The novelists under discussion here, in order of seniority, are: Kojima Nobuo, Shimao Toshio, Yasuoka Shōtarō, and Endō Shūsaku. The four are identified by Japanese literary critics as members of a subgroup within the senchū-ha, a makeshift literary association known as the "Daisan no shinjin," or the "Third Generation of New Writers."

The quality of the literature produced by the Third Generation authors is high, but the significance of their contribution to postwar literature goes beyond any isolated works. The novelists of this generation have dismantled and reshaped the literary signifiers of narrative prose in Japan. They have taken apart the central "I" of autobiographical fiction, bending and then breaking the vertical pronoun that had seemed so sturdy and unassailable in the shi-shōsetsu of the twenties and thirties. That process of dismantlement begins with the stories of personal collapse, and in this chapter I will examine some of the individual experiences of these four authors as they will relate to their assaults on the "I" of their fictions.

Members of the Third Generation fell out of touch with home and heritage in their childhood, sacrificed their youth to preparations for war, survived the conflict, and returned to a disrupted society that held no place for them. Thereafter they struggled to live in the absence of values that had sustained their ancestors for generations. Having done virtually everything but fight during the war, they turned bellicose in peacetime and exiled themselves from a society to which they could not accommodate themselves.

Few of the Third Generation were more than ten years old when the sweeping Red Purges began to restrict intellectual dissent in Japan. They had been born a decade too late to develop a taste for any philosophical alternatives to the state socialism that was maturing even as they did. The only ideology they experienced firsthand was the creed of deracination. Rapid industrialization, increased social mobility, a weakening of the traditional family system, and the effects of a disciplined but increasingly dogmatic education tore these future writers loose from their roots. In their fiction there is a conspicuous loss of a sense of place, of a spiritual home from which they can derive solace or inspiration. Home becomes such an abstraction for them that it scarcely even serves as a stimulus for youthful rebellion. For them there was no more of the *shitamachi* (the old "downtown" section of Tokyo) that intrigued Nagai Kafū (1879–1959) however much it deteriorated; to them the Kansai region in western Japan had become merely a place of commerce, not of culture as Tanizaki Jun'ichirō saw it. And the lyric environs that take on symbolic life in the work of Kawabata Yasunari no longer moved the Third Generation to rhapsodize on their natural surroundings. They were one of the first generations in modern Japan to be cut loose from any ties with "home."

Among the writers of his generation, Yasuoka Shōtarō has written most frequently and most evocatively of this loss of home, of the initial uprooting process that prepared this generation for the greater losses of war and defeat. The collapse of home and family ties echoes incessantly in the ears of Yasuoka's characters, like the flapping wings of a moth that has lodged in the eardrum and is slowly gnawing its way toward the inner brain.[6] Maturation is the most difficult of endeavors for the Yasuoka character, since it is a process that exposes the myth of a past home and requires that he begin to create something of a resting place for himself in the present. The experience of the past, however, has taught him to be highly skeptical that such a spiritual nest can ever be fashioned.

With the expansion of Japanese imperialism to the Chinese mainland in 1931 and 1932, the tolerance for political and intellectual diversity at home quickly shrank. The Peace Preservation Law of 1925 had already prescribed penalties of ten years in prison for participation in left-wing extremist activities; further edicts through the early thirties sharpened the teeth of these laws and restricted personal freedoms even more. The effects of growing repression upon the Third Generation were indirect; they were forced to look on uncomprehendingly as young men just a few years their senior were either shot or jailed and pommeled until they recanted their seditious liberal beliefs. Born exactly between the Marxists and the Kamikazes —after the death grip had begun to choke out leftist ideologies, but before the nationalistic indoctrination had taken firm hold—this generation was ill-prepared either to participate in or to criticize what was happening all around them. One critic, Hattori Tatsu, has described how the difference of just a year or two affected the intellectual and emotional development of this generation:

> The influence which the war had upon all of them is first apparent in the fact that their spiritual molding took place during the war. . . . Violence was the common state of affairs in the outer world, and their minds were shaped within that climate. Slightly older men had the leisure to steer clear of the violence and create a tiny world for themselves in some remote corner. But the younger men were less blessed with the unique set of circumstances that would allow them to create such a world.[7]

Because they had no private corner in which to retreat either emotionally or philosophically, the distaste which the members of this generation felt for the increasingly fascist orientation of their government tended to be visceral and private, as Yasuoka's memoirs demonstrate:

> In March [of 1938], I graduated from middle school and traveled to Shikoku to take the entrance exams for Matsuyama Higher School. As I had anticipated, I failed the exams, but the newspaper which I picked up at the test site reported that Hitler had successfully annexed Austria. Then in 1939 I went to sit for exams at Kōchi Higher School in Shikoku. Again, as I half expected, I failed, and once again Hitler's Germany, in the wake of the victory in the Spanish war, had invaded Czechoslovakia and turned it into

> a protectorate. In this manner, each time I set out on a foray to a provincial high school and was turned away in defeat, for some reason Hitler was able to send his troops into a neighboring country and achieve victory. I had no choice from my standpoint but to consider Hitler a personal jinx.[8]

If Yasuoka's reasons for disliking Hitler seem overly subjective, consider the manner in which, as a devoted fan of foreign movies, he became disillusioned with his own government:

> *Grand Illlusion* is about some officers in the French air force who are taken prisoner by the German army in World War I. After several attempts to escape from the camp, they finally succeed and flee across the border to Switzerland. In and of itself there was nothing about the movie that made it "inappropriate to the times." Even in Germany, Göring, who was commander of the air force and second in authority to Hitler, was said to approve of the film as a flight officer. But Göbbels, Minster of Propaganda, resolutely banned the movie, declaring that it "profoundly insulted the German military." Thereupon Japan, determining that it would be best to forgo the showing of a film that might besmirch the honor of the people of federalist Germany, finally banned all performances of the movie.
>
> I was truly incensed. Unlike the cancellation of the Olympics, the proscription of *Grand Illusion* was scarcely noted in the papers and prompted little public discussion, but to me it was a considerably larger problem than the Olympics. I was used to censorship, having seen many blank spaces in newspapers and magazines since my childhood, and had resigned myself to the practice. But no matter how hard I tried, I couldn't understand why a movie that had originally been passed for showing was suddenly banned at the whim of the German Minister of Propaganda. Just what had happened to the system of censorship in Japan? Were we to assume that our officials could not think or make decisions on their own, but passed judgments for our nation only after hearing the opinions of the ministers of foreign countries?
>
> To stretch the point, I think perhaps I was intellectually awakened at this juncture.
>
> Until this time, I had liked Germany, and I had nothing against Hitler or the Nazis. Since its resignation from the League of

> Nations in 1933, Japan had been isolated from the international community—that was a source of grief even to a young man like myself. That's why I felt a sense of gratitude when Germany as soon as it came under Nazi control summarily withdrew from the League of Nations. And when General Franco staged a rebellion in Spain, I cheered for him, hoping that his forces would quickly overcome the government troops. I imagine the majority of Japanese people felt the same as I did. And if I had not been a movie fan, I probably would have gone on feeling that way for a long time. But when I was robbed of the opportunity to see Jean Renoir's film, which was being hailed as an immortal classic, I at once developed a hatred for Göbbels, and came to despise Hitler and Germany. And it suddenly troubled me deeply that Japan was beginning to ape the ways of the Nazis.[9]

By the time the members of the Third Generation were ready to go away to college, just before or during the war, most of the voices of protest had been stilled in Japan. The intellectual climate in which they received their higher education had grown sterile and monotone. The form of education that slowly but persistently hounded this generation was known as "Shūshin," variously translated as civics, ethics, or morals education. Herbert Passin writes:

> A minimum of one hour per week of morals was mandatory in all classes, from elementary through the secondary school. But apart from the formal morals course, the ideas were woven into the curriculum and into school life in any way the ingenuity of the educators could devise. Whenever subject matter permitted, they were to be worked into the textual material.[10]

By the mid-1930s, educators had found many ways to incorporate nationalistic propaganda into the daily instructional material. Thus when history was taught, it was the mythical history of Japan as a country literally descended from the gods and thereby morally superior to the nations of the West. Geography was also distorted to give the students the impression that Japan had an inevitable mission of leadership to perform in the East Asian sphere.

Throughout such classroom texts as *Kokutai no hongi* (The Japanese National Polity), promulgated in 1937 as the master plan for Shūshin education, emphasis is placed on the uniqueness of Japan in all her aspects (a central tenet of the Nihonjin-ron, treatises on the essence of Japaneseness), the superiority of Japanese to occidental ways, the fallacies and pitfalls inherent in the "dangerous" social concept of individualism, and the need for Japan to benefit from the material culture of the West while rejecting its spiritual roots. But the Third Generation would have just been finishing middle school when *Kokutai no hongi* and the new morals texts were introduced in the lower grades. And so, like virtually everything else about their lives, even their indoctrination was done in half-measures. These crumbs of force-fed dogma caught in the throats of the Taishō-born youths, and it is no surprise that they had difficulty swallowing their educational diet. They could not put the reasons for their distaste into words, but it smelled bad, somehow.

By the late 1930s, when the Third Generation had attained the age ripe for plucking by the military, patriotic songs were blaring out over the radio waves with jingoistic messages bleeding through the lyrics. One ditty, commissioned by the Cabinet Information Board (Naikaku Jōhō-kyoku) in 1937 and officially recommended by the government, sold over a million copies in the record stores.[11] It is titled "Patriotic March" (Aikoku kōshinkyoku), and had words by Morikawa Yukio set to the music of Setoguchi Tōkichi:

Look! The sun over the Eastern Sea is clear
The morning sun shimmers on high
The heavens and earth brim with vitality
And hope leaps up
In the great Country of Eight Islands.

Ah! The outlines of Mount Fuji
Soaring in the bright clouds of dawn
Are the pride of our homeland—
Flawless, unshakable Japan.

Arise! Living in Light forever
Under one unbroken line of sovereigns,
We His subjects all
Comply with His authority—
This is our great mission.

Go! Bring the eight corners of the world
Under one roof

Guide the peoples of the four seas
And fight to establish righteous peace.
Fragrantly our ideals blossom
Together with the flowers.

No matter how often
The storms of trial rage over us
Firmly we will defend what is right.
There is only one road
We must pursue.

Ah! Marching in time with the footsteps
That have thundered forth since the remote Age of the Gods,
Into the distance our grand procession goes,
And glory be always to
The Imperial Nation![12]

Even more insidious in the way it brings militaristic ideology down to the personal level and glorifies patriotic death, was the "Bivouac Song" (Roei no uta), written in 1937 by Yabuuchi Kiichirō, with music by Kozeki Hiroyuki. Within six months, a recording of the "Bivouac Song" had sold 600,000 copies.[13]

Since I bravely vowed
Before I left my homeland
That I would fight courageously,
How could I possibly die
Without achieving glory?
Each time the bugle sounds the march,
Before my eyes I see a wave of banners.

Trudging across the endless wildernesses
Of flaming earth and vegetation,
The Rising Sun and the helmets advance.
Stroking my horse's mane, I wonder—
Who can know
If he will still be alive tomorrow?

When we bivouac
Sometimes bullets and tanks and bayonets
Are our pillows.
In a dream my father appeared,

Urging me to die.
I awaken and glare at
The enemy's sky.

In the battle today
My buddy, bathed in red,
Smiled broadly as he cried,
"Banzai to His Majesty!"
How can I ever
Forget that voice?

Those who go to war
Have long since resolved to die.
Do not cry for us,
Insects in the grass.
If it be for peace in Asia,
Why should we begrudge our lives?[14]

Despite the persuasive combination of educational propaganda, governmental advocacy, and even musical encouragement, the students preparing in 1937 to enter the university or a technical higher school felt little urge to die. Their sense of bewilderment, in fact, left them unable to do much of anything but drift. The few meager sources of pleasure allowed them were gradually being stripped away. With the passing of the National General Mobilization Law (Kokka Sōdōin-hō) in March 1938, it became dangerous to read proscribed books or even to utter unguarded thoughts. Both Yasuoka and Shimao Toshio tried their hands at writing short stories during their early days at the university, and both had their publications banned. Shimao's experience, which occurred at Kyushu University in 1937, was the more extreme of the two:

> After we finally put the first issue together, we received notification from the Ministry of Home Affairs that sale of our journal was prohibited. This had come about because, in accordance with the prevailing laws, we had dutifully sent them two presentation copies for inspection. The five of us were summoned to the special political section of Nagasaki Police Headquarters and were interrogated in separate rooms. The reason for the proscription was primarily that several expressions in the stories Kawakami [Kazuo] and I had written were said to be in violation of the provisions in

> Publication Law 14 . . . concerning the corruption of public morals. But it seems to me that we were primarily grilled about whether we had any antiwar sentiments and if we had the backing of any left-wing associations. . . . I was dumbfounded at the exaggerated suspicions of the political police, and it frightened me to discover that the powerful judgments of the authorities could invade even my private thoughts. Since I had not made any advance mental preparations for this sort of thing, I was left defenseless in my fears. I don't know how my coeditors felt inwardly about this whole incident, but on the surface, in exchange for retracting their suspicions and letting us return home, the officials made us promise that we would not publish another issue of our journal. Thereafter an agent from the special police dropped in from time to time to check us out. The incident was also reported to our school, and the principal responded by giving us a lecture, and we agreed to his stipulation that we were to write no more stories or poems while we were in school.[15]

At the universities many foreign books were banned; liberal teachers were being accused of lèse majesté; and textbooks were being rewritten one after another to declare from every imaginable disciplinary angle the need for Japanese domination of Asia. Yasuoka, with an eye ever ready to point out the absurd, notes that in 1942 a particularly ridiculous example of this tendency cropped up in language textbooks after English was declared an "enemy language":

> I opened up the new French language textbook and stared in amazement. There were selections from writers like Alain Fournier, Fabre, and Prosper Mérimée, but the rest was an unbroken succession of essays by such famous French rightists and ultranationalists as Maurice Barres, Léon Daudet, and Charles Maurras; the text even included the commemorative speech given when Field Marshal Henri Pétain, the World War I hero who became the head of the Vichy government in the Second World War, was inducted into the Academy. With materials like this in the textbook, I felt as if the schools were using the French language to teach us about fascism.
>
> Perhaps it was not pointless to hear the opinions of French rightists and royalists as a means of understanding French and European society. But their use of such materials to teach the

basics of language provided the best possible excuse for me to skip class.[16]

Compulsory military drills became an uncomfortably familiar part of the curriculum at virtually every educational institution. As the war machine ground its way forward, the amount of time devoted to training the draftable young men in military technique was increased, infringing upon time for academic subjects. Army officers on active duty were posted at each school to insure proper discipline and enthusiasm for the drills. Against their will—though they were never quite sure what they willed—the young men of the Third Generation in Japan were being forced to shape themselves into potential soldiers. Little wonder that many of them lost interest in the process of education altogether. The only feeble protest they could muster was to cut classes as often as they could get away with it. Endō Shūsaku describes both his own lack of motivation for study and the physical reprisals that were a common part of classroom discipline:

> Thinking back on it now, it seems as though I went to school merely for the purpose of taking catnaps and pulling pranks, and then to be scolded and beaten by my teachers.
>
> Corporal punishment was severe in those days; the teachers beat us soundly. Pommelings with the flat of their hands or their fists were common, and we were sometimes even beaten with the corners of wooden triangles. The most painful of all was being whacked with the edge of the hard attendance book. Of course, I have no call to bear a grudge against them, because it was my fault for doing things that prompted the beatings. In almost every class, I buried my head in my arms and dropped off to sleep; I never did my homework; I brought stray cats into the classroom; and I set off alarm clocks without warning. It was perfectly natural for even the most benevolent teacher to want to lift his hand against a student like that.[17]

Even the practice of cutting school was rendered futile after around 1942, when university classes were often canceled, and the students yet to be conscripted were shuffled off to munitions factories to do labor service.

Of the young men from this generation who went away to war and came back to write, few fit the stereotype of the fiercely loyal, inexplicably brutal Japanese soldier. Our four novelists are ample proof that not every conscript conformed to such a model. A brief look at their wartime experiences should be sufficient commentary upon their individual and collective bewilderment. Kojima and Yasuoka both had only fleeting glimpses of the enemy; Shimao spent his wartime career preparing to meet an opponent who never materialized; and for Endō the adversary was ideological and had a Japanese face.

Kojima Nobuo, an avid reader of Gogol and Pushkin, graduated with a degree in English literature in 1941. When he went out job-hunting after he received his diploma, the best offer he could find was a position teaching English at a private middle school. It probably did not escape his notice that, as he was settling into a career of teaching the English language, Japan was rapidly moving toward war with most of the English-speaking nations of the world. He was drafted shortly after he began teaching, and during basic training was ordered to forget every word of the hated enemy tongue.

> I was taunted on occasion because I had graduated from the university and because I wore glasses, but since it was an all-male society, I was also doted upon. Nearly every night for five months, a certain senior soldier who wanted to treat me kindly invited me to drink with him. Liquor was poured down me, and I became the butt of his drunken jokes until morning. At dawn I was released and returned to the barracks just an hour before reveille.
>
> My ranking within the barracks was the highest of everyone, but of the thirteen men in the regiment who applied for officer candidacy, I was the only one who failed. . . . Thereafter all the rejects were lumped together and trained to be cipher readers. . . .
>
> When we went out on punitive expeditions . . . I always felt a great sense of futility. Of course, it would be futile to be killed in battle, but it was truly miserable to be scrambling around looking for an enemy. Whenever we went out hunting for them, it was always after they had already run away.
>
> In the spring of 1944, I was transferred to a communications unit in Peking. We were given new facilities at Yenching University, and our job was to intercept transmissions from the American

> air force installations in China. Eventually I became responsible for conveying the information to headquarters. Some of those reports were based on decoded transmissions, but a good half of them were products of my own imagination.[18]

At the Yenching University unit, Kojima worked alongside half-blooded Japanese, several Chinese, and one Nisei PFC married to a German woman. Their mission entailed a second irony, for Kojima was now being ordered to remember the English he had been commanded to wipe from his memory. And with what must have been an unusual mixture of relief and shame, Kojima soon after learned that his former battalion had been annihilated in the fighting against MacArthur's forces at Leyte between October and December 1944. By the end of the war, Kojima was teaching his commanding officers such useful English phrases as "Would you care for a drink?" and "I am not a war criminal."

Yasuoka's father was transferred by the army to Central China in 1939 for a tour of duty. Except for a couple of brief furlough visits back to Japan, he saw nothing of his family again until 1946. But Yasuoka was not particularly saddened by his father's absence:

> As a child, I never wanted to discuss my father.
>
> It embarrassed me beyond measure when my father was mentioned in front of other people. Why? My father was a soldier, but he cut an insufferably poor figure. Even a child can see the humor in a soldier who appears drab even when he is decked out in all his medals and brandishing his saber. And it pained me to see him riding a horse—he always looked like he was holding on to the horse's neck for dear life, ready to be thrown off at any instant. Worst of all, my father was a veterinarian for the army, and it humiliated me to hear him called a "horse doctor" by the people in Tōhoku. . . .
>
> To me, my father seemed like the fountainhead of all shame, the matrix of all my sensitivity. Everything ugly, everything disgraceful, everything painful was assimilated into the image of my father.[19]

With his father out of the picture, Yasuoka may have sensed that he would fall yet further under the sway of his doting, protective mother. To counterbalance her influence—and perhaps to express some of his ambivalent feelings toward the trend of the times—he got into some "bad company"[20] and formed a Fūten Club (which can be interpreted as either the "Insanity Club" or the "Juvenile Delinquents' Club") of young men who let their hair grow long in the Western style, read Kafū and Tanizaki, and tried to mimic their bohemian lifestyles:

> In place of textbooks, we stuffed our schoolbags full of yellow-covered picture books or romances by Tamenaga Shunsui. We swaggered about triumphantly, spouting off in the language of a comic storyteller. One day F announced, "I'm going to learn to sing in the Sonohachi or Itchū style." We all followed suit and wanted to learn. But those styles of singing were prohibited, and not a single adult was studying them. Since we had no options, I decided to make do with the Kiyomoto style, and went to see a woman teacher named Kiyomotonobu, who lived in a tenement building in Inari-chō.
>
> She decided to teach me how to sing "Evening Showers." But what humiliation! No sooner had I launched into singing "The e-e-evening showers—" with a purple face than she shook her head, peered over her glasses at me, and said, "That's terrible. Absolutely terrible. Have you ever thought of studying the Gidayū style?"
>
> . . . I left the tenement thinking, "Damn, I can't handle Kiyomoto!" The wind blew across my crew-cut hair. It was bitterly cold.[21]

Yasuoka managed to avoid military service until March 1944, but even after he was sent to Manchuria for boot camp, he managed to create a "tiny corner world all my own . . . one that I could not hope to find anywhere around me in the outside world, where I secluded myself away."[22] The little world he created for himself in the military, however, was not the philosophical retreat which Hattori had described as the spiritual salvation of the previous generation. Yasuoka's place of solitude was centered in the latrine. He developed a persistent (and quite likely self-induced) case of diarrhea during basic training, and retreated to the toilet to take refuge. He collapsed from illness the day before his regiment was transferred to the Philippines, and from the hospital where he stayed until the end of the war, he received precisely the same news that Kojima had—that his regiment had been annihilated in the fighting at Leyte.

One of a minority of volunteers from the Third Generation, Shimao Toshio entered the Japanese navy upon receiving a degree in Asian history from Kyushu University. Shimao's experiences call into question the entire concept of volunteerism during the war:

> At the time America had some small fighting ships called torpedo boats which caused Japan considerable anguish. I understand that Japan decided to create their own fleet of torpedo boats in response. I knew nothing about the background behind any of this, but volunteers were sought from among the student inductees to serve on these new and dangerous combat vessels. As lip service alone, I perfunctorily put down the torpedo boats as my third and final choice, but I ended up being assigned to them. I was trained to sail on the torpedo boats, but . . . I think perhaps the navy was unable to produce them as they had anticipated. That left two hundred of us without a commanding officer. . . .
>
> One day—I think it was in April or May of 1944 . . . when we were sick to death of the unchanging routine of training for the torpedo boats, suddenly there came an order for muster. Many of us among the student inductees were filled with worldly desires and lacked technical skills, so our training was carried out with much upbraiding: we were told that we were not fit to be young officers in the navy, that "too many oarsmen make a boat go up a hill." But at muster, the instructor in command of our student unit said, "Your earnest dedication to your training has been rewarded, and at long last you have become full-fledged young officers. The navy has given special recognition to your accomplishments and has granted permission for some of you in the torpedo boat unit to volunteer for a 'special attack' unit. Today we will suspend all training and give you the leisure to think this through; then you will write down whether or not you will volunteer for this special unit."
>
> At the time, all we could think of was that we wanted to do something different, no matter what it was. Since our training was canceled and we had the whole day to rest, our first reaction was to feel liberated. We then felt an urgent need to think, but I have no idea what I thought about. We did not have the energy to think

> about what would happen to us after we volunteered for the special attack unit, and we spent the entire day walking aimlessly along the beach, eating sea urchins, doing our laundry, and then falling into bed. It was a totally uneventful day, but it felt like an extraordinarily long day. According to the tallies announced the following day, every one of the just over two hundred students in the torpedo boat unit had volunteered for the suicide squadron. . . .[23]

After another period of training, Shimao was sent to one of the tiny islands in the Amami group south of Kyushu as the commander of a suicide squadron. For ten months he led his squadron of 183 men in a regimen of daily life directed toward preparation for death.

> A suicide unit participates in battle only once. Once that occurs, everything is over. And so I ended the war without seeing battle. . . . On normal days we engaged in no dangerous battle maneuvers of any kind. I had no experience of mingling with the enemy in pitched combat. All we did was wait—wait for the enemy to come. You could say that waiting composed the entirety of my war experience. . . .[24]

Each day they waited for the signal from naval headquarters to board their one-man torpedo boats and propel themselves toward the invading enemy fleet. Only the knowledge that death was certain and imminent gave any meaning to their everyday activities. "Until the orders to attack came down, we led a life of ease. Our rations were good, the food was far better than that allotted to any other unit, and promotions came rapidly."[25] In what must be one of the supreme ironies of the Pacific War, Shimao's orders to prepare for launch arrived on the evening of August 13, 1945, and he and his men waited in full battle regalia for the final command that never came. Little wonder that the war as a psychological state has never really ended in Shimao's fictional world.

The emotional scars of war cut deep even for those, like Endō Shūsaku, who were able to avoid the draft. Endō, who had been baptized a Catholic at the age of eleven at his mother's instigation, was kept from serving in the army by persistent lung problems. But the war remained for him an intellectual struggle. He had never been truly comfortable with the foreign religion he donned as a child, and it was really not until his university days that he came to grips with its meaning in his life:

> Christianity for me was like a Western-style suit of clothes that my mother put on me in my youth. . . . But when I reached adolescence, I began to be bothered by the fact that the Western suit was not the right size for me. . . . Parts of it were baggy, other parts too short on me. When I came to that realization, I tried several times to remove the suit. . . . But in the end I was unable to do so. Until I could do so with assurance and self-confidence, I could not bring myself to cast off a set of clothing given to me by someone I loved. . . .
>
> Later I decided not to try to remove the suit. Instead I would try to refashion it into Japanese-style clothing that would fit me. . . . When I realized that I would have nothing to wear in its place if I took the suit off, I began to write novels. . . . To stand naked and find a set of clothes for yourself, to make that choice on your own—that is literature. But I came to feel that literature also exists in the lifelong effort to take a suit of baggy clothes that someone has given you and tailor it to fit your own body.[26]

As a student at Keiō University, Endō lived in a Catholic-run dormitory managed by the Christian philosopher Yoshimitsu Yoshihiko. Under Yoshimitsu's influence, Endō began reading Rilke and Maritain and started pondering the position of Christianity in Japan and in his own life.

But as he records in his reminiscences of the period, "In the factory and at school, it became an everyday occurrence for the drill instructors or my fellow students to taunt me with questions like, 'With Japan at war, how can you go on believing in an enemy religion?' or 'Whom do you revere more, the Emperor or your God?' "[27] Besides the jeers of classmates and the suspicions of the authorities, Endō also had to contend with frequent bouts of self-recrimination for adhering to the enemy's religious faith, and with doubts about the placidity with which the priests each Sunday intoned their "Thou shalt not kill"s without taking a firm moral stand against the war itself.

Each of these writers has treated the war in his fiction, but certainly the most harrowing accounts of the personal wounds of that conflict are to be found in the fiction of Shimao Toshio, if only because the battle for him continued to be waged for four decades within his own heart. Although he missed his appointment with death on the battlefield (critics have not missed the comparison with Dostoevsky's mock-execution experience) Shimao through the act of writing found new settings where the fighting could be continued, and other enemies to engage.

Three of our four writers went to war, but it is interesting that none ever saw battle with Allied troops. Kojima alone of the three, as he intimated above, engaged in some minor skirmishes with Chinese soldiers, but these were all a "waste," since the enemy had always fled by the time the Japanese troops arrived. The true enemies were the senior soldiers quartered in the same barracks. They were the immediate threat to the younger ambivalent soldiers, who became the targets of harsh corporeal abuse.

These were, in short, warriors who never became involved in the actual business of war. Trained not so much to kill as to die, and armed with the instruments of their own annihilation, they were sent forth on a mission they loathed and ultimately failed to accomplish. And though they may have been pleased to fail in the deepest recesses of their hearts, they were also publicly embarrassed by that fact. The rush of circumstances made them into almost unwilling survivors, since the death that was supposed to be their goal and their national duty had conveniently eluded them. From the Japanese perspective survival can only turn a soldier into an unwelcome anomaly. Those who returned alive, for whatever reason, had somehow failed in their calling, had managed to incur shame without committing a shameful act. For this generation, the stigma of survival, the return to a ruined and defeated homeland from which they could no more retrieve their youth, and the humiliation of foreign occupation all combined to complete the uprooting process. Yasuoka recreates his thoughts on the night of August 14, 1945:

> I could not get to sleep that night. Was the eight-year war that had started with the China Incident finally coming to an end? I was relieved at the thought and felt as though I were dreaming. But when I tried to go to sleep, the air-raid sirens blared out. When I turned out the lights, the explosions from the B29s echoed through the darkness. What if the Emperor, in his important broadcast tomorrow, announced that the final battle on the main-

> land was about to commence, and that the people were all to steel themselves for a fight to the death? That seemed unthinkable to me. I was more troubled by thoughts of the face of my father, who was serving on the battlefield in the South Seas. If Japan surrendered, it was possible that all the high-ranking officers at the front lines would have to commit suicide. In fact, that was undoubtedly what would happen. The chief officers who had told their men "Die rather than be captured" would not be allowed to become POWs and get away without cutting their own bellies open just because Japan had been defeated. At that moment, I suddenly had a vision of myself shouldering a honey bucket. If my father died, I would be responsible for taking care of my mother. . . . In reality, this was a far more serious problem than the question whether my father would have to commit suicide. Foolishly enough, until that moment it had never occurred to me that the end of the war for which I had so earnestly yearned would mean that my father would be unemployed, and that the entire financial responsibility for my family—even if that was just my mother and myself—would fall upon me.[28]

The mixture of shame, exhaustion, and physical destruction to which these men returned in late 1945 meant that the urge to transfer personal experience to paper did not well up immediately. There was an almost six-year lag after the surrender before most of them brought some sense of order to their lives and began careers in literature. The uncertainties of existence in postwar Japan at that point did not seem qualitatively superior to those of the war years. Yasuoka's reminiscences about his repatriation just before the end of the war are informative:

> In truth, my liberation from the army at that time could be called incomparably good fortune, but in another sense I felt as though I had suddenly been cast adrift on the wayside. When our house was burned [in the Tokyo fire bombings], my mother had not evacuated any of our belongings, so I had neither a place to live nor anything to wear. . . . The people [in the Asakusa district] had suffered as cruelly in the air raids as they had during the great earthquake; yet they had all returned to live in the same place they had lived before. Was this some kind of basic instinct? Or was it merely that they had nowhere else to go? But if there was some

> sort of primal urge to return to the original home, that urge seemed to be lacking in me. Although I did a great deal of wandering through various neighborhoods of Tokyo, the only place I had no desire to visit was the Setagaya district where the charred remains of my house stood.[29]

Perhaps it is not too much of an exaggeration to suggest that the unwavering reliability of the self was also destroyed in the war. Certainly the confidence to assert themselves in artistic form was not available to most young writers in 1945. The authors who set to work recording their experiences immediately after the defeat were mostly those of the previous generation, writers who had had a taste of Marxist philosophy in the early thirties. They still believed in ideals, in the efficacy of philosophical values, in the importance of placing blame for the atrocities of war. This group is known in Japanese literary history as the "Sengoha" (après guerre) faction.

Here we must grapple with one of the vague intricacies of literary jargon. Both the authors of the Sengoha and those of the Third Generation are technically members of the senchū-ha or "war generation." The Sengoha were the first significant group of new writers to emerge after 1945, to be followed by a second wave of newcomers and then, shortly after the outbreak of the Korean War, by the Third Generation. But the Sengoha, though they share the war experience with their younger colleagues, were old enough before the commencement of hostilities with the Western world to have tasted of intellectual alternatives. No such luxury was afforded the men of the Third Generation.

When the war concluded, the Third Generation had no faith in either themselves or in debunked creeds. They were naturally skeptical too of the new banners of "democracy" and "revolution of the proletariat" that were waved before their eyes during the early Occupation years. They were, frankly, weary of gazing at banners of any sort. Yoshiyuki Junnosuke, one of the charter members of the Third Generation, voiced the attitudes of his contemporaries when he wrote:

> The writers who came before me [the Sengoha] spent their youth in league with communism, but mine was spent very differently. As a result, my concerns are unlike theirs. During the war, I couldn't bring myself to sacrifice my life for the sake of any single

> philosophy, even if its ideals might be realized at some point in the future. Many willingly made that sacrifice, but the very thought repelled me. The idea of becoming a sacrifice gave me no pleasure. I considered myself an "individualist"—not an egotist, certainly, but something more refined. In those days the word "individualist" was considered equivalent to "traitor," but I bravely used it to describe myself anyway.
>
> . . . Communism enjoyed a great wave of popularity shortly after the war. . . . But the innate resistance I felt toward that philosophy was the same resistance I had felt toward the militarism of the war years. I could not bear the thought of putting on another uniform when I had just taken off the previous one and thereby liberated my individuality. Neither did I care for the thought of martyring myself for the sake of some ideal that might possibly be realized in some distant future.[30]

Cut off from the world of postwar ideas, this Third Generation might have considered seeking guidance or at least consolation in the rich body of literature that makes up the classical Japanese tradition. But just as their education and their war tours had taken them away from their families—a severance made more acute by the physical destruction and death that followed in its wake—it also caused them to lose touch with the wellsprings of indigenous culture. Traditional roots had run deep for earlier generations, sustaining them and providing them with a sense of national continuity. But for this generation, the controlled education of the prewar years had provided little leisure for contact with Japan's literary and cultural heritage. The only "literature" their drill instructors could recite from memory was the *Hagakure,* an eighteenth-century samurai guidebook to honorable death.[31]

Trammeled with a utilitarian education and sent out to face certain death, this generation may have found insufficient solace in the fragility and gentle melancholy of classical Japanese poetry and fiction. With what little time they did have for literary pursuits before the war, they seldom found the impetus to delve into the classics. To Kojima, the term "classical Japanese literature" *(koten bungaku)* connotes nothing earlier than Natsume Sōseki's 1910 novel *Mon* (Mon, trans. 1972);[32] at any rate, he was more interested at that point in the biting satire of Gogol than the gentle sensitivity of *Genji.* Shimao at the time was reading Dostoevsky, Endō the French Catholic novelists and philosophers, while Yasuoka was caught up in the bohemian dandyism of popular writers from the late Edo period, such as Tamenaga Shunsui.[33]

In this respect the writers of Japan's Third Generation were wrenched away from literary roots more decisively than their predecessors. To a large extent it had been an affinity with the classics that had sustained writers who had already established their reputations before the war. Nationalist sympathizers could tune in to the mythological tones of the *Man'yōshū,* while those less enthusiastic about Japan's involvement in the war could also draw upon different facets of their literary heritage to console themselves. Thus Tanizaki Jun'ichirō took refuge during the war years by creating his own *Genji* world in his novel *Sasameyuki* (The Makioka Sisters, 1943–48; trans. 1957). Kawabata Yasunari, Nagai Kafū, and even Dazai Osamu were equally engrossed in studies or recreations of earlier writings.[34] Their closeness to tradition in a sense helped them bridge the difficult war period and make the transition into the new postwar age with some feeling of continuity.

The Third Generation writers had no such luxury. They sensed a vast gulf separating them from writers like Tanizaki and Kawabata. They even felt distant from the Sengoha authors, who were right at home discussing ideologies, or the relationship between politics and literature, or metaphysical theories of literary form and style. The new writers had no experience with abstractions. So much of their lives had been spent focused on the consumption of scanty meals and the inadequate satisfaction of other physiological needs that they could cling to nothing but the tangible realities that lay directly before them. The dialectical, usually left-wing concerns of the après-guerre faction left them cold.[35] Yasuoka describes the distinction between his generation and the Sengoha in the following terms:

> [The Sengoha] had all been adults during their school days, and after the war they were beginning to work at respectable jobs. From my perspective, they were a group of unthinkably precocious individuals. But in fact, this was not a problem of individual temperament or ability relating to precociousness or late blooming; rather it had to do with differences in the circumstances of our generations. . . . Hotta [Yoshie], who entered the preparatory de-

> partment at Keiō University in 1936, the year of the February 26th Incident, inherited some of the traditions of the Meiji period university students who sported handsome moustaches on their upper lips. But my generation, who entered the same school some four or five years later, was forbidden not only to grow moustaches but even to let the hair on our heads grow. On our close-shaved scalps we wore school caps that were mere imitations of army hats, and once each week we had to show up at school with gaiters wrapped around our trousers.
>
> In and of itself, it was a trivial matter to be forced to shave our heads. But for a university student to have to crop his hair in the style that had previously been a symbol of elementary and middle-school students was more than a simple question of appearance. To put it in other words, we were not allowed to become adults even though we had become students at the university. Until our generation, once you became an adult you were as a matter of course allowed to go into bars and lounges for recreation and entertainment. But for us these were prohibited, and in the entranceways to bars and coffee shops hung signs that read "Off limits to students and minors." Of course, we were able to drink as much as we wanted on the sly, and we were hardly ever punished for going into bars or coffee shops. But the limitations on the scope of our activities and the refusal to treat us openly as adults hampered our emotional development to some extent. Thinking back on it now, it seems to me that the impact of this upon us was disproportionately large.[36]

The writers of the Third Generation remained distrustful of anything outside their own unreliable egos. As Yasuoka notes elsewhere, "No book I read had any profound influence on me, and no desire to initiate a philosophical revolution motivated me. It was just that, even though I considered myself unreliable, I couldn't depend on anything outside myself either. I had no choice but to cling to my unreliability as long as I lived."[37]

As a result, these embryonic writers felt at home in the disjointed chaos of the postwar years, where they were free to vacillate between humiliation over the foreign occupation and stubborn pride at being Japanese. So the surge in the Japanese economy that got under way during the Korean War years provided them with no cause for rejoicing. There was no place for them in the new business-centered, success-oriented society. Their attitudes were like those of Charlie in Fitzgerald's "Babylon Revisited": when a bartender says, "I heard that you lost a lot in the crash," Charlie replies, 'I did . . . but I lost everything I wanted in the boom."[38] This Japanese generation's sense of loss too was intensified by the coming of prosperity.

A mood of relative contentment and stability had settled over the Japanese populace by the early 1950s. Much of the confusion and deprivation of the immediate postwar years had been resolved, and Japanese political and economic structures had been reshaped under the stern but inspired guidance of MacArthur's GHQ. Idealistic hopes for a revolution of the working class had dwindled, and the attention of the Japanese people had turned from guilt-ridden recollections of the war to a concern for the everyday struggle to make a living and establish new foundations.

New hopes and a fresh supply of national goals persuaded the populace at large that an economic miracle was within reach, and a sense of unity in working toward that end for the most part brought the nation back together again. But fragmentation remained the dominant theme of the new writers. Their lack of enthusiasm for the new integrative forces in society, as much as it might seem to be at odds with the new spirit of the age, actually gave voice to a vague uneasiness that lay concealed under all the external successes. However much Japan may have boasted of the initial miracles, beneath the surface a gnawing sense of inferiority and guilt continued to flow. It was this spirit that the Third Generation captured in their literature. There can be little doubt, whatever portrait of the new Japan was being sketched from the raw data of economic development and political stabilization, that many readers of fiction in the early fifties were sympathetic to the darker portrait of spiritual decline that was beginning to appear in the writings of the Third Generation. The visages their words described were morally pock-marked, and such a picture resonated within the experiences of many readers. While Japan was beginning to pull herself together economically, her new authors were starting to write of the great falling apart that was within themselves.

They were uniquely suited to the task; the postwar years too had been taxing for them. Yasuoka came back from his military hospital in 1945 and went straight to bed with a case of spinal caries that crippled him and left him unable to do any kind of gainful work for nearly a decade.

> The doctor told me that I would have to stay in bed for seven or eight years. My family didn't have the money to pay for a doctor for such a long period. Even if I were able to recover completely, there seemed little likelihood that I could go out into society and find a respectable job. But oddly enough, once I realized where matters stood, I felt somehow at ease. From the beginning I had doubted my ability to lead a decent, self-supporting life. Once I had contracted this disease, I felt that I had at last assumed the status of a normal human being.[39]

For Yasuoka, the disease that had twisted his back out of shape was merely warping his body into a form that accurately reflected his inner vision of himself and of the times in which he lived. He worked briefly as a "house guard" for the Occupation, halfheartedly keeping watch over vacant houses set aside for use by U.S. military personnel; that he has described as "the only job where I could work lying down."[40] From his prone position, Yasuoka began writing stories about people inept at dealing with life in the postwar age.

Kojima Nobuo returned from the war to find that his home had been reduced to ashes by the Allied air raids. When he finally located his family several days later, he had his first glimpse of his son Kazuo, already nearly four years old. At first unable to find a job teaching English, he did liaison work at the prefectural office. Before long, he had decided to uproot his family from their native Gifu and move to Tokyo, where he hoped to become a writer. Because of their economic circumstances, he often had to live apart from his wife and children; when they were together, it was in a high-school dormitory where his wife was always scrapping with the other housewives. But to Kojima's mind, the outstanding symbols of the postwar period were the packed trains racing back and forth to the capital, and his own many and futile attempts to build a modern house with Western-style appurtenances that would meet with his wife's approval:

> Why is it that I feel that each time we have moved or remodeled our house, our living space has shrunk and become more uncomfortable? The layout of the rooms must have something to do with

> the fact that a house just over 700 square feet feels more cramped to us than one a little more than 400 square feet. . . .[41]

The postwar period for Endō was a time of adventure. In 1950, he and three other students were selected to be the first Japanese to study abroad after the war. He set sail on June 5 aboard a French passenger ship. It was hardly the exalted sort of exchange program that operates today. The ship had just deposited a group of repatriated Japanese prisoners-of-war in Yokohama, and was proceeding to France with a score of armed black African soldiers in the cargo hold, where the four Japanese students were also lodged. They were not allowed to disembark at Hong Kong, where the Japanese were still considered war criminals, and at Manila the four were interrogated at gunpoint by Filipino authorities. Undoubtedly Endō and his shipmates hoped that France would provide a refuge from the humiliation they had endured as defeated Japanese; the scars of war-torn Asia might have a chance to heal at such a distance. But Endō describes an incident two days before their boat docked at Marseille:

> Late that night I got out of bed and went up on deck all by myself. I gazed at the dark ocean. Suddenly in the distance a pillar of fire shot up into the sky, scattering a million sparks in all directions before it suddenly died out again. It was the Stromboli volcano. Never before and never since have I witnessed such a violent eruption. Just then a ship's mate clattered noisily across the deck. He asked me if I were Japanese, then reported, "War broke out in Korea today."
>
> Another pillar of fire shot up, showering more sparks through the sky. My emotions, which were beginning to undergo a change aboard ship, were dealt a decisive blow that evening.[42]

The shock to Endō, and the realization that he could not easily cut himself off from the contemporary experience of his homeland, dampened his hopes that the European interlude would somehow resolve all his personal conflicts for him. The nearly three years Endō spent in France reinforced his feelings that Western culture was essentially unlike Japanese, and that he had assumed an enormous personal burden when he adopted Christianity.

Shimao Toshio, after missing his appointment with death on August 15, 1945, was repatriated to his home, but less than half a year later he returned to the island where he had been stationed and married a young woman he had met there; she had put on mourning clothes and vowed to die when his orders to launch came through. The couple returned to the Japanese mainland, where Shimao taught Asian history at a variety of colleges and commenced a career as a writer. His early stories clearly indicate that he felt bewildered and isolated; they were filled with nightmarish surrealistic techniques and characters who wander on "solitary journeys." Like Shimao, his characters feel that "When something inauspicious occurs, I am quick to assume that the worst possible outcome will result. . . . My posture is simply to wait for that to happen."[43] It seems almost as if the phantom of death that Shimao eluded on the south seas island continued to pursue him into the postwar world. That nightmare became a reality for him in the summer of 1952, when his wife lost her mind. Beginning in 1956, at approximately the same time that Shimao embraced his wife's religion and was baptized a Catholic, his fiction shifted to depictions of the extraordinary strife that her madness brought into their marriage.

Of the four writers, the sharp, satirical bite of Kojima Nobuo's fiction has been most effective in capturing the agonies and absurdities of the Occupation years. His stories vividly capture the pandemonium, the deprivation, and the panic that swept across the islands after the surrender declaration. An old order that had been considered sacrosanct had been wiped out of existence almost overnight. Without that order people were reduced to a state of chaos, uncertain whether they would be alive tomorrow and not convinced that they cared. Kojima's characters attempt to go on living in a world that has been stripped of meaning, but the best they can do is hobble along like partial cripples, cutting figures at once amusing and pathetic.

The Third Generation ignominiously survived twice, eluding first the bullets of war and then the despair of peace. Certain that they belonged in neither environment, yet unwilling to make the choice Dazai and later Mishima Yukio made, they endured without knowing how they would or should live their lives. They recognized only that whatever moral standards might eventually be adopted for the new Japan, they would not be totally comfortable with them.

Though superficially Japan has changed a great deal since the late 1940s, the sense of loss, if anything, grew more pronounced in the writings of this generation. Perhaps the most significant aspect of the mature fiction of these four has been their sharp, relentless examination of the ultimate human battlefield, the ground upon which the most painful conflicts are waged, and where human relationships are subjected to their most poignant tests. That setting of course is the home, and it is no coincidence that several of the finest novels written over the last twenty-five years by members of the Third Generation have been classified as *katei shōsetsu,* "domestic" novels. These largely autobiographical works often use the motif of insanity to characterize the emotional rift between parent and child, husband and wife.

In the final analysis, it may be that, in their quest to deal with everyday, experiential reality, these authors have delved as perceptively as any into the spiritual roots of contemporary Japanese society. This is certainly the case in the domestic novels of Kojima, Yasuoka, and Shimao. And the search for an understanding of the spiritual basis for human relations lies at the heart of the fiction of Endō Shūsaku, who has examined his own life during and after the war and found that he, like many others he has observed, is a weakling who needs to rely on some higher power to endure the challenges of modern existence.

There are indications in more recent works of these four writers that, having passed through the inferno of complete loss—the loss of a spiritual home, the ravages of war, the humiliation of defeat, and the collapse of the familial order—they are moving toward a sense of resolution, of "reconciliation," to borrow Shiga Naoya's term, within their fiction. But it is a posture that is possible only after the recognition of loss, and their early postwar works, which deal with their own sense of bewilderment and dislocation, will likely remain the most eloquent testimonies of the agony which the modern experience has inflicted upon an entire generation in Japan.

II

Collapse of the Literary Group

THE MOTIF of displacement, so prominent in the writings of the Third Generation, is scarcely a recent phenomenon in Japanese literature. Modernists may seek, within the narrow confines of their own studies, to identify Bunzō in Futabatei's *Ukigumo* as the first "lost" soul in Japanese fiction. But they had best be prepared to argue that claim against the classicist, who will undoubtedly suggest that the honor belongs to Niou and Kaoru in *The Tale of Genji*.

In like manner, the modern Japanese novelist could be described as an individual "cut off from the outside world and . . . completely excluded from power itself,"[1] even though the quotation happens to have been directed at Murasaki Shikibu. With this sense of incertitude so rampant throughout the literature, the important distinction for the Third Generation becomes the manner in which they have transformed their experience into new literary signifiers. But before I examine that achievement, it is necessary to describe the manner in which the creative ego was, for perhaps the first time in Japanese literary history, left totally in isolation by the demise of its traditional support group, the literary coterie.

The history of any literature is, of course, fashioned by the interplay of two distinctive currents—the surge toward individual literary expression, and the drive to integrate that solitary voice into a larger chorus of tradition. What is significant in the Japanese case, however, and pertinent to a discussion of postwar writing, is the special relationship that existed in the premodern tradition between the individual artist and the literary community. Granting voice to private experience most often was the aim of the writings, of course, but that process was tinged with a lingering sense that solitary documentation was a socially disruptive, degenerative activity. As a result, authors of the classical age often sought means of compensating for the subversive substance of their verses and narratives. Those means ranged from the formal—the mythic *jo* of Hitomaro's *chōka,* the associative integrations of the classical poetry anthologies, the group art of the *renga*—to the social—the *hiden* or secret traditions of classical poetics, the established schools of poetic orthodoxy. Structural integration of their individual literary creations into larger, group-centered genres, or social integration into groups of like-minded artists, were the methods they often adopted to atone for the lonely intimacy of their creations.

With the passage of time, however, the author has fallen further within the ranks of society, and the contravening urge toward integration has withered. Writers have come to consider themselves more as outcasts, but at the same time, the means available to blend in with a body of creative activity have slipped from their hands. Although various stages of collapse in the relationship between author and tradition, or even author and text, are apparent throughout the history of Japanese literature, the scope and intensity of the deracination that confronted the Third Generation are extreme. One aspect of this literary dislocation can be seen in the dismantlement in the 1950s of the literary group traditions. The formal literary coterie is a product of the last century or so in Japanese letters, but the concept of group-centered, even group-authored literature can be traced all the way back to the sources of classical Japanese poetry.

With the Meiji Restoration of 1868 and the opening of Japan to the West, the old stable sociopolitical order collapsed, and a new period of individual initiative and its accompanying anxiety was ushered in. It is no coincidence that the most important writers of the age, from Futabatei to Sōseki and Ōgai, focused on the agonies of isolation that resulted from Japan's entry into the modern world, or that the first truly "modern" novel in Japan has as its theme the uneasy adjustment that a group-oriented people had to make into a new individualized society. In literary terms, all the old methods of integration had been debunked. Japan had been severed from its classical roots by rapid industrialization and internationalization. Except for the already splintered haiku, few of the traditional literary forms survived the transition into the Meiji period. It was clear that some new means had to be found to prevent individual authors from becoming totally, suicidally isolated not only from the society—the recluse tradition had, after all, inured them to that—but from their fellow artists as well.

The solution, however feeble it may have been, lay in the creation of a new strain of literary "groups," of coteries of like-minded writers who shared common techniques and philosophies of literature. Much of the history of the last century in Japanese letters can be described in terms of the rise and fall of these formal salons of composition, the modern heirs to the factional "schools" tradition of the medieval age. Surveys of modern Japanese literature regularly center around the interplay between such groups as the Kenyūsha of the 1890s, the Romantics and Naturalists, the antinaturalists, the elitist Shirakaba-ha, the Neosensationalists, and the two groups which dominated literature between the late twenties and the advent of the Second World War: the Proletarian writers, and their adversaries of the Neoaesthetic school.

Amid all this hubbub, it was often the case, as in the medieval period, that those who belonged to none of the established factions—double outsiders, in a sense—were the ones producing the best works of literature. Names that cannot be affiliated with any of the exclusive coteries stand out for their brilliance as authors—Tanizaki Jun'ichirō, Nagai Kafū, Akutagawa Ryūnosuke. Even Kawabata Yasunari, though early associated with the Neosensationalists, broke away from the pack and established himself as an independent voice. But it would be a falsification of modern literary history to minimize the important role which the literary groups and their various organs of publication—the *dōnin zasshi,* or coterie journals—have played in the development of modern fiction in Japan.

Certainly the largest and most ideologically unified literary group ever formed in Japan was the Nihon Bungaku Hōkokukai (Japanese Literature Patriotic Association), organized on May 26, 1942. Over four thousand novelists, dramatists, poets, and essayists were officially "encouraged" to join the association, the aims of which were purely propagandistic. It may well be that the bitter taste this particular "literary group" left in the mouths of many of its participants after the war was the first step toward the collapse of any residual integrative tendencies in modern Japanese literature.

The final demise of the literary coterie did not come, however, until the mid-1950s. It happened when an entire generation of the disoriented was forcibly thrust together, only to find that they were too isolated from one another to speak with a common voice; thereafter the literary group ceased to have anything other than a socializing function. The coterie lost its artistic function in Japan when the Third Generation debuted, creating a final chasm of loneliness for the writer that has not been, and perhaps cannot be, filled.

In the early 1950s, as now, the surest means for a hopeful young writer to achieve widespread recognition and attract the attention of publishers was through receipt of the Akutagawa Prize, an award for new writers conferred semiannually by a committee of established authors. At that time, though, in the confused and boisterous flurry of literary activities that the Occupation had made possible with its more liberal attitudes, it was no easy task for a new writer to decide what, if any, stand to take vis-à-vis literature and life.

There seemed little point, for instance, in trying to topple the established deans of fiction—writers like Tanizaki, who had maintained a stubborn silence during the war years and then published his masterpiece, *The Makioka Sisters,* between 1946 and 1949. Kawabata Yasunari too, declaring that he would henceforth write nothing but elegies for the lost Japan, in 1949 began serializing his finest work, *Yama no oto* (The Sound of the Mountain; trans. 1964). These and similar writers were virtually above challenge after the war; their familiarity with classical tradition, their seasoned fluency of style, and their sensitivity to the misery of their contemporaries rendered them both invulnerable to attack and beyond imitation for a young writer who lacked their breadth of vision and experience.

A new proletarian literary movement had gotten under way soon after General MacArthur opened the prison doors to liberate an entire generation of Marxist protestors. But the movement itself suffered as the new Japanese Communist Party was weakened by the Red Purges of 1950 and an intellectual rift that eventually split the Party. The primary reason the neoleftist literary faction crumbled, however, was the death of its finest talent, Miyamoto Yuriko, in 1951. At any rate, the aspiring writers born around 1920 knew and cared too little about liberal dogma to want to join such a movement. Proletarianism, after all, was just another in a long string of -isms they refused to trust.

The most vociferous group on the literary scene in the early fifties was made up of men in their midthirties who had dabbled in Marxism as youths and witnessed the suppression of intellectual dissent during the war. These were the Sengoha (après-guerre) writers, who claimed to speak for literary orthodoxy in the post-1945 society. Essentially they were the last viable literary "group" in Japan, their coming together a result of common war experience and roots in the prewar proletarian ideology. However much individual diversity existed among the Sengoha writers, they were held together in a cohesive literary movement by philosophical bonds, common goals, and their own journal *Kindai Bungaku* (Modern Literature). As Shindō Junkō, one of the critics who has affiliated himself closely with the Third Generation, notes:

> The Sengoha writers shared the same philosophy or the same educational background, or at least had banded together into a group of like-minded individuals. They were warriors who espoused new artistic or enlightenment causes. It is reported that Takeda Taijun once exploded, "Each separate writer is an individual! Critics have to give each of us individual consideration!" But even a writer like Takeda cannot easily be separated from his image as "Takeda of *Kindai Bungaku*."[2]

The barrenness of the literature that had bowed to political domination by the military was obvious to the Sengoha. In their manifesto for a new literature, they rejected the notion that political concerns should take precedence over literary ones. They promoted an existential view of life and rejected the narrow, egotistical vision of the prewar Naturalists. Perhaps foremost among their goals was a desire to expand the scale of fiction, to place human beings within a Marxist "historical perspective" and treat human experience from a variety of philosophical, political, and historical angles.

The Sengoha tended to reject traditional, native forms of literary expression. Some, like Nakamura Shin'ichirō, wanted to sweep away the existing traditions in Japanese fiction (specifically, the prewar "I-novel") and replace them with the ideals of nineteenth-century European fiction. A few even proposed that Japanese poetry be reshaped into rhymed sonnet form. One critic associated with the Sengoha rejected the haiku as a "second-rate" art form, while another called the viability of the entire body of Japanese lyric expression into question.[3]

The Sengoha writers and critics left a distinctive mark on postwar literature, filling *Kindai Bungaku* with essays and stories aimed at the establishment of a new, "individualistic literature."[4] The fiction produced by the Sengoha novelists is impressive both in its dense philosophical content and in its sheer volume. Few authors in the history of Japanese literature have written such sustained and lengthy narratives as the Sengoha. And in the profound questions about personal guilt and the meaning of human existence which they raise, few war novels can rival Ōoka Shōhei's *Nobi* (Fires on the Plain, 1952; trans. 1957) or Noma Hiroshi's *Shinkū chitai* (Zone of Emptiness, 1952). Similarly, Haniya Yutaka's *Shirei* (Spirits of the Dead, 1946–48; final chapter 1977) is distinguished by its attempt to cope with the relationship between politics and the individual. The example which the Sengoha set for their contemporaries was nothing if not daunting.

The subsequent Third Generation of writers was, in fact, easily intimidated by both the Sengoha and the established deans of modern fiction. Nothing in their experience had prepared them to ponder life in the philosophical fashion their seniors had adopted. Their brush with war and death had not inspired them to study questions of guilt but merely taught them the need to scramble for survival. By 1952, when they were ready to settle into literary careers, the public mood in Japan had changed perceptibly. The peace treaty ratified that year brought the foreign military occupation to an end, and the "postwar" period personified by the Sengoha writers essentially came to a close. The focus shifted from national/philosophical to individual/bread-and-butter goals once again—perhaps for the first time in over two decades. The concerns of everyday life rather than existential crises were what occupied the thoughts of the commoner in Japan. And the new writers—the Third Generation—were those who gave voice to this new public sentiment, echoing not only its external features but also the anxiety buried beneath.

The Emergence of the Third Generation

IN THE January 1953 issue of the leading literary journal *Bungakkai*, an article appeared entitled "Daisan no shinjin" (The Third Generation of New Writers), marking the first appearance of the term "Third Generation." Unfortunately its precise meaning was never clarified. Yamamoto Kenkichi, the author of the article and a leading critic, wrote the piece on assignment from the editors of the journal. His initial remarks indicate the vagueness of the term:

> The editorial staff assigned me to write under this title about the newcomers who have appeared over the past year. But I am not at all sure what this "third generation" business is supposed to mean. They probably thought up the name after seeing the movie *The Third Man.*[5]

In fact, about a year earlier the critic Usui Yoshimi had published a brief article in *Bungakkai* titled "Daini no shinjin" (The Second Generation of New Writers), and obviously the editors had simply expected Yamamoto to comment on authors who had debuted over the past twelve months. Thus the provenance of the term itself is easily explained; but it is the manner in which the appellation "Third Generation" came to be used that is significant. And Yamamoto—perhaps unwittingly—pointed the way by making his offhanded reference to the Carol Reed–Graham Greene film.

The motion picture *The Third Man,* first released in 1950, had attracted popular audiences in Japan by 1952. But as Kojima Nobuo, one of those who came to be numbered among the Third Generation, has pointed out, there was no "third man" in the film. "He" was an expendable figment of a criminal imagination—a leftover, a man of no consequence once his insubstantiality was confirmed. In that sense, anything in Japan labeled "the third" this-or-that in the early fifties came to mean a leftover, something or someone expendable, of no value or endurance. Yoshiyuki compares the usage with that of a "third-class ticket" or a "third-rate executive."[6] However Yamamoto or the *Bungakkai* editors intended it, in Japanese literary history "Third Generation" soon came to be used in a pejorative sense by critics who considered the popularity of these writers a transitory phenomenon.[7]

And yet, for all the offhandedness with which Yamamoto dismisses the relationship between the film and the new generation of writers, it seems to me that there is a significant—though clearly unconscious—artistic link between the two. The film's narrator, Holly Martins, is in many ways a pragmatic, detached "I," a newly arrived visitor among the ruins of war-ravaged Vienna who admits that he never knew the city in its days of glory. Vienna itself is torn into occupied foreign segments, and black-marketeering seems to be the chosen mode of survival. The war, and the chaotic rubble it creates, are coeval with the postwar present of the film. The most common setting for the film's action is the sewers, where the childlike child-killer Harry Lime ("He never grew up. The world grew up around him, that's all.") is eventually trapped and killed. Everything within the film seems disrupted, distorted. Even Reed's camera angles appear askew—we find ourselves gazing up obliquely at characters from a perspective near the floor.

However unwitting the connection, the narrative style of *The Third Man* has much in common with the literary techniques the Third Generation would adopt. The narrators in their fiction are often detached observers, wanderers who have witnessed destruction but not participated directly in it. The shambles of postwar Vienna are congruous with the rain-soaked, bloated landscapes where the Third Generation fictions are staged. Perspectives are generally distorted, and time most often has no meaning of any kind.

What I am suggesting here is not any sort of direct link between the cinematic techniques of Greene and Reed and the literary styles of these Japanese authors, but rather a substantive justification for labeling some of them a "third" generation. Their art has allowed them to build upon the rubble of their personal experience and to fashion literature which, like the film for which they were named, has an enduring, evocative quality.

A significant step in the attempt to create a new literary group was a round-table discussion among fledgling writers printed in the same issue of *Bungakkai* as Yamamoto's brief article. Titled "Shinjin sakka bungaku o kataru" (New Writers Discuss Literature), the panel included Yoshiyuki Junnosuke, Agawa Hiroyuki, Yasuoka Shōtarō, Takeda Shigetarō, Itō Keiichi, and Miura Shumon. Their conversations failed to produce earth-shattering comments on literary theory, but thanks to their participation, Yasuoka, Miura, and Takeda were asked by the persistent *Bungakkai* editors to draw up a list of new writers and critics who might be invited to participate in a social gathering which the magazine intended to sponsor. None of the three men felt familiar enough with the contemporary literature, so they went for help to the one man they knew was an avid, critically perceptive reader—Yoshiyuki Junnosuke. In Yoshiyuki's words:

> I was told that the editors at *Bungakkai* were planning to sponsor a get-together for new writers and critics. They wanted it to be a regular meeting, held once a month, and they had asked [Yasuoka, Miura, and Takeda] to agree upon a list of ten writers and five critics. . . . The editors requested that we include Gomi Yasusuke, who had just received the Akutagawa Prize, and Shimao Toshio. . . . So we wrote down the names of the ten people we thought should be invited on the left side of a sheet of paper; any other names that came up went into the right column. In our selection, we did our best to choose solely on the basis of the value of their writings. None of us had ever met Kojima Nobuo, for instance, but he went in the left column.
>
> The final selection was made by the *Bungakkai* editors, but they pretty much acceded to our wishes.[8]

Invitations were sent out to each of the candidates on the list.

The parlor-game manner in which the participants in a new "literary group" were chosen clearly indicates the degree to which the gathering itself was the result of external manipulation rather than an internally felt need. The image of four young men huddled in Yoshiyuki's apartment, debating a list of writers they were curious about but had not had the opportunity to meet, is a succinct commentary on the lack of cohesion within the Third Generation gathering. As with the label that was pasted on them, the group into which they were congregated—by the same journal editors—had no literary meaning in and of itself.

There is some question as to the exact date the first meeting was held.[9] In any case, within a month or so after the initial "Third Generation" article appeared in print, a group of young writers met together under the auspices of *Bungakkai,* at a restaurant called Hasegawa in the Higashi Ginza section of Tokyo.

Bungakkai editor Suzuki Susumu chaired the initial meeting. The first order of business was to create a name for the group. After some discussion, it was agreed that they would call the gathering "Ichi-ni-kai" (The One-Two Association), since their plans were to meet on the twelfth day of each month. "Not a bad name," quipped Kondō Keitarō, one of the invitees. "After all, it'll probably fizzle out after 'one' or 'two' meetings, anyway."[10] Kondō's forecast turned out something less than accurate, but his devil-may-care attitude toward the association conveys the degree of commitment some felt toward the get-together.

At this point in time, there was still no identification between the members of the One-Two Association and the literary term "Third Generation." The social gathering was attended by many writers who had not been mentioned in Yamamoto's article, including Yasuoka and Miura. Not until some two years later did critics begin to make a correlation between this group and the "Third Generation."

One of the distinguishing but somewhat peculiar aspects of the One-Two Association was that literature was seldom if ever a topic of discussion when the writers and critics met together. Kojima notes that the only subjects Kondō was interested in discussing were women and dogs.[11] Shindō lists their range of discussion topics as including women, the best bars in town, their wins and losses at gambling, and related themes.[12] In contrast with the stern, single-minded men who populated the *Kindai Bungaku* assemblage, these new writers seemed frivolous and not wholly dedicated to their craft. The nature of their association must, however, be taken into consideration. They had not come together because of common literary goals or out of a mutual desire to reform contemporary Japanese writing. There was no shared interest in European literature, no impassioned political philosophy, and no literary journal that would stand as a banner symbolizing their ideals. In short, none of the motivations that had brought the Sengoha writers together existed among these men. They came together because the editors of an important magazine had invited them to a free dinner. Their notions of what literature should be and do were highly individualistic, so much so that they did not feel comfortable discussing them in a "group" situation.

Bungakkai no doubt was hoping to be the sponsor and creative outlet for a new literary generation in Japan. But the writers themselves gravitated to the Higashi Ginza restaurant out of a peculiar mixture of envy and affection. The anxiety that another might be the first to produce an unexpected masterpiece, tempered by the knowledge that everyone else felt equally ill at ease—this blend of curiosity, caution, and camaraderie first brought the members of the One-Two Association together.[13] Eight of the nine new writers present had already been nominated for the Akutagawa Prize before the first meeting.[14] So in a very real sense the authors had come to that meeting to have a look at the competition. A lingering sense of rivalry may partially explain why literature was so infrequently discussed. When Yasuoka was introduced at that first meeting to Gomi Yasusuke, who had just received the Akutagawa Prize, his antagonistic greeting was, "I'm an artist right down to my pores!"[15] The same emotions that built barriers of rivalry between Yasuoka and Gomi may have put up walls around the topic of literature, one too sensitive to be discussed among men still uncertain of their own qualifications as writers, and still sending out hesitant feelers in search of friendship.

It is evident, then, that even at this initial meeting of the One-Two Association the new writers had no common literary goals to discuss. Their careers had begun separately and distinctly, and there was no reason any of them needed to belong to a literary group at this juncture. Having no shared philosophy, they needed no framework or forum from which to present their individual ideas. Takeda Taijun of the Sengoha may have been the one who spluttered "Each separate writer is an individual!" but it was the writers of the One-Two Association who best exemplified those words.

There are, of course, exceptions to such generalizations. Kojima Nobuo, of the assembled group probably the most familiar with both Japanese and foreign writings, had an earnest interest in literature and longed to trade ideas with others. So when each monthly One-Two assemblage broke up, Kojima would go out for a second round of drinks and debates with the critics from the group, leaving the other writers to go their ways with their discussions of women and the race track.[16] Kojima was the elder of the group, older than many of the Sengoha writers, but his distinctively bitter humor and his dissatisfactions with the literary aims of the Sengoha ranked him in style if not in temperament with the One-Two Association writers—though he too had an instinctive dislike for systems of classification.[17]

Shimao Toshio was another unusual selection for inclusion in the association, though as we have seen, he was invited at the insistence of the *Bungakkai* editors. Two years younger than Kojima, Shimao had worked on a coterie magazine named *Kōki* (Splendor) with Mishima Yukio the year after the surrender. He began publishing fiction in 1948, earlier than most of the Third Generation, and his literary techniques, centering on surrealistic-type dreams and a hallucinatory approach to reality, are closer to Abe Kōbō's than those of any other writers of the day. Only later, after his self-imposed exile to the islands south of the mainland, did Shimao's style and subject matter come to resemble that of others in the Third Generation. Perhaps his early social contacts with the One-Two Association writers helped shape the substance of his fiction after his estrangement from everyday life in Tokyo.

This uneasy gathering would have dissolved quickly, it seems, but several members of the group developed friendships among themselves, and Yoshiyuki's small apartment in Ichigaya became a gathering place for the most important new writers. If literature was discussed at all, it was in reference to their mutual hopes for the Akutagawa Prize.[18] And indeed, at this juncture a stranger to the group—success—intervened in the form of official recognition, providing the anomalous coterie with some superficial justification for sticking together. The One-Two Association had held six monthly meetings[19] when Yasuoka Shōtarō was awarded the Akutagawa Prize in 1953 for two of his short stories, "Warui nakama" (Bad Company; trans. 1984) and "Inki na tanoshimi" (Guilty Pleasures; trans. 1984). It was the beginning of a trend. A year later, Yoshiyuki received the prize; Kojima and Shōno Junzō, another member of the association, shared the award later the same year, and Kondō was the recipient in the first half of 1956. Once public recognition had come to one after another of these writers, it was inevitable that literary critics would begin to focus attention upon them. The coincidence that each of the Akutagawa Prize winners for several years running was a member of the One-Two Association did not escape notice, and very naturally critics started searching for areas of common interest and influence among these newly honored authors. It was not immediately apparent to the critics that whatever similarities might be found in the writings of the One-Two Association members had developed considerably after the organization of the group; they seemed oblivious to the fact that the assemblage itself had not been formed out of common literary aspirations.

Not all the critical voices were enthusiastic. In February 1954,

Hirano Ken of *Kindai Bungaku* expressed what was to be a common criticism of the writings of the group:

> [This month] I read several works by the writers in the "Third Generation" group (?)—Shōno Junzō's "Enji" [Rouge] and Yoshiyuki Junnosuke's "Shūu" [Sudden Shower] in *Bungakkai,* Yasuoka Shōtarō's "Sābisu daitai yōin" [Personnel of the Service Squadron] in *Shinchō.* . . . But I felt that none of the stories had the depth that lingers with the reader after he has finished it.[20]

Two interesting points emerge from this critique. First, Hirano's well-placed question mark suggests that he too had doubts whether these writers constituted a true literary group in the sense of the term to which he had grown accustomed through his associations with the Sengoha authors. Second, it is worth noting that the Yoshiyuki story Hirano mentions, "Shūu," is the story for which Yoshiyuki received the Akutagawa Prize. The fact that Hirano found the story shallow indicates the difficulty he had accepting the view of literature—or, as he saw it, the lack of viewpoint—expressed in the writings of this generation. A stern advocate of large-scale writings with heavy social and historical content, Hirano was displeased also with the selection of Yasuoka as the Akutagawa Prize winner in 1953.

Hirano was not alone. Ishikawa Tatsuzō, one of the members of the selection committee for the prize, opposed the majority consensus that Yasuoka should be the recipient.

> I had not even considered the possibility that Yasuoka's two stories would be nominated so it came as a total surprise to me when they were awarded the prize. Since I had opposed the selection, I felt a responsibility to defend my stance. The day after the award was announced, I reread both of Yasuoka's stories, but I still had no idea why they had been chosen.[21]

Few of the Sengoha authors or critics could empathize with the reduced scale of the new fiction, or the weak, ineffectual characters who populated it. Unaffiliated critics like Yamamoto Kenkichi saw in the narrowed world of their fiction a reflection of the gap between the experiences of their generation and those of the Sengoha writers. Responding to Takeda Taijun's angry insistence that each individual writer be treated as separate entity, Yamamoto sought to defend his use of the term "Third Generation."

> I too am opposed to the idea of ignoring the differences between individual writers and applying a label to them. But I feel that in the case [of the Third Generation], that label was spawned out of a desire to come up with evidence of similarities linking the new writers together. Takeda's generation was called the Sengoha because they had similar motives, and Takeda himself did not object to the appellation. . . . It was with a view to the current sufferings of those who survived the war and have now come into prominence that the term [Third Generation] was applied to them. I think that we must clearly recognize the changes in the nature of suffering that must be endured by the Third Generation—the generation which is in every sense a product of the war.[22]

With the literary world still fundamentally dominated by the critics of the Sengoha, it was only natural that considerable negative criticism heralded the advent of the Third Generation on the scene. They had many detractors at this early point, and few defenders. The major critics of their own generation were absorbed in studies of earlier literature, often, ironically, that of the Sengoha writers. Shindō Junkō's major work of the early years, *Sengo bungaku no kishu* (The Standard Bearers of Postwar Literature, 1955), dealt with the writings of Takeda Taijun, Mishima, Noma Hiroshi, Ōoka Shōhei and Shiina Rinzō.[23] Okuno Takeo was obsessed with his study of Dazai Osamu; and Muramatsu Takeshi, an avid student of French literature, was tracing the influence of Valéry on contemporary Japanese fiction.

Transition to the Conceptions Society

WITH VIRTUALLY no influential champions, and with the entire *Kindai Bungaku* coterie seeking to tear down the very foundations of their literature, the Third Generation in the mid-1950s had arrived at the brink of their first identity crisis. After auspicious debuts and Akutagawa Prizes for a majority of its members, the One-Two Association began to fall apart at its none-too-tight seams. This was only natural, since the group had never possessed any real purpose beyond obtaining recognition of its participants. The initial sense of distrust and rivalry had been abated by receipt of the prize, and a few members of the group began to consider some literary goals for their association. There was talk about creating a coterie magazine along the lines of the Sengoha's *Kindai Bungaku,* but the journal, which was to have been called *Kōsō* (Conceptions), never got off the ground. The One-Two Association simply did not have a unified view of literature to present before the reading public. Unlike the prewar Shirakaba-ha[24] or the proletarian literary movements, which had offered valid antitheses to the prevailing literary attitudes of their days, the Third Generation did not confront the Sengoha establishment with a fresh approach to literature or a new flag to wave.[25] They were united only in their dislike for any single philosophy of literature. But such a disjointed, ragtag unity can scarcely provide the inspiration required to put together a coherent literary journal.

From hindsight it is clear that the members of the Third Generation were not conscious of the significance of their writings. They may have felt as though they had nothing new to offer, but they were too close to the situation to realize that they were presenting a significant if somewhat poorly organized alternative to the dogmatism of the Sengoha generation and the staunch traditionalism of established writers like Kafū and Kawabata. They could not have known that, in their rejection of wholesale Western literary imports, they were restoring Japanese literature to its traditional course. They were not aware that, by shifting the focus from exalted ideas and elaborate surface decoration to petty human activities and restrained prose, they were moving closer to a more detailed study of human frustrations and agony in the chaos of modern society than had previously been attempted.

Although the journal *Kōsō* was never published, the discussions about the possibility of a consolidated literary effort were sufficient motivation for the members of the One-Two Association to restructure their meetings and do some shuffling in the membership. In February or March 1954 the One-Two Association was dissolved (after somewhat more than "one or two meetings") and then immediately replaced by the "Kōsō no kai" (The Conceptions Society). There were advantages to the change: the gathering took in some fresh blood —Hattori Tatsu was invited to join the Conceptions Society because of his active support for the writers of the group. Endō Shūsaku, who had returned from three years of study in France in 1953, had just published his first collection of essays, *Furansu no daigakusei* (University Students in France, 1953). At a party after his book was published, Endō happened to run into one of his old classmates from Keiō University, Yasuoka Shōtarō. Yasuoka had, in fact, crashed the party to determine whether the scraggly student he had seen polishing shoes on the Mita campus after the war was the same Endō who had written *University Students in France*. He was astounded to find that they were one and the same person, and Yasuoka invited Endō to attend the Conceptions Society meetings.[26]

Three of the critics who had belonged to the One-Two Association —Okuno Takeo, Muramatsu Takeshi, and Hino Keizō—declined the invitation to join the new group, and instead struck out on their own with the creation of a journal of literary criticism, *Gendai Hyōron* (Contemporary Criticism), which began publication in 1954.[27] The loss of these critics was a symptom of the internal slackness of the outgoing One-Two Association. Yoshiyuki asserts that the writers who formed the new Conceptions Society purposely ousted the critics from their number. In retaliation, the *Gendai Hyōron* group rejected most of the writers from the Conceptions clique, allowing only Kojima and Shimao, the authors they considered "serious," to attend their discussions on literary theory. The Conceptions men claimed that these critics had no understanding of literature; the critics retorted that the Third Generation had no acquaintance with ideas.[28] This rift was serious for them. It was the final break with critics of their own age, those with the greatest potential sympathy for the thrust of their writings, and it assured them that they would be even further isolated from the literary world. This schism partially explains why the writings of the Third Generation have been almost universally ignored in Japan until recent years, when younger commentators such as Ueda Miyoji, Akiyama Shun, and Etō Jun began to examine their contributions to postwar literature.

The one obvious benefit accruing from the creation of the Conceptions Society was that the membership rolls were finally crystallized; critics today generally equate affiliation with the Conceptions Society and membership in the Third Generation. Endō was the last arrival to be included, and he made it under the wire as a critic, not a novelist. He had always aspired to write fiction, however, and felt he could not qualify for the Conceptions Society if he did not at least try to produce a piece of imaginative writing. In November 1954 he published his first short story, "Aden made" (As Far as Aden). The reception was mixed, but in May his short novel *Shiroi hito* (White

Men) stirred up considerable discussion, and two months later he received the Akutagawa Prize for the work. It was a precocious beginning, one that assured him a permanent position in the Conceptions Society.

One significant change in the Japanese literary climate served to bring the names and activities of these writers before a larger reading public than ever before. By 1955 the mass media had infiltrated many homes in Japan. There were television sets in 53,000 homes throughout the country that year.[29] Between 1954 and 1956, Japanese newspapers serialized almost two hundred novels written expressly for popular audiences.[30] Of the Third Generation, the first to write a newspaper novel was Shōno Junzō, in 1955. Yasuoka followed suit in 1958. Endō, one of the all-time champions of the medium with nearly a dozen newspaper novels to his credit, wrote his first in 1959.

Only writers who felt comfortable on their own could take full advantage of the new expanded audience. The Sengoha writers were more at home in their group, and it therefore devolved upon the Third Generation to assume the role of literary popularizers via the mass media. In 1955, control over the literary world had clearly slipped away from the grasp of the *Kindai Bungaku* coterie; no literary work of any significance came from the Sengoha writers that year.

The retreat of the Sengoha did not, however, automatically signify that the torch of literary orthodoxy had been passed directly into the hands of the Third Generation. Younger runners had joined the marathon, as if in response to the assertion that the Third Generation was racing toward oblivion. The Akutagawa Prize for the latter half of 1955 went to Ishihara Shintarō, a young unknown who "did what he liked . . . in the way he liked,"[31] thereby offending virtually every established writer with his iconoclastic, self-centered style and his eager association with the journalistic media. Ishihara posed for magazine photographs like a model, appeared on television, set new fads in hair styles, and went on to act in and direct film versions of several of his novels. He was the first example of a writer who had completely capitulated—in the view of the old guard—to the temptations of the popular media. The critic Togaeri Hajime doubtless had Ishihara in mind when he surveyed the chaotic individualism of the world of letters in 1956 and lamented that "the literary establishment has collapsed!"[32]

Somewhere in between the group-oriented, cautiously conservative older writers of the Sengoha and the brash new wave of authors symbolized by Ishihara stood the Third Generation, in the middle once again, isolated but yearning to communicate with those around them. The Third Generation were likely the first Japanese novelists to have the combined resources of television, newspapers, and weekly popular journals available to them. This afforded them the opportunity to reach a wider audience than had ever been available in Japan before. It also allowed them, if they wished, to overuse or abuse the media as they saw fit. Though they have collectively avoided the extremities of bad taste in self-commercialization reached by a Truman Capote or a Norman Mailer, still the fact that some of these writers have faces readily recognizable to the average television viewer indicates the manner in which media exposure has proved a mixed blessing.

Writers in Exile

AS THOUGH they sensed that it would be television and newspapers and not the literary journal that would carry forth the names and activities of the Third Generation, the editors of *Bungakkai* withdrew their support from the Conceptions Society at the end of 1954, declaring publicly that the gathering of writers they had fostered had "served out its purpose."[33] Although the publishers at Chūō Kōron stepped in and offered to take over sponsorship of the group, negotiations broke off when the proposed journal *Kōsō* failed to materialize. The Conceptions Society was converted into a self-sustaining organization, supported by donations from its members. *Bungakkai* had been forced into the tacit admission that they had failed in their attempt to create a cohesive literary group that could bring prestige to themselves and rival *Kindai Bungaku.* The Conceptions Society became, in short, a social club.

Meetings continued on a monthly basis throughout 1955 and 1956. Endō has described a typical meeting of the Conceptions Society:

> Topics such as the relationship between politics and literature, which were invariably discussed at gatherings of young critics at *Gendai Hyōron,* were almost never debated by the Conceptions Society. Instead we devoted our full attention to a piece of fiction that one of our group had written, discussing it from a variety of

> angles, or relating some unusual event we had seen or heard about. . . . We all paid close attention to what our fellow members were writing. We influenced and were influenced by one another. It might be an exaggeration to call it friendly rivalry, but something very near to it always lay at the heart of our conversations. At any rate I for one was always interested in anything one of the group had to say, no matter how mundane the topic. At the same time, this was a gathering of men of very strong individuality, and I often had to pause and wonder how I could carve out a course uniquely my own.[34]

One significant difference between the One-Two Association and the Conceptions gathering was that literature was no longer a taboo topic for conversation. Clearly the writers were feeling more at home with their profession and more confident of their own talents. But the strong outlines of individuality continued to dominate the meetings of the new society, and the mention of continued, though friendly, rivalry suggests that whatever discussions of literature may have taken place, the definition and refinement of individual tastes still lay at the heart of their debates.

Despite the growing sophistication of their meetings together, however, all was not well in the careers of the Third Generation. Their initial literary statements about everyday life in postwar Japan had been made by around 1955. They had detailed the frustrations, the humiliations, and the absurdities that crowded the life of the modern Japanese Everyman. But it was growing increasingly evident to several of their number that they could not go on endlessly repeating the same refrains, chronicling the same failures in the same forms. Critics had earlier expressed doubts that they would be able to sustain their literature along the same lines for any extended period of time. Now the writers themselves were beginning to share those doubts.

In the midst of this crisis, one of the members of the group defected. Although he had not been a central figure in either group, his self-imposed exile underscored for every member the literary impasse most of them had reached, and at the same time suggested a possible way out of the artistic cul-de-sac. Shimao Toshio was the exile. When his wife developed severe emotional problems, they shipped their children off to her family and went into an asylum together. After six months of treatment, Shimao withdrew totally from the Tokyo literary scene, and the couple went to live on Amami Ōshima, a tiny island far removed from the southernmost tip of the Japanese archipelago. Shimao had always been a loner, even in the precariously assembled One-Two Association, but the others had recognized him as a distinctive literary talent. With Shimao gone, those who were left behind were forced to stare openly at the underlying weaknesses in their own writings.

Critics did not hesitate to predict the fate of the Third Generation. One suggested that "The 'Third Generation' are trapped in a valley between the Sengoha and the new forces led by Ishihara. I think they'll probably be swallowed up in that valley, never to be seen again."[35]

One could argue it was sheer coincidence that, just as such forecasts proliferated, both Shōno Junzō and Kojima Nobuo left Japan and were "swallowed up" in the United States. Or it just might be possible that the path of "expatriation" Shimao had chosen began to appear attractive to others of the Third Generation. Both Shōno and Kojima received and accepted invitations from the Rockefeller Foundation to travel and study in the United States. While such an invitation might seem from the Western perspective to be something of an honor, given the keen competition in the Japanese literary world and the need for a writer to be in the thick of things in Tokyo at all times, the possibility that both men were eager for some kind of "distraction" to take their minds off the stagnation in their own writings seems highly plausible.[36] Their study abroad was in a sense a retreat, a disengagement from pressing literary demands to allow for retrenchment, rethinking, and perhaps a remodeling of the forms their literature was taking.

Exile for the Third Generation, then, was not essentially a process of recoiling from the realities of the society in which they lived. It was more a realization that their initial dismantling of the literary ego had been achieved, and that their subsequent fiction needed somehow to confront the void that remained. The sometimes stifling atmosphere of the Tokyo literary scene was no place in 1957 for deep self-reflection. The writing that Shimao began to do a few months after his retreat to Amami Ōshima is a clear testimony to the value of self-exile; his Amami works include some of the finest fiction that has been written in Japan in the twentieth century. And though

America as a nation plays a minor role in the postexpatriate writings of Kojima Nobuo,[37] the opportunity to remove himself from his work gave him the margin he needed to strike out in bold new directions after his return to Japan. Certainly exile for the Third Generation was a positive experience that clearly transformed their literature.

With Shimao, Shōno, and Kojima gone, monthly meetings of the Conceptions Society were often reduced to three members—Yasuoka, Yoshiyuki, and Endō.[38] Requests from journals for short stories trickled to a halt (neither Yasuoka nor Yoshiyuki received a single request for a manuscript from the leading journal *Shinchō* between 1956 and 1958), and editors made it clear that they expected more substantive works from these writers.[39] Even former supporters seemed to be turning against them. Kitahara Takeo, an author and editor who had initially been an ally, complained that the Third Generation had "finally sunk to keeping food on the table by writing pulp novels."[40] After that harsh attack appeared, Yasuoka wrote a letter to Shōno in America saying: "The Third Fleet is sinking!"[41]

The fleet suffered another tactical blow in 1957 with the appearance of two more vibrant young writers, Ōe Kenzaburō and Kaikō Ken. Both men were hailed at once by critics and received the Akutagawa Prize within six months of each other. The acclaim for these fresh talents echoed dully in the ears of writers who could almost feel themselves being "swallowed up" with each passing moment.

It was, ironically, the last straggler to join the ranks of the Third Generation who provided the group with what little cheer they could muster in the bleakness of 1957. Endō Shūsaku, a self-styled "gob of curiosity"[42] and the Third Generation writer with the greatest affinity for the mass media, took the lead in guiding the members of the Conceptions Society on a series of frivolous expeditions into the world of movies, newspapers, radio, and television. Serious writers before this time had seldom displayed the desire or the ability to make use of media other than the printed page to promote their own works, much less their private personalities. Several of the Third Generation, at Endō's instigation, became perhaps the first authors whose faces became familiar to the average Japanese though their media exposure. These exploits into various media served to strengthen the views of the older generations of writers that the Third Generation were not truly "serious" about literature. "Akutagawa Prize authors" visiting a motion picture set or some such place began to appear in the major Tokyo newspapers.[43] On one occasion, Endō arranged for Yasuoka, Yoshiyuki, Miura, and Shindō to appear as guests on a radio network broadcast; participants were scheduled to discuss their wives' foibles and idiosyncracies before a nationwide audience. All the participants had assumed that Endō would be joining them as a panelist, but when the broadcast began to air they caught sight of Endō in the control booth, grinning broadly as if to say, "I've got you again!"[44]

Whatever the merits and failings of the escapades that Endō initiated in the late 1950s, his intention at that time was clearly to provide himself and his colleagues with a release—an escape, as it were, from the psychological burden of the bad press they were receiving from the literary critics. The comic relief Endō brought into their lives had an unmistakably medicinal effect. The releases from tension that he provided gave them a detached perspective on their situation, and afforded them the leisure to reshape their individual approaches to fiction. Without the excursions Endō planned for them, it is quite possible that depression and anxiety over their literary fortunes could have scuttled once and for all the ships of the Third Fleet. Shindō comments:

> It was, I suppose, fortunate for our mental health at that time that Endō Shūsaku was one of our number. . . . I imagine [those escapades] stick in my mind because they took place during the depressing period when the "Third Fleet was sinking." Endō then was constantly coming up with new forms of diversion. That was in his nature, of course, but it was with uncanny sensitivity to our situation that he filled his role as our jester.[45]

Exile assumes various guises, and in the case of those writers who were left behind in Japan by colleagues escaping to the United States or the islands of the sea, the most convenient and refreshing mode of exile was buffoonery. Not everyone in the group shared Endō's fondness for pranks, but those who did take part in the activities were able, if only in passing moments, to remove themselves from their roles as serious writers and get a breath of fresh air. When they returned to their writing desks, the respite seemed to have given them the energy to put words to paper in new, more interesting ways.

The Second Surge

IT WAS not solely as jester at the crumbling court of the "Third Generation" that Endō proved himself a welcome member of the group. He also was the first of the writers of the Conceptions Society to pull out of the creative slump that had come over them. Perhaps it was because he had started as a writer of fiction three or four years later than the others; possibly it was his indominantly active mind and curious nature; or it might have been the impetus of his search for a coherent grasp on his own religion that helped Endō take over the creative lead. At any rate, the publication of his *Umi to dokuyaku* (The Sea and Poison, 1957; trans. 1972) signaled the return of the Third Generation to critical and popular acclaim. Endō's novel was an unexpected success and received two important literary awards.[46] It assured Endō a position among the leading young writers of the day and gave his colleagues in the Conceptions Society new critical life.

Yasuoka was stimulated by—or envious of?—Endō's success in the longer form, and over the next two years he produced one long novel—*Shita dashi tenshi* (Impudent Angel, 1958)—and then a medium-length work, *Kaihen no kōkei* (A View by the Sea, 1959; trans. 1984), which received both the Geijutsu Senshō and the Noma prizes for literature. The hex seemed to be broken. In the decade beginning in 1957 the Third Generation writers were awarded one literary prize after another. In the wake of the "collapse of the literary establishment," literary awards had become the center of attention, and throughout the 1960s these authors repeatedly produced works that were honored with such distinctions.[47] Even critics who had looked forward with some relish to the demise of the group marveled at the maturity and durability of these new works. Others could only express their disbelief and dismay. When Ōoka Shōhei, one of the more irascible members of the Sengoha clique, returned from a half-year trip abroad at the end of 1962, he expressed surprise and disappointment at the discovery that during his absence the Third Generation had "come to roost" at the center of the literary world in Japan.[48]

In these maturing works, a distinctly new style and approach to literature are apparent, although the emphasis on the details of everyday life has not changed. The most prominent form these later works take is the *katei shōsetsu,* the "domestic novel" as it was employed by Kojima, Shōno, Shimao, and Miura. These novels open up new lines of exploration first suggested in the writings of Japan's earliest "domestic" novelists, Tokutomi Roka, Ozaki Kōyō, and later Shimazaki Tōson and Shiga Naoya.

What is most noticeable about these later works, however, is the degree of variety that exists among the novels of each writer. In the early years of their association, as they traded complaints about nagging editors or confided uneasiness about the progress of a forthcoming story, there was a sense of camaraderie, of a shared fate that linked these authors together. But such a period of mutual influence could not last forever. Maturity in a groupless literary society could only come through the final act of cord-cutting. It is remarkable that the Conceptions Society survived the exodus of Shimao, Shōno, and Kojima. But the meetings did in fact continue through their exiles and for a short time after Shōno and Kojima returned from the United States.

The year 1960 was a crucial one for the Conceptions Society, though not in the same sense that it was for many other authors in Japan. The members of the Third Generation were conspicuous by their absence from the many debates that arose in opposition to the renewal of the U.S.-Japan mutual security agreement. The so-called "Ampo riots" were a political and intellectual watershed for post-Occupation Japan, but the Third Generation writers displayed little interest in such matters. While some in Japan chafed for greater national autonomy from the Asian policies established in Washington, these writers recognized an ever-widening chasm opening between their literary concerns and the ephemeral permutations of national politics and economics. As the 1960 anti-American protests mounted, Yasuoka left for a year in Nashville; Endō was hospitalized for what would turn out to be almost three years. The group had survived earlier defections, but at this point the authors were forced to realize that their writings had grown far apart. The individuality that had always existed, whether they wanted to admit it or not, had blossomed in the early period of retrenchment and recovery. Accordingly the meetings of the Conceptions Society stopped. Yoshiyuki remarks:

> [By 1960 or 1961] the period in which we met together frequently and influenced one another had come to an end. As I write

> now in 1965, it strikes me as meaningless to try to place us within the confines of the Third Generation classification any longer. Still, I cannot shake the feeling that we ourselves best understand the truth about one another's work.[49]

Since the collapse of the Conceptions Society, however, Japanese critics have been less enthusiastic about the task of compartmentalizing writers or labeling abstract literary movements, and those groups which have been formed exist almost exclusively as social or media-directed organizations, not literary salons in which creative ideas are shared. The collapse of literary groupism in the fifties was an external as well as an internal phenomenon. Writers who did not know each other, and who were even suspicious or jealous of one another, were herded into a social gathering that had no ostensible literary significance. Within the space of six or seven years, that makeshift group had ceased to have any function and died a natural but belated death.

More significant, however, is the fact that the writers who belonged to the Conceptions Society came to realize for themselves that the age of mutual influence and group-derived literary goals had passed in Japan, and that the writer who was to have anything of importance to say to a postwar audience had to speak with his own voice. The Conceptions Society dissolved from within because groupism was no longer a viable basis for the expression of literary concerns in modern Japanese society. The Third Generation may have felt isolated from their predecessors, their peers, and their literary heritage, but in the final analysis that degree of solitude was necessary.

One unfortunate result of the death of literary groupism in contemporary Japanese letters is the fact that this generation of writers has had to bear the label of "new writers" throughout their careers. The original title "Daisan no shinjin"—Third Generation of New Writers—was applied to them on the assumption that they would be a flash in the pan, a phenomenon that would soon just go away. But the predicted disappearance never took place, and thus they remained newcomers.[50] Because there are no more literary "groups," writers no longer apprentice themselves to established authors to train their talents. The Third Generation had to write and publish on their own, without tutorial guidance. This has led to the publication of many immature works, and the writers have had no recourse but to learn through their own mistakes. The demise of the literary clique has also meant that an author seldom becomes a "sensei" anymore, and is largely without disciples of his own to teach and—more important, perhaps—to learn from. And so the newcomers have stayed eternal tenderfoots, literary warriors not only masterless but also discipleless.

That fate may, though, be somehow appropriate. These are authors who have written of the maladjustment of common people in the face of modern chaos; of cowards, cripples and clods who can never be at ease amid the frustrations that result from their shrinking capacity for action. The isolation of the individual author finds apt literary reflection in the "domestic" novels of the Third Generation, where the family as another traditional social group is depicted in a state of disarray and near-collapse, while the individual within that group has also been stripped of all conventional prerogatives. Perhaps the greatest achievement of the Third Generation has been the degree to which their novels have mirrored the actual crumbling of the Japanese family unit and the individual ego, while symbolically also emblemizing the dissolution of the literary clique.

So it is perhaps natural that these writers have been a long time establishing themselves as the old guard in the literary establishment. The new critics have seen them as "perplexing older brothers,"[51] and these authors have been forced to continue the struggle to prove themselves, to demonstrate that what they have to say, though it may be said in the language of everyday conversation, has a deep significance for individuals in modern society.

Critical Perspectives: Repositioning the "I" of Fiction

THE EARLIEST champion of the new generation of writers was himself a young unknown critic named Hattori Tatsu. He had never met any of the One-Two Association members when his first essay on their literature, "Shinsedai no sakkatachi" (Writers of the New Generation) appeared—ironically enough, in the January 1954 issue of the journal least sympathetic toward the Third Generation, *Kindai Bungaku*. Hattori was not an apologist for these authors; rather he was a perceptive student of literature who had a clear view of the nature of the change that had taken place in the transition from

Sengoha to Third Generation writings. He recognized the collapse of imported ideals and the efforts of the new writers to narrow their focus to everyday human activity. There they stood watch as the common person's ability to influence the surrounding society shrank to the microscopic.

Hattori published his article shortly after Yasuoka received the Akutagawa Prize, when there was still no clear-cut identification of the One-Two Association with the critical term "Third Generation." Thus Hattori's list of authors is not completely congruous with Yamamoto's.[52] He made his selection solely on the basis of "newness" to the literary scene; he did not distinguish according to chronological age.

Hattori in his essay suggested six fundamental characteristics that were shared by the "writers of the new generation." It is here that his critical perceptivity is most evident. The criticism has become standard, quoted in almost every subsequent study. What is perhaps most interesting about these characteristics is the fact that, until Hattori's essay was printed, few if any of the writers themselves had recognized how much they had in common. If anything, Hattori's study was most influential upon them after the fact; they began to see new directions for their work as a result of the critical comparisons Hattori had made between them.

Hattori suggests that the new writers have the following elements in common:

> the predominance of a "Biedermeier style";
> contrast with the Sengoha writers;
> a reliance upon simple, existential reality;
> adherence to the "I-novel" tradition;
> the weakening of a critical disposition;
> a lack of interest in politics.[53]

Likely few of Hattori's contemporaries really knew what he meant by a "Biedermeier style" in literature. The term was used in Europe to describe a period of German art in the early to mid-1800s; it primarily described a solid, comfortable design of furniture and house construction. The original derivations of the German term[54] suggest a touch of neoclassical conservatism. But most likely what Hattori had in mind was the aesthetic features commonly associated with

Biedermeier-style furniture: simplification and practicality. These are, in fact, highly appropriate terms in reference to the literature of the Third Generation.

Simplification in the new fiction took place in both form and content. Instead of the sprawling, comprehensive novels—often of ponderous length—that the Sengoha writers produced, the authors of the new generation (as if feeling there was less to say in an age when the circle of an individual's influence was narrowing rapidly) wrote short, almost lyrical works that limited their focus to the everyday, even petty experiences of less than superhuman people. Yasuoka and Yoshiyuki are known in Japan almost exclusively for their short stories, though both have worked extensively in the novel form. Endō Shūsaku has written few novels that exceed four hundred manuscript pages, or about 300 book pages, in length—which to a leviathan writer like Noma Hiroshi of the Sengoha would scarcely qualify as a short story.[55] Kojima Nobuo's best work is a short novel, and Shimao Toshio's most powerful creation, though it appears to be a long novel, is in reality a *rensaku,* a series of short stories related by character and theme.

There is a concomitant simplification in tone and subject matter. None of the Sengoha writers could have forced themselves to write about the war with either levity or sarcasm—the philosophical *issue* of war was more important to them than the examination of human entanglement in war's twisted paradoxes. The ability to treat the most debasing of human activities with lightness and self-directed (rather than self-centered) humor represents a major achievement of the Third Generation authors.

Practicality in the fiction of the Third Generation also suggests that the philosophical substance of literature so highly prized by the Sengoha was rejected by the new writers. This is, in fact, what occurred, and in talking of the "contrast with the Sengoha," Hattori is intimating this abandonment of systematic philosophical or ideological content in the novel. Yasuoka in an early journal forum most eloquently pointed to the way in which the new writers felt they differed from their literary elders. The Sengoha, he said, were like bulldozers making their way across the barren stretches of land scorched by the war. They were in essence starting over in Japanese literature, preparing the unfertile ground so that new seeds of creativity could be planted. This Sengoha bulldozer broke life up into large chunks with names like "war" and "guilt" and "responsibility," and left those chunks lying around for all to examine. Then along came the new generation of writers. They had no bulldozers—their paltry inheritance from the war years did not include any heavy machinery. Instead they came through with shovels and hoes, their task being to break down these enormous philosophical clods of dirt that covered the landscape and crush them into tiny handfuls of dust —the dust of everyday human activity.[56]

Thus the Third Generation did not come forth so much as an antithesis to the Sengoha but as a reduction in the scale of their labors. Feeling decidedly unqualified to ruminate on topics like "guilt" and "responsibility," the new writers sought greater specificity and less generalization in their work. They eliminated virtually all abstractions and examined only what they could physically lay their hands upon.

This is the "simple, existential reality" that Hattori cited. In the fiction of these writers, human experience is stripped to its primal layer—or perhaps a bit lower. Even when their stories are set in wartime, in a prison, or in foreign lands, it is the mundaneness, the endless sameness of those experiences that they emphasize. The Sengoha had seen the extremes of war and imprisonment as the ultimate evils of human existence, experiences that were anything but "everyday." But the new writers had grown up knowing nothing but war, pain, physical deprivation, and punishment. These for them had been everyday occurrences, everyday to the point of tedium. No sooner had they grown inured to such a life and even come to feel comfortable with it than the war came to an end and plunged them into a new, unfamiliar world in which they could never feel at home. Their literary task—their challenge—was to present the reality of their unreal experience to a reading audience that was beginning to accept the quiet gray tones of peace and rehabilitation as a new commonplace. The tactic which they adopted almost universally was to turn the entire concept of reality inside-out, to examine their own experiences through an inverted telescope. Intentional distortion of reality, the acceptance of nightmare landscapes as truthful, and the rejection of placid "everyday" scenes were the literary techniques that set this generation apart.[57]

We need look no further than the physical settings of the Third Generation literature to find this reshaping of everyday experience.

Their stories of army days do not describe life on the field of battle. That would require an outdoor setting, a sense of openness despite the potential for death. Instead, authors such as Kojima and Yasuoka set their wartime tales in dank brothels, where the holy Japanese warriors are contracting social diseases, or in the military latrines, where the enemy is not some foreign soldier but the workings of an unwilling recruit's intestinal tract.

The conscious selection of such materials as the centerpieces of their fiction is strong evidence of these authors' concerns with the base absurdities of an everyday existence that few of their readers have shared. This is a deliberate reduction of human activity. Unlike Tanizaki, who celebrates bowel movements as some sort of aesthetic evidence that the entire human body is a work of art, Yasuoka and his colleagues examine life in the toilet as a clear symbol of human baseness. There are too many bathroom scenes in the fiction of this generation to dismiss them as aberration. They are clearly intended as symbols of the degradation and defeat that the characters—and the nation—experienced in the war and Occupation.

Like the diarrhea that plagues the characters, rains fall with alarming regularity, as though the heavens themselves have been disrupted by some major calamity. Few incidents seem to take place in normal rooms on sunny days. The rooms where characters find their ridiculous lives being played out are often bilious and oddly colored; for example, the womb-like asylum cell in Yasuoka's *View by the Sea* is a lizard-green cave that almost seems to undulate like some bodily organ. These qualities are exaggerated even further in the writings of Shimao Toshio, who places his protagonists within landscapes that are straight out of the most horrifying nightmares.

Hattori in his critical essay suggested that a possible explanation for similarities in the writings of the Third Generation could be found in the varying nature of war experiences shared by generations only slightly separated in age. Thus, while many of the new writers were very close in age to the writers of the Sengoha, few if any of the later generation shared the same type of war experiences. Ōoka Shōhei of the Sengoha was a prisoner of war for almost a year; Noma Hiroshi fought at Bataan and Corregidor and in 1943 was imprisoned for pacifist activities. By contrast, Kojima Nobuo, born only five days after Noma, spent the war in China in the company of mixed-blood Japanese, decoding messages from the enemy camp and teaching

English to his senior officers. Yoshiyuki Junnosuke spent only three days in the army, being discharged after the military physicians discovered he was suffering from bronchial asthma. The significance of war experiences for both the Sengoha and the Third Generation cannot be overemphasized, but the fundamental differences in the nature of those experiences must also be highlighted. In essence the Sengoha went to war as a group, united by a common sympathy for Marxism and antipathy for Japanese militarism, while the Third Generation joined the fray as scattered individuals, emotionally rather than intellectually alienated from the military effort.

In a second article on these authors, Hattori attempted to create his own list of Third Generation writers, based on the characteristics he had delineated in his earlier essay. That list is surprisingly close to the one generally accepted today—including Yasuoka, Yoshiyuki, Kojima, Shōno, Miura, and Sono Ayako (the first woman to appear with the group).[58] Hattori's comments on the differences between the Sengoha and the new writers are salient:

> For a variety of reasons the Sengoha writers put their trust in concepts imported from Europe. But the "Third Generation" cannot bring themselves to believe in any of these creeds. When their youth—corresponding to the war years—came to an end, all that was left in their grasp was intractable, unvarying memories of a commonplace, petty "self" that could not assume any poses or muster the zeal necessary to believe in itself. As individuals they have survived to the present day burdened with that image of the self. They are further plagued by an inability to act purposefully. . . . And so for them, the postwar period—which should be an age of liberation—is instead a time to which they are ill-suited; they would almost prefer the thrills of air-raids, evacuations, and the lives of persecution they led as conscripts and soldiers during the war.
>
> Other writers in their thirties now [i.e., the Sengoha]—those who could be classified as superior intellects—were able to start writing immediately after the war, because they had found something to believe in. But what was left for the stragglers to do? They could only adopt the opposite tack. They could not believe in the outer world, in lofty, absolute philosophies, or even in the pull of their own emotions. They knew that they were not superior intel-

> lects, that they were instead mundane and base. Still, they could not wear the grave, all-knowing expression that the other I-novelists wore. . . . Which of these writers will rise to the top of the waves that break one after another for their age and their generation, and survive?[59]

The work of Japan's Third Generation represents a literature in flux, not only because the major figures of that generation continue their literary activities today but because the corpus of their achievements represents a rethinking of the foundations of modern Japanese fiction. If postwar Japanese fiction constitutes, as I will argue below, a fundamental reconsideration of the significance and potential of the I-novel form, then at least two major currents can be traced in the last three and a half decades.[60] The Sengoha writers (and those, like Ōe Kenzaburō, who have followed their example) were, in the broadest terms, a group who sought to sweep away what they felt was an embarrassing history of confessional novels, apolitical writings, and indefensible parochialism that kept Japanese literature from having any truly universal significance. Their goal was to start over from the very beginning, to remodel Japanese literature more along foreign lines and create thereby a product that could speak more directly and forcefully to the modern human situation. Their aims were lofty, and their achievements were often mammoth. To accept their work fully, however, it is necessary to accept their basic premise—that the I-novel no longer had any hope for regeneration.

Certainly the most problematic aspect of Third Generation literature is the tenacity with which these writers have clung to the I-novel form. To the Western reader, the fiction written in Japan over the past six or seven decades is likely to seem highly conservative in the forms it has allowed itself to assume. It is therefore crucial to understand the ways in which the postwar I-novels differ from their prewar ancestors. Without this understanding, the reader is apt to assume that modern Japanese fiction has been locked into a fossilized form of expression and has been unable to move beyond the limitations set for it over eighty years ago.

Although the external form has remained the same, and though to all outward appearances it would seem that the author-protagonist identification has not changed, in reality the subtle nuances of ironic perspective in the postwar I-novel (a perspective that seems to me to be absent from the autobiographical fiction of Tayama Katai[61] and his Naturalist progeny) afford a sharp contrast to the earlier confessional works. And it is in the writings of the Third Generation that this new perspective in the I-novel first appears.

In prewar Japan, the I-novel form was used by writers such as Shimazaki Tōson and Kasai Zenzō primarily as a mode of personal confession.[62] The assertion of individuality in opposition to a symbol of social oppression—generally the patriarchal family order or the nation itself—formed the core of this brand of literature. Shiga Naoya brought a new dimension to the I-novel: a powerful affirmation of the supremacy of the ego over any external concerns. The emphasis on confession combined with the virtual infallibility of individual emotions produced "novels" in which the protagonist was essentially indistinguishable from the author. Events that occurred in these works were generally drawn from the creator's own private range of experiences, and seldom if ever did the viewpoint or feelings of other characters enter into the substance of the novel. The "I" of the novel was always clearly at the center of the work, was the individual the author cared most about, and was the one whose feelings and attitudes were the ultimate measure of right and wrong. The prewar I-novel was, in effect, a deification of the Selfhood of the author/hero, a mystical glorification of his personal inner suffering, and a rejection of any authority—social, political, religious, or otherwise—outside that of individual will.[63]

Although the writers of the fifties continued to employ the I-novel form, their approach to life had changed so drastically from that of the prewar Naturalists that they are clearly writing a new kind of novel. No longer is the public airing of private laundry, dirty or otherwise, the intention of the novelist. The Third Generation authors introduce personal experiences not so that they can be deified through uncritical codification but so that they can be demysticized through artistic intervention. The complete identification between author and protagonist has broken down. Even when the subject of the novel is a writer, there is a clear layer of irony separating the author from his storyteller. These writers use personal experience in an attempt to assert the overwhelming importance of everyday life. No more do the great windmills of prewar fiction seem worth tilting at—at the end of the war, when legions of repatriated fathers returned to Japan physically and emotionally broken, it was evident that the traditional family system, like the Japanese landscape, lay in ruins; and whatever was left of nation or religion or society had been swept away by the bomb and the defeat, and had to be rebuilt from ground zero.

Believing as they do that the most fundamental roots of human behavior and interpersonal relationships can be traced to the common actions of common people, these writers seek within the limited range of their own experience for keys to understanding the nature of those relationships. Although the cast of characters in their stories may seem as limited as in prewar I-novels, an important element has been added—a realization that "other people" *(tanin)* besides the protagonist actually exist out there in the real world. In taking a tightly focused look at human relationships on a very basic plane—within the marital associations between husband and wife, or in the disrupted contacts between parent and child—the authors of the Third Generation take into consideration for the first time in the I-novel the feelings and attitudes of characters other than the masculine hero.

The "I" of this new fiction has ceased to be a local god of sorts—the Self, in fact, has fallen so far from grace that his personal convictions are no longer to be trusted, much less exalted. This erosion of the deified self actually got its start in the fiction of Kambayashi Akatsuki and, most important, Dazai Osamu, but it reaches its culmination in the novels of the Third Generation. The ego is lost now, unable to guide itself, much less serve as a mirror for the conduct of others. With the shattering of individual will, guidelines for behavior must emerge from the interaction between characters, particularly between husband and wife. The prevalence of strong mothers and wives in the fiction of the Third Generation is indicative of this subtle but significant aspect of the postwar I-novel. Authors now, even when writing about characters very much like themselves, are forced to take a step or two back from their first-person narrators. As a result, they can view the thoughts and actions of their protagonists with a new measure of irony, bemusement, and at times even scorn.

In short, then, in postwar Japanese fiction the I-novel and its self-centered protagonist have been ravaged by the forces of relativism. The form itself has ceased to be regarded as an absolute medium for the expression of individual emotions, and its main character no longer occupies the center of the fictional universe. The "I" has had to step aside and allow room for other egos to fill the pages of the novel. This shift from absolute to relative in fiction is completed in the writings of the Third Generation, and their achievement in breaking down the impervious prewar I-novel form deserves high marks, since it has set the stage for new and exciting experiments in the novel.

I would argue that, crippled though they may be, Japan's Third Generation writers have successfully transformed the I-novel and fashioned it into a form that can express much more range than it did in the prewar period. They have achieved this both by shattering the image of a reliable "self," a narrator who stands at the center of a quasi-fictional world, and by placing foils for the male "I" at the shifting center of their fictions. These foils are not necessarily independent characters (though in some instances they come alive) but serve rather as reflectors of the disintegrated "I" 's being. Thus, unlike the prewar I-novels in which the undiluted thoughts and feelings of a single masculine self constituted the entire substance of the work, in the Third Generation writings the "I" views himself in the mirror of an "other" and recognizes his own flaws and shortcomings therein. And perhaps the most significant aspect of these mirror "others" is that they are, in virtually every crucial case, women who are either maternalized or deified, or both.

The first Japanese critic to suggest the centrality of the Mother figure in the writings of the Third Generation was Etō Jun. His 1965 critical study, *Seijuku to sōshitsu: "Haha" no hōkai* (Maturity and Loss: The Collapse of the "Mother"), is both an enlightening piece of literary criticism and an absorbing approach to cultural anthropology. Drawing inspiration for his work from the psychological approach taken by Erik H. Erikson in *Childhood and Society,* Etō does a close reading of Kojima's *Embracing Family* (over half his study is devoted to this novel), Yasuoka's *A View by the Sea,* Endō's *Silence,* and two other novels by members of the same generation.[64]

In *Maturity and Loss,* Etō argues that postwar Japan is best characterized as a society in which the patriarch, the traditional cornerstone, has lost his authority over those who for centuries have obeyed his dictates without question. With lucid examples from *Embracing Family* and *A View by the Sea,* Etō demonstrates how the husbands and fathers in these novels, exhausted from the war and dazed by the recovery, have without realizing it relinquished their roles as helmsmen of the home and become, in essence, pater-unfamilias. With Erikson as a further guide, Etō goes on to suggest that the resulting relationship between mother and son becomes one of profound ambivalence. To compensate for (or perhaps simply as a reaction against) the capitulation/unconditional surrender of the father, the mother showers all her affection upon her son and places all her hopes in him. But this boy, as we will see, is every bit as bewildered as his physically debilitated father. He has never sought his mother's adoration, nor has he felt worthy of it. For the most part, he simply wants to be left alone, to be able to crawl into some dark, isolated corner and remain there safe and unmolested.

For this son to attain true maturity, Etō claims, he must reach the point of "betraying" his mother. He must break away from her influence and thereby assert his independence. He has to become a separate person, a distinct—but, by definition, lonely—"other." This "loss" of Mother is a painful but necessary prelude to "maturity." As maturation takes place, the home itself is subject to disintegration, for both father and mother are stripped of their traditional powers and are reduced to simple, unattached men and women. This process of individual isolation and the accompanying collapse of the family are the most important motifs treated in the "domestic novels" *(katei shōsetsu)* written by the Third Generation in the mid-1960s. Amid this chorus eulogizing the alienated self and the annihilated home, the writers of the Third Generation have retained their solo voices. None of them approaches the problem in precisely the same manner as any of the others. Yet there is a remarkable congruity in their focus upon the women who stand as the center posts within the crumbling familial houses. The maternal figures which appear with such remarkable frequency in these fictions suffer as a result of the crack-up, and as often as not insanity is one of the side-products as they stare into the pit of isolation after the fall of the home. Yet somehow their sufferings and their associations with the men who have been unable to stay the collapse elevate them to some kind of deified status.

Mother is clearly an important, controlling force in the fiction of Yasuoka Shōtarō. She is both thesis and antithesis, the font of life and the greatest obstacle to independent existence. Only by rebelling against her dictates, as Shintarō does in *A View by the Sea,* can a young man obtain any sort of freedom. Yet the very act of severing the tie between son and mother can be seen (as Yasuoka, though not Shintarō, sees it) as the destruction of any meaningful links between one human being and another. If individualism simply means the assertion of one isolated soul's ego in opposition to those of everyone else (as perhaps was the case in much prewar fiction in Japan), then a society that tries to build itself upon the foundation of such a concept of individualism is destined to suffer what Natsume Sōseki called the "loneliness" of the separate person.[65] And Yasuoka seems as pessimistic about the potential for the survival of such a society as was Sōseki. Yasuoka's Mother figure is, then, both an impediment to individual freedom and a powerful reminder that total liberation from the restraints of interpersonal relationships can be obtained only through the frightening sacrifice of all ties with the "others" who populate our world.

In his autobiographical writings, Shimao Toshio has also examined in considerable detail the minute exchanges between the separate individuals who make up one tiny household. Therein he has uncovered a complexity, a pain, and a longing for a seemingly impossible unification that the casual outside observer could never hope to view. Miho in *The Sting of Death* endures the ultimate agony of insanity as a result of gazing into the chasm where human bonds lie broken and bleeding. But her very torment elevates her to the position of a savior for her transgressor husband, for Toshio realizes the extremities of grief he has caused her, and he determines on the basis of that realization to "serve" her in the same way a devout individual would render service to a god. Viewed in this fashion, *The Sting of Death,* for all the torment the reader is forced to share with its protagonists, becomes something of a hymn of joy,[66] for Toshio has discovered a way out of the pit. Although its strains are certainly muted, that hymn is a definite part of the complex substance of *The Sting of Death.* And Miho's rule as both wife and deity is central to the essence of what Shimao is saying in his work.

Perhaps no male characters seem quite as helpless vis-à-vis the women as those of Kojima Nobuo. The *bokus*[67] and Shunsukes of his fiction seem no match at all for the wily, modernized, self-confident women who appear in the stories. Yet, just as America is in no sense the true locus of Kojima's attention in "American School," neither are the women who seem to be so much in control really the characters Kojima wishes to focus upon. The domineering Tokikos are drawn the way they are not to demonstrate how the tables have finally been turned on the Japanese male chauvinist; Kojima is not producing proto-feminist fiction here. Rather they appear to demonstrate that these men have lost the ability to make decisions for themselves, and their only option is to rely upon someone else—anyone would do, really—and leave the important matters to an "other." The focus remains upon the crippled men, not because they are men, but because they are handicapped.

Endō Shūsaku, who often seems like an anomaly in this generation, fits in very comfortably with his other three colleagues here in terms of the "maternal deities" he creates. His uniqueness perhaps lies in the fact that the emphasis in his religious ("serious") novels is less upon the relationship between one human being and another than upon the association between an individual and God. But this does not disqualify him from membership in the Third Generation. For after Endō discovers, as he does in *Silence,* that his God is not an unyielding Father but a compassionate Mother, his entire vision of human relationships is transformed. It is in his "middle-brow" *(chūkan)* novels that Endō pursues these concepts on the human plane; there he attempts to demonstrate the need for a redemption in human relationships through a debasement of the opportunist and an exaltation of the virtues of the weak. He can do this because his Mother-God has forgiven him for his own weaknesses and demonstrated to him how important it is for him to show the same degree of compassion for others. Thus it is characters such as Mitsu in *Watashi ga suteta onna* (The Girl I Left Behind, 1963) and Gaston in *Obakasan* (Wonderful Fool, 1959; trans. 1973) who stir Endō's sympathies, for they are characters more maternal in their actions than others. It is this caring, maternal side of Rodrigues that Endō elevates in *Silence.* And the most gripping evocation of this ethic can be found in that story most appropriately titled "Mothers."

In sum, then, these four writers have converged in their image of a maternal deity which somehow justifies, forgives, purges, or accepts the frailties and shortcomings of men who have always felt themselves lost in the society to which they were born. The creation of such figures was, perhaps, an inevitability for authors who could see no other way to survive the absurdity of their position—caught precisely in the middle between the war and postwar periods. Their fiction has, in a sense, tempered the overwhelming egotism of the prewar I-novel, and set the stage for a fiction which can present a broader narrative perspective, a more complex irony in the voice of the discourse, and the portrayal of more than one central personality.

The chapters which follow have as their aim an examination of the new literary signifiers in the writings of these authors, signifiers which have had their meanings altered as the social environment of Japan has undergone radical change over the past half-century. My analysis of individual works will assert that the use of "I" (in whatever form, be it *watakushi, boku, ore,* or any other variant) can no longer be compared to that which prevailed in the heyday of Shiga. The major contribution of the Third Generation to contemporary Japanese literature has, I think, been their labor of redefining and recasting such signifiers and making them available to subsequent writers. I am convinced that the kinds of transformations which the Third Generation have made in the I-novel form, in the layers of duplicity, and in the relationship between author, text, and reader, have been the real groundwork that has allowed later writers to engage in the exciting sorts of experiments that they have undertaken.

I seriously doubt, for instance, that the innovations which Ōe Kenzaburō has brought to the I-novel would have been possible without Yasuoka Shōtarō as his immediate literary ancestor. This is not to suggest either that Ōe acknowledges Yasuoka's contributions or that there is some sort of direct influence. Neither is necessary to my assertion. By the mid-1960s, Yasuoka and others of his generation had done enough hammer work on the boulders of fiction left by the Sengoha that Ōe and others were able to keep the I-novel form alive and pliant.

Of equal significance is my strong sense that the current crop of younger writers of boldness both in language and technique may owe some unpaid debts to the work of these four. It cannot be mere coincidence that some of the leading women writers of the last two decades—including Kōno Taeko and Ōba Minako (who in 1987 became the first two women authors ever elected to the selection committee for the Akutagawa Prize)—have begun to focus more intensely and believably on the relationship between men and women since Kojima and Shimao published their stories. Nor do I think it inexplicable, in the wake of the dismantling of the literary self accomplished by the Third Generation, that writers such as Takahashi Takako and Tsushima Yūko are undertaking a thorough redefinition of the "I" of fiction.

In like manner, a handful of important writers who have chosen to rally around the banner of literary satire—Inoue Hisashi and Maruya Saiichi, to name only two—cannot help but be counted as tacit disciples of Kojima's work. And one can only wonder what might have become of that unique phenomenon known as the "Japanese Christian writer"—a category that now includes Miura Shumon, Sono Ayako, Sakata Hiroo, Yashiro Seiichi, Mori Reiko, Takahashi Takako, Ōhara Tomie, and others—without the intellectual and artistic guidance of Endō Shūsaku.[68]

Thus the contributions of the Third Generation to contemporary Japanese fiction, though still largely unsung, do not lie solely in their labors of dismantlement. They "came home" from the war as repatriated egos, and their initial literary task was to demobilize the conception of narrative self that had not survived recent Japanese experience. As they have toiled to pick apart the "I" of their fictions, however, they have discovered new ways to express individuality, new angles from which to view their characters and stories, and suggested new potentials within the mode of narrative prose which they and their younger successors continue to explore.

III

The Loss of Home: Yasuoka Shōtarō

Yasuoka Shōtarō, 1981

I wondered why eggs had to be and why from the egg came the hen who again laid the egg. The question got into my blood. It has stayed there, I imagine, because I am the son of my father. At any rate, the problem remains unsolved in my mind. And that, I conclude, is but another evidence of the complete and final triumph of the egg—at least as far as my family is concerned.

—Sherwood Anderson, "The Egg"

So we beat on, boats against the current, borne back ceaselessly into the past.

—F. Scott Fitzgerald, THE GREAT GATSBY

THE BIRTHPLACE and birthdate of Yasuoka Shōtarō are clearly noted in every chronological appendix to his published works. A glance at any of these will elicit the information that he was born on May 30, 1920 at a hospital in Obiyamachi, Kōchi City on the island of Shikoku. But to Yasuoka himself, whose literary trademarks were to become insecurity and repeated failure, the inherent weaknesses in his constitution can be traced to the uncertainties surrounding his birth.

> I have no place that I can unequivocally call my hometown. Of course this is not unique to me—certainly a majority of the people now living in large metropolises feel the same way. . . .
>
> Actually—and this is something I learned rather recently—my age as well as my hometown is open to question. In the family register, my birthday is listed as May 30, 1920. But I am told that it was actually sometime between the 10th and 20th of April. Then other say, no, maybe it was sometime in March. My father and mother are dead now, and I never had any brothers or sisters, so I have no way of finding out the truth. It shouldn't make any great difference either way—but somehow I feel that I have had to start

> life out burdened with a typographical error. It's almost as if my noncommittal nature and my flair for prevarication had their start there.[1]

It is singularly appropriate that Yasuoka's life should begin without a fixed home. For there has been a persistent accumulation of "being without" experiences that form the undercurrent in his fiction. Just as he claims to be without physical or chronological roots, he would later profess to be without teachers who influenced his life, without friends in the numerous schools he attended as a child, without the physical stamina necessary to subsist on a human level, without skills sufficient to obtain steady employment, and without the ambition necessary to follow up on his early successes as a writer.

For some, such an array of losses—or absences—might be emotionally devastating. And certainly some pain seeps out between the lines of what Yasuoka has written about himself. But most often he does not lament these gaping holes in his life; instead he has come to take a certain gloomy pleasure ("inki na tanoshimi," the title of his Akutagawa Prize–winning story) from his situation. Writing about his own many failures as a human being first brought him success as a writer, and so Yasuoka chose the only logical path—he began to revel in disaster and to glory in defeat. And this was fine for a time. It was a note that his literary contemporaries had not sounded as well or as humorously. But eventually the prospects of fame and success in his new career began to instill fear in his heart, and at that point Yasuoka had to do some serious pondering about his writing. The result was one of the finest short novels of the postwar period—*A View by the Sea*.

Although Yasuoka has always been branded a Kōchi product and has come to think of himself as such in recent years, in actuality he never spent more than a month at a time in his "hometown" and could not speak anything other than a bastardized version of the local dialect.[2] Less than two months after his birth—whenever it was—his mother Tsune brought her new baby to Koiwa in Tokyo, where father Akira had begun working as a veterinary surgeon for the army. It was the first in a long series of disruptive moves for the young child. Moving became such a frequent motif in his youth that Yasuoka would later write:

> I feel as though I have been riding on a train since the day I was born. That is no hallucination; it is a graphic sensation that is

> mingled with childhood memories of myself weeping and wailing aboard a train in midsummer, my face covered with prickly heat rash.[3]

With military animals in need of care in Tokyo, northern Japan, Korea, and China, Akira's chosen profession provided little stability for his family members. In the space of four years, Yasuoka Shōtarō had been enrolled in six different primary schools in three separate cities and two nations. The emotional strain for the young boy was tremendous. He had lost friends (and eventually stopped trying to make new ones), he had been forced to live in a rural town where he could not even understand the dialect, and he had lost all confidence in his ability to perform scholastically. In "Utsukushii hitomi" (Beautiful Eyes, 1959), one of the many young boy characters in the early Yasuoka short stories says soon after the family moves from Korea to northern Japan:

> My mother did nothing each day but heave deep sighs. Every time she saw me playing with the new maid, she cried out hysterically, "Come over here and play by yourself!" She told me the lice in the maid's hair would lay eggs in mine.
>
> But I needed to play with the maid. I was stunned to discover that I couldn't understand a single thing anyone said to me when I went to school. . . . So naturally I had to have the maid beside me to double as playmate and interpreter.[4]

No sooner had Yasuoka picked up the local dialect than the family was back in Tokyo. In April 1931 he was enrolled in one school; two months later he was placed in a different school, the Aoyama Minami Primary School. There he "hit the real rock bottom,"[5] placing seventieth in a class of seventy students. The provincial accent he had just mastered formed a barrier between him and his fellow students, and they made fun of the way he spoke. Another character, this one in "Kokyō" (Hometown, 1955), comments:

> We had been in Tokyo for two months when I started feeling as though I was the only one at school who talked the way I did. I realized that when I spoke, everyone else fell silent and listened to the way I talked. I tried to imitate the way they spoke, but then I felt like I had an extra tongue inside my mouth.[6]

The displacement that characterizes Yasuoka's recollections is perhaps only a magnification of the situation which many of his generation found themselves in as Japan whisked through a vast range of social changes in the 1930s. One of the finest of the early Yasuoka short stories—and there are many gems among them—is the sensitive 1952 "Shukudai" (Homework), his third published story. It is set further back in his youth than any of his other works, and it crystallizes not only how Yasuoka felt about his own insecure childhood but how many of his generation came to feel about the insubstantiality of their familial homes.

The structure of "Homework" is characteristic of Yasuoka's stories. It is made up of tiny, essentially unconnected vignettes, crowded together in tight proximity to one another. Each finely honed scene is a microscopic study of failure or perplexity, sufficient in isolation to convey the nuances of character and situation which we normally expect from an autobiographical story. Yet the amassing of many of these anecdotes within the fragile structure of a single short story creates an exaggerated, distorted effect, clearly a distension of reality that draws our attention to details we might not have noticed in a more naturalistic presentation.

"Homework" is, essentially, an amalgamation of these youthful failure experiences. Yasuoka begins his narrative in familiar I-novel fashion, presenting the first-person account of a young primary school boy very much like himself, who has just transferred from Hirosaki in northern Japan to the Minami Primary School in Tokyo. The boy is a mass of insecurities because he has been moved from school to school a number of times. He naturally has learned to loathe school and to feel inferior, out of place, and alone. His emotions fluctuate between poles of hatred for his classmates and yearning to be accepted by them. He wants to please his mother—or, rather, he wishes to avoid incurring her wrath—but his youthful sense of adventure constantly impels him to do things he knows would not meet with her approval.

Just as this boy's expectations will be betrayed as the story advances, the expectations that Yasuoka builds within the reader by feigning a straightforward I-novel approach are destroyed as his literary technique unfolds. We anticipate from the I-novel tone of the story that Yasuoka will lead us down a path of scrupulous verisimilitude. And, in fact, the first two or three events of the plot reinforce such a view. Yet as the narrative picks up momentum and the instances of humiliation increase, we begin to lose our bearings and experience a feeling of loss similar to that of the young boy.

The central event in "Homework" is the schoolboy's embarrassing inability to complete his summer homework assignments, but Yasuoka heaps a seemingly infinite number of other debasing experiences on his hapless narrator. Failures crop up like minor battlefield skirmishes that will eventually escalate toward the ultimate defeat. There is only one fleeting (but crucial) mention of the Second World War at the end of the story, but surely the narrator's array of private disasters mirrors the traumas which the nation was simultaneously experiencing.

One typical example of the many subsidiary failures in the story will demonstrate not only the underlying absurdity of the boy's situation, but also the central role played by his overpowering mother, a woman whose relentless gaze serves as a constant reminder to him that he is less than the perfect boy she expects him to be.

> My cousin Sadaka's wedding took place during summer vacation that year. It was held at the Gakushi Hall. Once before I had eaten a Western-style meal there with my father and mother. After the meal, my mother had informed me that my manners were atrocious and that I had embarrassed her in front of the waiter.
>
> On the day of the wedding, I was so worried about eating the food properly that I couldn't think about anything else. That was my downfall. I saw my first Shinto priest that day. He wore a peculiar blue robe, a black hat, and tall, lacquered clogs. He reminded me of a magician in the way he ordered around a woman dressed in a white robe and red *hakama.* When he waved his white purification rod over my head with a rustle, I was sure I had smelled the aroma of the gods. Finally he turned toward the altar and began bellowing a bunch of gibberish. The sound was so bizarre that I couldn't imagine it was coming from anywhere except outdoors.
>
> "How funny! I can hear a cow mooing, mom!"
>
> My mother turned white as a sheet and sternly shook her head at me, but it was too late. Laughter infected the entire room. I was expelled from the ceremonies as an irreverent heathen. Totally shamed, I fled to the roof in a daze. As I peered down at the ground, so far away it made my eyes swim, I saw cars and trains scurrying about like ants. Suddenly the wedding banquet that had been such a source of anxiety to me came to seem unbearably enticing now that I wouldn't be allowed to eat it.[7]

It is summer vacation, a time when the normal pressures and anxieties of youth should be diminished, when a truce should be called in the adolescent's battle with the forces of society. School, of course, is the customary symbol of that society, and summer homework is the typical form of control it attempts to exert over a young man. But in this passage, it is clear that the boy is also perpetually intimidated by his mother, and that she has an uncanny talent for making him feel inadequate. She is like the "magician"/priest who calls out strings of commands to his pure (dressed, as she is, in white robes) but inferior assistant. The Shinto priest here is, in fact, a surrogate for the boy's mother, representing the formal, "acceptable" aspects of society and emitting from his hands the "aroma of the gods." This is an authority that should not be challenged. And yet this priest is only one in a string of authority figures, beginning with his mother and later opening outward to include his teachers and the principal at school, and finally the entire Japanese war effort. In the presence of these domineering figures the narrator feels so utterly inferior that he cannot help but blunder.

The boy's inability to understand or accommodate himself to the conventions of society is neatly capsulized in his innocent but unacceptable identification of the priest's holy chants as the lowing of a cow. It is altogether fitting that in his confusion the human and animal realms are combined. Yasuoka's characters have recurrent difficulties making distinctions between the two, signifying a belief that the recent experiences of humanity have, in fact, dragged us all down to the bestial level of existence. There is no malice intended in the boy's outburst, but he manages to incur the wrath of his mother and gets himself expelled from the social gathering. From his place of exile on the roof, he recognizes that his failure to abide by the rules has solved the problem that initially agonized him—having to eat the banquet food with proper decorum. But now, compared with his current situation as an outcast, the thought of sitting at the banquet table comes to seem most attractive.

The scene is a compact summation of the narrator's entire dilemma, and we recognize that the remainder of the story will simply intensify the boy's uneasiness and his withdrawal from the necessary but frightening human contacts around him. Yasuoka blows these pieces of perfectly formed glass and pours them full of humor, pathos, and a sensitive understanding for the gnawing, unfulfilled desires of his characters.

In "Homework," the boy is caught in the trap that so many of Yasuoka's characters fall into. Unable to cope with the outside world, he has retreated into a tiny world of his own creation. But this journey inward does not locate a safe or pleasant retreat. The demands from the outside cannot be muffled, and he finds himself unable to sit comfortably in either realm. Yasuoka's characters all seem to be squirming uneasily in their chairs, clawing at itches that lie just out of scratching reach, wishing they could be somewhere away from it all but longing all the same to be accepted where they are.

The narrator of "Homework," unable to find acceptance in the classroom once vacation ends, plays hookey in the graveyard but soon is driven out by fleas and rainstorms. He is without refuge. Rejected by both the cradle of learning and the graveyard, he seeks a last resort. Home should be able to offer some comfort, some understanding. If he cannot be accepted for what he is at home, where can he turn? But his mother has learned of his truancy, and she is furious with him. He has not lived up to her expectations; instead the boy threatens to turn out as worthless as her "horse doctor" husband.

The conclusion of the story finds the boy wandering the streets aimlessly. At this point Yasuoka strips away the last suggestion that his story is a simple autobiographical recollection. He vaults the level of the narrowly personal and gives his piece a temporal context by concluding it with a subtle but telling intimation of war. This is actually the first inkling we have that the story takes place after Japan has invaded China. The bewildered narrator stumbles across a mimeographed poster that reads, "Stop the war!" glued to a wall. He tries to tear it off, thinking first that a war should be the ideal solution to all his problems. His teachers and principal—the true "enemy"—would all be drafted and killed, and the students could burn down the school building. But somehow he senses that political or military decisions will not solve his personal dilemma, and his thoughts turn inward again. If he tears at the poster, perhaps some miraculous intervention will save him. He claws frantically and imagines that a policeman has come up behind him to congratulate him for his patriotism.

> He told me I was a praiseworthy child. He wrote my name in his notebook, and the next day at school the principal commended me. . . . I peeled off another poster and continued my fantasy—

my fantasy that this student who had brought honor to his school had been excused from doing any of his summer homework; from now on he could sit comfortably at his desk in the classroom.[8]

As the two passages from "Homework" demonstrate, one of Yasuoka's finest talents as a writer lies in his ability to tell a simple, childlike story of earnest but helpless innocence and to overlay it with a mature, ironic understanding of how society dishes out its rewards and punishments. Stories like "Homework" reverberate with the tension between the two sets of eyes which observe the fictional incidents. One pair, reminiscent of the myopic vision of the prewar I-novelists, sees only the objective facts as they are presented to the reader. This is the adolescent perspective, a submergence within the experience itself that sometimes rendered authors such as Dazai Osamu incapable of final detachment from their narratives. To this, Yasuoka adds a pair of analytical eyes, a sadder reflective vision. This unobtrusive but strongly felt narrator knows that a *deus ex machina* has ceased to operate in the modern world, and that characters like the boy in "Homework" must continue to writhe and hope for some magical salvation—such as the fantasy policeman—that never seems to come.

Many such stories from the 1950s assert—in equally inventive terms—Yasuoka's painful knowledge that, no matter how hard his immature protagonists may search, they will never encounter a comfortable nesting place. And yet the search for a home continues, and the characters pursue their wanderings like members of a troupe of circus performers (the circus being another recurrent motif for Yasuoka) who must pass their lives on the road. One story from this period finds a young man pursued by strains of "Jingle Bells" until it seems to be ringing endlessly in his head; another gets a moth in his ear and persuades himself that it will lodge in his brain forever; still another is pictured as a warrior in a sword dance who must fight his opponent while he struggles under the weight of a child strapped to his back. All these characters share the relentless torment of the boy in "Homework." Upon close examination, it becomes evident that such burdens are imposed upon these characters because they have no roots, no home that they can go to for help, relief, or even love.

The motif of a lost home appears in various forms in Yasuoka's stories. Often it is epitomized by the lack of love between his mother and father; by her scorn for her husband's chosen profession, or by her insistence that her son grow up to be different from his father. The attitudes and demands of the mother character dominate virtually all Yasuoka's fiction. And it is the realization that this mother is overly demanding, far too cruel toward a husband who sincerely loves her, and much too unrealistic in the requirements she makes of her lackluster son that forms the core of many stories. As Etō Jun has described it, it is the "loss of mother,"[9] the recognition that she is as fallible a creature as her son, that forces Yasuoka's characters to grow up and, at the same time, leads them to the realization that their images of home have been illusion.

The confusion and ambivalence which characters like the schoolboy in "Homework" feel toward their mothers/homes is intensified as they encounter the sexual frustration of midadolescence. The normal feelings of desire for the opposite sex are tainted by the experiences they have had with their mothers, the central females in their lives up to this point. Mother has become an oppressive, omnipotent existence in their lives, and young men like Juntarō in "Aoba shigereru" (Thick the New Leaves, 1958; trans. 1984) know that they must cut the bonds with their mothers before they can establish meaningful relationships with any other women. The initiation scene so central to literature must be played out as part of the maturation process. Juntarō has to accept and exhibit his lust for a woman or be sucked forever into the womblike vacuum of his mother's control.

Home and family were frequent objects of rebellion in the autobiographical fiction of the 1910s and 1920s, but independence and self-affirmation were such overweening goals that the sense of betrayal which accompanies the exodus from home was scarcely if at all felt by the characters in those novels. With Juntarō and his brethren, however, the guilt is overpowering. Because patriarchal authority has vanished from within the home, Mother has blossomed into a figure of almost mythologic power, and her centrality in the life of her son cannot be denied.

The primary narrative concern in "Thick the New Leaves," for instance, is whether or not Juntarō is going to pass the entrance examination into higher school. Already he has failed in three successive attempts. It seems to him that swarms of women—all of them linked to his mother in one way or another—are dancing around him, announcing his shortcomings to the world. His fourth failure notice is delivered as the story opens.

> So, this year he'd failed again. It was an odd feeling.
>
> Juntarō had lain in bed awake that morning and listened to the maid come up the stairs. Her footsteps were lighter than usual, almost as if she were keeping time: a suspenseful footfall.
>
> The tip of this maid's nose was repulsive—always red and spotted with big pores, as if only that part of her face had been steamed. But if you could stand this she wasn't totally bad looking. There was the little dimpled chin, the slim and graceful neck above her sloping shoulders, and then those narrow eyes that would sometimes flash up at him so crossly. . . . Juntarō lay with his eyes shut waiting for the sliding door at his head to open, quite as if he expected that at any minute this figure would roll right into his bed.
>
> —Hmmm, I wonder if she'd ever take it into her head to get in bed with me—oh but what am I thinking. . . .
>
> Still, it isn't necessarily out of the question. Isn't that the real reason she's coming up to the second floor this early in the morning when I'm the only one around?[10]

Without the opening line, this passage would be a simple expression of male adolescent fantasy—a young man sleeping in late, imagining that every woman who approaches him is willing and eager to end his pent-up sexual frustration. But Yasuoka has raised a red flag before he introduces the fantasies, and before the maid ever appears we know that Juntarō is in no danger of attaining a successful initiation into adulthood. Yasuoka underscores this secondary disappointment a page later, after the maid has delivered a failure notice rather than her body. Juntarō staggers to the bathroom, looks down at his crotch, and mumbles: "Wouldn't you know, today it's not up." (p. 32).

The announcement of failure—stamped in purple with the word UNSUCCESSFUL—has come from a woman; a woman, moreover, in his mother's employ. However much he may wish to keep his inadequacies to himself, Juntarō never seems to be able to deceive the women who are linked to his mother. It is almost as though these women are determined to keep his failures foremost in his mind. His intellectual shortcomings spill over and affect him physiologically as well.

Juntarō seems to recognize the need to break with his mother, but he lacks the ability to find a way out of the home. All this is complicated by the fact that his sexual feelings are repeatedly tracing a pathway back to his mother. The maid is one such channel, since she is older and a household employee. But there are more obvious signs of Juntarō's confused wish to extract himself from a relationship which has such a magnetic pull on him. His chief reason for wanting to stay in school really has little to do with the fact that Japan is at war and he might be drafted. Rather it provides him with an excuse to absent himself from a home where he must confront his relationship with Mother.

> . . . There was another thing, though it wasn't something he liked to talk about: Juntarō's mother wore her clothes badly. A shirt-front or the hem of a robe would be left carelessly open for any length of time. Especially in the summer. Maybe this shouldn't seem so bad once a person got used to it; but it just wasn't the same as taking a bath together when you were little. [p. 44]

The intimations of a potentially incestuous relationship between mother and son infuse this story with yet another undercurrent of frustrated passion—not only is Juntarō unable to sustain a morning erection as he fantasizes about the maid, he also has to contend with the blatant, slovenly sexuality of his own mother. He is being pulled in many directions at once, but consistently the strongest attraction comes from within the home.

As in many of his stories of youthful entrapment, Yasuoka in "Thick the New Leaves" takes the slender fabric of his own experience and weaves it into a quilt of far thicker substance, linking the events of his private life to the context of Japanese external history and to an even larger network of shared human experience. The images he employs in this particular story all involve Juntarō's attempts to cut the cord. These images are significant at once on the personal and the public levels, and serve as both narratorial and metaphorical devices.

The first of these images appears after Juntarō, no longer eligible for a draft exemption because he cannot gain acceptance into school, is driven by his mother to apply for naval accounting school. But he fails the physical examination:

> Within an hour Juntarō had walked out the gates of the naval school of accounting. He stood leaning on the railing of the Kachidoki Bridge with the river breeze blowing in his face.
>
> The test had begun with a physical. First they had measured his height, weight, chest size, and grip strength, and then there was a short-arm test and rectal examination. Juntarō went in behind the screen where an army doctor, sitting with his thighs arrogantly spread apart, was belting out in a voice that echoed through the whole gymnasium,
>
> "Since when do you think you're going to be an officer in the Imperial Navy with a thing like that?"
>
> How ridiculous, Juntarō thought. What right does he have to insult somebody who's just here to take a test and isn't even in his division yet?
>
> Juntarō was next. He stood in front of the doctor, a captain who reminded him immediately of a man who used to come over to visit his father, Junkichi. That man was probably doing something along the same lines right now in some other gymnasium somewhere. While he was thinking this, Juntarō pulled on the cord to his trunks, and promptly had a knot in his hands.
>
> "Cut if off! If it's that long cut the damn cord off!"
>
> But Juntarō only slowed down the more. He purposely took his time undoing the knot just to aggravate the doctor.
>
> After leaving there, though, he went to the chin-up station, and somehow he could not get in the mood to lift his own weight. He hung lifeless from the horizontal bar.
>
> "What's the matter with you!" the officer in charge yelled, and as if that were his signal, Juntarō let go of the bar. The rule was, if you failed one item of the physical, that was it for the exam. Wonderfully efficient.[11] [pp. 55–56]

The parallelism Yasuoka often employs in situation and imagery is evident here: as at the story's opening, we see Juntarō first in the aftermath of failure, then trace back to the causes of his defeat. This allows Yasuoka to infuse his text with irony, both blatant and covert. The oft-defeated Juntarō is leaning on the railing of the "Kachidoki"

Bridge. While this is an actual placename, it is accentuated in the text by placing it in *katakana* rather than Chinese characters—a technique which Yasuoka employs liberally in his writings—and has the subtextual meanings of both a "cry of victory" and "a time to win." Both of these are of course sharply ironic in context, and become more so in the parallel situation with which Yasuoka concludes his narrative.

Secondary echoes in this passage of text can be discerned in the officer's derisive comments to the potential cadet. The reference to an inferior "thing" dangling between the candidate's legs is clearly to be paired with Juntarō's deflated examination of his own private parts at the outset of the story, and then again just before the navy physical, when he studies a photograph of himself naked and discovers that "the only assertive thing about him was his navel, strangely and conspicuously facing forward; and then, where his bowlegged thighs came together, the painfully contorted thing strangled in the fresh underwear . . ." (p. 54). The protruding navel is mentioned almost as an aside, but it becomes of vital importance as Yasuoka sews together his references to several different kinds of "cords," all of which eventually tie Juntarō to his mother. In contraposition is his male organ, which should be the part of him that finally establishes independence from her: that instrument is feeble, "painfully contorted," "strangled," and, as we will see, ultimately unable to procure for him the desired freedom.

The most significant aspect of this loaded passage, however, is the unexpected shift in Juntarō's attitudes toward the physical examination. Things had been going normally for him until the officer made a remark about another candidate's penis. Abruptly his thoughts turned from his aim of succeeding at just one test in his life. His thoughts, in fact, turn to home, specifically to his inept father. It is at this moment that Juntarō's opportunity to establish himself as a separate existence from his mother slips from his hands. Instead of adroitly slipping off his shorts and baring the lower regions of his body, he tightens the cord, as if to camouflage his maleness and subvert his own individuality. Once that is done, all he can do is hang "lifeless," much like his own organ, and accept the inevitability of failure.

Yasuoka closes the circle of image and situation and fastens the umbilical cord tightly to Juntarō's navel in the concluding scene of the story, in which Juntarō makes one last desperate attempt to assert himself by sleeping with a prostitute at Tamanoi:

> She untied her sash. Juntarō stared wide-eyed. This was where the miracle would begin. But the woman stayed on her feet, stuck her hand up under her kimono and fussed about for a while.
>
> "I get cold so easy, you know," she said, and pulled out a piece of black wool cloth from under her hem. So that was it. He had thought she looked too thick from the waist down. While Juntarō was wondering if a cat might not jump out from between her legs next, the woman lay down on the bedding with her inner gown still fastened, spread her thighs, and said, "Well. Show me you're a man."
>
> But Juntarō just stood there where he was, shocked, and didn't lift a finger. Was that what he had been dreaming about all these years, this black thing stretched out under the white stomach? It was ugly, even grotesque, but he did not turn his eyes away.
>
> "Why aren't you taking off your pants? Hurry up, your underwear too. . . ."
>
> The woman's words reminded Juntarō of the doctor at the naval accounting school. [pp. 58–59]

There are numerous layers to this passage that provide a resonance far more moving than the simple events of the plot. The slovenly, lackadaisical prostitute seems to offer hope to Juntarō—she unties her sash, loosening one kind of cord that he imagines will free him from the restraints of another. The chance to finally get an uninhibited, unembarrassed glance between the folds of a kimono, reminiscent of the garment that his mother has often worn in blatant disarray, seems like the beginning of some grand "miracle" to Juntarō.

Yet there are troubles within those folds. The woman appears thick from the waist down, a physical description that could very well be applied to a pregnant woman, a potential mother. Her refusal to remove her garment completely can only remind Juntarō of his mother's careless manner of dress. And when the prostitute lies down and spreads her thighs, her taunting challenge is, "Show me you're a man." This has been precisely the sort of taunt his mother has rained upon him. He must succeed in his school entrance examinations, or in his application to the naval academy, so that he can demonstrate to her that he is a "man," not a mousy horse doctor like her husband.

That unaswerable challenge is compounded by the disappointing, "grotesque" panorama between the woman's legs. And finally, added to all these layers of defeat are the words which echo the bark of the doctor at the naval school. Juntarō has not been able to cut the cord; when the opportunity has presented itself, he has had to keep his deflated organ covered and admit thereby that he is not ready to leave his mother.

He abandons the prostitute and wanders the streets of Tokyo, coming across a second bridge that he does not cross. With the ironic "cry of victory" of Kachidoki Bridge still echoing hollowly in his ears, Juntarō confronts the "Shirahige Bridge." Yasuoka writes this in a softer, more feminine *hiragana* script, but there is nothing soothing about the meaning of its sounds. "White beard" here, in addition to recalling the beard-like "thing" between the prostitute's thighs and linking her even more tightly with the image of his slovenly mother, surely posits that Juntarō will remain under his mother's sway for the rest of his life.

One further stylistic element of this story deserves comment to demonstrate the care with which Yasuoka selects and assembles the pieces of his stories to form finely etched wholes. The seasonal references which he sprinkles through "Thick the New Leaves" provide a significant subtext of movement, change, and revitalization against which Juntarō's inactivity and desperation are brought into sharp focus. Juntarō's failures are cyclical, and have become linked to the alternation of the seasons in his mind. The familiar, dependable pattern for the past three years has been: spring—take tests; fail; endure the wrath of Mother until the cherry blossoms have scattered; then relax around the time the young leaves begin to sprout.

Juntarō, then, has learned from experience that he does not share Sei Shōnagon's aesthetic tastes in seasons: "haru wa akebono" (In spring, it is the dawn that is most alluring).[12] Dawn in spring for him is the time when failure announcements come from schools, when his manhood refuses to blossom, and when he must listen to his mother complain that he is not a real man if he seems likely to follow in his father's footsteps. Yet even this ironic perception of the seasons is reversed when Yasuoka brings his narrative to a close. Once he catches a glimpse of "White Beard" Bridge, "Juntarō walked on along the bank, turning this over in his mind, walked on beneath a row of cherry trees dense with damp, heavy leaves. And kept walking." (p. 60).

For the first time in his life, the luxuriant leaves of midspring have not brought a release from the specter of blunders that blight the season. This year the sprouting leaves do not even attract his attention. He is too caught up in the realization that he has not been able to succeed at the most important venture of his life—freeing himself from his mother's sway and becoming a separate person. It is as though Juntarō recognizes the source of his personal grief and sense of failure—the inordinate demands of his mother—and yet cannot bear to cut the cord decisively and finally. For that cord is knotted as tightly around him as the string in his shorts that keeps him a somewhat unwilling virgin. Until he can make that painful but necessary move, the green leaves of spring will continue to fill him with remorse and remind him of his failure.

The subtle and ironic intimations of the title in "Thick the New Leaves," with Juntarō's development running against the currents of nature and the seasons, clearly mark this as a "good" story. But there is one final code implanted in the subtext of the story which adds further poignancy and significance to the work and elevates it to a stature high within the ranks of postwar short fiction. The title refers not only to Juntarō's inverted responses to the seasons but also to a popular song of the war years, "Aoba shigereru," by Ochiai Naobumi.

The song centers around the final farewell between the medieval warrior Kusunoki Masashige and his son Masatsura, just before the famous warrior departs for what will certainly be death in battle for the imperial cause. Masashige was, of course, one of the prime patriotic culture heroes paraded before the Japanese populace during the Second World War, first for his unquestioning loyalty to the emperor and later for his willingness to die for the nation. Yasuoka's ironic usage of the first lines of the song as the title of his story thus has the effect, for his contemporaries, of playing a patriotic war anthem softly in the background of his text.

The song itself, with its touching association between father and son (one who, like Juntarō's father, has gone off to war; the other the son who must remain behind, treated to the end as a child), reverberates so consistently through the story that it bears quoting in full:

Evening draws nigh at Sakurai's leafy ford
As in the shadow of the trees [the hero] stops his horse

And deeply ponders what the future holds in store.
Are they tears or drops of dew
That splatter on his armour's sleeve?

Wiping away his tears, Masashige calls his son.
"Your father," says he, "is bound for Hyōgo Bay,
And there he will lay down his life.
You, Masatsura, have come with me thus far,
But now I bid you hurry home."

"Dear Father," replies the boy, "whatever you may say,
How can I leave you here and go back home alone?
I may indeed be young in years,
Yet shall I come along with you
On your journey to the world beyond."

"Not for *my* sake do I send you hence," the father says.
"Soon, when I no longer live,
This land will be in Takauji's hands.
You, my son, grow quickly and become a man
So that you may serve our Emperor and his realm!

"Here is the precious sword
That His Majesty bestowed upon me many years ago.
Now I am giving it to you
In memory of this, our last farewell.
Go, Masatsura, back to our village,
Where your aging mother waits!"

Father and son exchange sad looks as they wend their separate ways,
And through the early summer rain
They hear the mournful call of the *hototogisu,*
Who, when he cries, sheds tears of blood.
Ah, who would not be moved by such a song?[13]

Here the "leafy ford" *(aoba shigereru)* of Sakurai stands in stark contrast to the death that awaits Masashige, but it is an appropriate image for the son who will remain alive. Juntarō too is a survivor, but not in any heroic sense. He cannot follow where his father has gone, either to war or to bed with a woman, and thus Masashige's injunction to "grow quickly and become a man" is biting, whether it is taken privately or politically. Juntarō cannot become a man either by separating himself from his mother or by going off to war. All he can do is go back to the village where his "aging mother waits." The Masashige-like courage that was touted during the war years has no meaning in Juntarō's life. The pull of mother at home is stronger than any desire to follow in the steps of his less-than-ideal father.

It seems highly unlikely that Yasuoka was unfamiliar with the historical postlude to the events described in the song. According to the *Taiheiki,* Masatsura bowed to his father's will and returned home, but when his father's severed head was sent back from the battlefield, he seated himself in the Buddha Hall, loosened the strings that bound his skirts, and pulled out his father's sword in preparation to commit suicide. The image of strings that overlaps with Juntarō's two failed attempts to attain maturity is stark and powerful. Even more compelling is the fact that the *Taiheiki* goes on to record that Masatsura's mother comes rushing in at the critical moment and talks her son out of killing himself.[14] Yasuoka has forged a stirring shadow-image of the Masatsura legend, etching his ironies sharply into the bedrock of his subtext and producing a story filled with resonance.

The Juntarō stories are admired in Japan for the sensitivity with which they portray the anguish and frustrations of the *rōnin,* that special caste of students caught in limbo, still waiting to pass an entrance exam and get into a college. But "Thick the New Leaves" and the succeeding stories about Juntarō are more than just an accurate glimpse into the pit of the Japanese "examination hell." They are a portrait of the failure as a young man, a study in how the innately insecure can have their doubts reinforced time and time again, until they are convinced that they do not qualify even for a starting position in the human race. The conflicting and irrational demands of his mother, his friends, school, and society—all these work together to make Juntarō sure, just in case he ever doubted it, that his low estimation of himself is, if anything, too charitable. Not that Juntarō is a blameless victim. He speeds up the process of dehumanization by actively refusing to take responsibility for his life, and by passing up the few chances for success that do come his way, if only because he knows his apathy will wound his overly demanding mother. It is impossible to determine whether Juntarō's was the original failing, or if society (or Mother) took the first initiative by making an inordinate request of him. Yasuoka shows how failure breeds upon failure, inaction upon inaction, pushing Juntarō further and further away from a home that never really wanted him, into a society that has no special use for him either. And ironically, what waits for him "out there" in society, lurking like another specter of potential failure, is a war that is eager to use up his youth for its own purposes—just as Juntarō's mother has used him to get back at her husband.

It is no coincidence that a character like Juntarō—rapidly losing his grip on his own life, less and less able to make decisions for himself—has the narrative of his actions set in a period of modern Japanese history when the reins of individual freedom and choice were being snatched away by a growingly powerful military elite which eventually sent the nation hurtling into failure. With pungent irony Yasuoka hammers away at military society as an extension and corruption of home life, making it evident on the level of discourse that his quasi-autobiographical fictions are not to be taken merely as private records of ineptitude.

When Yasuoka's fictional characters enter the army, we can be assured that the result will be both humorous and subtly painful. For his war stories might aptly be subtitled "Juntarō Goes to War." Although the main character in Yasuoka's first full-length novel, *Tonsō* (Flight, 1956), is named Yasugi Kasuke,[15] in temperament he is a blood brother of Juntarō. Like Juntarō, he is a born failure, inept at everything he sets his hands to do. He is one of the last of his generation to be drafted; after all his friends have gone off to war, he feels that the only ones remaining at home are himself and those he thinks of as good-for-nothing Koreans. Although he is not particularly happy at home, he certainly has no desire to be a soldier, and no idea why a war is being fought in the first place.

It seems almost a misnomer to call Kasuke a soldier, or to describe *Flight* as a "war novel." There is not a single scene of fighting with the "enemy" in the book. But that is not to say that no conflicts take place—more than enough combat goes on within the barracks. Kasuke's greatest and most tangible enemies surround him every moment of his military life; it is no wonder that "everyday" existence comes to mean physical and emotional pain to Kasuke. His enemies are the "others"—the unwanted compatriots in the unfamiliar atmosphere into which he is unwittingly thrust—a situation very much like home for Yasuoka characters. It is no accident that one of the author's fine war stories is titled "Katei" (Home), or that it should be prefaced by a statement from the handbook for military conduct: "The barracks is home to the soldiers who share in one another's joys and sorrows, life and death."

The most remarkable aspect of *Flight,* Yasuoka's only full-length work to treat the actual war experience, is the author's relentless focus upon the animalistic traits of the protagonist. There is a distinct flavor of homeliness—in both senses of the word—about Kasuke's war experience. Yasuoka selects only those elements of his character's barracks life that are distortions or exaggerations of the everyday experience of a soldier. The emphasis is upon the activities which reduce a human being to the lowest common denominator—eating, defecating, and groaning in essentially subhuman protest that society (either civilian or military) asks us to do anything more.

This distortion might seem, on the most superficial level, to have philosophical protest as its intention, but a careful examination of the text of *Flight* does not bear out such an interpretation. Yasuoka relentlessly denigrates his character so that he may be seen as the homeless mongrel he is. Moral postures such as heroism or antimilitarism are utterly foreign to a figure such as Kasuke, who can scarcely rise above concern with his own diarrhea. He is an individual controlled not by his mind but by his bowels. Small wonder that such a person can be so easily snatched away from a familial home in which he does not feel comfortable, and can never be forced to fit into his new home in the army's barracks.

There is a mother in the new home, Group Leader Hamada. Like the maternal figure back in Japan, Hamada serves as a disapproving witness to Kasuke's misdeeds. Nothing has really changed for Kasuke, except for the identity of his watchman. If he has been unable to form any true relationship of mutual interchange in his home and seems unlikely to succeed in the army, it is because of the

> unrelieved tension that comes when one is under constant surveillance. The more the body and nerves stiffen, the more desolate the mind becomes. In the interest of self-preservation [Kasuke] must keep others under "surveillance." But such "surveillance" reduces those other individuals to mere objects, evaporating his ability to interact with them. This frantic struggle to stay alive ultimately robs him of all sensation that he is in fact a living being.[16]

Over the course of the novel, Yasuoka weaves together three separate but interlocking images of almost bestial isolation and degradation that underscore Kasuke's bewilderment and his inability to resolve his dilemma by any process of mental reasoning. The first of these is a concentrated dissection of the daily rituals—the events in the "everyday life" of a soldier—which strike Kasuke as existing solely for the purpose of breaking the rookie soldiers of their sense of independence and their youthful impulse to resist authority. They are, in short, like household chores that are intrinsically meaningless but which serve the purpose of undermining any questioning of authority. For Kasuke, the most senseless of all the ceremonies is the requirement that every soldier wrap his shins in special army-issue leggings. This, of course, must be done in the few moments before the soldiers are ordered to fall in each morning. Yasuoka describes the ritual in comic terms worthy of William S. Gilbert.

> Why would nearly every army in the world adopt something so bothersome to put on and take off? At the very least, it would take one minute for even the most seasoned soldier to wrap the things tightly around both legs. Even if you had three minutes to spare before the order to fall in, it would take at least a third or a half of that time to do up your leggings. That's assuming, of course, that everything goes smoothly. You have to bend over at the waist to coil the things around, but when you do, your gas mask and all the other paraphernalia dangling at your chest start doing flip-flops all over the place, and your hands refuse to follow instructions. We had a strict order that our gas mask was *never* to be removed from our person, so you can't take it off and lay it down just because it's in the way. If you really concentrate and finally succeed in getting the things wrapped as far as your kneecaps, all of a sudden comes the cry: "Attention!"
>
> You look up, and far off in the distance, no bigger than a bean, you see a booted officer advancing toward you. You have to snap to attention and "Present arms!!" And of course, your half-wrapped leggings slither limply down around your ankles.
>
> . . . As he pulled his leggings up and began to rewind them, Kasuke visualized soldiers all over the globe—in China, Germany, France, and Brazil—bending double like shrimp just as he was, and doing battle with these infuriatingly cumbersome strips of cloth. . . . After all, weren't most of the responsibilities heaped on soldiers around the world just like these leg wrappings? Useless actions repeated over and over again without end pervaded every

aspect of life in the barracks. And they were all rationalized in the name of "discipline."[17]

As this passage demonstrates, the act of "doing battle" for a soldier like Kasuke is unrelated to his interaction with outsiders. His struggle is self-contained, a fight to the death with the accouterments of daily subsistence placed before him in the shape of such useless objects as leg wrappings. Kasuke's mind reacts to the absurdity of his situation not by rebelling but by imagining that this must be the status of every other soldier in the world. He is not the only shrimp bent over double—they are to be located all over the globe. Kasuke can accept the meaninglessness of his own routine only by magnifying it in his mind to a cosmic level.

Once he has determined that the universal lot of the soldier is to spend his days in skirmishes with his personal gear, Kasuke can absorb himself in that endeavor and not bother his soul with the large, uncomfortable questions of war, death, and killing. He can turn inward. This Kasuke does, concluding that

> when a man is placed under complete restraint twenty-four hours a day, there is only one location where he can act freely and in accordance with his own private will—in the inner workings of the various organs that lie beneath his own skin. The only actions he can undertake without supervision are eating, digesting, and producing waste material. [pp. 254–55]

Once the potential for self-assertion has been reduced to virtual nothingness, daily life becomes an exercise in absurdity. Kasuke has lost all control over his own actions when mastication and defecation seem the only human processes still under his guidance. He develops a marathon case of diarrhea, but he almost glories in the outcome, for it is something that he has done for himself, not had done to him by others. Furthermore, he now has a valid excuse for visiting the latrine, which he finds is the only place on the entire campsite where he can be alone, free from surveillance. The toilet becomes the "little separate world off in a corner" that the writers of Yasuoka's generation sought as the final, but illusory, escape. The single shaft of light shining through a crack in his favorite latrine stall seems to Kasuke to be the one ray of heavenly hope in his otherwise blackened experience. He wishes he could make the toilet his home, live and eat all his meals there, and there enjoy liberation from the demands of military life.

This is the second major motif which Yasuoka introduces in the novel, and it represents the first of several attempts that Kasuke makes to "flee" from the army. His actions are reminiscent of the young boy in "Homework," who for a time found comfort in a cemetery, or of Juntarō, who sought the dismal company of prostitutes when life at home became an intolerable reminder of his failings. Yasuoka's characters always come at life like animals, their actions reduced to such primal functions as defecation and copulation. Kasuke too, unable to perform well as a soldier or to master even the simplest of military tasks, follows his first impulse to flee from the pressures placed upon him. The only possible reaction for him is physiological, and therefore feeble and self-abasing. The latrine is not the most pleasant refuge (the association with primary bodily functions again calls up recollections of Juntarō's failed initiation rite), but it is surely a more cheerful place for Kasuke than the barracks or the exercise ground.

After situating Kasuke in his newfound home—the toilet—Yasuoka introduces a third major symbol of Kasuke's spiritual predicament: the braying of a donkey. The new soldier is ordered one day to carry a tub of discarded food rations to a dumping spot. Kasuke and a comrade place the tub on a pole and carry it on their shoulders. As they stumble along, the pole gouging into their frail shoulders, Kasuke hears the cry of a donkey.

> The braying of that beast of burden . . . was the first sound he had heard upon his arrival in Manchuria. It was truly a unique sound, one that defied comprehension. That "hee-haw, hee-haw, hee-hee-hee-haw" was like the sound of an old locomotive suddenly applying its brakes along rusted rails, or the sound of a child scraping its fingernails along a tin can. That bizarre howl, like the cranking of metal machinery, would echo throughout the barracks for a half an hour, an hour. . . . Why did it bellow so loudly, so forlornly? The first time he heard it, Kasuke thought perhaps a Manchurian coolie was being flogged somewhere by a Japanese soldier. When he learned that it was the braying of a donkey, he was convinced that some Manchurian peasant was whacking the animal's rump with a log or a stick. But he was wrong again. The

> donkey was braying for no reason at all. Its reins tied loosely to a poplar tree, it shook its head as if from tedium and howled out, "hee-haw, hee-haw, hee-hee-hee-haw!" It was almost as if the donkey was crying out for sport, or out of habit. The sound was annoying and unpleasantly foul. But then, the donkey too was unable to run away from its distasteful duties; if it couldn't rebel, what else could it do but bray?
>
> Out of breath, Kasuke swished his tongue around inside his parched mouth and absently pursued this idea. And unwittingly he found himself repeating the same sort of cry within his head.
>
> —There's nothing I can do. After all, I was dragged here to a place I didn't want to come to. [pp. 211–13]

At this point, the identification between man and animal is complete. Kasuke feels as if he too is lashed to a tree, unable to escape "distasteful duties" but totally unequipped to rebel. His escape valve is braying, reproducing in words the vocal protests of the donkey. But braying will not make the chores go away. Just as the homework refused to go away for the boy in Yasuoka's earlier story, or the entrance exams that never ceased to plague Juntarō, the requirements of everyday life in the military will continue to hound Kasuke.

The three central motifs of the novel—meaningless daily routine, diarrhea, and animal-like braying—are brought together at the center of the novel. The concentration of the three elements into one pivotal moment in the narrative provides much more than a dramatic conclusion to one of the threads of plot. It underscores the spiritual dilemma of a man who can only be comfortable in his surroundings if he ignores ("flees") the promptings of his soul and surrenders himself totally to his body.

Kasuke's unit is about to be transferred to the battlefield, and he puts on full battle dress for the first time. When he is completely attired, he can scarcely move under the weight. It is as though the military gear carries the burden of every soldierly duty; beneath it Kasuke all but topples to the earth. Once the men assemble on the parade ground, the battalion commander begins to deliver a final address on the moral responsibilities of the Japanese warrior. Kasuke's bowels protest almost at once, and he can only wish that the entire parade ground would be transformed into a giant privy. When the "at ease" order is finally given what seems a thousand years later,

Kasuke bolts for the toilet. The scene Yasuoka molds here is a work of mastery, for it is slapstick comedy that also distills all the stylistic elements of his text.

He made it in time.

The signs posted on the latrine doors to his right read "Non-coms" and "Infirmary Patients," so he yanked at the third door. It opened. But he could not go in. That was to be expected. About his body dangled the trappings of full battle array, and in his right hand he clutched a weapon that no soldier would ever let out of his possession. Propelling his body straight forward, like a fugitive attempting to break through a solid wall, and raising his arms vertically in front of him, Kasuke eventually forced his way in.

But when he tried to crouch down, the metal helmet that was attached to his backpack next to the canteen rebounded against the rear wall. Kasuke stumbled forward, colliding with the door and jamming his gas mask into his chest. The scabbard of his sword got wedged against the wall to his left.

The moment he finally managed to unlace the cord in his trousers, he felt a warm trickle slithering down the insides of his thighs. With a mixture of disgust and relief, Kasuke wearily muttered, "Up to now, I've used my bowels to take revenge on the army. Now my weapon of vengeance has turned on me."

When Kasuke had finished his business and packed away his soiled clothing inside his backpack, he went outside. But the torches of the battalion had disappeared.

It was incredible. There was not a soul to be seen in front of the barracks.

He raced to the parade ground, but not a single truck remained.

Now what should he do? . . . He returned to the barracks and collapsed onto a bed. Everything had been cleared out; not a single sheet or blanket remained. But what a pleasant feeling of restfulness this was! The winds of "freedom" he had experienced only in the toilet up until now seemed to blow briskly and consistently here.

Somewhere he could hear a donkey braying. It was not the usual irritated cry, but rather an inviting voice that called up all manner of pleasant memories. Lying flat on his back, he tried to

> imitate the voice. Then Kasuke dropped off into a deep sleep. [pp. 266–68]

The latrine, the braying donkey, the potential for flight are all merged to highlight Kasuke's isolation from the society to which he has been assigned by imperial command. "Now what should he do?" is the unanswerable question that reverberates at the core of the Third Generation's fiction. While Kasuke has been evacuating his bowels, the entire camp has been vacated and the soldiers are on their way to the Pacific front. He is left bewildered—which is nothing new for him—and he doesn't know whether he should try to follow them or wait where he is for further instructions. He is at a complete loss, just as he was when he tried to decide whether to escape or to become a model soldier. Ironically, the army has deserted him. He is left close to delirium; he has contracted a lung disease, and when he is finally discovered, he is taken to an army hospital.

The remainder of the novel depicts Kasuke's transfers from one Manchurian hospital to another, as he inches away from the battlefield and closer to Japan. At first Kasuke is led to believe that he has been freed from the rigid discipline of the military and can relax in the hospital environment, but eventually he comes to discover that, even if his battalion has fled from his presence, he has not necessarily found a comfortable refuge where he can peacefully roost. Kasuke is destined to remain homeless; there are no more havens left in Japan or Manchuria, and he himself lacks the ability to align himself with any of the pseudo-homes that remain.

Even when he discovers his name on a list of patients who are scheduled to be sent back to Japan, the images of "back home" that come to Kasuke's mind are anything but attractive. Home to him at this point means

> schools that pretend they're the army; coffee shops that serve you saccharine candy; a house and family deprived of all material goods. . . . Even if he did return "back home," all that awaited him there were the same hospital ward supervisors and aides and army medics. If he were sent "back home" to his mother, all that awaited him there was—
>
> Just then the radio suddenly brought news of the war situation into the darkened hospital room. . . . Our troops are engaged in

fierce fighting on the southern battlefields; cities "back home" are beginning to fall victim to localized air raid attacks. . . .

The radio switched to a hospital frequency. "The following men are to bring their belongings and report at once to the square in front of the hospital in preparation for their repatriation to Japan. . . ."

To his surprise, Kasuke's name was repeated twice. . . ." [pp. 286, 352]

Yasuoka again administers a marvelous, massive dose of irony. Only after Kasuke has abandoned all hope do the orders for repatriation come. Kasuke has by then realized that not even a return "back home" will be an escape for him. For it is not really the army that he wants to flee. It is the web of restrictions which have come at him in his state of ineptitude to plague him in the military, but none of that will change once he returns to Japan. He will go on being clumsy and bumbling within the Japanese social framework. He does not need to escape just from the barracks; he also needs to get away from home, from society as a whole, from the demands that naturally result when one has to interact with other people. There is no escaping the need for that association—certainly the boy in "Homework" wanted it as desperately as Kasuke does—but Kasuke cannot flee from the fact that he is poorly equipped to interact with other people.

The knowledge that escape is impossible, however, does not provide Kasuke with the means to cope with other human beings. He remains in a state of social infancy (literally and figuratively frozen[18] at the anal stage of psychosocial development), still caught up in the satisfaction of his own selfish needs. It is as if he never had a home, a place of nurturing where he could learn the skills necessary to survive in human society. And indeed he has been without a home, though perhaps he does not come to see it in those terms. He does get a glimmering when he realizes that "back home" holds no pleasant associations. Escape becomes impossible when he recognizes that he has nothing to flee *toward*—he loses interest in getting out of the army because he has nothing better to go back to. In the final analysis, it is this lingering agony of homelessness that is Yasuoka's concern in *Flight* rather than the exigencies of life in the Japanese army. At the conclusion of the novel, it seems doubtful that Kasuke will ever be able to meet the minimal requirements for social intercourse. He is returning to Japan no better prepared to cope with what he will face there than he was to deal with the demands of life in the military.

In a perceptive essay on the writers of Japan's Third Generation and their relationship with American literature, Kojima Nobuo draws comparisons between Yasuoka and Sherwood Anderson.[19] The comparison is apt, particularly between the main character in Anderson's "The Egg" and many of Yasuoka's fictional heroes. Not that Anderson directly influenced the course of Yasuoka's literature—it is doubtful that Yasuoka ever read anything by Anderson until very late in his career. But if there is one story in the mainstream of American literature that catches the underlying tone of Yasuoka's fiction, it is "The Egg." The bumbling, well-meaning father in Anderson's story is a close approximation of the father who appears in so many of Yasuoka's stories about the dismal postwar years. That father, in fact, becomes the central character in the mature works of the late fifties and early sixties.

When he turns to an examination of the postwar years, Yasuoka's focus expands beyond himself—another indication of a perspective broader and more critically refined than that of his main characters—to include the members of his family. The tragedies of loss, both the physical losses of war and the emotional drainage that accompanies them, extend to every member of that family. These stories are perhaps the finest, most perceptive Yasuoka has written, and they lead very naturally into the creation of his supreme literary achievement, *A View by the Sea*.

"Kembu" (Sword Dance), written in 1953, is a story of people enervated not so much by the war and the defeat as by their own incompetence, and shamed by that inadequacy into isolation from their neighbors and ultimately from one another. In this basic sense, the story has much in common with "Homework" and *Flight,* but the inclusion of a father and mother along with the inept son (modeled, of course, after Yasuoka himself) expands the range of the tragedy and emphasizes the collapse of the family bonds.

"Sword Dance" is one of Yasuoka's best short stories; it is at once spontaneously amusing and pathetically sad.[20] It is a perfect whole, opening with a near cinematic image of a sword dance; then moving without pause into the main events of the story; and fading out with a repetition of the initial image, which has now been given deeper meaning by the events that have intervened.

Although the specter of a father absent because of the war hung over most of Yasuoka's early stories, in "Sword Dance" and "Aigan" (Prized Possessions, 1952; trans. 1977) he finally attempts to depict his father in fiction. Clearly the young men in Yasuoka's stories are relentlessly dominated by their mothers. Despite that fact, though—or perhaps because of it—they come to resemble their drained fathers more and more as the years go by. The father character in Yasuoka is likely to be an army veterinarian who becomes one with his patients after the military machine collapses. When the war comes to a halt, this man has lost his grip on life. He has known no life but wandering, no career but the now defunct army. He is set reeling uncontrollably in the unfamiliar environs of the postwar period. And most debilitating of all, he no longer commands the respect of his wife and son. In fact, he barely knows them.

Yasuoka's father characters are essentially mute, static figures who move aimlessly from one doomed venture to another. They seldom speak out in defense of themselves or in criticism of others. They exist to be maligned, to be accused, to be hated by their loved ones. But in the end, as a result of the literary fabric that Yasuoka has woven about these motionless characters, we as readers understand the agony they feel and recognize that they do not deserve the abuse that has been heaped upon them. We sympathize with them, and we identify with them. In his ability to create this kind of character with so few strokes of his brush, and in his skill at drawing our sympathy toward the father even when he is viewed through the critical eyes of his unappreciative son, Yasuoka is unsurpassed in his artistic usage of autobiographical materials.

The central metaphor of "Sword Dance" is illustrative of this subtle portrait of the father, sketched, as is so often the case in Yasuoka's stories, by a son who has eyes to see but no critical perspective to interpret or empathize:

> Among the hazy recollections of my youth is one of a sword dance I once saw. A man with a floor cushion strapped to his back to represent a child goes to battle with his foe, wiping away the tears from his eyes. His opponent is formidable, and because of the child on his back, he cannot wield his sword freely. Neither can he abandon the child. I know he must have groaned beneath that burden. This dance had seemed the height of boredom to me then—why would it remain forever in some portion of my brain?[21]

Such questions are never answered in the surface text of a Yasuoka work, but the narrative sandwiched between the two appearances of this sword dance scene is an implicit response. The father is displayed in a variety of poses, none of them flattering. He has spent over thirty years as a career soldier, but now that hostilities have ended, his life has been rendered meaningless. Japan's public defeat has also signaled personal failure for him. He is repatriated to a wife and son who regard him as a meddlesome stranger, yet who feel free to demand economic support.

Through the eyes of a son crippled by disease and unable to leave his bed, Yasuoka allows us to examine this man in a variety of vignettes: waving a hoe in their barren garden, where he can grow only noxious tobacco from leaves he brought back from the battlefield; raising chickens, but spending all the family's money on feed, with the result that he has to gobble down the hens' eggs himself, literally eating up their profits; mixing together water, salt, MSG, and caramel coloring to brew bogus soy sauce in the backyard, but so lacking in business acumen that he tries to sell "clear soy sauce" to the neighbors when the coloring agent runs out; hiring on as a house guard for the Occupation forces, but rankling when his boss asks him to wear a U.S. Army uniform.

By piling these absurd, heartrending images one upon another and assaulting the reader with almost more humiliation than one story can sustain, Yasuoka takes the bland sword-dance image that begins the story and infuses it with the lifeblood of the father's struggles to survive in a world that has no place for him. We are left at the end of the story with understanding and sympathy for this man, far more than his own family will extend toward him. When the sword dance scene is echoed at the conclusion, as the narrator son chats with a friend who has grown fat eating American food and plans to travel to the States to learn the art of baseball, the dance now blazes in full color; instead of the lifeless outlines of the opening, we see the son as the helpless burden strapped to his father's back. And, dressed in the uniform of the conquering army is the father himself, defending his home not with a sword but with the hoe he uses to hack away at the sandy earth in their impotent garden.

"Sword Dance" succeeds as a tale of failure and disorientation because the touch of ironic detachment allows Yasuoka's readers to understand much more than his selfish narrator. The author moves from comedy to pathos without interrupting the flow and style of the story, and he pulls all the elements together by means of a graphic image that at once introduces and summarizes the course of the action. At the heart of his narrative is a tiny family, poorly equipped to cope with the changes in the world around them. Their almost childish attempts to establish, if nothing else, an economic link with the outer world are absurd—near slapstick at times—but beneath the sound of pratfalls is a desperate cry of loss, as three people realize the need to reach beyond themselves yet shrink back after each inept attempt. Like Kasuke and many other Yasuoka characters, they live like animals in a zoo, set off from others, embarrassed by the curious stares of the onlookers but no more capable of freeing themselves than any of the other prisoners on display. They have lost everything: their home, their source of livelihood, and—most serious of all—their self-respect.

In his fiction of the late fifties and sixties, Yasuoka continues to examine the enervated, clumsy characters he created earlier. But the incapable sons have grown older in this middle period; they have finally cut all ties with home and set out to create their own families and careers. They do so with understandable apprehension, since their youthful experiences have prepared them for failure. Yasuoka's narrators possess little self-understanding; we as readers can discern the causes for their failures much better than they.

Yasuoka's conclusions about the human maturation process are not particularly optimistic. With little retouching, his portrait of the failure as a young man becomes a study of the incompetent as a husband and wage-earner. The traits seem almost hereditary, for as the son ages, he comes to resemble his bumbling father more and more. The new generation of husbands and fathers continues to repeat the mistakes of the past, the mistakes rooted in their own diffident natures.

Perhaps it is coincidental that, soon after Yasuoka's own mother died in a Kōchi sanitorium, the jaunty humor of his early period rapidly drains from his stories; certainly stories less obviously humorous in intent had been written before her death. But from this point, there is a distinct swerve in the direction of Yasuoka's work. In previous stories he had been able to look at human beings who lack the impetus or the talent to associate with others of their own kind, and he had chuckled at them. But by 1959, with the composition of

A *View by the Sea,* Yasuoka is considerably more tormented by the selfish acts that keep one person from reaching out to another. He stops viewing these human failures with humor, and a sense of desolation, a despair that renders humor frail and hollow, permeates Yasuoka's masterpiece.

In its broadest conception, this short novel distills everything that came before it in Yasuoka's work. In the "view by the sea" that the main character has at the end of the work, the past is no longer a separate entity to be glanced back upon as a curio item. It comes rushing in to join with the present and infuse it with ultimate meaning. Yasuoka is less flippant in this novel because he has more clearly defined the distance between himself and his material.

What Yasuoka is pursuing in this work is more than simple failure on an examination, sexual disfunction, or rodent infestation (the subject of an amusing 1957 story, "Mogura no tebukuro" [Moleskin Gloves]). With precise attention to detail and a flawless juxtaposition of past and present, Yasuoka defines the inability of his main character to fulfill the minimal requirements for membership in human society. To betray the expectations of society—as Kasuke and the boy in "Homework" do—is one thing; but the narrator-son in *A View by the Sea* proves himself unable to establish a decent human relationship within the confines of his own family. He and his parents can be called a family only because biology, social convention, and economic necessity have forced them to be so. But this is a ruse—in fact, they have never had a home in the spiritual sense, and the war and defeat merely exacerbate the process of decline that eventually pulls them apart. Whatever emotional ties may have been assumed to exist between parent and son are only a travesty of affection; when those bonds are stretched to the breaking point, it becomes clear that they are composed of hatred and selfishness.

Using a fictional approach quite unlike the one Kojima Nobuo employs in *Embracing Family,* Yasuoka arrives at strikingly similar conclusions about human life. In the postwar worlds of both these authors, the most tragic loss is not the defeat by a foreign power but the collapse of the bonds that have traditionally held both family and society together. In Kojima's novel, the tension ripping those bonds apart becomes evident only when infidelity and disease assail the family. In *A View by the Sea,* insanity and death release a flood of memories that washes away the hypocritical sham that has concealed the erosion of those emotional ties.

The novel is narrated in the third person, but every "view" is through the eyes and perceptions of the son, Hamaguchi Shintarō, who has made a journey to his native Shikoku to watch over his mother Chika in the last painful hours of her life. Once again Yasuoka manipulates his narrative technique to allow us to see things through a character's eyes while maintaining our critical posture toward that same character. This is clearly a narrative voice more sophisticated than that in the standard Japanese I-novel. A couple of examples of this technique in operation will demonstrate the control which Yasuoka exercises over the information which passes between text and reader unfiltered by the narrator's limited perceptions.

The first view we get through Shintarō's eyes is of his father:

> Shintarō stole a glance at his father Shinkichi in the next seat. Sunburnt neck craned forward, Shinkichi was gripping the back of the driver's seat for support. His temple was a blur of dark splotches, and his rigidly profiled cheek was creased as if to suggest a smile. It had been a year since Shintarō had last seen his father's face. He noticed three whiskers his father's razor had missed, one on his adam's apple and two under his temple, that had grown almost half an inch. The eyes were too small for the large head and were the color of old glue, and they shone feebly as the eyes of an unfortunate would. [p. 105]

There is little in this passage to suggest that Shintarō and Shinkichi are father and son. The son's perceptions are unrelentingly negative. Shinkichi is described as though he were some enfeebled chicken (an image echoed more concretely later in the novel), unable to support his own weight, much less that of the rest of his family. What appears to be a smile on his lips seems singularly out of place, since he is on his way to an asylum to watch his wife die. This is the first glimpse of Shintarō's feelings about his family. We will be given many other views as the novel progresses; at this stage, however, we have no grounds to suspect that Shintarō's evaluation of his father is anything but accurate.

Although the narrative perspective is Shintarō's throughout the novel, Yasuoka makes careful use of flashbacks to help us understand how this man's judgments have been formed. His unflattering assessment of his father, in fact, turns out to be merely an echo of the reaction his mother had the first time she set eyes on Shinkichi. This is how she related that important day to her son:

> After all, I was married off without ever having met him, you know. When I saw this round-headed bald man come shuffling up to me the day of the ceremony, I thought, my goodness, this wedding is so countrified they've even invited the temple priest along, and believe me, when I found out that was the bridegroom I nearly ran off right then and there. [p. 117]

A mutual conspiracy of loathing for Shinkichi is established between mother and son. This broken triangle is emphasized at so many points in the text that we first marvel at its durability and finally are disturbed by its implications. Chika and Shintarō are so unwaveringly repulsed by Shinkichi and so united in their perceptions of him that their association almost comes to seem like a jealous love triangle, with Shinkichi as a threatening outsider. Although Shinkichi's absence from the home throughout the war years has stimulated the development of this quasi-incestuous relationship, it is evident from Chika's account of her wedding day that the seeds of familial discord were planted far earlier.

One of the functions of the flashback scenes in the novel is to clarify for the reader if not for Shintarō that this relationship which developed between Shintarō and his mother during Father's absence has not been "normal." Mother and son had been living blissfully in a borrowed house at Kugenuma together, almost like lovers, supported by the money they received each month from the father overseas. For this idyllic life (one of the little worlds of unreality shared by so many Yasuoka characters) to continue, however, it is necessary that Shinkichi remain at the battlefield. His repatriation a year after the defeat spoils all that ("It was only after Shinkichi's return that Shintarō and his mother really began to experience Japan's defeat," Yasuoka ironically notes [p. 137]), and Shintarō realizes that he no longer wants to live with his parents. They are a burden to him, particularly now that his exhausted, incapable father can do nothing but putter around the garden.

It is, in fact, no longer a "father" but merely a "man" who has come to live with them. In his mind, Shintarō strips his father of all patriarchal privilege, without realizing that he thereby strikes a blow at the foundation of his own family unit. This sense of familial collapse is heightened once every scrap of food has vanished from the house. Only when that happens does Shinkichi announce that he will go to the family home in Kōchi to "consult." It seems reasonable to mother and son that reliance on the extended family, the nucleus of Japanese society, will be a simple enough matter. But in one of the most vivid scenes in all of Yasuoka's fiction, and one emblematic of the collapse of home and family, Shinkichi returns from Kōchi carrying nothing more than a solitary chicken in a cage. That is all the assistance they can expect from "home." Shinkichi seems the one about to lose his mind after a cat kills their precious chicken.

The total disintegration of this family seems imminent. Shinkichi has ceased to be a "father," and Shintarō behaves less and less like a "son" each day. All that remains is for Chika to appear as something less than a "mother" in Shintarō's eyes, and it will all be at an end. That happens when Chika will not permit Shinkichi to go on pretending that he is her husband. If he cannot be their financial mainstay, neither will she allow him to be her lover. Shintarō awakens one night to angry voices, and the next morning he discovers his mother's bedding spread out in a separate room, "twisted like a dead snake" (p. 140). At this point, though he tries to suppress the thought, Shintarō senses the presence of a "woman" within his mother's body, a woman who has rejected the physical advances of the man he once knew as his father.

What remains now is merely an assemblage of two men and a woman.[22] Shinkichi is denied his final prerogatives as a husband; he has never commanded the respect his position as father should merit. Shintarō has let his mother down simply by coming to resemble his father physically. And Chika now seems like a "woman" and not like his mother. All their relationships are conditional, and this builds barriers between them, giant unscalable walls that eventually crumble under pressure and leave their home a pile of rubble at their feet. Shintarō announces that he is sending his parents back to the country, while he will stay by himself in Tokyo.

This is the final threat to the potential illicit bond between mother and son. Once Shintarō makes the move to sever the cord—moving beyond the hapless attempts of Juntarō—and leaves Chika alone with a man she cannot abide, her mind snaps. When Shintarō visits them after a long absence and verifies with his own uncomprehending eyes that Mother has indeed gone insane, he feels no sense of guilt for her plight. Nor does he understand what her relationship with him has meant to his mother.

> Once in the night Shintarō heard something bump against the sliding door of his parents' room and wondered if she was having another attack; but over Father's thick drowsy voice he heard mother say, "I'm going to the bathroom," and the door slide open. . . . When he realized the footsteps in the dark hallway were advancing toward his room, Shintarō was so terrified he thought his blood would run backwards in his veins. A shadow fell across the dimly visible *shōji* screen before him.
>
> Just then, "No, no. The bathroom's this way, it's the other direction," he heard Father.
>
> "Really? Did I go the wrong way?" came the unexpectedly meek reply, and this time the footsteps receded off in the direction of the bathroom, where the cedar door creaked open. [p. 182]

The incestuous implications of this scene are striking, but in a manner that the reader has come to recognize, Shintarō does not have the will or the desire to try to understand what has happened to his family. This is one of many instances where Yasuoka circumvents his narrator and speaks directly to the reader through suggestion, situation, and irony to convey to us the degree of Shintarō's spiritual blindness. Repetition of scenes of this sort have the cumulative effect of discrediting Shintarō's perceptions, and we are left to scrutinize and evaluate this crumbling household from the pieces of information which Yasuoka scatters through the narrative.

It would, in fact, be instructive to chronicle two or three instances in the novel where Shintarō is embarrassed in the presence of the reader. This is a device central to Yasuoka's purpose—to present, challenge, and then redefine the meaning of selected "sceneries." The ability to present a specific scenery is a gift that any decent novelist possesses, and it was the talent which the I-novelists drew upon most frequently. Shintarō shares these autobiographical writers' abilities to recall images of past and present with convincing accuracy. He lacks, however, what they too were often missing—the ability to sift those sceneries, to question and examine their meaning, to place them within meaningful contexts that go beyond the borders of individual experience and open out onto an entire ocean of human existence. Yasuoka's consistent ability to convey both the content and shortcomings of Shintarō's perceptions to the reader through the technique of paralepsis[23] is strong witness to the degree of control he maintains over his narrative.

The clearest metaphorical expression of Shintarō's limited viewpoint is the location in which virtually all the novel's action takes place. When Chika was placed in the Kōchi asylum a year before the novel opens, the family had requested a room with a view of the fairytale bay. A tiny, lushly grown island lies within the maternal embrace of a spit of land, and unconsciously Shintarō had hoped that a view of this tender scenery would satisfy his mother and atone for the emotional loss of her son. But when Shinkichi and his son return for the last vigil, Chika has been moved to a room without a view. The justification is that she is now blind. But somehow it is appropriate that Shintarō is locked in this "blind" room for a period of nine days until his mother's death.[24]

> Outside the window was a playing field that faced the sea. As the window was small and the wall thick, Shintarō's view was severely limited. All he could see from where he sat was a section of ridgeline and one face of the mountains that surrounded the hospital on three sides. Now, however, the sunlight filled the whole window, making it so bright he couldn't even look in that direction. Sometimes Shintarō heard the echoing shouts and laughter of the regular patients; when he got up to look, he saw them dashing barefoot across the blindingly bright field at mad speeds, gripping bundles of laundry under their arms. The sight, clipped by the square window frame and glittering in the sun, made him think of a single frame of movie film. From the hospital room it looked like a piece of a scene snipped from another world. [p. 130]

Yasuoka places Shintarō in a position of virtual solitary confinement. Because he has no official duties or responsibilities toward his dying mother, he has the leisure and the motivation to meditate on the bond that has joined him to Chika. But his reflections are all superficial, distorted views, like his blocked angle of vision out of the window of her room. Yasuoka states, very matter-of-factly, that "Shintarō's view was severely limited." By implication we understand that this refers to his insights. He cannot see the little island that is hugged by the shore outside the window; the suggestion is that he is also oblivious to his mother's embracing warmth. He sees individuals and relationships in two-dimensional, static poses, like the scene on the beach that reminds him of a single frame of movie film. He is not sensitive to the movements of time, the shifting of emotions, or the need to nurture and protect an intimate relationship if it is to remain alive. The brightness of the outer world is anathema to him: "he couldn't even look in that direction." Later, in fact, he constructs a makeshift blind to block out that painful light ("It wasn't only the heat that Shintarō couldn't bear, but also the fact that he could see straight into his sleeping mother's mouth" [p. 153]).

The static, sightless vision is further emphasized by Shintarō's inability to form a link between her room and the outside world. The spiritually blind son and the physically blind mother face one another, though she cannot see him and he does not want to look at her. He must at all costs avoid placing this room, this relationship, in any larger context. He must keep this to himself, conceal it as a private world removed from society at large. Otherwise he will have to begin asking himself questions. Even when the doctor makes a rather scathing statement about his family, Shintarō refuses to consider the significance of the remark.

> "In other countries they bring people to an institution right away, old people included; but here—call it belief in the family, or a case of underdeveloped individualism—most of them are kept at home and never sent away like that. . . ."
>
> All of a sudden Shintarō felt as if the hallway in front of him had stretched out infinitely, and for an instant his feet stopped moving.
>
> Shintarō was dizzy with confusion. He didn't know what had caused it. All he knew was that the green door to the room where they had just left his mother seemed to be cut off from the long hallway, cut off from the yellow varnish and white walls and green window frames, and getting infinitely distant and small . . . and that all the while there rang in his ears the echo of a soft, sweet, light voice, like a musical instrument, repeating the words, individualism . . . belief in the family. . . .[pp. 123–24]

The inherent struggle between individualism and belief in the family, between egotism and responsibility, lies at the root of Shintarō's tattered association with both his mother and father. But he cannot probe that struggle or consider himself a participant in it. Instead he seals off his mother's room, cuts it off from the rest of the hospital, and places it in a vacuum where he will not have to ponder such weighty matters. He may hear an angelic chorus singing to him about individualism, but somehow the sweet, airy nature of their voices removes any trace of discord between his own selfishness and the state of his family ties.

One other misperception on Shintarō's part prepares the reader for the inevitable confrontation between mother and son. Yasuoka has assiduously warned us that Shintarō's views are not to be trusted. We observe him time and time again examining an object without probing it. He sees people walking on the beach, and to him they are merely part of the landscape. "It wasn't a scene you could look at for very long." But then,

> Shintarō suddenly remembered these were not normal people—and for an instant the thought shocked him. Shintarō did not understand what that shock meant. Was it surprise that he could have been so deeply engrossed in the landscape? Or was it that he had only now sensed that madness really lurked in these patients? Leaving the question dangling, Shintarō turned his attention to his surroundings in an attempt to puzzle out the enigma that was his mother. [p. 134]

We have no confidence that Shintarō will be able to unravel the enigma of his mother, for he leaves all the important questions dangling. We grow so used to his descriptive approach to a scene that we no longer hold out any hope that he will follow it up with an analytical interpretation. Shintarō has several encounters with a man at the hospital who wears a bandage around his neck; but it is quite some time before Shintarō notices that the man has a glass tube in his throat, and even longer before it dawns on him that this man is also a patient at the asylum.

All these sceneries, described but not defined, come together at the two central moments in the novel. The second of these is, of course, the death of Chika, which I will deal with shortly. But there is another death, a spiritual rather than physical one, that takes place midway through the narrative. It is as moving as Chika's death and infinitely more surprising, both to Shintarō and to us. Yasuoka has prepared us for it, but we are still caught off guard and are moved and relieved that we have been allowed to witness something that slips past Shintarō almost totally unawares. This moment occurs when Chika comes close to recovering consciousness as the orderlies move her from one bed to another to help soothe her bedsores. The move is very painful for her, and Shintarō looks on without emotion until she speaks the first words he has heard from her in over a year. But they are the last words he expected to hear her utter.

> Mother continued to cry out until the open sores adjusted to the mattress. Her chest heaved as her whole body worked to draw in short, violent breaths between cries. A nurse told Shintarō to take his mother's hand. He did as he was told. The fair-skinned attendant spoke to her as he had on that first night.
>
> "Mrs. Hamaguchi, Mrs. Hamaguchi, it's your son. Your son's holding your hand now."
>
> But Mother just kept crying, "ow, ow," between gasps for air. As Shintarō stood there, feeling the incredibly tiny, soft palm of the wrinkled hand he held within his own, he was conscious of a vague memory just outside his grasp. But while he was still fishing for it, the attendant's voice broke his line of thought.
>
> "It's your son, your son. . . ."
>
> Mother's breathing began to calm down a little. She closed her eyes. Footsteps sounded outside the room, and Father appeared; he came in and sat down beside her. At this her cries of "ow . . . ow . . ." gradually subsided until she was only muttering softly as if half asleep. Then, in a hoarse, low voice, she said it.
>
> "Father. . . ."
>
> Shintarō felt as if something had just slipped out of the palm where he had been holding onto his mother's hand. Father wore the same faint smile as always, as he looked down at his now peacefully sleeping wife. [p. 152]

As he clutches his mother's hand, Shintarō fishes for a "vague memory just outside his grasp," a long-forgotten affection for her. But as always, he lets it slip away. Then the loveless son who has always been confident of his own filiality is struck dumb by the name his mother calls out in her moment of agony. The name he expects to hear, of course, is his own. With a mixture of anger and incomprehension he instead hears her call for her husband, for a man he had blithely assumed she could never love. The last tie between him and his mother, a tie that he has been hacking away at through his actions for many years, has finally been totally severed. He feels betrayed and empty. Though he imagines he should now sense that a great burden has been lifted off his shoulders, he rather feels only numbness. His mother, the only person in his life who had never betrayed him, has cast him aside and called out for a man he is certain she has hated since she first set eyes on him. This is a puzzle too complex for Shintarō to unravel. Indeed, given the shallow affection he has felt toward his parents for so many years, it seems highly unlikely that he would expend the energy to solve this riddle.

This scene creates only confusion for Shintarō, but it has the opposite effect for the reader. All the unreliable clues and impressions that Shintarō has been scattering before us are swept away, and he is left to stand in isolation, a self-imposed exile from home as a result of his willful rejection of his parents. At the same time, we can exult in the link that has been forged between mother and father. Our perceptions of Shinkichi, dim and uncertain until this point, are solidified, and we recognize him for the decent, devoted—though certainly feckless—man that Yasuoka has hinted he might be. The barrenness of the emotional landscape is redeemed by Chika's one uttered word, and love is rescued from the ruins of this home.

For the remainder of the novel, Shintarō will blithely grumble about how "stifling" *(oshitsukegamashii)* his mother has been throughout his life; even the lullaby she sang to him as a child seems to express this oppressiveness:

> Have you forgotten the days
> When you were young and knew no wrong;
> When your mother would rock you to sleep
> And calm your fears with a song?
> In the spring there was rain on the eaves,
> And dew in the garden in fall—
> With tears never dried I would pray for you.
> But you don't remember at all.[25]

Shintarō hears no affection in the song, only the heavy burden of his mother's disappointment in him. And he feels as though he has reached an important level of understanding in their relationship: "Finally, what bound mother to child was sheer convention" [p. 146].

That "convention" by itself is not enough to sustain Shintarō's interest in his parents. Congenitally blinded to whatever positive traits his father might possess, he is equally deaf when relatives come to the hospital and rave on at how "wonderful, truly wonderful" Shinkichi has been in his ministrations to his deranged wife. With an excess of patience he has struggled to bring her back to reality, to help her realize that her nightmares are of her own making, a result of her obsessive attachment to a son she must set free, and of her irrational hatred for a husband who sincerely loves her. But this is not the Shinkichi that Shintarō has known, and he refuses to admit the possibility that what his aunt says is true. He can only see his father as a helpless, ineffectual animal crouching in a dark corner of the sanitorium room. Rejecting outright the possibility that his father might have been truly "wonderful," Shintarō ultimately cannot understand why his mother called out for her husband instead of her son in her single moment of lucidity in over a year.

Two days after Chika calls for her husband, she dies in the presence of Shinkichi and Shintarō.

Yasuoka does not tell the reader whether Shintarō has been able to put together the pieces of his past and realizes that the strain upon the already frail bonds between husband and wife, mother and son have wrenched his mother from the world of sanity. But Yasuoka has provided us with enough "views" to allow us to judge for ourselves. Our perceptions and evaluations are confirmed in the moving scene that we are shown—once again, through Shintarō's eyes—at the conclusion of the novel. Yasuoka demonstrates Shintarō's selfishness and at the same time vividly depicts the shallow, hollow chasm that is his inner self. As Shintarō, drained of life, stares out at the ocean at ebb tide and sees the desolate scene there—a perfect reflection of what is left of his human feelings—he still seems unable to understand that a family must be more than just a group of people who happen to live under the same roof.

> Nine days. Exactly what had he accomplished during that time? To what end had he locked himself up in that room filled with a mixture of sweet and stale odors? Had he thought that he could if nothing else make up for everything that had passed by living in the same room with his mother for a mere nine days? Even supposing such an atonement was incomplete, what exactly was it he hoped to atone for? What was he attempting to recompense? In the first place, the idea that he needed to repay his mother for something was ridiculous. A son repays his mother in full just by being her child. A mother makes recompense merely by having a son, and the son pays off his debt by being his mother's child. No matter what they do to each other, no matter what passes between

them, mother and son settle all accounts between themselves, and no one else can intercede.

Absorbed in these thoughts, Shintarō wandered about the exercise ground. So everything is finished. How indescribably pleasant it felt now to be able to walk freely about the landscape he had viewed through that window scooped out of the thick walls of her sickroom, without having to feel diffident or constrained toward anyone. Even the sun that shone directly over his head was no longer an annoyance. He wished he could use that sun to burn up every layer of clothing he wore, each steeped in that gloomy odor. . . . Shintarō looked up at the scene that stretched before his eyes, and in shock he came to a stop.

It was a familiar enough scene, with its fairy-tale islands floating lightly in the embrace of the promontory. But now it brought him to a halt, for on the surface of the sea, waveless and calmer now than any lake, hundreds of wooden stakes poked blackly up as far as the eye could see. . . . For an instant, every object of nature ceased its movements. Only the sun beaming overhead splashed its yellow-streaked splotches of light here and there. The wind was stilled, the scent of the tide gone, and everything seemed to have dried up with one motion in response to the bizarre scene that had just surged up from the depths of the ocean. As he gazed at the row of stakes—like the teeth of combs, like grave markers—it was apparent to him that he had caught hold of a single "death" in his hand.[26]

With firm but unobtrusive control, Yasuoka is able to bring all time and all movement to a standstill in this scene. It would be merely a clever literary trick if Yasuoka did not use the device to bring perfect symmetry and focus to his narrative. But when action and the surge of time come to a complete stop, every betrayal, every selfish whim, every thoughtless move that Shintarō has made comes bubbling up from the depths of the ocean view before his eyes to indict him for his lack of love. When time ceases to flow in a Yasuoka work, past and present become one, and the human failures that clutter the landscape are transformed into universal accusations. Shintarō can witness the scene before his eyes and be unable to make much of anything out of it—"death" is all that surfaces in his mind, without any thought of his part in it—while from our perspective we are able to place his actions into a frozen framework of time and see him for what he really is.

In that cessation of movement and time, Yasuoka rivets his gaze on his individual characters, and all the agonies of shattered love, lost youth, homelessness, and deceit come together in a stark, gloomy portrait of modern man in his empty state. The scene before Shintarō's eyes is the shallows of his own soul laid bare on the sands of the seashore. Like the waters of the ocean, he has dried up inside, and only a row of wooden grave markers remains to indicate where the daily little deaths have taken place. The scene is one of total devastation, the dismemberment of a human being who has trusted only his own ego and in the end is left with no other companionship.

Shintarō's failure is more extreme than that of any of his predecessors. He has failed at the most fundamental and most vital of endeavors, that of communicating with his fellow human beings. Ironically, the only character in the novel who comes anywhere near succeeding as a human being is the one we had always been led to believe was no better than the animals he treated—the father Shinkichi. He has not let his wife's spite or his son's contempt poison him as well. He may have had his failings as a provider and a patriarch, but in his tender nursing of his blind, crazed wife, he has demonstrated that he has within him resources of love that Shintarō utterly lacks. And he has justly been rewarded for his efforts by a single utterance of his name. That word brims with affection such as Shintarō will never know.

A View by the Sea is an agonizing portrait of failure, an anguished view of the lowest levels of human relations. But it is the high water mark of Yasuoka's achievement as a writer, and surely one of the finest short novels written in Japan in the modern period. It is the best piece in which fragments of his own experience are welded into a framework of enduring power. This novel reflects undiluted his own sense of a lost home and a splintered family, themes that lie at the heart of his fictional world.

After *A View by the Sea,* Yasuoka wrote two full-length novels which reiterate the views of human life expressed in the earlier work, and which rely heavily on the same literary techniques. In both *Maku ga orite kara* (After the Curtain Falls, 1967), over which he anguished for five years, and *Tsuki wa higashi ni* (The Moon Is to the East, 1971), Yasuoka employs the technique of time suspension. What distinguishes *After the Curtain Falls* is the fact that the entire novel is built upon a complete identification between past and present. The suspension of time seems to place the protagonist on an endless turntable of perpetual ineptitude. Indeed, Yasuoka's fundamental thesis is that human action is a series of repeated blunders; that people do not learn from past mistakes, but go on repeating them time and time again; that the plot of the play of life does not change a whit after the curtain falls.

The novel is filled with striking visual vignettes like the concluding scene to *A View by the Sea,* perhaps the best at the opening when the ambivalent protagonist, the artist Kensuke, is appearing onstage in an amateur Kabuki play, portraying a woman student of the Meiji period. Onstage, he sweats profusely under the bright lights; the weight of his costume and wig and the thick odor of the many-layered makeup he wears oppress him, rendering him all but immobile—again the stoppage of movement. Kensuke does not realize that offstage, in his everyday life, he sweats as profusely under the dazzling lights of reality, and that the burden of his multilayered failures, past and present, leaves him as emotionally paralyzed as he feels upon the stage. In this hot, damp, timeless spotlight of inactivity, Kensuke catches sight in the audience of a woman he had had an affair with many years earlier. Thus the familiar chain of past recollections mingled with present exasperation begins again for a Yasuoka character.

The end of the novel finds Kensuke sitting immobile in a coffee shop just twenty-four hours after he had performed in the Kabuki play. His marriage seems about to come apart at the seams, and he knows he should be with his wife, trying to prevent the dissolution of his own family. But he continues to sit, pondering:

> Ah, I want to go home! If I go home, there'll be beer and sushi and cream puffs—so much on hand I'd never be able to eat it all!
>
> Kensuke rose from his chair.
>
> . . . No matter what, I have to go back to my own house. Even if there aren't any sushi or beer or cream puffs, it is my own home. . . .
>
> Kensuke . . . walked slowly toward the cashier at the door. He was numb from his thighs to his buttocks, and as he limped toward

the exit, his reflection in the glass door reeled unsteadily with each step, distorted and growing increasingly larger.[27]

As Kensuke's distorted image staggers toward the glass door, he recognizes the resemblance between himself and his limping, inept father. When the curtain fell on the war years, Kensuke's father—like Shintarō's in *A View by the Sea*—must have uttered the words, "Ah, I want to go home! If I go home, there'll be beer and sushi and cream puffs. . . ." The words are reminiscent too of Kasuke's phantom longings for home as he sits in his barracks in Manchuria. It is the yearning common to virtually every Yasuoka character—for the simple physical comforts of a home that has never existed except in the deepest recesses of their imaginations.

The Moon is to the East is less successful than *After the Curtain Falls* because of an inherent redundancy in Yasuoka's technique and theme. The tenacity with which he clings to this motif of lost home, however, is indicative of the degree to which he is absorbed by it. Perhaps the most intriguing part of this novel—aside from the usual sharply etched vignettes—is the derivation of the title, and its relation to Yasuoka's fondness for freezing time. Although Yasuoka gives no reference (one must always suspect titles in Japanese that scan as five or seven syllables) and has always claimed total ignorance of classical Japanese literature, his title in fact comes from a strikingly pictorial haiku by the eighteenth-century poet Yosa Buson. The poem, composed in 1774, reads as follows:

Na no hana ya
Tsuki wa higashi ni
Hi wa nishi ni

Rape-blossoms!
The moon is to the east,
The sun to the west.

This remarkable bit of fanciful cosmology suggests that the field of rape-blossoms that Buson has stumbled across seems so expansive that it could be a self-contained universe. The concepts of space and time are distorted as the sun and moon are brought together at differing ends of a natural landscape. In Buson's verse the emphasis is visual, highlighting the scope of the field of flowers. For Yasuoka, the more important part of this vision is the subjugation of the advance of time.

Yasuoka's literary activities since the publication of *The Moon is to the East* in 1971 suggest that he was searching for a new mode of expression in his writing. Perhaps he recognized the stale pall of redundancy that hung over *The Moon is to the East.* In the five years after the appearance of that novel, he published a handful of short stories, but no sustained works of fiction. He also engaged in a variety of creative endeavors during that period—he lectured on Japanese literature at Toronto University, wrote literary criticism for a prominent journal, participated at the invitation of the American government in a 1976 lecture tour of Japan to commemorate the American bicentennial, cotranslated a novel by Marcel Mouloudji, and joined the selection committee for the Akutagawa Prize—but it was not until 1976 that he again went to work on a major piece of literature.

It is significant that the first installment of this new work appeared just a few months before Yasuoka published a collaborative translation of Alex Haley's *Roots* into Japanese. For the work that Yasuoka finally put into book form in 1981, *Ryūritan* (Tales of Wanderers), is in many senses a continuation of his own long search for roots. In *Tales of Wanderers,* Yasuoka turns—uncharacteristically—to a remoter past, to the mid-nineteenth century when Japan was in turmoil after the first coming of foreigners. There he begins his search for kindred spirits among his ancestors in Tosa province, specifically his forebear Kasuke,[28] a minor historical figure who participated in a political assassination and then fled from home and family.

It goes without saying that Yasuoka felt a strong kinship with Kasuke, who lived in an age of upheaval, never quite able to fit in or feel comfortable. Kasuke was ultimately executed for his part in the assassination; he was in fact the only member of the conspiracy sentenced to death. Here too Yasuoka seems to be locating the same traits of uncertainty, clumsiness, and humiliation that have wracked his own soul in the modern age. Time again stands still for Yasuoka, and just as Kensuke at the conclusion of *After the Curtain Falls* saw a reflection of his father in his own image in the glass door, Yasuoka in *Tales of Wanderers* has encountered yet another likeness of himself in an earlier generation.

In *Tales of Wanderers,* Yasuoka employs a wealth of actual historical documents, letters, diary entries, and descriptions of his own visits to sites important in Kasuke's life. With this technique, he reduces the distance between historical event and contemporary reader, and draws us into his narrative with his own fanciful, sometimes wry musings about facts of history. With this work, which Japanese critics have blithely labeled a "novel" for want of any better term, Yasuoka has opened up new vistas, redefining the I-novel by including the historical "I" alongside the contemporary one. But for all the innovative technique in this work, one can only be struck by the fact that the initial posture of the author has not changed at all. We are still confronted with the young boy wandering about the cemetery, wishing he could go back home.

IV

The Eternal War: Shimao Toshio

Navy lieutenant Shimao Toshio, summer 1944

Is the knowing all? To know, and even happily, that we meet unblessed; not in some garden of wax fruit and painted trees, that lie of Eden, but after, after the Fall, after many, many deaths. Is the knowing all? And the wish to kill is never killed, but with some gift of courage one may look into its face when it appears, and with a stroke of love—as to an idiot in the house—forgive it; again and again . . . forever?

—Arthur Miller, AFTER THE FALL

THE SUICIDE boats (*Shinyō*, or "ocean shakers") introduced by the Japanese navy late in 1944 were just over fifteen feet long and three feet wide. Constructed of thin wood and powered by an automobile engine, these tiny launches displaced 1.4 tons of water and could advance through the waves at a velocity of 23 knots. Designed for only one man to operate, each boat carried in its nose a 250-kilogram explosive, which the pilot could detonate by pulling a handle at the moment of impact with an enemy vessel. Over 6,200 of these torpedo launches were constructed before the end of the war, but their effectiveness in battle was minimal.

A majority of the Shinyō squad members survived the war. Seven divisions of suicide launches were destroyed at Corregidor and another six sunk elsewhere in the course of battle, while many of the men scheduled to pilot the boats were killed in hand-to-hand fighting on Okinawa. Others died in freak explosions at the launch bases, the most tragic of these killing around 180 men in Tosa Bay on the day of the surrender.[1]

Hundreds of men were selected to pilot the "ocean shakers," only to be released with the defeat of Japan. At least one, the novelist Shimao Toshio, continued to carry an armed torpedo around with him inside his head. As the commander of a suicide unit on the tiny island of Kakeroma in the Amami chain north of Okinawa, Shimao passed nearly a year of his life amid enormous contradictions. While the war in the Pacific raged all around them with an ever-mounting fury, Shimao and his men were required to sit still on their island, waiting for the order to die. In the day, they hid beneath heavy camouflaging, apprehensive of enemy reconnaissance flights. Though they were equipped with antiaircraft guns, they did not dare use them, since a single bomb from an enemy plane could detonate all their torpedos. All their training for death took place under cover of darkness.[2]

Theirs was essentially a life of ease; knowing that these men were soon to make the ultimate sacrifice, headquarters treated them to rations of far higher quality than the ordinary combat troops received. Yet Shimao had been a reluctant volunteer,[3] and once he was made commander of the suicide squadron, his personal anxieties mounted. Recognizing that the order to launch could come at any time, his greatest fear was that he would lose his composure as he tried to dress in his full battle gear while communicating orders to his men. Irrationally he worried that he might forget to take along the final ceremonial meal that was to be placed in his own torpedo launch. To stave off this concern, Shimao often awoke in the middle of the night and, while his men slept, rehearsed the task of dressing in his battle regalia.[4]

An excessive concern with the totally meaningless details of everyday life when they are just preparations for death is a twisted psychological subtlety that infuses much of Shimao's fiction. In his most autobiographical story about the suicide corps, "Shuppatsu wa tsui ni otozurezu" (The Departure Never Came, 1962), Shimao wrote:

> If the order to launch had come the previous evening, I would have been able to fight bravely as a suicide pilot. . . . But tonight was different. In the space of one bizarre night, I felt as though I had been treated with contempt. I had plumbed to its very depths the feeling that, even if I were to survive, I would never be able to endure the day-to-day existence in a world surrounded by the threat of extinction. . . . I could not bear the weight of the daily life that would press down upon me if the order to launch never came. If I hurled myself toward death, I would be free from the

past; but so long as I had to remain in the midst of daily life, I would never be able to sever my ties with the past. . . . I want to set out now, before I regain any of my attachments to life.[5]

I dwell upon this aspect of Shimao's past because, in a sense, the literary distillations of his personal experiences can be summarized as a process of dressing in battle gear. At least three distinct, extended encounters with death since childhood served to convince him that the course of an individual's life is determined primarily by such exigencies. At the age of six, Shimao fell seriously ill, and though the doctors could not provide a clear diagnosis, they were certain the child would not live. Shimao's mother took him and her other children from Yokohama to the family home in Fukushima, hoping that the change of scenery might effect some cure. The day Shimao's father left Yokohama to join the family, the Great Kantō Earthquake struck, demolishing their house. Though Shimao eventually recovered, he continued to suffer from frequent headaches and impaired vision throughout elementary school.[6] His war tour, culminating with the orders to prepare for launch on August 13, 1945—orders that were never followed by the command to launch—left its indelible mark. He was, in more than a literal sense, left on the day of the defeat with his engines racing, prepared to leap into the void of death but never allowed to do so. When he began his career as an author shortly after repatriation, Shimao began writing about characters who have no point of contact with normal life, for whom "everyday" existence has no meaning. Trained during the war to believe that there could be no life for them in peacetime, they return to wander the ravaged streets of postwar Japan with utterly no sense of purpose, no vision for the future, no tangible grip on the moment. Only by summoning back the war, donning their emotional battle gear, and recalling the endless anxiety of approaching death are they able to feel a part of the emerging society.

There is another aspect, more frightening, to the experiences which Shimao has transformed into literary materials. In each unresolved brush with death, Shimao was the beneficiary of an unusual and perplexing Providence. Each encounter was paradoxical, combining special privilege and extreme anxiety. In wartime, Shimao was treated by circumstance as something better than he was or could hope to be. A complex web of expectations embraced and entrapped him. He was treated with deference because he was expected to "save" the nation. The kamikaze warriors ("divine wind," connoting something innately superior about these pilots) were considered to be "gods without earthly desires,"[7] a role more easily assumed by a dead soldier than by an unwitting survivor. In the gap between his presumed role as savior-god of the nation (or at least of Kakeroma Island) and his awareness of himself as a duplicitous, egotistical mortal Shimao found the central conflict for his literature.

Shimao's wife Miho, in her own evocation of the war years, has described what she and her fellow islanders expected of "Lieutenant Shimao":

> Because of his generosity and solicitude, the people of the island began calling this twenty-seven-year-old commanding officer "our benevolent father" *(waakyajuu),* and they gave him their affection.
>
> From about the time news began to reach us of the severe attacks on Okinawa, raids by enemy planes became daily more terrible; elsewhere in the Amami Islands, two or three houses built on the beaches were bombed and burned, and there had been some human casualties. But the inhabitants of Nominoura and Oshikaku, near the Shimao squadron, held a conviction so firm it approached religious faith, that "Lieutenant Shimao will protect us, so everything will be all right." They were convinced that the enemy planes that crashed at sea or in the mountains had all been shot down by the antiaircraft guns of the Shimao squadron, interpreting those successes as certain proof that Lieutenant Shimao was their guardian deity. And strangely enough, the villages of Nominoura and Oshikaku continued to survive unscathed. This fact intensified their devotion to the commanding officer. People were inspired by the soldierly way Lieutenant Shimao carefully collected the bodies of enemy pilots whose planes had crashed, burying them with proper grave markers in the village. "That man must represent the ultimate in human existence" *(Anchuukusa, ningin tushi, umarekahannu chuu daroyaa),* they proclaimed, and there was even a popular song that went, "See, what did I tell you? Lieutenant Shimao is both compassionate and heroic . . . for you would we gladly lay down our lives"; one heard it in the mouths of toddlers barely old enough to talk. . . .

> More than twenty years have passed, but even today at Nominoura inlet you can see the decaying remains of the base, and the people of the island still have a group that meets to talk of Lieutenant Shimao; they sing the "Lieutenant Shimao Song" and reminisce about those days. And every once in a while, Lieutenant Shimao appears in my dreams—to the evident chagrin of my husband.[8]

The pressures of having to play God; the fear of being found out (made more real by the likelihood that enemy bombs would eventually fall on Kakeroma); the yearning to be regarded as a fallible individual, coupled with the wish to retain the comfortable perquisites of deification—these struggles lie at the core of Shimao's texts, creating a literary discourse that speaks to more than just the bizarre experiences of a suicide pilot—that stretches out to include each of us who has peered into the chasm separating our honest realizations of ourselves and the exalted and unreachable expectations that others have for us.

In sum, then, the "commanding officer" experience merges with the motif of an unworthy God to create a total inversion of the concept of "daily life" for the characters in Shimao's fiction. Combined with this is the temporal illusion of uninterrupted warfare. Shimao's imagery is filled with deep pits of despair, with heads that constantly itch from imaginary sores and stomachs that twist with a pain both physical and psychological. And always the wanderers—the metaphorical repatriates who become hallucinatory travelers, searching for some familiar face or doorway from the past but never able to locate them. At times the quest becomes a dream, merging fuzzy reality with surreal fantasy. By the mid-1950s, this metaphor of wandering assumes new dimensions. The characters, now more closely identified with their creator (generally named "Toshio," in fact), find themselves suffocating in marriages that have too much of that mundaneness that fills them with terror. So they begin wandering outside the home in search of new love, a love fraught with some of the dangers of war because of the potential for discovery. And when the inevitable discovery comes, the battle resumes—this time a struggle between a man and wife who wage their own private war as though their lives depended upon the outcome. As, indeed, they do.

Shimao's codification of personal experience, then, essentially involves taking the fluidity of the prematurely terminated war-suicide and solidifying it into the bedrock beneath all placid postwar experience. To illustrate this implantation of an underlying code, I will turn briefly to an emblematic little scene in the 1959 short story titled "Haishi" (Ruins). The narrator is, predictably, a former commander of a suicide boat squadron, and the story follows him as he undertakes a postwar pilgrimage back to the island where he was stationed. He is unaware that he is still known to the islanders as the "Commander," since nearly ten years have elapsed since the surrender. Much has happened to him in the interim; he returns, in fact, accompanied by his wife, who is now mentally deranged. Somehow, though, there has been a disruption of temporality, and the narrative lulls us into ignoring the passage of time. The Commander's chief mission at this time is to take apart the physical setting of his past activities, to locate some tangible evidence that the island base has been altered and that all traces of the war have been obliterated by the passage of time. This will allow him to begin dismantling—or, perhaps, disarming—the psychological vestiges that linger malevolently in his psyche and that of his wife. This attempt to destroy past codes—by acts of violence, if necessary, since these characters were stopped short of their self-destructive, conclusive launches in wartime—so that new foundations for behavior and relationships can be established is the central literary undertaking of Shimao's fictions. The eventual realization that such disarmaments are impossible brings a true pathos to the narratives.

Initially in "Ruins" it would seem that such a restructuring is within the realm of possibility: on the beach, there are no traces of the barracks. It is high tide, suggesting that nature and time have been able to wash away every trace of that intrusive past.

> I wanted to stand on this beach forever with Kesana. Eventually the entire bay would be filled with sea water.
>
> With that thought, I shifted my eyes toward the shore. I realized that the outermost edges of the caves where we had concealed our launches were protruding far out into the bay, gaping somewhat unnaturally like the beaks of gigantic waterfowl. These were the mounds of earth that were pushed out toward the sea when we originally dug those caves.

When our division first arrived here at N Bay, precisely the same air of tranquillity had hovered over the place.

With the passage of ten years of time, N Bay had recovered its original repose. But the staring eyeballs at the entrances to the twelve caves were unchanged, as were the beak-like mounds of earth in front of them. The ocean waters had not touched the granite rocks that we had pounded into the beach so that the tires of the trailers carrying our five-ton launches would not sink into the sand. Gazing through narrowed eyes at the two tracks of granite that remained, I was swallowed up by an inexpressible feeling of desolation.

The fading light of evening was preparing to trade places with the dark of night. We stepped back, making up our minds to take the mountain path to O Village. Kesana and I both hoped that we would be able to reach the cemetery under cover of darkness, unnoticed by the people of the village.[9]

The placidity of this scene is deceptive, but it conceals a duplicity common in Shimao texts. Initially the narrator appears to be yearning for some kind of emotional harmony—with his past as well as with his stricken wife. As he gazes at the landscape, he seems to want to obliterate temporality and be subsumed into the calming, conscience-numbing embrace of the ocean. As those waters had meant self-annihilation to him during the war, they now also promise to erase the pain he has experienced since the surrender, a pain which has brought him back to scenes of the past in quest of an ultimate solace —through the death either of his memories or of his own consciousness. But it is the curse of the intellect that it is tirelessly associative, and thoughts of the ocean force him to shift his gaze to the beach. There we no longer encounter soothing images. Instead we have lurking caves and the "unnatural" beaks of enormous creatures from the past that seem ready to pounce upon the Commander and Kesana. But these monsters are unnatural only because they were created upon the beach by the Commander himself, when he and his men transformed this innocent scene of nature into a base for war.

With this, the narrator is swept back, and the gentleness of peacetime is easily converted into the calm that hovered over his squadron as they awaited certain death. The dual quality inherent in tranquillity—that it can both assuage and expose pain—and the association of peace with death are central codes. In the final paragraph of this scene, Shimao makes it clear that the natural setting has maintained a neutrality that transcends time, and that the potential for horror in the past and the almost palpable terror of the present ("staring eyeballs," "beak-like mounds of earth") have been imposed upon that blank scene by the duplicitous acts of men, specifically by this Commander. Once he realizes that the enemy to repose lies within his own soul, and that the past is ever-present because nothing has changed for him internally, he is "swallowed up" not by the lullaby waters of the ocean but by "an inexpressible feeling of desolation." That single description of the Commander's feelings bears the entire weight of past and present narrative, and to undervalue it or ignore its inherent pain is to miss all that Shimao has invested in this story. That recognition and its accompanying desolation make it impossible for the narrator to have any further contact with the living. He must now avoid the villages where he is worshiped as a savior of the island. Only darkness and the cemetery can provide a sufficient cloak for his emotions. The god of the island has returned with his lunatic consort to the scene of his creations, but because of the human frailties that choke his soul, he has not been able to pronounce either the works of his hands or even himself "good."

The gods may have fallen from grace in "Ruins," but the granite pedestals upon which their images were enshrined remain to torment them. There are, metaphorically, granite buttresses concealed just beneath the surface of virtually all Shimao's fiction. The soils he uses around these structures are composed of varied elements and textures, but the shape and consistency of the granite beneath remain, for the most part, unchanged. Whether in war or in tranquillity, the fallen god can neither escape his past nor endure his present.

I would like to carry this one step further by suggesting that there is a prototypical scene in several of Shimao's war tales that also rumbles beneath the surface of many other stories which seem at first to have nothing to do with the Pacific War. This scene can be defined in terms of familiar Japanese sociological types—*uchi* and *soto* ("inside" and "outside" the group or home). The *uchi* in Shimao's stories is a home base which is the source of a clearly delineated set of duties, expectations, and requirements. It is here that a soldier is expected to be a god, and a father is supposed to be an unwavering savior. In the war stories, the *uchi* is obviously the military base, the locus of operations aimed at one simple goal: vicarious salvation of others through their proxy death. Because of the ominous, forbidding, life-threatening nature of this "home," the soldier who narrates Shimao's war stories is constantly attempting to flee, to extricate himself from these fatal duties or at least to take a brief, unauthorized furlough from them. He does this by sneaking off the base under cover of darkness to meet with a young woman who lives on the island. The assignations on the beach provide fleeting relief to the soldier, but he can never be totally at ease—the home base hovers in his consciousness like a summons to death. There is a desperate quality to these emotional encounters between man and woman—both know that he could receive orders to die at any moment. The intensity of the situation is further heightened by the guilty realization that he could be dallying here when the call to battle is sounded, and that he will end up an AWOL god who has lost his saving powers.

The eternal war in Shimao's fiction is this struggle between sublimity and sensuality, madness and rationality, expectation and disappointment. His writings can be superficially divided into those which deal directly with the war experience and those which focus on his family in the postwar period, but there is a striking similarity to the frameworks around which all these stories are constructed. The home base/*uchi,* whether a military encampment or a tiny rented house in Tokyo, is a constraining, overly demanding presence to be avoided and eluded at any risk. The narrator, whether a suicide pilot or a struggling novelist, is driven by an aimless, irresistible urge to flee the demands of home and wander as a solitary sojourner *(tandoku ryokōsha)* in the uncertain realm outside the home *(uchi no soto).*[10] He is torn between this urge to wander and an unpleasant but equally undeniable "homing instinct" (*kisōsha* impulse) which fills him with guilt over his indiscretions. And of course he knows that death hangs over him if he is discovered absent without leave. The young woman who waits on the beach in the war stories is transformed into the trusting wife who waits at home in the postwar fiction (and through a marvelous, factual irony, they are one and the same woman). The housewife is as ready to dress herself for death beside the family hearth as she had been on the island.

The themes of war and fallen godhood are continuous in Shimao's fiction. One of his earliest stories, "Tandoku ryokōsha" (Solitary

Traveler, 1947), is an expression of the displacement his protagonist feels after returning from a daily association with death in the military to an everyday world where death seems to play no part. Untrained in accommodating himself to such surroundings, he continues his roamings, hoping for some sort of revival of the emotional intensity of the war period.

"Solitary Traveler" consists of several episodic fragments, described in short, disjointed paragraphs. The splintered form of the work conveys the crumbling within the protagonist. The structural and philosophical parent of this story is, of course, Dostoevsky's *Notes from Underground.* The influence of Dostoevsky, in fact, can be seen in a great many of Shimao's works. That influence can be overt, as in the stomach or liver disorders of the protagonists in "Solitary Traveler" and "With Maya," echoing the social biliousness of the Underground Man. Or it can be absorbed into the fiber of Shimao's writing, as with the agony of "hyperconsciousness," the spiritual malady which afflicts both Dostoevsky's and Shimao's antiheroes. The result for both sets of protagonists is an acute inability to participate meaningfully in the simplest acts of human intercourse.

In *Notes from Underground,* the narrator's degradation of Liza amid the "wet snow" is the experience which has emasculated his soul, making it impossible for him to deal with the activities of everyday life. For Shimao's solitary traveler, the brushes with death, betrayal, and his own fallibility during the war have robbed him of the capacity for true exchange with another person. One of the first things we realize about this character is that he has an almost comic fear of doing mundane things. Actions that come as second nature to a normal member of society send this young man into almost catatonic states of fear mingled with defensive hostility. Early in the story, he decides—after much hesitation—that he must board a bus.

But this is no easy task for someone so removed from reality. He cannot bring himself to speak to the clerk behind the ticket window, so he stares absently at the departure schedules, which mean nothing to him. Soon he is gripped by an unassailable urge to relieve his bowels. Not until he emerges from a "filthy" bathroom can he muster the courage to buy a bus ticket.

> Most of the events that can possibly take place on the road are mere trifles. Why then am I so uneasy? Once again I have been

> anxious and jittery. I suppose the path ahead of me seems shrouded in darkness because I don't know where I'll be staying tonight. If I could just decide upon some place as my residence—no matter what kind of place it is—then I could crawl into bed without uttering a word to anyone. But right now, before I can even steal a few moments of slovenly sleep, I have to come up with the proper actions and figures of speech to deal with other people. And that is what seems to be making me uneasy. It is painful for me to have to prepare my words and actions in advance and store them away for later use.[11]

Shimao does not tell us the context of this man's loss. We don't know whether he had no home to return to—was it destroyed by bombs? was he banished by relatives? is he suffering from war-induced amnesia? We are as helpless as he is to discover the roots of his homelessness. But just as he has no distinct origins, he also has no fixed destination. Part of the reason he has so much difficulty mustering the courage to buy a bus ticket is that he has nowhere to go, no end to the road he travels. This relates directly to the second major component of loss described here—the collapse of the language of communication. The narrator's concept of a place of repose is a residence where he doesn't have to "utter a word to anyone." This is a flag to us that something of major proportions has gone wrong within this individual. He is rejecting the basic activity—speech—that normally makes life within human society bearable and satisfying. He is tormented by griping pains in his intestines simply at the prospect of "coming up with the proper actions and figures of speech to deal with other people." This is a radical break in the chain of human interaction, an inward death of sorts. Such an attitude makes it doubly painful for us as readers to be hearers of his tale, for we are repeatedly reminded even as this man tells us his story that "having to prepare [his] words and actions in advance and store them away for later use" is a source of constant pain to him. The act of storytelling becomes a form of self-flagellation for the Shimao narrator.

Unlike *Notes from Underground* or Natsume Sōseki's 1914 novel *Kokoro,* which show us the present tragic immobility of their antiheroes and then conclude with a revelation concerning the roots of that emotional paralysis, Shimao here concentrates on the "middle period" of his protagonist. We learn very late in the story that he is a former suicide pilot who "can't seem to make anything turn out right" (p. 112). But Shimao is here not so much interested in the causes of his dilemma or his eventual surrender to it; the author's focus is upon the period of wandering, when his narrator still feels as though there should be some potential in human contact, still some logical place of rest available.

Yet the wanderer seems certain to fail as he tries to establish contact with several individuals over the course of the story. Shimao intimates through the use of names that his protagonist's visit to some Russian immigrants he knew before the war will lead nowhere. The husband and wife are given the names Nikolai and Alexandra, positioning them within a collapsed order which cannot be rebuilt. And their lives are too commonplace, too normal. They have become a part of the ordinary flow of life after the war, and they have no point of contact with the narrator's war experience.

Nothing is to be trusted. Recurrent stomach pains convince him of the unreliability of his physical body, while unsatisfactory encounters with the antipathetic "others" persuade him that neither are his emotions to be esteemed. Then, in what seems an abrupt turnabout, he has a chance encounter with a young woman and not only is able to strike up a conversation with her but eventually spends the night with her. This is an inexplicable lapse in the internal logic of the narrative unless we examine the substance of the relationship in some detail.

Shimao describes the hotel where they come together as

> out of place in this humble fishing village. It appeared to have been built long before the war, when times were still good, as a retreat where foreigners in Shanghai could come to escape the heat. . . . An Occidental hotel seemed terribly inappropriate to this fishing village, and yet once it was actually built, it seemed like a perfectly harmonious landscape. Because of the historical background of the nearby city, one could unexpectedly come across a Western-style bungalow on a mountain path outside the village at M Bay. Back when I lived in the city, I often went walking in the suburbs, and many times I would see old, white-haired European men who were living like hermits with Japanese women who had been overseas but were now totally changed back into middle-aged oriental women. The fishermen of the region were no longer surprised by the

unpleasant sight of mixed-blood children. . . . And so the hotel, too, was a peculiar juxtaposition of hostility and harmony, and suited the fishing village well. [pp. 81–82]

There is more than a little ambivalence to this setting. Although Shimao is never explicit about the location, it is clear from the "historical background of the nearby city," from the later reference to the city as "N," and from the narrator's question to the woman: "What were you doing on August 9?" that the story takes place in the outskirts of Nagasaki. The scene of atomic disaster has implicit significance for the narrator in two ways—we learn that he attended a commercial school there before the war, and we know that the explosion that transformed the lives of the people in the region is something that was supposed to be a part of his life but never was. It is as though he feels a need to continue showing up for his missed appointment with death. He seems to go out of his way to seek out this area because of its "juxtaposition of hostility and harmony," as if he requires those two elements working together in order to function at all.

The foreignness of the setting and the frequent mention of *konketsuji*—half-breeds—also add to the ambivalent atmosphere. This is carried over into the narrator's perceptions of the woman, who is described successively as "a warbling parakeet," a "blue dragonfly," a "foreigner" or "half-breed" herself, a "cat," and a "loner." In a further set of contradictions and contrasts, the narrator reports:

> Her coquetry most likely sprang from the air of a geisha that she had about her, and so it seemed that she should fit in best with a small tatami room and props like a shamisen and a red mirror stand. Yet that was not the case. For some reason the foreign *(batākusai)* furnishings in her room—the two twin beds, the white enamel pitcher, the large mirror in a decorative frame—gave it the air of a ship's cabin and brought a peculiar harmony to the scene, making us feel all the more like characters in a play. [pp. 89–90]

More than once in the course of the story, Shimao uses language that suggests some sort of stage performance, with "props" and "characters" and "furnishings" that remove us more and more from the realm of reality and create for the narrator a situation which he can infuse with any kind of atmosphere he chooses. All that is lacking, once he has set the stage somewhere other than present-day Japan, is for his imagination to reconstruct the feverish anticipation of his war experience, in the faint hope that a return to that abnormal psychological state will allow him to reestablish human contact.

This former kamikaze warrior achieves just such a transformation of time, place, and situation both passively and actively. We learn through the woman, "There were Occupation soldiers staying in this hotel until just the other day. They told me at the desk that we're the first guests the hotel has had since the troops left" (p. 92). She describes her room, which is a mirror image of his, as "frightening," and asks him to stay there with her. There are ominous footsteps in the hallway; they turn out to be those of a "wraith-like" maid who asks them to sign the hotel register. (Both use false names; his, "Shirohata Hachirō," connotes a white flag of surrender.) When they sit on the twin beds (pushed together in her room), he sees a bright blue light outside the blinds and seems to associate it with an explosion. Moments later an engine turns over nearby.

> A sound just like those that tormented me during the war. Eventually I realized that it was the sound of an automobile engine. What, an automobile? Now I was wracked by a different fear. The sound was of an engine left running in a car parked at the front of the hotel. Had the police come to raid the place? Did that kind of thing still happen? Or had the Occupation forces suddenly been mobilized? Would someone be coming into this room? [p. 104]

No real suspense is built up by his anxious musings. The absurdity of his fears is evident in the context of the story. We have no reason to believe that a car running outside the hotel poses any danger to the man or to his liaison. The associative processes of his mind are clearly those of a person suffering from "hyperconsciousness." And the woman who shares his room is oblivious to his state of mind. It seems likely, then, that he is injecting this twisted psychological climate into the room as an attempt to do battle with his pathological fear of normalcy. And by treating the entire situation as a drama of potential discovery and even death, he is able to make love to the woman. Even more indicative that his projection of wartime onto peace is necessary is the fact that, when he awakens the next morning, his diarrhea has subsided.

It is thus precisely because this brief affair is without logical origin and lacks any future that the narrator can accommodate it when he cannot cope with anything more ordinary. Through a process of mystification, by selecting for his private little minimelodrama those elements of setting, situation, plot, and player that are as far removed as possible from the realities of his everyday postwar experience, he transforms the reality into a near-illusion. Thereby he is able to consummate a physical relationship with a woman who has, for him, become a nonperson, or at best half human. He substitutes this liaison for the consummation he was denied as a suicide pilot.

"Solitary Traveler" is one of the first postwar works to confront the problem of spiritual homelessness that beset the war generation. It is filled with a keen, undiluted anxiety, a terror of everyday contact, and an aversion to life that becomes tangibly physiological over the course of the story. Elements such as the diarrhea are employed in nonrealistic ways. Unlike Yasuoka's characters, who develop intestinal problems in every conceivable situation, Shimao's characters suffer from the disorder only within the confines of everyday existence. Once they can make a leap of the imagination back into the war, they cease to be tormented by these physical and emotional discomforts.

This paradox, initially startling to readers who imagine themselves comfortably integrated into the contemporary world, becomes a fascinating, disquieting concept to ponder. While there is a certain unfamiliarity to the situations that characters encounter—the trauma surrounding the purchase of a bus ticket, for instance—at the same time, fundamentally they ring true, and with a little effort one can superimpose the fear and disengagement which lie at the base of those situations upon one's own experience.

In stories like "Solitary Traveler," Shimao is searching out—as a solitary literary sojourner himself—some of the motifs and techniques that better-known writers would latch on to in the early fifties. The first stories of Abe Kōbō, for instance, bear a striking resemblance in both theme and approach to the works Shimao was producing in the three years after the defeat. Abe's "Akai mayu," (Red Cocoon, 1950; trans. 1972) for example, shares with "Solitary Traveler" the same sense of displacement, and concludes with some of the same surrealistic effects Shimao employed in stories like "Yume no naka de no nichijō" (Everyday Life in a Dream, 1948; trans. 1985).

Because of its surrealism, "Everyday Life in a Dream" is a much more difficult work to explicate. It belongs to that category of stories which the author has described as works he composed "with [his] eyes shut,"[12] as opposed to the more realistic stories of later years. Yet in both his realistic and his surreal stories, Shimao's aim—the inversion of reality and fantasy, of war and peace—remains the same. Still, Shimao makes it difficult for the reader to distinguish between the two poles by eliminating any clues to the points of transitions. The story is, for all intents and purposes, set within the mind of the protagonist, which roams at will between waking and sleeping nightmares.

This story has some traits in common with "Solitary Traveler." The time frame is similar; "Everyday Life in a Dream" also takes place in the years immediately after the war. We are not told overtly that the protagonist has been a suicide pilot, but there are several cryptic references to "that incident" or "that day," and once again we find ourselves at the mercy of a painfully reticent storyteller.

A unique aspect of "Everyday Life in a Dream" is that we are given an occupation for the narrator. Though he is as much a wanderer as the protagonist of "Solitary Traveler," we have here a pretext for his journeys—he is an aspiring "novelist."[13] The story can, in fact, be read as "a statement on the relationship between life and art,"[14] though it seems to me that the relationship is one characterized by a considerable distance and ambivalence. The career of "novelist" is an ideal one for a Shimao protagonist. Although we normally think of a novelist as an individual who attempts to reproduce some aspect of human experience through the medium of literature, in this story the occupation allows the narrator to participate in life without being directly involved in it. The "novel" serves as a barrier, a shield between the frail individual and the frightening realm of actual experience. It is as though literature is an emotional prophylactic.

The same fear of words that we encountered in "Solitary Traveler" may be found in this man who must rely upon words as the tools of his profession: " 'verbal expression' became so heavy a burden that I almost abandoned my trade," before he has a story in print. "Reading back what I had written, I found that it was extraordinarily unclear. I had simply strung words together; there was no sign either of divine guidance or of satanic inspiration" (p. 57). Surely the abstraction of his writing stems from the fact that his work exists in a void, relating neither to the author nor to outside human experience. He is, in fact, persuaded that he will have no self-identity until his work appears in print. But he is also convinced that he will have nothing more to write unless he has an actual, "everyday" experience. So he sets out to join a gang of juvenile delinquents; but he is there only as an observer. He has carefully maintained a distance between them and himself, just as the young gang leader has an attitude of "deliberate rudeness, always keeping people at arm's length" (p. 59). Once again we have an attempt to be a part of the world without being touched by it. And the same insecurity, the same sense that this individual has been seriously wounded by past experience, lies at the core of his hesitant flirtation with the mundane:

> What I intended was to become a member of the gang . . . I was convinced that I would have psychological security: with the gimmick of being a novelist, I myself could not be hurt no matter what happened. This double-edged blade drawn, I had also provided the backup snare that I might thus be considered a practicing "humanist." What is more, the account of my daily activities and the "fiction" based upon it would become my second literary work . . . though I was intermittently knocked flat by the prospect of the vast, insipid task of putting it into words. [p. 58]

This attitude—of going out into the world in search of experience and using literature as a shield—seems almost a parody of the I-novel tradition. The annals of twentieth-century fiction in Japan are filled with anecdotes about established writers whose creative imaginations dried up when their lives took on a semblance of tranquillity. Conspicuous examples are Shiga Naoya, who deliberately had an affair with a maid to provide himself with some literary material, or Yasuoka, who "wrote his first good novel after his mother died, his second good novel after his father died, and now that his wife is ill. . . ."[15] The ironic inversion for Shimao is that his narrator is doing just the opposite: he is seeking for a moment's peace by a distant contact with bizarre experience because he has found everyday life too frightening.

Another recurrent pattern is rootless wandering. The protagonist has managed to burn all his emotional bridges in one way or another —though we are not told how. "By now I had not a single friend in this town. Where were my father and my mother, I wondered? I had lost track of them both" (p. 62). Being without family, he concludes that "there was apparently nowhere for me to rest my bones. The families I had known slightly had passed into a new generation" (p. 63). This is a clear reminder of Nikolai and Alexandra in "Solitary Traveler," and that narrator's rejection by them.

Neither are friends or acquaintances likely targets for communication. When the "novelist" runs into an old elementary school acquaintance—not a friend, he is quick to point out—Shimao gives us several layers of separation between the two men. First, of course, is the barrier of time, since this man is nothing more than a ghost from the past. Then there is the bizarre disease with which the man is afflicted—leprosy, an ailment which, of course, spreads through physical contact. And finally, there is the man's reported mission in coming to see the "novelist"—he has brought him a supply of "a certain article made of rubber" (p. 60), which he proceeds to finger and stretch. The prophylactics are a tangible representation of the many spiritual barriers separating the novelist from everyday reality, and from those individuals both familiar and unfamiliar who populate it.

If even acquaintances from the past are unwelcome visitors, how much more disconcerting are total strangers:

> People passed by; they all seemed insubstantial, had pale shadows. It was dark, but it was certainly not evening. There was the sun, high in the sky, and it was dark. People walked by in droves. Oh, give me the thick heaviness of lying on a beach in the blazing, glaring midsummer daylight I once knew. [p. 67]

There is no shortage of people who might be contacts, but everything is turned inside out. There is darkness in midday, and normal associations do not seem possible with beings that are "insubstantial." Even the anxiety of waiting on the beach is preferable to everyday life outside dreams.

Linked to this opaque view of others is a lack of trust in himself:

> Suddenly, I sensed that since that day my flesh had begun to give way and was no longer sound. . . .
>
> I had resolved to put no faith in my spontaneous emotional reactions. It had been that way ever since the day of that incident. [pp. 64–65]

As a final hermeneutic code, Shimao inserts three major images of wartime that help this "novelist" find a measure of comfort in postwar everyday life. The building where the gang meets is a bombed-out shell; the house in Nagasaki where the narrator finally locates his mother is described as being at the epicenter of the bomb and in a state of ruin; and a final, cumulative scene brings the past firmly into the present.

> I was walking through the streets of the town. I was always walking. Ever since that time, planes had been flying overhead. Countless planes flew above me, and I trembled in fear. The very idea of metal flying through the sky alarmed me, but I was even more frightened at the thought that something might fall out of them. So whenever they came, I would look up at the sky and plan what to do in that event. From time to time aluminum gasoline barrels would be dropped. They struck the earth with a metallic thud and lay motionless. This was reassuring, but there was no way of knowing what would fall from the skies next. The planes gradually increased in number. At lower and lower flying altitudes, they buzzed around the skies over the town like an invasion of locusts, their hard bellies gleaming in the sunlight. I began to feel that the end of the world was near. [p. 61]

Thus the streets of placid, postwar Japan are transformed into a wasteland still menaced by swarms of war machines.

These recurrent patterns of image, character, and situation in Shimao's early fiction indicate a desire to give some kind of literary shape, however bizarre, to personal experiences that were equally bizarre. The process of inversion is particularly effective in the concluding passage of "Everyday Life in a Dream," a difficult but well-conceived distillation of Shimao's literary art.

> I felt my scalp with my hand. Big sores, like calcium rice crackers, had formed all over my head. I shuddered and was assailed by the unpleasant sensation that all the blood in my head was freezing and withdrawing to the center. I tried peeling off the scabs. They came off easily. But afterward, the itching was completely out of control. Able to stand it no longer, I began to scratch and claw uncontrollably all over my head. At first, it felt intoxicatingly good. But immediately, a violent itching returned. This time

it was not just on my head, but an itching that seemed to well up all over my body. There was nothing I could do to assuage it. It was a horrible sensation, as if my body were submerged in ice and slugs were crawling all over my neck, like the lukewarm shampoo you get at the barbershop after a haircut. Whenever I stopped to rest my hands, the sores grew like mushrooms. With the strange feeling that I might at any moment be about to abandon the human race, I scratched and scratched the sores on my head.

At the same time I felt a violent pain in my stomach. Like the wolf who had his belly stuffed with stones, I seemed to reel, and I felt unable to walk straight. Gathering my courage, I thrust my right hand into my stomach. Then, still madly scratching my head with my left hand, I tried forcibly scooping out what was in there. I felt something hard adhering stubbornly to the bottom of my stomach, so I pulled at it with all my might. And then the strangest thing happened. With that hard kernel uppermost, my own flesh followed up after it. So desperate at this point, I was beyond caring what happened to me, I kept pulling. Finally, I had turned myself completely inside out like a sock. The itching on my head and the pain in my stomach were both gone. On the outside I was like a squid, smooth and blank and transparent. Then I realized that I was submerged in a pure, murmuring stream. It was a shallow stream, apparently in the open fields. Still steeping my body in the murmuring stream, outside I saw an old tree—what kind I do not know—completely bare of leaves, on each of whose thick bare branches perched a crow holding on with its wide open beak. Looking more carefully, I saw that on each and every branch were not one but swarms of crows with their beaks open wide. They looked as persistent as plant parasites. I had the sense that these crows would remain just as they were, in that position, for ever and ever. The only sign that they were alive was the way they occasionally moved their upward pointed tails and softly spread their wings. But they kept right on clinging fast with their beaks to the thick, dry, leafless branches. Still bathing my body, I thought how much I wanted to strip those crows, those scale insects, from the tree. [pp. 69–70]

Consistent with the writer's attitudes toward reality—that an inversion has taken place, and that daily life is a painful state not to be endured—his body is turned inside out. Once he has achieved that state, his discomfort, his pain, and his fears of others all dissipate. He is submerged into a flowing current of limpid water, losing the identity that separates him from others and ignites his anxieties. Only in this condition, it seems, is he able to feel at peace with his surroundings. Only by living his daily life as though he were dreaming, and by accepting his hallucinations as though they were reality, can he continue with the near-hopeless process of survival.

But even this complete inversion is not a solution. As his inside-out body flows like a river, he encounters a tree with withered branches. He examines it closely, and discovers that there are crows perched on every branch. As though they were a symbol of everything that torments him in his daily life, he is struck by a desire to rip the crows off the branches, the way one would tear a snail from its shell.

And there this remarkable story ends. The image of crows resting on withered branches is a familiar one to Japanese readers; it derives from a famous verse by the seventeenth-century master Bashō:

Kareeda ni
Karasu no tomaritaru ya
Aki no yūgure

On the withered branches
Crows have perched—
Nightfall in autumn

The two distinct elements brought into tense contrast with one another in this monochromatic verse are unchanging constancy (the autumn dusk; a *fueki,* or permanent aspect) and fleeting fluidity (the crows, stationary for but a moment; the aspect of *ryūkō,* or transient movement).[16] By ending his story in this manner, Shimao is suggesting—again, in a highly surrealistic blending of modern metaphor and classical allusion—that the seeming solution reached by his narrator, a solution that is little more than self-annihilation, is not a permanent resolution to his dilemma at all, that it is, in fact, a gesture as ephemeral as the crows precariously perched on the withered branches. The inner peace which he has achieved can at any moment be reversed, just as the crows can take flight with any change of the wind. The tension which Shimao creates with this image—the potential for the destruction of the narrator's happy state of nonexistence—underscores his complete inability to bring himself into any sort of compromise with the human society that surrounds him.[17]

Stories such as "Solitary Wanderer" and "Everyday Life in a Dream" earned Shimao the admiration of many of his colleagues in literary circles, but they did not attract the popular audience which, for instance, began to display an interest in similar works by Abe Kōbō. I would suggest that Abe's early surrealist stories, which are a mixture of science fiction, humor, and the motif of homelessness, are more appealing precisely because they mute the pain of alienation through their formal facetiousness, and because they introduce but do not probe the ramifications of the modern dilemma of loss. Shimao's stories are at once more complex—both in form and in philosophy—and more demanding. Ironically, however, in a manner which parallels the later literary career of Ōe Kenzaburō, Shimao's literature was transformed and turned to more realistic (that is, more autobiographical) directions once he—and his protagonists—eventually formed a close personal relationship through marriage. The nightmarish view of everyday life embedded in the early stories becomes more immediate for the reader once Shimao's conception of daily life shifts from the abstract delusions of a wanderer to the torment of a man who has to cope with the demands of a wife and children. As with Yasuoka and Kojima, Shimao's best work came as he shifted his focus to the family situation. The series of works beginning in 1954 with "Kisōsha no yūutsu" (The Melancholy of Homecoming)[18] are among the most intimate, painful chronicles of interpersonal relationships written in the postwar period. They derive to a large extent from the horror of Shimao's own brushes with death, and they dramatically reconfirm his belief that everyday life—particularly the daily associations between man and wife—can be infinitely more terrifying than war.

Stories such as "The Melancholy of Homecoming" suggest that the addition of a tangible, constant "other" (so often identified in Shimao's fiction not merely as a "separate person"—*aite*—but as a "foe"—*taishu*) to the distorted formulas of everyday life for his protagonists serves only to intensify the sense of inadequacy and guilt that torments them. Once we have gotten to know Shimao's early wanderers and to recognize how ill-prepared they are to form a permanent relationship, it is simple to imagine the conflicts that will be set in motion once these men have a reminder of their weaknesses living with them under the same roof. In a supremely felicitous blending of actual experience with literary irony, the woman who marries Shimao's suicide pilot/novelist is none other than the island girl who was the soldier's clandestine lover during the months he awaited the orders to die. Thus the person who in wartime was his occasional escape from responsibility beyond the confines of the encampment *(uchi no soto)* is the new center of his obligations (a new *uchi*). The relationship must, by definition, be a strain upon both of them, for both are aware of the ironic inversions of her role and of his potential—even need—for duplicity. Thus the dethroned god of the island under siege has before him, enshrined in his own house, a perpetual reminder of his guilt and fallibility, a yardstick of the distance he has fallen. The presence of such an altar to his failure drives him out of the home, of course, but it also eventually requires him to seek out a new, reliable "god." This is the process that shapes Shimao's mature fiction, and in the following analyses I will attempt to delineate the significant elements of that quest. For it is indeed a pilgrimage of biblical, even religious, import to Shimao. The language of discourse which he adopts is clearly aimed at the recovery of a lost relationship with deity in the hope that such a bond will allow him to look without horror at his own face and at those of his family members.

Shimao's quest can also be described as a movement toward recognition of the separation, a vision of the gulf that separates human and human, man and god. The journey into the inferno is what forms the core of his writings. The central character in "The Melancholy of Homecoming" is given a bizarre, emblematic name—Kannō Miichi, written with characters that seem to mean "a serpent that curses God." Yet *kannō* in Japanese can also mean both "carnal pleasures" and "answer to prayers."

Even as he pursues the fleshly aspects of his name, Miichi is cursed with an imagination—conscience?—that gravitates toward the worst possible eventuality, the most painful consequences of his actions. When he deserts the home after an argument with his wife Nasu, he almost turns back several times when he realizes that Nasu and the children have gone to bed with the *kotatsu* heater still on.

> Again he thought of the fire in the *kotatsu* and was on the verge of starting back home. But if he went back and Nasu and the

children woke up, it was likely he wouldn't be able to leave again. So he continued to walk, without really knowing why. Then in his imagination he saw something catch fire, and in an instant his house was enveloped in a hell of flames; Nasu, without uttering a word, was burned to death, and the children cried out tearfully through the blankets of smoke.

He could not possibly endure the malicious looks from his neighbors, whose houses had also caught fire.[19]

Miichi, like so many of Shimao's characters, torments himself over the possibility that his worst nightmares might become reality. His capacity for translating the inflated anxieties of his imagination into everyday terms is boundless. He lacks the slender wall of reason that allows the common man to distinguish between actuality and illusion. Thus he is always confusing the two.

In this work there is a distinct sense of conflict between selfish human desire and a nobler conscience, a homing instinct that acts almost like a protector of the relationships between one individual and another. Miichi condemns this "god," asserting his own independence from his wife and children, but he cannot deny that the urge to unite himself with them resides somewhere within his heart. There is something of a Fall here, a knowledge that at some point in his life he has lost the ability to form a lasting contact with another human being. For Miichi, that knowledge likely came during the war, when he could trust only the tangible presence of death hovering just ahead of him. With death such a certainty in his life, the urge to establish some kind of tie with an island girl became all but absurdly futile. But he continued to slip out of camp each night, defying the imminent threat and reaffirming his existence through her. The struggle between the two urges remains the foundation of Miichi's relationship with Nasu, though both of them recognize how tenuous such an association must be.

The blueprint of human relationships established in the war thus has determined the manner in which the marriage of these two is constructed. This transference of a distorted concept of reality onto the postwar situation is the source of excruciating pain for Miichi and Nasu, and there seems to be no power that can alter the course of their relationship. Miichi repeatedly leaves his house but continues to be drawn back to it, like a living ghost. Nasu persists in condemning Miichi for his lack of responsibility and is tormented by the fear that someday he will leave for good, yet she clings to the shreds of love and trust she feels for him. Seemingly only madness or death could shake them free. And these are precisely the elements which Shimao introduces into his stories in the late 1950s.

The second wave of Shimao's spiritual battle commenced in the summer of 1954, when his wife Miho began suffering from lunatic attacks and demanded that he curtail all activities outside the home and remain with her and the children. Shimao successively severed all ties with the literary world (clinging the longest to his friends in the Conceptions Society), resigned his teaching positions, and moved the family to several different houses around the Tokyo area in an attempt to escape the demons that pursued Miho. Finally in the spring of 1955, they sent their two young children to live with Miho's parents in Amami, and Shimao and his wife entered an asylum together. Released that October, they moved to Amami, where they would live in total isolation from the literary scene for over twenty years. That same October, the first of Shimao's "byōsai-mono" (stories about an ailing wife, an important subgenre in the I-novel tradition in Japan)[20] was published under the title "Ware fukaki fuchi yori" (Out of the Depths I Cry).

"Out of the Depths I Cry" was the first work to treat Shimao's domestic situations in essentially realistic, autobiographical terms, and the first foreshadowing of his growing reliance upon Christianity (he was baptized a Catholic in December of 1956, a little over a year after this story was published). This concern is evident in the story's title, which is, of course, a reference to the Latin "De Profundis," the opening section of Psalm 130: "Out of the depths have I cried unto thee, O Lord." The biblical antecedent, like many of David's songs, is both a recognition of human guilt ("If thou, Lord, shouldest mark iniquities, O Lord, who shall stand?" in verse 3) and a plea for forgiveness, a literary duality of purpose that is matched in Shimao's work.

Although Japanese critics have consigned this series of stories to the generic class of byōsai-mono, the suggestion that the "madness of the wife" is the cause of the rupture in the home of these characters is to read them without sensitivity: one might as well label Shimao's war stories works about the "madness of Tōjō." The battles that are waged in "Out of the Depths I Cry" and the other domestic pieces are remarkable precisely because of their balance between self-recrimination and clear victimization for both parties. There are no "good guys" and "bad guys" here; there are only two individuals standing naked before one another, knowing they have been banished from the Garden and desperately wounded by their mutual complicity and shame.

The initial sin is, of course, that of the husband in these works, and it seems to me that a more fitting generic category would be "byōfūfu-mono" (stories about an ailing couple). Shimao's literature is almost unique in modern Japanese fiction by virtue of the manner in which it foregrounds and sustains its interest in the wife's position in the relationship as forcefully as it does the husband's.

Shimao's literary production after 1955 becomes largely a very personal record, written as though his audience were limited to Miho and his two children. There is a therapeutic quality about these works,[21] and at times they seem like sacrificial offerings to some onlooking god. The initial work of this period is titled "Tsuma e no inori" (A Prayer to My Wife), a supplication addressed *to* Miho, not merely in her behalf. The identification of his wife as some sort of judgmental deity plays a major role in Shimao's work after this turning point.

This offertory function is apparent in works such as the 1961 short story "Maya to issho ni" (With Maya; trans. 1984). On the surface this is a moving, gentle story about the special though troubled relationship between a father and his retarded daughter. But it is also a disturbing study of a man completely unable to function on his own in normal human society; even more heart-rending is our recognition that this man is also ineffective at caring for those closest to him. Maya is one of the residual victims of the losses this father experienced during the two wars—the international conflict in 1945, and the domestic one in 1954.

The story is, like Maya and its narrator, almost too fragile to bear up under scrutiny. It is related by the father, who has left his haven on a tiny island and traveled to a city on the mainland to take care of some business. But he has not felt confident enough to go there on his own, and he has taken his ten-year-old daughter Maya with him. While there he visits a clinic to have some tests on his stomach, and he arranges for Maya to be examined for her speech impediment. Ever since the family left Tokyo and moved to their remote island,

Maya's speech has become slurred and mumbled and virtually incomprehensible to anyone outside the family. Doctors have been unable to suggest any causes or cures for the dysfunction. While at the outpatient clinic, the father allows Maya to wander off to the bathroom on her own, but she soils her pants there. Not until several days later does he discover that there is blood mingled in the stain, a discomforting indication that Maya is passing into young womanhood.

If "With Maya" were merely a story about a bumbling male ignorant of the changes in his daughter's body, it would be a realistic but familiar enough tale. Shimao lets us know at the outset, however, that there is more to the substance of this story than the simple recognition of normal physiological changes accompanying maturation. For in the end it is a story about total immaturity in human relations.

We learn at the very beginning of the story that this father is no ordinary man; that, in fact, he considers himself to be of a lower species than others.

> The patients, who leaned against the corridor walls or sat on sofas waiting for their doctors, resembled fish that dwell at the bottom of the ocean. They wore expressions like fish that know their bodies will shatter if they come too close to the bright surface of the sea, and suffer from the sharp difference they can see between their own faces and those of fish that move in shallower waters. I felt an affinity with that look, realizing that it mirrored my own nature perfectly.[22]

Before we even know what kind of hospital we are in or what kind of disorders are being described, we are alerted that this man feels out of his element, that he is uncomfortable—even physically distressed—when he is away from his home and the familiar presence of his wife and children. When he leaves his home "at the bottom of the ocean" and goes out to mingle with those who dwell in shallower waters, he cannot help but feel threatened and sense a vast distinction between himself and others. In the company of outsiders, he suffers as though he had entered a realm of different atmospheric pressure. This state of mind is clearly abnormal, for he is engaged in the most mundane of activities and he does, after all, take his daughter with him everywhere he goes.

The notion that this father is somehow detached from the workings of normal society is heightened by his impression that the doctors and nurses who pass up and down the corridor are unconnected to his situation; by the fact that the two doctors who come into his examination room seem either not to notice him or to speak a dialect he cannot understand; and when the nurse (who impresses him as cold and uncaring) sticks a rubber tube down his throat and then proceeds to ask him questions he cannot possibly answer.

This final absurdity, however, is delicately echoed in the father's association with his own daughter, Maya. Because she has difficulty communicating, he often has to put words into her mouth, words that frequently tell us more about him than about Maya:

> "After they take some of Daddy's stomach juices, it'll be your turn to see the doctor. We have so much to do! What do you think Mommy and your brother are doing now? I bet they're thinking about Maya. Are you worried about Mommy? You don't need to be. You're with Daddy now. Do you wish we were back on the island right this minute?"
>
> "Nope." She gave the pat answer, but after a moment's thought she revised it to, "A little."
>
> "You wish you were back home a little? Well, Daddy wishes he could go back now, too. . . ." [p. 199]

Because of her reticence, Maya's father often seems to use her as a sounding board for his own anxieties, particularly with regard to his duties toward his family. Maya is capable of at least monosyllabic response, but he seldom waits for her to answer. Whether Maya is worried about her mother (why she should be worried, we are never told) is immaterial; the key here is that the father brings up the potential for anxiety and tries to assuage it before it surfaces. It is a blatant ruse to cover his own fears.

In a most telling scene, one reminiscent of other Shimao stories in which the narrator imagines the worst possible outcome from a trivial set of circumstances, the narrator muses:

> Whenever I travel away from home, I am tormented by a concern that what I'm doing may prove, at any given moment, to have been a mistake. That feeling intensifies abruptly in the evenings, when I've been released from my duties at work. Inevitably I end up thinking that I've made an inexcusable blunder simply by being

> somewhere far away from my family. I know I have left them to look after a home in a place quite surrounded by water and separated from me by overwhelming distances. If some frightening, unforeseen calamity should occur in my absence, I could not rush to their aid. Before word of the mishap could reach me, a legion of futile hours would have slipped away. No one would know where to contact me from the time I left my hotel in the morning until I returned at night. Even if news reached me quickly, the ocean stretching between K City and our island was a daunting barrier. Were I lucky enough to make the ferry connection just as it sailed from the dock, I would still have the crossing to contend with: fourteen or fifteen hours of slow, eddying time. The simple effort it took to imagine such things all but tore my emotions out of the realm of reality. [pp. 206–7]

Because Shimao prefaces such utterances as these in metaphors of deep-water fish who cannot survive at the surface, and succeeds them with scenes of a father who cannot supervise the simple activities of his handicapped daughter, they have an empty, agonizing ring to them. He portrays himself as some kind of hero, even savior, within the framework of his daydreams, but in fact the physical distance that separates him from his wife and son is not nearly as significant as the emotional gap that prevents him from exerting any kind of patriarchal authority.

Even more important, there is no evident threat to his family members back on the island. He has succeeded in turning his private anxieties inside out—much as the protagonist of "Everyday Life in a Dream" turned his body inside out—and thereby imposes his specious inner turmoil on the outside world. His lack of self-confidence is transmuted into a fear that his family will fall victim to some calamity in his absence. His internal reality, utterly divorced from external fact, is superimposed onto the realm of phenomena through his fertile but twisted imaginings.

Shimao gives us a view of the internal workings of this man—sterile in terms of the outside world, poisonous to his mental functionings—when the nurse extracts some of his gastric fluids.

> Though it was a part of me, I was disgusted at the sight of this heavy, viscous liquid that came from deep within my body. It tickled the walls of my esophagus as it made its lukewarm way to

> the outer world. Yet the nurse did not seem disturbed. I marveled that she didn't seem to react even when some of the fluid spilled onto her fingers as she fiddled with the tube. If it had been me, though the juices were my own, the nerve endings in my fingertips would have recoiled. [pp. 201–2]

What is perhaps most pathetic about this man, and what is described with such effective irony by Shimao, is his firm yet false conviction that he is Maya's protector. Without the illusion that he is the mainstay of his family, he would be a wanderer. It is the single pin that connects him to everyday reality. He meticulously goes over each item on his daily schedule, deluding himself into believing that he is a master at the details of life, and he is able to view himself as a strength to his disabled daughter. Yet he confesses, without realizing the significance of his revelation, that Maya is the member of the family most able to deal with such details: "Her memory for everyday matters was the most vivid in our household. We were amazed by her precise recollection of appointments her parents had forgotten, or of places where we had tucked away coin purses and the like. When we lost something, Maya would nonchalantly announce its whereabouts in sparing phrases, then silently lead us to the spot" (p. 205).

Even in the examination room, he tries to persuade himself that he is a support to Maya, that she is comforted by his presence, but in fact just the opposite is the reality. In many ways he is the feeble child desperate for reassurance, and she is the silent, understanding parent allowing him to fend for himself but remaining just within earshot should something unexpected occur. Being "with Maya," in fact, is more of a necessity for him than it is for her.

Because Maya is the true parent and he the child, there are several places in the story where this father has the feeling that he is in fact out on an excursion with his wife. Many of his descriptions of Maya are cloaked in language reserved for adults. When we first see her in the hospital corridor, she is dressed in an oversized jacket made by altering one of her mother's old overcoats. She swings a little handbag with a beaded string back and forth, and looks "tall for her age" (p. 198). As they are going into the examination room, they cross paths with a "young woman . . . helping a feeble old man out of the room" (p. 200), another reflection of their own situation. Later, describing Maya's appearance as they sit in the hospital waiting room, he notes,

"There was a full-blown femininity in her face, the look of a grown woman in miniature" (p. 209). When Maya goes off to the bathroom by herself, her father begins to panic when she does not return right away. He has delusions of her lying on the bathroom floor, bleeding, and that image immediately overlaps with that of his own deranged wife. As the story progresses, more often he makes connections between Maya and his wife, as though they were the same personage, a figure clearly a mainstay in his life. His final observation about Maya indicates that he really understands little about her: "I found myself wondering if Maya didn't in fact know everything that was going on, and when she was away from us and around other people, if she didn't speak quite clearly and bustle about like a hardworking housewife" (p. 216). It is as though he cannot bear the thought that Maya is in fact better at getting along with outsiders; he almost demands that she be as fearful and inept at human contact as he. In this sense, he seems to need her to remain tongue-tied. She is a support to him because she is so much like him.

He does have aspirations for her improvement, of course. When a nurse tries to get her to talk, he is deeply moved at the sight of Maya struggling with her entire body to make some sort of utterance. What he sees is an image of himself attempting to break out of his self-created shell of isolation. Maya is never totally successful at communicating to an outsider, and that is both a relief and a discouragement to her spiritually retarded father.

All the duplicity imbedded in the discourse of "With Maya" reaches its painful culmination when Maya does in fact begin to display signs of maturation. When the father discovers streaks of blood in her soiled underpants, he wonders if perhaps she has been sexually molested (in a marvelous unspoken inference—"Lots of people together. Daddy's friends. One was nice to Maya. Maya tried to go bathroom, fell down. Hit head" (p. 217). But there is no evidence, in either story or discourse, that anything abnormal has occurred. The horror for him is that Maya is becoming an adult, growing into an individual whom he can no longer use as a shield for his own inadequacies. The normality of Maya's passage into womanhood is most disturbing to him. His words of comfort to Maya at story's end, rather than soothing us as readers, are sufficiently self-conscious and insecure to provoke tears: "Go to sleep now, Maya. There's nothing to worry about. Go fast asleep" (p. 217).

We would very much like to believe that all will be well in this family, and we are concerned about Maya's physiological impediments. But most of all we are struck by the frailty of this man's efforts to reach outside himself, particularly in comparison with Maya's brave ventures into the "frightening" world outside her family circle. Maya does come out seeming like a girl who will be able to fend for herself adequately, if not smoothly, in her contacts with others. Her father is the one in need of sympathy, for his is the greater affliction.

"With Maya" provides an unusual perspective on Shimao's private situation; it is an examination of the crumbling of his family seen from a unique angle—the relationship between the father and Maya. It is as though Shimao came up for air after an extended underwater battle with his wife and produced this story during a lull in hostilities. It is one of his most affecting stories, filled with stabbing moments of irony, subtly expressed insights into the nature of human insecurity, and a balance of depth and simplicity that can perhaps be attained only when the main characters are a less than secure adult and a mute, enigmatic child. It has much in common with another of the most touching and delicately crafted stories of the postwar period, Ōe's "Sora no kaibutsu Aguii" (Aghwee the Sky Monster, 1964; trans. 1977).

If "With Maya" emerges from a lull in the storm, *Shi no toge* (The Sting of Death), a series of twelve linked stories written between 1960 and 1976, places both author and reader directly in the path of a literary maelstrom. *The Sting of Death* synthesizes and surpasses everything Shimao had written before, and it stands as the most agonized portrait in postwar Japanese fiction of the pain two individuals can inflict upon one another in the name of love. The novel, as it will loosely be styled here, is the most vivid account of the torments of human isolation and the human potential for destructiveness written in Japan since Natsume Sōseki's *Kokoro* appeared in 1914.

Shimao's title alludes to Paul's famous discourse on human duality (1 Corinthians 15:55–56).[23] After a lengthy comparison of natural (or carnal) and spiritual, corruptible and incorruptible ("flesh and blood cannot inherit the kingdom of God; neither doth corruption inherit incorruption"), Paul chronicles the "mystery" of resurrection and then issues the ultimate challenge, "O death, where is thy sting?" His response is "The sting of death is sin" *(Shi no toge wa tsumi de aru).*

The novel is about individual responsibility, and the anguish over sin that lies at the root of betrayal. The husband Toshio has been covering up his extramarital indiscretions for nearly ten years when the novel opens, but his days of secrecy and discreet individuality come to a swift end when he returns home from his most recent assignation. The second paragraph of the novel begins abruptly, after the fall:

> I had slept away from home the previous night. When I returned home the following afternoon, the wooden door to the rotting, half-collapsed bamboo fence was locked. My heart began to pound, and I slipped through our neighbor Kaneko's gate into the narrow garden of my house. I rattled the front door and one at the side of the house, but they were locked and would not budge. The window looking into my four-and-a-half-mat work room was clearly visible from both Kaneko's and Aoki's houses, being right next to a picket fence we had set up between us. I put my eye to a break in the glass and peered inside. An ink bottle had been knocked over on top of my desk. Feeling a tightening in my chest, I went around to the kitchen door in back. Our two hens had laid eggs, but I had no desire to collect them. Behind our house was a tiny factory, separated from us by a path so narrow that one had to turn sideways to pass through. With my body vibrating from the hum of the machinery and with the sound of shredding iron reverberating in my ears, I picked up a fragment of brick that was lying on the ground and smashed one of the panes of glass in the kitchen window. I felt much like a criminal, and a shudder surged upward from the soles of my feet. Dishes lay untouched in the sink, and I knew that the day of judgment had finally come. My body and heart both felt as if they were suspended in midair. I walked from the entranceway through the two- and six-mat rooms and on into my study. As I stood frozen there, I felt as though I were examining the graphic scene of a crime. Ink was spattered on the desk, the tatami and the walls like bloodstains. And my diary, sordidly discarded in the midst of it all.[24]

There are numerous gaps in the semantics and logic of this passage. At first reading it seems almost a non sequitur. As innocent, detached observers (though we lose our innocence over the course of the novel), we at first have no idea why a locked door should cause the narrator's heart to "pound," or a spilled bottle of ink cause a tightening in his chest. And just what is the logical connection between "Dishes lay untouched in the sink" and "I knew that the day of judgment had finally come"? Should we assume that this man at last will be punished for leaving dirty dishes in the sink? Are we really supposed to accept the shaky association that is made between spattered ink and blood spattered as if at a murder scene? These holes in the logic of the narrative are warning signs to us that the symbols of everyday activity can be infused with horror when there is a sizable gap between appearance and reality.

Much of the "melancholy" associated with homecoming for Toshio derives from the imprint of his contorted mental state upon the inanimate features of his house. Frequently our attention will be directed toward the "rotting, half-collapsed bamboo fence," which is a rather obvious representation of the condition of the owners. Less blatant but clearly a signal of disorder is the anxiety Toshio feels when he discovers the door locked. Of the range of possible explanations for a locked door—the family has gone out shopping; there has been a rash of thefts in the neighborhood—Toshio's mind immediately gravitates toward the most self-incriminating, most pessimistic conclusion: his wife has discovered his infidelity and fled the house to do something drastic. The house itself seems to judge him, to resist his attempts to elicit a response. And he is physically shaken and aurally assaulted by his neighbor, the factory. Finally he has to expose himself as a criminal to gain access to his own house.

Once he has broken into his home, he seems to expect to find carnage. His wife has discovered his infidelity—that must be obvious from the discarded diary he glimpsed through the window. Has she murdered their children and then slit her own throat (a not uncommon occurrence in such situations)? He does indeed find havoc—dirty dishes in the sink, ink splattered all over his study. These mundane acts are suffused with heady emotional connotations that have their origins in Toshio's guilt.

The opening scene is a compact presentation of expository material. In its language, irrationally setting a scene far more sanguinary than the physical realm would seem to warrant, it establishes contrasts between sanity and madness that will characterize the entire novel. We are treated to pounding hearts, tightening chests, vibrating bodies, shudders, and near-swooning—all over a locked door. Before the novel has rattled to a climax, we will have witnessed this scene repeated in a wide array of variations, always with the slightest ripple of movement in everyday life triggering the most desperate emotional reactions. Shimao has succeeded in capsulizing that process in this opening scene. He demonstrates how the warped mentality of his protagonists implicates even their surroundings in guilt. The fence is rotting; the doors are recalcitrant; the very foundations of the house are being shaken by vibrations from the neighboring factory; the dishes are soiled and suggest that Toshio's wife has abandoned her responsibilities; the study looks as though a murder has been committed there, though we learn that the weapon was the words of private confession in Toshio's diary; and that weapon itself lies "sordidly discarded" *(kitanaku suterarete iru)* in the room. Taking advantage of the elastic capacities for ambiguity in the Japanese subordinate clause, Shimao even manages to involve his character Toshio in the mayhem, for the final sentence reads "kitanaku suterarete iru watakushi no nikkichō," making "sordid" and "discarded" serve as modifiers both for the "diary" and for "me."

All the essential elements of the "story" of *The Sting of Death* are contained within this remarkable paragraph. We need only add the wife, Miho, to the formula; she will challenge and resist and mentally "vibrate" Toshio in an attempt to remove all deception from his body and soul. But in the meantime, she too will be shaken from the realm of everyday that is the special province of the Japanese housewife and be forced to join Toshio in his psychological hell. There they will use the "thorns" that are a secondary connotation of the novel's title to stab at one another and at themselves.

Miho's insanity is established in the first few pages. Knowledge of Toshio's crimes all but shatters the relationship. For all her derangement, however, Miho has nothing in her life that can replace her ties with Toshio. She must cling to that relationship, even if it means causing them both the most excruciating pain imaginable. She mercilessly interrogates Toshio, demanding to know every last detail of his many affairs, essentially requiring him to slit his soul open, to commit a sort of emotional *harakiri,* and display every inch of it to her.

This of course is an impossible request. No matter how scrupulously honest Toshio vows to become in order to restore her sanity, there are always pockets of private deception that he cannot reveal without utterly surrendering his selfhood to her. She will, though, be satisfied with no less, and early on in the novel there is a complete role reversal within the family. A lunatic Miho demands that Toshio call her *anata-sama* (your highness) and submit to her in every aspect of his behavior. Over the course of the novel, this takes many forms. At first there are the questions about his past. Then she demands that he take over the nurturing of their two young children, Shin'ichi and Maya. Subsequently she will not allow him to leave the house alone—he must always take the entire family in tow. This stipulation eventually forces him to resign his teaching job at the night school, and whenever he tries to write a piece of fiction for publication, she insists that he first submit it to her for revision and censoring.

In essence, then, the plot of *The Sting of Death* traces in minute detail the burgeoning demands which Miho makes upon Toshio, and Toshio's ever fainter attempts to assert his individuality against these "commandments" from a vengeful god. She seems to be trying to subsume his will within her own. He struggles, but before the novel concludes, he seems almost to welcome this annihilation of his ego. He has fully accepted the fact that his own sins were the direct cause of Miho's inner torment, and self-annihiliation comes to seem the only means by which he can atone for his transgressions.

The tempo of the novel is determined by the rise and fall of Miho's lunatic attacks. By adopting such a format, Shimao runs the risk of overtaxing the patience of his readers and inviting tedium. Surprisingly, such a danger never materializes. There is sufficient variety in the details of each attack, and a subtlety of interplay between Toshio and Miho that renders each experience unique. Besides, the repetition of these scenes of lunatic encounter numbs the senses of the reader in the same way that Toshio becomes inured to them, so that finally we come to accept the premise that fierce, violent lunges toward and away from the brink of death are as much a part of everyday experience as answering the telephone or opening the mailbox. We are tempted to recoil from such a conclusion, but Shimao's relentless reiteration of his point eventually forces us to submit, much as Toshio is driven to accept Miho's control over his life.

Another unique and extremely effective facet of the novel is the recurrent use of war imagery to reinforce the intensity of the struggle between Toshio and Miho and to draw attention to the ferocious underbelly of placid everyday life. Early in the novel, when Miho is in the midst of an attack and slaps Toshio, he retaliates in kind. "When I tightened my fist and struck her in earnest, there was a dull clap of flesh, and I remembered how it had felt when I had beaten a subordinate in the military" (p. 17). At this early stage in the reformulation of their relationship, Toshio still sees himself in the dominant position.

As his confidence in his own contribution to the relationship wavers, however, he feels more and more apprehensive about the outside world, and less certain about the sanctity of the decisions he has made in his life. His betrayal of Miho in particular stabs at him—like a sting of death resulting from his private sins now made public. When she gives expression to a rare moment of affection at the conclusion of a fit of madness, Toshio's memories are ineluctably drawn back to the days when they first met—when he was a soldier on her remote island.

> She enfolded her husband with both arms as though she were clinging to a pillar. Then she slid down his body to the floor.
>
> "I nurtured and formed these hands and feet. You would have died a long time ago if I hadn't worried about feeding you properly. I don't want to give you to anyone else. No one. No one! But you ignored me and did whatever you wanted. And not just for one or two months. For ten years. I've tried and tried to endure it, but I can't go on anymore."
>
> Half in tears, she chanted the words like a rehearsed monologue. She sat on the floor, alternately stroking the sole of her husband's foot and pressing it against her cheek, all the while weeping out of control.
>
> Suddenly I thought of the war days. I was stationed at a naval base near her home. Late at night when I went to see the still youthfully plump girl, she had groped in the darkness for the stars on my uniform, run her hands along my jacket, and knelt to stroke my combat boots. The memory persuaded me that the aroma of beach crinum had wafted all the way to this backstreet house in a corner of the capital. I'm not sure what combination of circumstances made me grow distant from my wife in the turbulent chaos after the defeat. But I couldn't help seeing in the tiny figure of my wife sobbing at my feet an image of the past that was an irrefutable part of my experience. [pp. 45–46]

The interpolation of war imagery here is interesting, but equally fascinating is the uneasy shift of perspective in the third paragraph. Toshio is relating this experience through his own eyes, but suddenly we discover Miho stroking "her husband's" foot, as if Toshio had suddenly retreated from center stage and become a mere player among the crowd. This is another strong indication that his individuality is gradually peeling away from him, and that his sense of control over his life is slowly crumbling. I am tempted here to associate this with previous instances in which we have seen Shimao's characters literally or figuratively turn themselves inside out in order to relieve their inner misery by exposing it.

More explicit images of the battlefield are injected into the narrative as this tiny family attempts to venture out into the world of strangers. To evoke the sense of dread that grips Toshio and Miho as they set out on a train ride or to the shopping district, the "others" they encounter along the way are sometimes referred to as "the enemy" (*taishu,* again, rather than the more common *aite*). And the family members are described as dressing up in their "battle gear" *(busō)* when they leave the relative safety of their home. On one particular occasion, irrationally fearing that the other woman might come with an escort of thugs while they are away, Toshio comments:

> I thought of the white wooden fence surrounding the house we had just left behind. There was every likelihood it was under attack by someone at this very moment, but I could not imagine what form that attack was taking. But the sensation of the attack penetrated by body with raw lucidity, and I could not escape its clammy grasp upon me. Although my entire family had donned its battle gear and set out for the world outside, Shin'ichi was still far too young to carry a rifle, and my wife, who should have been the bond holding us together, seemed likely to have a lunatic fit and turn her gun on me the moment she spotted the enemy. [pp. 111–12]

The fundamental story line in *The Sting of Death* suggests comparisons with a work such as Fitzgerald's *Tender Is the Night.* But the moral considerations which lie at the heart of his novel make Arthur Miller's autobiographical play *After the Fall* a more fitting Western counterpart, particularly insofar as the use of war imagery is concerned. Miller (drawing his story, interestingly enough, from autobiographical sources—his failed marriage to Marilyn Monroe) pursues the meaning of the pain-ridden relationships in his life and ultimately compares his own destructive capacity with the nightmares of Auschwitz. The lookout tower at the death camp is, in fact, an omnipresent element hovering over the progatonist's attempts to sort out the causes behind the many betrayals that have characterized his associations with others. Similarly, as Toshio questions his own responsibility for what has happened within his home, images of war and impending death spring to mind, and the language of war is integrated into the fabric of his narrative.

The inevitable culmination of this process is, of course, for Toshio to "surrender unconditionally" to Miho's demands. The overlap of wartime defeat and marital discord is intentional and central to Shimao's intent in the novel. With the potential for death—for final "separation"[25]—a constant reality for Toshio because of the unrelieved intensity of Miho's insanity, the only possible reaction for him (other than the morally unacceptable flight) is the sublimation of his own will to hers. This process echoes the manner in which Shimao's wartime "lieutenants" had to submit themselves totally to the control of their superiors, while the specter of death hovered continuously over them. The only conceivable release from the tension of that situation was through a "departure" that literally signified death. And yet it was precisely the inconceivable, the "unendurable" that took place on August 15: the launch into death was called off, though the boats remained armed and ready. And thus the stinging potentiality for death continued coeval with the everyday activities of those who were sent defenseless into the postwar era of peace. In many senses, the situation in which Toshio finds himself in this novel is congruous with that of his wartime shadows.

Yet Toshio is aware that he can never fully live up to his superhuman promise to open himself to Miho's scrutiny and control. The gulf between the ideal relationship they would like to have and the flawed one that exists between them ensures that there will be no release from the cycle of self-inflicted torment. They are trapped in a timeless void that threatens to open up into a negation of their very existence.

> A person could not survive without the provisionary belief that each individual day had severed its ties with the previous ones. But

> for my wife and me now, each thread from the past has wound itself around the present, tangling itself about our exposed nerves and giving off bluish sparks. I had no idea when those sparks might burst into an uncontrollable conflagration and consume everything. Once we had grown accustomed to the repetition of her attacks, the interval during which they were subdued began to reek of death. [p. 257]

There seems little chance of resolution to the conflict between Toshio and Miho; he cannot fully annihilate his selfhood, and she cannot accept him any other way. Avenues of hope are closed off one after another. Miho cannot go on living in certain parts of Tokyo, because they remind her of locations where he has taken his other women; these neighborhoods take on almost mythological overtones, reminiscent of the directional taboos prevalent in the Heian period. These two people cannot communicate with the outside world in any reasonable fashion; this is borne out by the receipt of threatening letters from Toshio's former lover. There is, however, a supreme irony at work here. The reader eventually catches on to the fact that the letters are written and placed in the mailbox by Miho herself, but Toshio never seems to realize this. His life is more completely manipulated by Miho than he can ever imagine. She is, in short, controlling his life like some sort of offended deity who will demand the payment of the last farthing before she will release him from purgatory.

Perhaps the best way to illustrate the degree to which this man and wife have cut themselves off from the rest of the world, as well as to demonstrate the stylistic techniques which Shimao employs to highlight the relationship that has formed between them, is to examine a passage that comes near the end of the novel, when the other woman visits their house. It is long and tortuous, but it provides so many insights into Shimao's technique and sketches such a stark, immediate portrait of this couple that I will quote it in full. I might note that the level of emotional intensity in this passage is typical of the entire novel.

> "Mr. S." I heard the diffident voice of a woman call my name. I quickly drew my hand from the lock, turned on my heels, and scrambled back toward my wife's room.

The woman's voice pursued me. "Mr. S. Wait. There's something I want to talk to you about."

What should I do in this situation? No definite ideas came to mind, and I did not have the composure to evaluate this unexpected new reality. My head seemed about to split open. A southerly wind softened the evening air in the wake of the rain, and the aroma of newly budding plants permeated the cool atmosphere.

"Mr. S." The voice that called my name reanimated an oppressive past that I thought I had exorcised. I had the illusion that a separate self had detached itself from me and was unlocking the gate and walking toward the woman. I wondered if she had brought some thugs along with her, but I was more afraid of how my wife would react to this situation. I planted my trembling feet outside her room, struck by the thought that perhaps the final judgment had come. My wife was poised like a cat peering through the darkness, and in a relatively calm voice she asked, "Is it her?"

"Yeah," I answered, and at that my wife scrambled into the yard in her bare feet and ran toward the gate, calling to me, "Hurry up, hurry. We can't let her get away. Grab her!"

I returned to the gate, but I could not see the woman anywhere. My wife nimbly unfastened the lock and raced out onto the street. I shouted: "Miho, if she's gone, let her go. Don't go chasing after her." But she ignored me and continued on. I peered through the darkness ahead, reminding myself that I must remain calm, and walked after her.

My wife called the woman's name, and I heard a woman's voice reply "Yes?" There was not the slightest tension in her voice; it seemed like a conversation between two friends who hadn't seen one another for a long time. Soon I heard sloshing footsteps coming back toward the house, and the hesitant woman returned with my wife holding one of her wrists. No one else seemed to be out there.

Seeing me, my wife said, "Toshio, you hold onto her too."

"What are you doing? I'm not going to run away. Please let me go." Seeing them side by side now, my wife looked much larger.

Unable to wait even for the woman to remove her overcoat once we were inside, my wife asked, "What have you come here for?"

"Mr. Z asked me to come." As she spoke, she untied a furoshiki and took out a small wrapped box of pastries. I saw an envelope tucked beneath the ribbon.

"What is this?"

"Mr. Z and the others collected a little money to help with your doctor bills, and I brought it over."

"*Money?*" My wife's voice betrayed her excitation. "There's no reason we should take sympathy money from you people."

"But we all came up with the idea . . ."

"Please take it back. Such a petty gesture anyway. It's fine for you to destroy someone's family and then come talking about sympathy money."

"But I have it here for you." The woman looked at me. I could say nothing, since I was powerless to control the situation. Because I stood there mute, my wife's suspicions mounted.

"I get it, I get it. You've drummed up a good excuse to come here and threaten us, haven't you? You left those ridiculous letters at our house in Koiwa, but that wasn't enough for you. Now you've come forcing your way in to have a look at the madwoman. That's it. That's it! I know that's what you're up to!"

The woman appeared to waver a bit. "Why would I . . . ? Mr. Z simply asked me to . . ." She appeared to be sliding back toward the door as she spoke.

"If you were bringing sympathy money, why did you try to run away?"

"I didn't run away. I didn't think anybody was at home."

"Liar. Liar! Toshio, grab her. Don't let her escape!"

I blocked the door and reached out for the woman, but when we touched one another, I could not bring myself to apply force. Yet, if I held her loosely, it would appear to my wife that I wanted to set her free. So I tightened my grip. But that seemed to incite my wife even further.

"Toshio, do you really love me?" At the unexpected question, a foreboding whisked before me like a flash of light.

"I love you."

"Do you love this woman, or hate her?" she pressed. I gazed into the woman's eyes, and finally replied softly: "I hate her."

"If that's true, then you can beat her while I watch, can't you? Do that for me." Her tests were multilayered traps. Realizing that my wife's reaction would be identical no matter what my response, I felt my paths of escape closing off. Determinedly, I struck the woman across the face. I could see the blood racing beneath her skin.

"Too weak. One more time."

Unable to oppose her, I drew my hand back with exaggerated flair and struck the woman again with my open palm. She looked at me with scorn in her eyes.

"Do you think that's good enough to cure my madness?" My wife grabbed the woman and dragged her to the far side of the room. With a frightened expression the woman asked: "What are you going to do to me?" When she had pushed the woman up against the wall, my wife clutched her hair and fiercely began beating her head against it.

"Ouch, ouch! Mr. S, help me!" That plea elicited only greater violence from my wife.

I tried to intercede. "What do you intend to do if you break her head open?"

My wife turned up her eyes at me. "Oh, I see. She's more important to you than I am." But she faltered a bit, and I knew she was considering the import of my question. The woman was utterly dispirited and at the mercy of my wife. All she could do was cry for help. But then she found a break and brushed away my wife's hands. As she ran, one of the rotted floorboards snapped under her feet. Staggering frantically, she ran headlong into the yard and toward the gate in her bare feet. But she could not shake off my wife, who nimbly pursued her.

"Toshio, hurry and lock the gate!" I went to secure the lock. I felt that I had no choice but to watch matters develop for a while. My wife placed her legs between the woman's and flipped her to the ground, then coiled her hairs around the fingers of her right hand, pressing her face into the dirt and pinning her down.

"You came here thinking I'd be off at the crazy hospital instead of at home. You won't get away with a trick like that. I knew you'd come some time, so I've been watching for you. You'll never get away now."

"I told you I brought the money because Mr. Z asked me to. I was going to give it to you and then leave."

"I know exactly what kind of plot you had in mind, coming all the way out here this late at night." She seemed to be choking the woman's neck with her left arm.

"I can't breathe! Help!!" Her voice was strangled. They were grappling on soil that had been soaked by the rain, so there was every likelihood that they were both covered with mud, but it was too dark to see clearly. The mud that clung to their cheeks and foreheads looked like sticky blood. My wife could not conceal her heavy breathing as she railed at the woman. Each time the woman squirmed, my wife moved with her. Before long they had rolled over near the fence by the neighbor's house. As this went on, I stood watching with folded arms and said nothing.

"Mr. S, help me! How can you just stand there watching?"

I could not reply.

"This is all your doing. Take a good look! You're just going to stand by and watch while two women kill each other, aren't you?!"

Madly my wife repeatedly pounded the woman's head into the ground.

"Help me!!" With yet another cry, the woman stretched out both of her legs, flipped her body over, and began a counterattack. Her skirt was twisted, and the familiar legs leading to the white lingerie were just below my eyes.

"Toshio, hold her legs down. My fingers are stiff and I can't move them. Surely you're not going to take her side?"

I crouched down, but I felt guilty as I restrained the woman's legs. If I let her go, though, I would be going against my wife's wishes. Torn between bizarre feelings of confusion and disobedience, I grudgingly threw myself on top of the woman's legs. I did not know how to deal with the pleasure I felt at touching something forbidden. It was an eerie sensation, as though the last support left to me was on the verge of collapsing.

"I know—let's tear off her skirt and panties. Toshio, hurry, hurry!"

My wife spoke in earnest, but I felt as though my ears had invented those words on their own.

"What are you waiting for? Are you that fond of this bitch?"

Spurred on to action, I was intrigued at the idea of stripping the woman, and I reached my hands out toward her waist. The instant my fingers touched something resilient beneath her lingerie, the woman summoned all her strength and kicked me away. For some reason I had thought that the woman would yield herself to my touch, so I was at a loss to understand what was happening when she kicked me away, wriggled free, and stood up. My wife barked an order at me, and eventually I was able to wrestle the woman to the ground again.

"If we hurt her, we'll have nothing but problems later on. Why don't we let her go now?" I ventured, but my wife showed no signs of compliance.

"We'll drag this bitch through the mud!" My wife took one of the woman's legs and had me take the other. We dragged her across the ground for ten feet or so, but she was surprisingly heavy, and we could not go any further. Once again my wife twined her fingers through the woman's hair and pressed her head to the ground.

"I'll kill you," she said. They were both exhausted, their movements languid, their breathing heavy. From time to time, as if she had just remembered to do so, the woman would cry,

"Help!" or "Murderer!" or "Someone help me!!" [pp. 287–91]

One of the many remarkable features of this passage is the extent to which Toshio is syntactically absent from the action. This is not fully evident in English, with over a hundred references to "I/me/my" in our strongly referential language. Japanese, however, characteristically enables a narrator to disappear as the subject of an utterance in the linguistic equivalent of humility. It is therefore not surprising that Toshio should intrude himself less frequently in the narrative in the original Japanese, but the extent of his withdrawal in this particular scene, and the nature of his limited participation, is peculiar, and tells us a great deal about the literary substance of *The Sting of Death*.

A structural examination of this long passage provides some interesting insights. In the Japanese, equivalents of the first-person pronoun or any other direct reference to Toshio appear only eighteen times in the narrative portion of the discourse. Only seven of those times is Toshio the grammatical subject of some specific action; four of those times his actions can be categorized as passive, a nonaction. To illustrate:

Passive Actions
I heard
I peered through the darkness
I stood watching with folded arms and said nothing
I could not reply

Each of these nonactions is expressed in the "Watashi wa . . ." + verb pattern, which deemphasizes the actor and shifts attention to the action. Here, however, both actor and action are static.

There are three patterns in which Toshio does take action as a participant in the narrative, and these can be categorized as overt actions.

Overt Actions
I blocked the door and reached out for the woman
I struck the woman across the face
I went to secure the lock

These, again, are expressed grammatically as "Watashi wa . . ." + verb. The significant aspect of these three seeming actions, however, is apparent only syntactically. In context, we find that they are all done in response to direct commands (all expressed in a strong, essentially "masculine" imperative in the Japanese) from Miho. Toshio neither thinks up nor carries out these actions of his own volition. Furthermore, with only a couple of exceptions, every verb describing Toshio's actions or nonactions is written in the *hiragana* script rather than in the appropriate and more commonly employed *kanji* character. As in some of Yasuoka's work,[26] the use of such a mode of transcription has the effect of draining the verb of some of its force, of reducing its visual power. This becomes a subtle discursive commentary upon the ineffectuality of the protagonist.

The other appearances of the first-person pronoun in the quoted passage involve one of the women looking at Toshio (three instances), the woman kicking him, and a second "self" creeping out of Toshio's skin and moving toward the woman. There are five remaining instances, with Toshio receiving some action (a plea from the woman that incites Miho to increased violence), being impelled toward some action (my wife . . . had me take the [woman's] other [leg]), or, again, merely observing what is going on. It is worth remarking that not a single instance of the "watashi ga . . ." construction appears in this lengthy passage. Among other usages, that pattern signifies the active participation of an agent in the discursive flow. The total absence of such an actor in Toshio's case—a feature not uncommon in Shimao's style—suggests a considerable degree of syntactical withdrawal on the part of the narrator.

In short, then, it is impossible to find a single instance in this extended and crucial section wherein Toshio acts of his own free will and choice. He has relinquished all his prerogatives as an individual to Miho, and he can act only upon command from her. He is no longer an agent unto himself, either narratorially or rhetorically.

Or so it might appear. While we are astonished and somewhat abashed at the image of this man standing with folded arms and simply watching while the two women he has slept with thrash about in the mud, shouting "murder" at one another, the male reader at least is almost guiltily aware that something within Toshio has not completely relinquished his sins. Even as the ruckus erupts around him, providing concrete evidence of his indiscretion and the pain it has brought to Miho and the woman, a fallible, unrepentant something within Toshio continues to be moved with desire toward his former lover. The stirrings of that passion at this point in time, after all he has suffered through with Miho, can only serve to persuade Toshio of the futility of his attempt to surrender every part of himself to his wife. That guilty and yet pleasure-laced recognition of human weakness is deftly described by Shimao in this and many other scenes in the novel. This ritual repeated time and again in *The Sting of Death* persuades us of the novel's ultimate truthfulness in its description of the marital relationship specifically, and of all human interaction in a more general sense.

But to examine the novel more for its technique than for its content, I would suggest that the ultimate persuasive power and literary distinction of *The Sting of Death* lies in the complex web of relationships which Shimao creates between author, narrator, characters, and reader. I will mention just one intriguing aspect of this complex interchange. Toshio as a literary character is a participant in the story. As a fictional creation he is limited to a specific range of thoughts and actions as they are chronicled in the narrative. These are, primarily, shaped by his relationships with Miho and the woman, who is never named in the story.

At the same time, however, Toshio is also narrating—that is, reconsidering—the events of the story. On this discursive level, we as readers are drawn into a more meaningful role as participants. We are invited witnesses to Toshio's continuing emotional infidelity, as he is at turns tormented and tantalized by the revival of erotic feelings toward his former lover. Presumably—at least insofar as our overt relationship with the narrator is concerned—this is privileged information, relayed to us because we are privy to Toshio's innermost feelings, those very feelings he so desperately wants to keep concealed from his wife. As privileged onlookers, we assume the role of coconspirators (or at least voyeurs), and are thereby subtly allied with Toshio in his mental indiscretions. We end up as enemies to Miho as a result.

But how well are we able to keep our evil secret? Does the discourse suggest that there are more layers to our complicity? Is the only contract established by this narrative the one between narrator Toshio and the reader? I would suggest not. We have been told on numerous occasions within the text itself that Toshio has had to submit all his writings to Miho for her censure and revision. And she has, over the course of the novel, taken on goddess-like proportions, exhibiting a remarkable ability to see into her husband's mind and demanding control over all his actions and thoughts. This would suggest that even the normally private exchange between narrator and reader has become subject to the scrutiny of Miho—the character whom we have mutually betrayed. We are caught in the trap laid by Miho, whose power as a character seems to extend beyond the bounds normally set within a text. We begin to feel that our words "spoken in darkness shall be heard in the light; and that which [we] have spoken in the ear in closets shall be proclaimed upon the housetops" (Luke 12:3). Even as he validates the secret contract between storyteller and listener, Shimao is letting us know that an act of duplicity on our part, shared through the textual exchange between Toshio and reader, has violated the covenant of fiction and left us open to and deserving of punishment.

Such a technique of narration invites us—in fact, almost impels us—to share in Toshio's torments. It also challenges all our assumptions about our own secret dealings, suggesting that if our acts are indeed observed in the same manner as the movements of characters in fiction, then we cannot escape ultimate responsibility for what we do. Shimao manages to invert the entire question of "author as god," placing both himself and his readers at the feet of a larger, textually omnipotent judge. He thus manages to be thoroughly moral in this narrative without even a trace of didacticism. We all meet unblessed, on a hill of skulls, as Miller's Quentin would express it. And Shimao's structuring of relationships between characters and between discourse and reader persuasively embodies that view of human existence.

Once Shimao has effectively established the complicity of all parties within and without his narrative, there remains only one simple conclusion. We must all enter the asylum together. In terms of the narrative, it becomes clear to Toshio and Miho that the only way they can maintain the tenuous bond between them is to allow it to develop in total isolation from the outside world. They must shut themselves away and devote themselves exclusively to the fostering of their fragile, mutual love. They will send their children to be with Miho's family on the tiny southern island, and the two of them will commit themselves (in both senses of the word "commit") to a mental asylum. Yet even this drastic move does not provide a full, immediate release from all their anxieties. Toshio is forced to realize that, just as he can never completely subsume his will beneath that of Miho, the two of them will never be able to escape entirely from the enemy world that surrounds them.

> I felt a kind of relief and a strange sort of pride that I had at last entered a mental institution. But I had imagined it would come equipped with a sturdier metal door, and I felt a bit dissatisfied at being in this dilapidated wooden building. Had I supposed it would be a stone building tightly sealed off with bolts, like some impenetrable prison? Perhaps I had been hoping for an isolated spot totally removed from the outside world. [p. 337]

Toshio begins to see—however faintly—that there will never be any absolute separation from his need to interact with other human beings. His life until the inciting crisis of the novel had been one of avoidance, a refusal to consider what it means for one individual ego to chafe against another. Over the course of the work, he comes to recognize his own inability to form and nurture a relationship, as well as the potential he has for causing pain to those who would draw near to him. By the end, he has accepted the responsibility to work at just one basic relationship—that with Miho. He has jettisoned everyone and everything else to devote himself to this struggle. He adopts his posture of "unconditional surrender" not merely out of despair but from a complex mixture of love, guilt, helplessness, and a belated but sincere yearning for harmony. It would be an oversimplification to see Toshio's submissiveness as an unadorned expression of love for his wife. Yet certainly love is one of the elements that comes to play in the confused tangle of emotions that sends him into the hospital beside Miho. An overwhelming desire to have someone else—even God—assume the burdens that he can no longer bear brings him to this final point of self-denial. Simultaneously, there can be no question of his devotion to Miho and his earnest hope that he can exorcise the devils that haunt her. The impulse toward self-preservation and the desire for self-immolation join together with a sense of complicity in Miho's tragedy to drive him to his act of ultimate compassion.

The conclusion of *The Sting of Death* gives no indication whether Miho's (and Toshio's) madness will be cured. But it is enough to have Toshio recognize that by losing his life for Miho (and for himself), he will in the end save what remains of the relationship that has bound them together. At the very end of the novel, Miho has demanded that Toshio turn over to her all the love letters he had received from his mistress. This is yet another thorn of guilt that stabs at Toshio, and when he leaves Miho in the hospital room while he goes back home for their bedding, he fleetingly savors the taste of freedom. But in an instant, he realizes that he can never leave Miho.

> As I walked along the street and got onto the train, I felt a surge within my body, a rush of freedom fluttering inside. The world and the people in it came to life in my eyes, and everything seemed to regain its customary assurance and warmth. Energy coursed through my body; I felt like working again! My body seemed almost weightless. But seared into the depths of my eyes was an image of my wife—there in the hospital ward with locks on every door, she sat on a bed in an empty, unfurnished room with bars criss-crossing the windows to prevent escape; suppressing her loneliness, she had pleaded to me with her eyes as I left her behind there. That image of my wife—a woman thrust down into a desolate hell when the only man she ever loved betrayed her—gripped my soul and tugged at my body, refusing to let go. My wife was in a mental ward, awaiting my return. I could not imagine that I had any other work to do than to live together with my wife in that hospital room. . . .
>
> My chest began to pound with anxiety after being separated from my wife for even a short time, and I could not relax. I had to see her again, even if it meant being caught up in another of her attacks. I felt we might even be able to start out on a new life *(atarashii shuppatsu)* if we were in our asylum room separated by

> locked doors from the outside world. Though a dark shadow was cast over that hope because I could not think of a way to dissuade my wife from trying to get back those letters. [pp. 337–38]

There is, certainly, a glimmer of hope that opens up in this concluding portion of the novel: Toshio is abandoning virtually every prerogative of his own life in order to dedicate himself to Miho's recovery. This "atarashii shuppatsu"—quite literally a "new departure"—is surely a positive note at the end of what has been a harrowing narrative. But only a careless reader would miss the allusion to Shimao's earlier story about his suicide-pilot days: that "departure" never occurred ("Shuppatsu wa tsui ni otozurezu"). We are thus left with lingering intimations of an anxiety of the soul that admits no simple, human solution.

Shimao's transferral of his personal experience into literary form in some ways resembles the manner in which an author such as Ōe Kenzaburō has struggled to reshape the I-novel. Both writers began as avant-garde experimentalists consciously attempting to break away from the autobiographical roots of modern Japanese literature, until personal tragedy (in Ōe's case, the birth of his retarded son) transformed their attitudes toward literature and sent them back into a reexamination of the potential within the I-novel.

Even though *The Sting of Death* is a reconstruction of the rift that entered Shimao's own marriage in 1954, the novel so dramatically transcends the stifling limitations of the autobiographical narrative form that such a pat classification cannot be countenanced. In many ways the work is almost a perfect antithesis of the traditional I-novel. First of all, Shimao employs anything but a technique of clinical realism. The influence of his early surrealist works can be sensed strongly in the undercurrents of this novel: the incidents of everyday life take on a nightmarish quality, and time is stretched beyond recognition. There is also a decisive aesthetic distance between the frantic, hallucinatory situation and the calm, intellectual voice of the narrator. It is quite possible to doubt the sanity of the character Toshio in the novel, but the narrator never seems out of control—he is always coolly detached from the lunacy going on all around.

Furthermore, the main thrust of the I-novel was an attempt to accept or rationalize the tragedy of life by reducing it to a matter of everyday experience.[27] As we have seen, Shimao achieves precisely the opposite effect—the experiences of everyday life are blown totally out of proportion and elevated to the level of tragedy. Yet this metamorphosis takes place precisely because mundane events evoke such suffering. But most important is the total dismantling of the protagonist's "self." Autobiographical writers such as Shimazaki Tōson and especially Shiga Naoya placed concern for the integrity of the individual ego above all other considerations. Any and all actions of the hero in a novel could be justified so long as the character was behaving in a manner consistent with his quest for self-definition. This meant that the main character had every right to run away when things did not turn out as he wished, and that no characters other than the first-person narrator were given anything beyond cursory, superficial consideration. Precisely the opposite is true in *The Sting of Death.* Toshio's individuality is gradually but irrevocably extinguished as he more fully realizes the depth of his sins, and without the presence of Miho, he would not be able to go on living at all. This is not to suggest that Miho is a fully developed fictional character; in fact, because she is to some extent deified by Toshio, her individuality suffers in the novel. But there can be no doubt that she is essential to Toshio in his attempt to cope with the agony of everyday existence.

The style of writing Shimao adopts in this novel is further evidence that he is concerned with more than the simple reliving of private experiences. He creates uncommonly long sentences and seemingly interminable paragraphs (some running as long as five pages). The vocabulary in them is evocative, metaphorical, and at times almost cryptically intellectual. A second noteworthy and seemingly paradoxical feature of the style is the inclusion of an enormous amount of commonplace detail—what the characters eat at each meal, what positions they lie in when they go to sleep, etc. The diary-like precision about routine activities seems incongruous in a novel about extraordinary circumstances, especially when they are described in such a lofty, almost pedantic diction.

Yet these two remarkable elements of style work together to give the novel a cohesiveness and a power that could come in no other way. The ponderous length of the syntactical parts and the erudite vocabulary bring a touch of stability, a sense of anchoring to the narrative. The rational, intellectual style Shimao uses to describe these highly unstable, psychotically emotional exchanges plunges his readers into the vortex of the conflict and convinces us that this abnormality is actually normal, and that the complacency of our own everyday lives is perhaps the true aberration. This delicately balanced contrast between madness and sanity—reflected in the style with steady, convoluted sentences describing bizarre, disjointed acts—sucks us into the narrative and involves us in it in a manner that a more matter-of-fact approach could never hope to achieve. At the same time, the contrast between medium and message makes it clear that no degree of intellectual attainment can provide a solution to a dilemma that derives essentially from a cancer of the spirit.

Finally, the conscious learnedness of the style, along with the apparent deification of Miho in Toshio's eyes, are a clue to a yet deeper layer of concern in *The Sting of Death.* The remarkable detachment of the narrator from the turmoil within the narrative gives us the impression that we are observing the situation from an exalted perspective, as if man is being observed from God's vantage point. This perspective adds a heavy touch of irony, for the exaggerated struggle between Miho and Toshio after a time comes to seem rather absurd even to themselves. From our safe, distant position we recognize that however much we may sympathize with these two people, their sufferings are a result of their own errors—sins, in fact—and that the "sting of death" is a torment which individuals bring upon themselves and inflict upon others, and which they are responsible for resolving. From such a perspective, escape is clearly an unconscionable act; only the courage to confront the problem directly can make a solution possible.

The inescapable conclusion here is that Shimao's attitudes in this novel are essentially religious. The biblical allusions in the title of the work and in several chapter names give us further hints. It cannot be a misreading of *The Sting of Death* to consider it as a metaphor for man's separation from God, enacting the torments that betoken that lonely state. The deification of Miho in Toshio's mind is but a part of this process. The reconciliation which Toshio seeks with her; the unattainable absolution for which he yearns; the self-denial which he accepts; and the torments of the inferno that he suffers for being separated from her—all these experiences are as applicable to Toshio's relationship with God as they are with his wife. Japanese critics have compared *The Sting of Death* to *Medea, Faust,* and *Crime and Punishment.* While these are all apt, it is the biblical analogy that gives Shimao's novel its consummate power.

In the final analysis, Shimao Toshio may be the most "lost" of all his literary generation. Removed both physically and spiritually from his colleagues in the writers' circles, he had to carve out his own private fictional territory and defend it with little support from contemporary critics. His personal experience may be vastly removed from that of the dark-suited businessmen who commute into Tokyo each morning, and his complex, dreamlike style may not make him a popular seller in bookstores. But the determined purity of Shimao's vision, and the evident torment of his participation in a war that never ended—a war, in fact, that seems to have eternal implications—guarantee him a lasting position in the chronicles of postwar literature.

V

Human Handicapped: Kojima Nobuo

Kojima Nobuo, 1969

> **Ours is essentially a tragic age, so we refuse to take it tragically. The cataclysm has happened, we are among the ruins, we start to build up new little habits, to have new little hopes. It is rather hard work: there is now no smooth road into the future: but we go round, or scramble over the obstacles. We've got to live, no matter how many skies have fallen.**
>
> **—D. H. Lawrence,**
> **LADY CHATTERLEY'S LOVER**

SATIRE IS a literary form particularly well suited to periods of social disruption, since it attacks the idealized romantic vision of an orderly world. But it is a mode that has flourished only sporadically in the Japanese tradition. Few authors have been removed enough from either the mainstream of society or the accepted channels of literary expression to be able to mount such a cynical assault upon the underpinnings of their culture.

The war and Occupation, however, provided conditions ideal for the germination of satire. The first true satirist to arise from the ashes was Kojima Nobuo; others, such as Inoue Hisashi, have followed in his wake, but Kojima was the groundbreaker. The roots of his satire are imbedded in his highly individualistic views of modern society. In Kojima's eyes, moral gravity has ceased to operate. The world in which we live has begun to spin wildly out of control; though his characters continue to try to steady themselves by grasping hold of some support, each lifeline proves illusory or breaks off in their hands. Yet still the struggle to find a handhold persist. Those unreliable grips may be actual handrails, as in "Kisha no naka" (On the Train, 1948), or hierarchical stars of rank on the collar of the ambivalent soldiers in "Hoshi" (Stars, 1954; trans. 1985).

The instability in Kojima's world is most clearly manifest within the relationships that exist or ought to exist between one human being and another. Even the bonds that once held society tenuously together have come loose. In the modern period few writers (Endō Shūsaku and Shimao Toshio being notable exceptions) have found the strength to focus on the relationship between a human being and some superior force, be it Nature or God or the Society. Most authors over the last century or so have lowered their focus to the maze of relationships that one individual forms with another. Even the I novelists of the prewar age had as their concern the manner in which one individual was expected to maintain associations with the world around him.

But for Kojima, even this fundamental approach to the study of human nature has collapsed. No longer does the individual himself, the "I" of fiction, adhere to a single fixed point of identity. "I" has become an inconstant, unreliable and unstable, no longer sure how to react with other human beings and thereby define his own identity. A comparison of Kojima's first-person narrators with those of Shiga Naoya indicates the degree to which the reliability of the "Self" has crumbled away in Kojima's fiction. Shiga's protagonists, such as the title character in "Han no hanzai" (Han's Crime, 1913; trans. 1957), have unshakable faith in the reliability of their own private judgments; even Shiga as author considered himself an unimpeachable judge, and earned his title as "the god of fiction" by placing himself above his narratives and intruding upon them, as in "Kozō no kamisama" (The Apprentice Boy's God, 1919), whenever he felt they were not responding properly to his directives. At the center of every Shiga "fiction" stands the Creator, Shiga, his feet planted firmly upon ground of his own cultivation.

The god-author has fallen from his throne in the writings of Kojima, and the stories I will examine below will detail the degree to which both author and narrator have been forced to abdicate their positions as final arbiters of right and wrong. If the standards of judgment in Shiga's day were individualized and internal, they were snatched from private hands by the war, then shattered by the defeat. The result, in Kojima's satirical world, is an entire population of bewildered wanderers, the reins of control taken from them and no longer discernible in the outside world.

This is most clearly manifest in the disjointed relationships between man and wife, superior and subordinate, parent and child—none of which satisfy the traditional expectations. The Kojima character has no emotional yardstick by which to measure his performance as a human being. Lacking that guide, these characters lapse into embarrassed silence, too unsure of themselves to take any meaningful plunge into the mainstream of life, too diffident to solve even the most pressing problems that confront their families. They are, in short, perfect specimens of the prototypical modern creature, Human Handicapped.

In an early essay appended to a collection of his short stories, Kojima clearly indicates the predominant character type he creates:

> As I look at my stories lined up one beside another here, it becomes apparent that all my stories are about "partial cripples." Because of my nature, I suppose, I have drawn a veil of humor over them; without that protecting veil, I would have been too embarrassed to take up my pen.[1]

Unable to define their relationships with others and too embarrassed to try, Kojima's characters hobble through life, each step a painful exercise in humiliation. Even as he observes their stumbling, Kojima is able to laugh at his creations. Or rather, his own embarrassment requires that he inject humor into his narratives. His satire, as dark as it may be, derives not from the supercilious laughter of the healthy pointing a finger at the afflicted. Rather it is the self-recriminating chuckle of a fellow cripple, one who sees a reflection of his own absurd struggles to walk erect. Kojima's fiction is both a descendant of and a challenge to the I-novel tradition. Revoking the authority of the "I," Kojima succeeds as a satirist in the same sense that the Russian formalists perceived the role of the parodist—as one who lays bare the problems inherent in the literary tradition through a distortion of its formal weaknesses. Kojima achieves this by placing the weighty burden of narration upon his protagonists' already twisted backs.

Kojima's reading of Gogol had an important impact on his satire. Even though his major in college was English literature and his graduation essay on "Thackeray as a Humorist," Kojima was most moved as a young man by his encounter with Gogol. The first reading material he sought out after his return from the war was the fiction of Gogol; certainly the absurdity of his experiences in the military had reinforced his own innate cynicism. The satiric pessimism of Gogol must have had even greater appeal for Kojima after he had witnessed the military's complete about-face regarding his English ability, once they had a means of using it for their own benefit. Like Gogol, who in 1828 made up his mind to move from the Ukraine to St. Petersburg to become a writer, Kojima in 1947 quit his job in Gifu and uprooted his family to move to Tokyo.[2]

The pessimism of Kojima's early stories, the bizarre, almost farcical distortion of reality in search of a higher truth, and the absurd consequences that result from each character's attempt at a meaningful action, are all reminiscent of Gogol's satirical writings. As one student of Gogol has observed:

> without analysing reality or even criticising it, [Gogol] selects and rearranges his material so that in the end we have a grotesque world where nothing has value, where no logic applies, where all is illusion and deceit. . . . Tragedy comes through the magnification and extension of the very trivial and banal and for this reason we have a vision of life as absurd and meaningless.[3]

No more appropriate description could be given for Kojima's first story after the war, "On the Train." The world he depicts there is indeed "grotesque," and the story finally fades off into a fog of "illusion and deceit." Kojima's voracious reading of Gogol both before and after the war played a significant role in the formulation of his early fiction.

Other important influences on Kojima include Dostoevsky (indeed, it is difficult to locate a modern Japanese writer who does not trace at least a few of his literary roots to *Crime and Punishment*) and Franz Kafka, whose works were just beginning to appear in Japanese translation when Kojima started writing. Most interesting to Kojima was Kafka's assertion that human beings are little more than insects.[4] Kojima had no difficulty correlating Gogol's pessimistic view of society with Kafka's belief that formless, oppressive forces block the path between individuals and their aspirations. His task as a postwar writer was to give expression to these sentiments in a uniquely Japanese fashion.

If Kojima appropriated a sense of distorted reality from Gogol and Kafka, his sensitivity to the details of everyday life may owe something to his fondness for William Saroyan. Though it is difficult to imagine two writers less similar in literary temperament than Saroyan and Kojima, certainly the emphasis which Saroyan places on the seemingly petty events in the lives of his characters can also be seen in Kojima's work. Like most of the other authors of his generation, Kojima is fascinated with commonplace details, particularly as they manifest the true nature of close human relationships.[5]

Although Kojima returned from the war convinced that human endeavor was basically a study in absurdity, for all their ridiculous acts, he could not abandon his characters in the pit of meaninglessness. The close identification between Kojima as author and his half crippled characters requires that he see a certain dignity in their feeble struggles to survive. Whatever indignities life may hand them, the characters in stories such as "On the Train" or "Amerikan sukūru" (The American School, 1954; trans. 1979) continue to wage the battle for self-preservation. They are humorous because they do not see that many of the absurditites that encumber their lives are of their own manufacture.

> While the stories I wrote after the war attempt to point out the absurdities of life, they also focus—especially after the defeat—on things which struck me as absurd during the war or after the surrender. . . . I started out with the impression that these absurdities were external, lying outside myself. But this is not necessarily the case—some seem to groan inside me in undiscovered regions.[6]

Kojima's fiction attains its highest levels in these vigorous, unrelenting portraits of human foolishness. Kojima clearly maintains a love-hate relationship with his characters, and his very ambivalence toward them as their creator jibes perfectly with his views regarding the relativism inherent in modern life. The focus of his satire is sharpest when he catches his characters off guard, in the moments when they are most human and therefore, by Kojima's definition, most ridiculous. His critical eye studies these moments in many realms of mundane behavior, whether on the battlefield or in the confusion of the postwar period. It is in his views of the chaos after the defeat that Kojima is most adroit at dissecting the debilitating struggles for survival, but he does have a number of curious works set in wartime.

In some of Kojima's central works about the Second World War, one can discover the germs of cynicism that blossom in his postwar writings. Somewhat earlier than Yasuoka, Kojima was already writing about the inconsistencies, the absurdities, and the lack of courage that abounded in the life of the Japanese soldier. He may, in fact, have been the first Japanese writer to focus directly on the ludicrous realities of the soldier's existence. And most convincingly, Kojima has written of the individual soldier's ambivalence toward the entire war effort, in stories such as "Stars" and novels such as *Bohimei* (Epitaph, 1960). In these works, Kojima blithely dismantles the standard stereotype. Some of his recruits flee the unbearable barracks life through intoxication, some by actual escape; others eagerly prepare for new lives after what they consider inevitable defeat. In this logical gap between ideal soldier and actual human being, Kojima finds amusement, cynical though it may be.

Kojima employs a technique of exaggeration in both "Stars" and *Epitaph*. The protagonist in each work is a second-generation Japanese-American who has the misfortune of being in Japan when the war breaks out and finding himself drafted into the Japanese army to fight against his own countrymen. These figures are inherently absurd, though Kojima was in fact personally acquainted with an American-educated Nisei who served in the Japanese army.[7] But Jōji "George" Sugihara of "Stars" and Tomio "Tom" Hamanaka of *Epitaph* function as more than wartime aberrations. Torn between an inborn love for America and a sense of duty to Japan, they are perfect symbols of ambivalence, the epitome of the inability to choose. By presenting his characters with situations in which any rational choice is likely to lead to further problems, Kojima demonstrates that he has no faith in purposive action, and it is a foregone conclusion that only laughable results will emerge from his characters' attempts to succeed.

In "Stars," George struggles mightily to make his actions conform to the Japanese army's expectations, which are symbolized by the single star he wears on his collar. The star motif, in fact, is a subtle and complex image in the story; the manner in which Kojima traces George's fluid relationship with the stars of hierarchy, and the final unreliability of those stars themselves, are the most successful literary aspects of the work. Initially, for instance, when George has been drafted into the military against his will, he feels only bewilderment in the presence of the stars:

> When I thought of the long chain leading upward from private second class to general to field marshal, my eyes swam as though I were peering up a ladder to heaven. The gulf was so incredible; one could never skip a single rung of the nearly twenty steps above. And a swarm of single stars like an ocean surrounding me. Moreover, this miserable single star acquired new life as it became two, then three stars. Suddenly on the next level a stripe was added. Then a silver stripe was joined by a silver star. Next the design changed and was given lively borders. And thereafter. . . . Thus, the higher you got, the more decorative and resplendent your uniform became. I suppose a conference must have been called to decide all this. One can imagine how inspired the delegates had been by the belief that the Great Ones must be suitably adorned.[8]

At first only the gulf separating his own lonely status from the glimmering top of the hierarchy rivets George's attention and causes his head to swim. He has not yet assimilated himself into the system or accepted it as the guiding principle for his own life. For acknowledgment of the system is tantamount to admission that he is the least exalted member. "Even horses," according to army legend, "can recognize rank" (p. 104), and thus George finds himself in the uncomfortable position of needing a support system to direct his life but not knowing if or how he fits into the star hierarchy of the Japanese army. It is only when George encounters another lowly one-star soldier, Hikida, that he can advance himself a rung on the star ladder and plug himself into the system. This comes with his recognition that Hikida is inferior to himself both physically and mentally. He accepts the system when he is no longer the army's prime whipping boy, and finds vicarious joy in standing back as Hikida is pummeled and abused by the senior soldiers. "Hikida was indispensible to me," he admits. "He was less a human being for me than a sort of star" (p. 109).

It is clear from the subtly shifting definition of stars here—from an external order to an internalized source of self-definition—that Kojima is playing tricks on his characters. As readers we are rather swiftly persuaded to dislike George, because he appears to accommodate himself to the new system rather effortlessly once it can work to his advantage. It is less comfortable for us, however, when we realize midway through the work that Kojima is not confining his observations to the military pecking order, and that his concerns in "Stars" extend to any and all systems of social organization that offer incentives to those who can muster the greatest selfish ruthlessness.

Kojima here has begun to employ a literary device that he continues to wield throughout his finest writings. He introduces a central character who is initially perplexed about his position in society, the home, whatever institution he may feel should embrace him. We are kept at an emotional distance from these characters by Kojima's calculating techniques of narration—his characters describe their situations and their actions in the most straightforward, unemotional manner possible. We are thereby forced to withhold judgment of these individuals until it is too late—until we have come to recognize some part of them that is a portrait in miniature of ourselves. At that point, we can no longer laugh at or despise these creatures without mocking ourselves. It is a bitter trap, but one which succeeds at emphasizing the painful irony of our lost circumstances.

In "Stars," Kojima does not restrict his focus to those on the bottom of the hierarchy. He also is at pains to point out the absurdity of those who are locked into the system at higher levels. The clearest representation of this is Captain Inoma, an officer who takes in George as his "housemaid" and attempts to turn him into a model Japanese soldier. Yet the model itself is patently ludicrous:

> He was twenty-two or three, with nothing special to recommend him aside from the fact that he was an officer. His chief claims to fame were the manner in which he could spit vigorously out his window each morning after I brought in his water, and the fact that he could drink the murky Chinese tea. He was, in short, a model officer. Bedecked in his officer's stars, he looked at least thirty years old. Strangely enough, when a man acquires two stars, his age seems to advance in concert with his promotion, as though even his years were subject to the rule of the stars.
>
> Brought into close contact with these distant stars, I felt not hatred but something more like adoration. I wondered if, as a result of all the anguish I'd been made to suffer in the midst of those inferior starts, I hadn't come to feel that life had greater meaning if I surrendered to the star system and regarded myself as worthless. I had indeed come to believe that stars had an intrinsic value to them—that a PFC was truly superior to a buck private, a lance corporal better than a PFC, a noncom greater than a common

> foot soldier, and an officer vastly more exalted than a noncom. I had become convinced that those of a higher rank than my own were an inherently different breed of human being. Particularly an officer. How could I even imagine that Captain Inoma—this lofty being for whom I washed laundry every day, delivered meals, and poured tea—belonged to the same species as myself? There was even a brief period when I embraced the peculiar notion that he was my superior by virtue of the fact that he belonged to a race of vegetarians. Perhaps I had fallen short of the mark because I had lived in America and been corrupted by the consumption of animal flesh. [p. 112]

This passage concisely summarizes Kojima's satiric technique. There are two layers to the discourse—George's implicit acceptance of the star system because it is, in wartime, his only ticket to survival; and his jaded, intellectualized perception of the system as an irrational promoter of mediocrity. Because we are not sure at this point exactly when George is relating these experiences, it appears that he harbors these two ambivalent views—an intellectual rejection of the system and a visceral dependency upon it—simultaneously. Thus the obvious humor in his depictions of Inoma (equating a model soldier with the ability to spit and drink insipid tea) and of himself (as belonging to an entirely different species from his superior, and perhaps invalidated as a member of the hierarchy by his dietary heritage) is tempered by our suspicion that he may have an emotional need to believe in these logically ridiculous perceptions. The fracturing essential to irony is presented here by Kojima as a complete severance between the mind and the emotions of his main character—a split that, in addition to representing the collapse of Japanese society as it pursued a logic-defying drive toward war, epitomizes the technique of literary dichotomy central to Kojima's writings.

George's cynicism toward the star system is brought into clearest relief when he attends Captain Inoma in the bath. His implicit acceptance of the system is challenged when he sees Inoma naked for the first time, stripped of the stars that normally adorn his uniform collar and define his status vis-à-vis George.

> Why should I be so stunned to see the captain nude, without his uniform? Who in fact was this naked man before me? He was muscular, to be sure, but was there such a great difference be-

> tween me and this man with the close-cropped hair when both of us were in the buff? After he climbed back into the bath, he launched into one of his recitations of Chinese poetry. I sat abstractedly holding his towel and soap. The sound of his chanting reawakened in me the realization that this was indeed Captain Inoma before me, and I returned to my senses. But I had a sluggish, uneasy feeling, as though a cog had slipped out of place. I wanted to get both the captain and myself back into uniform at once. [p. 116]

Identity and status so clearly defined by such externals as clothing are obviously unreliable, and George's eagerness to get both himself and Inoma back into the symbols of their relationship indicates his own shaky but desperate faith in those symbols. But the horrifying realization that such status distinctions may be fleeting—as easily cast off as the jacket of a uniform—fills George with an anxiety, a sense of betrayal that is not easily assuaged. His later attempts to test the dependability of the system he has adopted as his guide to life only reaffirm his suspicion that an external set of principles is of doubtful value. The only thing that saves him from a forced disembowelment in the story is his shocked, bemused discovery that his own navel is shaped like a star—a suggestion that, even without the external system, he could, if he wished, find means within himself to establish a suitable code of ethics.

The most telling scene in the story, and the one which displays Kojima at his ironic best, comes as the war ends and George, Inoma, and many other repatriate Japanese are aboard an American transport ship heading back to their homeland. Kojima avoids pointing out the implicit irony that George's true homeland is America; it would seem that his reliance upon the now defunct hierarchy of stars has left him without a true home to return to. After a group of U.S. Marines comes into the hold of the ship and takes some of the Japanese insignia as war souvenirs, some of the Japanese men themselves begin ripping off their uniform stars and tossing them into the air.

> Unable to endure the spectacle any longer, I stood up and shouted, "You mustn't tear off your stars. They're priceless! Stop it!!" I repeated the words again and again, until those around me stopped hurling their stars about and gathered around me. One of them cried, "Who is this bastard? I'll get his!" He lunged and

ripped off my insignia, then trampled on the three PFC stars with his boot and knocked me to the floor.

I climbed up onto the fiercely rolling deck. Inoma, bereft of his stars, stood there smiling.

"George! [Sergeant] Brown took my knapsack and boots."

In their place he wore a pair of American army boots. Suddenly I recalled that his feet were larger than average.

. . . Inoma and the other soldiers were now looking for new stars.

With a list of its prow and a blast from its whistle, the LST entered Sasebo Harbor. Hills came into view through the morning mist. Their color seemed so familiar that I became almost frantic to identify it. I paced back and forth on the deck, wanting to ask people, "What color is that?" Then I stopped in my tracks. I realized that the hills were the color of the khaki uniform I wore. [p. 130]

Inoma has both the innate ability and the inherent need to adapt himself to whatever new system of order comes along. He is a ready survivor, more than willing to beg his subordinate George for a job on the family farm in America. He is both a parody of the Japanese who is more than eager to adopt new ways of life from the West—a figure that stretches back to the early literature of the Meiji period in works such as Kanagaki Robun's *Aguranabe* (The Beefeater, 1871)[9] and Futabatei's *Ukigumo*—as well as a not completely unsympathetic portrait of the self-degradation required of those who maintain a will to survive.

George is another matter. His initial values, those he acquired as a student in Fresno, were taken from him against his will, and he was placed in a totally alien environment offering none of the supports to which he had grown accustomed. "Stars" carefully traces his reactions to and against the new system of order that is thrust before his eyes—the star hierarchy of the Japanese army. Feeling at first used, then abused, until finally he is able to find himself a niche in the system, George struggles desperately to make the cloth and metal of his uniform collar a part of his own skin—a skin which is, itself, a mixture of differing textures. But the experience of his nakedness, physical and moral as he attends Captain Inoma in the bath fills him with the anxious fear that he may never be able to make this system an integral part of him. His return to Japan—stripped of rank; reduced, in fact, to the status of an international hybrid once again through his appointment as a "Potsdam" PFC—is a return to a home that is not his true land of origin. But he must make the best of his circumstances, and attempt to stay the destruction of the star system that is his only means of self-definition. This is why he cannot endure watching as the other soldiers so casually toss away their stars. And while he can acknowledge the fact that some, like Inoma, are able to find satisfying replacements in symbols of the new culture—American army boots—George cannot so easily begin looking for "new stars."

His first glimpse of his unfamiliar "homeland" suggests that Japan itself is in the same moral quandary. If the hills of home are indeed a khaki color, the same hue as George's starless uniform, then Kojima would seem to be suggesting that as a nation Japan has been deprived of its governing codes of morality, and that George's dilemma can be expanded into a vision of the national calamity. While it is true that there are signs of possibility—though perhaps not "hope" in its most positive sense—in the moral flexibility of men such as Inoma, there are also clear indications that the period of social transition will take its toll upon those, like George, who invested all their souls in the defunct systems because they had nothing else.

Perhaps the supreme irony of the story lies in the fact that the one character who most fully adopted the code of stars was, in fact, never totally Japanese from the outset. Because of his dual origins, George would seem at first glance a likely candidate for rebellion against the imposition of a single system of status. But it is his very genetic ambivalence—an ambivalence which Kojima is surely proposing as a metaphor for the multi-cultural Japanese citizen of the modern century—that drives him to seek unwavering foundations upon which he can build his life. A quest for absolutes in a frantically relativistic world makes the process of adaptation all the more difficult for him, and makes of him a character of rich suggestivity.

Another striking image of this ambivalence is to be found in *Epitaph*. Tomio, after learning to adjust to the Japanese military society, is ordered by his superiors to dress up in an American uniform and act as decoy for the Japanese troops fighting in the Philippines. Tomio wears the American uniform over his Japanese one. This outward symbol of his innermost confusion continues to haunt him until his unit is ordered to disband and fend for themselves. He removes both uniforms and begins wandering through the jungle. He freezes in his tracks when he sees a rifle pointing at him through the undergrowth. Uncertain whether the weapon is being held by a Japanese or an American soldier, Tomio cries:

> "I'm not Japanese! I'm not American either!!"
>
> A shot sounded. I heard some English spoken. I scrambled to remove my uniform, but I had nothing left except my own skin.[10]

In the end, Tomio's dilemma is that he cannot decide for himself what he wants to be. His situation is rendered impossible by conflicting demands. He is at last reduced to a parody of action—a decoy dressed in conflicting uniforms and set loose to wander between one side and the other. Kojima here has created a painfully vivid image of the ambivalent hero. At the end of the novel, when Tomio rips off both uniforms, his own indecisive flesh remains, unable to become totally Japanese or totally American. He is caught in the middle, rejected by both sides, and uncertain himself which camp he wishes to belong to.

As a survivor of the conflict, Kojima looks back on the war and offers up this literary "epitaph" to his generation with a peculiarly Japanese mixture of shame and relief—relief that he is still alive, shame that he did not die with the rest of his buddies who perished in Leyte. In his view of the war, the survivor is not the ultimate victor. The dead have, at least, been laid to rest. Survivors like George and Tomio and Kojima can know no rest. They must bear the infirmities that the war has bequeathed to them. With the defeat, all the Georges and Tomios and Nobuos were left without their "stars," without their easily identifiable though distasteful symbols of identity. The cessation of fighting did not mean an end to their search for new stars, their longing for something stable to cling to or merely lean upon. After he had buried these emotionally dead survivors and erected an epitaph to their memory, Kojima turned his gaze to the years that followed the war. There, not surprisingly, he found many like himself who still groped about, still labored under the handicap that ambivalence and a society in flux imposes upon those who yearn for some philosophy that will keep them from stumbling again and again.

More than forty years later, it is difficult to comprehend the pandemonium, the deprivation, and the panic that swept across the islands of Japan after the surrender declaration. Coping with the concept of defeat itself—an unfamiliar, horrifying prospect for the Japanese—required considerable adjustment in their ways of thinking. An old order, one that was supposed to endure for at least eight thousand generations according to the national anthem, had been wiped out of existence almost overnight. Without that order, the people were reduced to a state of chaos, uncertain whether they would be alive when tomorrow came, and not sure they wanted to be.

In Kojima's stories that treat the postwar period, characters are tortured by these feelings of loss and confusion. Being sensitive to disruption and used to regularity in their lives, they suffer perhaps more than the average person on the street. In the early "On the Train," a school teacher who tries to make his way to Tokyo just after the war undergoes intense mental anguish as he observes and then experiences firsthand the degradation and despair all around him. The entire story is set aboard a packed steam-engine train struggling from the provinces toward Tokyo. The sense of confinement is purposeful, expressing Kojima's attitudes toward the stifling emotional atmosphere of those days. To intensify the reader's sensitivity to this climate, Kojima stretches the reality out to the horizon of farce. The insecure hero caught in the squeeze—physically and mentally—is Sano *sensei,* a pedagogue who is moving to Tokyo to take up a new job, just as Kojima himself did after the war. Sano is a weary, self-deprecating man with a fragile ego under constant assault from his shrill, antiseptic wife.

Kojima establishes the mood for his story in the opening lines, which capture not only the crowding of the train itself, but also the claustrophobic confusion after the defeat.

> The Tōkaidō train bound for Tokyo was on the verge of collapse. For a full day and a night it had raced along since its departure from Kyushu. On the platform alone rode twenty people; another three dangled precariously from the step. After each stop the train reluctantly panted forward like a horse slapped on its rump, and the passengers fell silent and abandoned themselves to their destiny. But their clamoring in the interim was reminiscent of hogs running amuck in a slaughterhouse; even their voices echoed like the squeals of pigs.[11]

The war has ended, and the energy that the people had stored up to operate the military machinery has suddenly been drained from them. Moving aimlessly toward some vague goal, they can only squeal like swine rising up in rebellion in the slaughterhouse. But their protests are in vain, and they are left with nothing but a profound and chronic weariness, the most familiar product of the postwar era. Clearly the train represents a sense of progressive "collapse" that is beginning to overtake the entire nation. And in a blind, almost lemming-like rush toward modernization, symbolized by Tokyo, they are, ironically, moving to embrace the "America" that has directly caused their weariness.[12]

These tracks leading the debilitated train and its passengers to Tokyo, to a new "star" of hope, are in fact just one of the many "roads" in Kojima's fiction. He envisioned himself as an onlooker who observes life passing him by while he looks on in cynical mockery. This he attributed to the basic character of his native home in Gifu Prefecture. "Psychologically," he wrote of Gifu people, "they lie midway between Tokyo and Kansai, being positioned on the road between the two. They have been forced to taste the indignation of a people passed by, and the bitterness of the onlooker."[13] For Kojima himself, event after event in his personal life convinced him that he was not in control of his circumstances, that ruin would go on all around him no matter what steps he might take to stay its progress. But the Gifu cynic in him continued to see a dark humor in the desperate attempts of man to stave off fate. The long roads are pathways leading his characters to humiliation, frustration, and near-despair. These people are social cripples who can only hobble uncertainly down those endless, unbending paths. Yet they keep on walking.

Since the defeat, Sano has lost interest in living. The shock of loss and the subsequent shifts in the currents of society have desensitized Sano; the flames of ruin have burned his tongue, rendering him unable to taste life. He no longer trusts anyone, and he lacks confidence in his own abilities as an educator. To teach something, after all, requires that one have a firm grip on the subject matter; but in the wake of the war, Sano is not sure he holds anything securely within his hands. Sano's tale could easily be the story of how George Sugihara or Tom Hamanaka reacted to the postwar years—the same ambivalence and hesitation are built into his character.

Above all, Sano cannot abide the disorder (or the disrespect for order) that he sees all around him. Even though wartime society had been bellicose and repressive, at least there had been order. He feels that the certainties of a disciplined life are preferable to the ambiguities of freedom, and that people without a sense of order are reduced to beasts. The animals—pigs and horses, primarily—that appear with great frequency in Kojima's fiction can likely be traced back to the portraits of wartime decadence in Sakaguchi Ango's writings, particularly "Hakuchi" (The Idiot, 1946; trans. 1962), but they are fully integrated into Kojima's vision of the utter collapse of human dignity. Once Sano struggles into the train car, he begins a rambling, self-conscious monologue on the need for order in the midst of chaos:

> "I eat rice gruel and rotten potatoes twice a day and consider myself fortunate. You may make fun of me, suggesting that I'm good for nothing. Well, I intend to go on living a life of reason. My students say to me, 'Teacher, you talk so soft we can't hear a word.' 'Not a word?' I ask. 'Not a single word. We haven't been able to hear anything for a while now. We've seen your mouth moving, so we figured you must be giving a lecture.' Do you suppose students these days know how to speak deferentially to their teachers?—they treat us as less than their equals. 'Teacher, what's the point of talking politely? We pay an exhorbitant amount of money to commute to school, and we get shoved around on the trains and get our uniforms all wrecked. That's why we have the courage to tell you this. . . . Teacher, can you hear us?' 'There's nothing wrong with my ears,' I reply. 'This problem didn't start today, Teacher.' 'Do you think I talk softly on purpose? Can you hear me now?' 'Nope. Not a word. Just your mouth moving.' 'Really? Well, it can't be helped. It's not that I can't talk louder because I'm starving. It's just that this is the loudest I can speak. I have two children, and my second wife is suffering from gastric dilatation—I have to put up with her weeping and wailing until we can get her cured. I've sold off everything I have to sell. Once my clothes are all gone, I can't very well start selling my skin, can I? So what am I supposed to do?' . . . Today I was waiting for the train at S Station. I assumed we might have difficulty getting aboard, so I woke up in the middle of the night and got at the very head of the waiting line. How grateful I was for my own sagacity!

> I waited there for five hours, in a state of calm, resigned enlightenment. And what do you suppose happened when the train arrived? We were shoved to the very end of the line! Why did we both lining up? I ask all of you—why did we bother lining up! If it's a foregone conclusion that everybody's going to scramble madly to get on, what is the point of standing in line until the train arrives? . . . For what purpose did I wait five hours?!" [pp. 18–20]

Sano's diatribe against the collapse of order is both pathetic and amusing. Kojima's reduction of that collapse to the inability of a class of students to hear what their teacher is saying is terse and persuasive. What should be emerging from Sano's mouth, of course, are the old-fashioned axioms regarding proper ethical behavior, for it was the duty of the wartime "Sensei" to inculcate morality. Yet the teacher himself, who should be the embodiment of what he teachers, is so drained of all certitude personally that he cannot raise his voice above a whisper. There is a degree of justice in a teacher no longer inwardly convinced about the content of his lectures being virtually struck dumb in front of his class. At the same time, however, there is some ambiguity in Sano's remarks, a tantalizing suggestion that perhaps the problem with the collapse of the old order lies not in the fact that the old-fashioned teachers have lost the ability to talk, but rather that the young generation of students has stopped listening. Clearly they are lacking in respect for their teacher—the hierarchical relationship between intellectual and moral superiors and inferiors has been dismantled; the students now speak to their teacher in the same language they use to one another. "Democratization" is essentially equated with a lack of reverence, and the students' revealing reply to Sano's question "Can you hear me now?"—"Nope. Not a word"—splits the responsibility for the degradation of wartime morality evenly between Sano's unwaveringly didactic generation and the stubbornly iconoclastic youth of the postwar age. Little wonder that Sano no longer knows precisely what position he occupies.

This ambivalence is embodied in Sano's behavior on the train. From our initial view of him—dangling from a step outside the carriage, one foot precariously planted on the train, one hand grasping the handrail—to his open humiliation as a team of farmers working alongside the tracks burst into laughter at the absurd figure Sano cuts, Kojima showers the reader with image after image of a man in total, disjointed shame. The hand frantically gripping the rail is subtly linked to George Sugihara's yearning for a moral stabilizer in the stars on his uniform collar.

The final blow to Sano's dignity, and the most expressive of all his failed attempts at action, comes when he is overwhelmed by an urge to urinate. But there is no point in even attempting to struggle through the crowded aisle to the toilet—in this chaotic, enclosed society, the toilet seat itself is crowded with the bodies of at least seven squatters.

> What it all boiled down to was that this train really had no toilet. When no clever alternatives presented themselves to his mind, Sano yielded to the forces that were pressing in on his hips from either side and lifted up his bottom. His wife spoke up, as though she were cradling a howling, unruly infant.
>
> "Need to go to the toilet? I can't believe you!"
>
> He remained where he stood, fidgeting.
>
> "It's hopeless, professor." The old man's voice was the only sound Sano could hear. "You'll have to wait two more stops. We've got a fifteen minute layover at B Station. You'll have to hold on until then. There's no time to do anything at a little station, and besides, if you vacate your seat everyone'll come diving for it."
>
> "This is ridiculous." Sano's wife was as crestfallen as if this predicament were her own.
>
> "It's no good! I can't hold it anymore! I've got to—!"
>
> Sano scrambled, almost falling—this was no time to be fastidious about trampling on people's feet. He snatched up a canteen that was hanging by the window, yanked out the stopper, and plunged toward his desired goal. Once he had finished, he straightened up, both embarrassed and relieved. But he could not lift his head, and he listened absently, much as though his head were under water, to the derisive laughter of the passengers on the crowded train. [pp. 35–36]

Here the total lack of control over one of the most basic of bodily functions represents what one critic describes as the "absurd state of [Sano's] spirit."[14] And yet, as absurd and loathsome as Sano would appear to be from the manner in which Kojima describes him, there is also a subtle discursive sympathy for his plight. What is to be said about a gathering of individuals—a society, as it were—so suffocating that even the most basic of physiological needs cannot be met without painful humiliation? Sano wishes he could disappear, vanish from the midst of all these people. His innermost shame has now been exposed (as it were) to the eyes of every person on the train. To make matters worse, a man identifying himself as a "spiritualist" proceeds to tell Sano that "deficiencies of the body are all rooted in instabilities of the spirit" (p. 38), and the man launches into a lecture on the new "scientific morality" which he represents.

But every potential alternative to chaos is discredited as the train inexorably makes its way toward the final symbol of hope—Tokyo, the modern city. The spiritualist turns out to be a fraud, and the black marketeer who had befriended Sano and his wife along the way steals all their worldly belongings—including, most painfully, the contraband rice they have hidden in their bags—and flees the train.

Sano's wife reviles him for his ineffectiveness—something she has done throughout the journey:

> "You idiot! You're stingy and filthy, and you have no pride. But you're generous enough to let all your things be stolen. It's a wonder your own body wasn't snatched from you!"
>
> In fact, Sano began thinking how nice it would be if his own body had been taken along with everything else. He was impressed once again at how futile life really was. If I'm going to die anyway, what manner of death should I choose? Death is an unknown, but the world is full of such unknowns. Should I really take leave of it all? To die, and have everything come to an end—the thought did seem somehow cheerless. But if he prolonged his existence even one more second, nothing of any worth would emerge from that second. Should he then flee it all, and let everything melt into nothingness? Thoughts of his two children, of everything were receding into the distance—the passengers, his wife's voice, even her form were fading into a detached realm; and Sano himself was dissolving into a fleeting, shadowy haze, transforming into a veritable nothing. [pp. 53–54]

Yet it seems likely that Sano will be called back to life, by either the grating voice of his wife, or the piglike squeals of the other passengers, or the screech of the train's brakes when they reach their destination. Despite his disillusionment, something within him still clings to existence, however irrational such a posture may seem. Even when life seems robbed of all meaning, he cannot bring himself to abandon the struggle. He is weary and confused, but he will go on living as a "veritable nothing." And likely he will continue his search for some kind of order in his life, just as the Tōkaidō Line train on which he rides will pursue its panting journey toward Tokyo—toward a symbol of the modern age, filled with empty but intriguing promises of new dreams.

In a 1955 essay titled "Nikutai to seishin" (Body and Spirit), Kojima talked about the frustrations of a hopeful spirit betrayed and shackled by an ineffectual body.[15] This is part of Sano's problem in "On the Train"—whether he is dangling from the train step or urinating in the nearest receptacle, the stability for which his soul yearns is continuously thrust out of reach by the overwhelming (and debasing) demands of his flesh.

This struggle between the conflicting components of the human animal emerges again in the 1954 "Bishō" (Smile). Here, in a story he then described as his "most autobiographical,"[16] Kojima adroitly juxtaposes the physical maladies of a son with the related emotional cankers that develop within the father. Once the story has concluded, it is difficult to determine which is more of a cripple—the paralyzed boy or his spiritually handicapped father.

Kojima in "Smile" probes to the roots of human relationships, searching for the sources of parent-child affection but finding considerable egotism and instability there. The narrator is a father whose picture has just appeared in the local newspaper; he has been photographed in a swimming pool crowded with children suffering from infantile paralysis. The caption reads: "A smiling father in the pool."[17]

One of the handicapped youths in the pool is this man's own son, a boy he saw for the first time when he was repatriated after four years on the battlefield. His first thoughts upon seeing his limping son are for himself: "The feeling that flooded over me was not that this was 'my son,' but that this was my 'sickly son. . . .' Even before I felt pity for him, I wondered if I had adequately disharged my duties as a father" (p. 175). Even at their first meeting, the father is beginning to show signs of inner decay: spiritually he is limping as tangibly as his son is physically. He has come back from the war physically whole but emotionally scarred, and looking at his son in his present state is like looking into a mirror. Things are reversed, and the spiritual affliction manifests itself as a bodily handicap in the form of his own child.

So twisted are this father's perceptions of himself and so concerned is he with his own selfish status that he associates with his son as a means of winning the approval of the neighborhood, of demonstrating that he is in fact trying to make up for the lost years. Or more accurately, perhaps, to make up for the loss of himself during the war:

> About a year after we moved to Gifu, we found out that the boy was suffering from infantile paralysis. Essentially this condition could only be cured if the patient received spinal injections within three months of the onset of the disease; after that the only treatment was massage (which also had to be done by a professional). In fact, since my son had problems with one leg and one arm, they told me at the hospital that there was probably something amiss in his brain, meaning that nothing could have been done from the very beginning. . . . When I heard this diagnosis from the doctor, I felt a profound sense of relief. It was no longer my fault. It wasn't even the fault of the disease. It was the fault of the war that had fostered malnutrition. Since the war was to blame, we ought to consider ourselves lucky that he was even alive, I told my wife. I said this to her not to console her, but rather to bolster my own feelings of relief. Thereafter I often took my son out to play. I was wary of a self who would not do so. But I did not pity or grieve for the handicap of my son as he walked along; rather I sought to atone for my lack of love for him by showing others that I could take him out and endure their gaze upon me. [p. 177]

One of the distinguishing features of Kojima's narrators, as exemplified by this father, is their almost total inability to comment upon the events and feelings with which they are intimately involved. It is, in fact, a very cold intimacy between actor and actions. Kojima's writings are distinguished by a breakdown of the evaluative, judgmental level of discourse. It is as if the author has lost all his authority. The analytical portions of his characters' brains seem to have malfunctioned—information enters into the system, but it is not digested or sifted. Instead it is reflected back into the outer world, in the desperate hope that some sort of final judgment will be rendered externally. Thus all thoughts and feelings of the character are directed outward; hesitant feelers are sent out to determine whether thoughts or feelings are either socially acceptable or "shameful" (one is reminded of Yamada's perpetual refrain in "The American School"—"Oh, *shame*ful!"). Because of the moral vacuum they find within themselves, Kojima's narrators cannot find internal justification for their actions, and thus constantly seek some external approval system. Their problems intensify when no system readily presents itself.

In the passage from "Smile" quoted above, the father displays and apparently feels no affection for his son. As detached observers of this relationship, we could easily rush to judgment on this man. To an extent, no doubt, Kojima expects that of his readers. But the clear irony of a story in which a child's physical handicaps echo the emotional handicaps of his parent impels us toward a less hasty evaluation. For whatever reasons—be it the war, the defeat, or any other combination of factors—this father has been cut off from paternal emotions as sharply as he has been severed from any internal standards of moral judgment. The problem of his son—a problem doubly ironic in that his physical impairments seem to originate in his brain—is one which he cannot evaluate as a parent. He has, after all, arrived on the scene too late to be a true father. His personal experience, centered most recently on the war, has not trained him to confront circumstance in a fatherly way. The expectations of his wife and his neighbors are that he behave as a parent—and it is this that causes him anxiety and leads him to beat his helpless son. His sense of overwhelming relief at learning that the boy's disabilities have nothing to do with his own shortcomings as a father stems not from a hope that he can now relate to the boy but from a realization that the people around him will no longer hold him personally responsible. So long as he can superficially satisfy the expectations of the neighborhood—by taking the boy out to play—he has been able to protect the fragile shell of his ego, the single slim defense perimeter he has established between himself and the outside world.

One night the boy wets his bed, and the father, with some inner sense of relish, beats him for it. When the mother, now pregnant with a second child, comes in to stop the senseless punishment, her husband turns on her and his fingers close about her throat. Unable to blame himself for anything that has happened to him or anything he does, he turns against everyone and everything. She kicks him and screams, "What the hell are you doing!!" That voice echoes throughout the remainder of the story. This father cannot understand his own violent actions; it is as though they are being forced on him by some external power. Time and again he has to stop and ask himself, "What the hell are you doing!!" But he can never come up with an answer. The violence that has spilled forth into his own house baffles him. Never once in four years of military service did he raise a hand against anyone, friend or foe. Now, when he has left what should have been a violent battlefield and returned to a home where peace should prevail, he has suddenly turned vicious. It is as though his entire world—his values, his emotional perceptions, his sense of right, his affections—has been turned inside-out. Living in fear of death every day in the army and yet surviving unscathed, he seems at a loss how to behave in an everyday family situation. He is still at battle, defending and fending for himself, unable to care for anyone else. The only moral code he has been taught is self-defense and self-preservation; now that such a code is no longer necessary, he can find no other guidelines to direct the course of his everyday existence.[18] Because his crippled son is so much like himself, he lashes out at the boy at every possible opportunity, as if to punish himself.

Like Shimao's Maya, this young boy seems more tolerant of his father's spiritual infirmities than his father is of his physical limitations. When the father asks, "Would you like to get better, son?" the only response is an enigmatic, almost accusatory smile. "I wanted to understand the meaning of that smile," the father muses. "I felt as if I had been knocked right out of the ring each time I saw that smile of his" (p. 182). The boy's senseless smile irritates his father; it is as though the son can read his father's thoughts and has penetrated into the secrets of his heart.

At his wife's insistence, the father reluctantly takes the boy to the YWCA, which is holding swimming classes for victims of infantile paralysis. As usual, he is more concerned with his own position than the boy's: "I wondered how I appeared to the others. I was much more concerned about that than I was about my son" (p. 185). He is embarrassed by the boy's deformed hand and tries to force him to keep the hand in his pocket. When the boy screeches in agony, the father catches himself, wondering, "Am I the only one here that does this kind of thing?" (p. 186).

When swimming instruction begins, the father retreats to the safety of the spectator gallery—he does not want to be in the water with his son. There his gnarled perceptions again become manifest. He is annoyed to see his son frolicking in the water, as though he were not sick at all. Most irritating is that smile on the boy's face. It sours his father's disposition; he cannot allow his ailing son the luxury of a smile, when he himself cannot muster one.

The swimming instructor invites him into the pool. Conscious of the social mask that he must always wear, he reluctantly agrees, but once in the pool he avoids approaching his son. Instead he helps the most infirm boy in the group. Again he is angered that the boy seems to depend so much on him, but people are watching, so he smiles and praises the boy for his efforts. He glances over at his son and reflects:

> No matter how hard I tried, I could no longer think of him as my own son. There didn't seem to be room for me to squeeze in between him and his instructor. I was sure that if I went over to him, this boy who was struggling so hard to float would sink to the bottom of the water. [p. 187]

The scars he has concealed in his heart and brought back with him from the war have in effect contaminated any normal relationship that this father might try to establish. He realizes that he cannot help his son, because he does not know how to help himself. If anything, he is a hindrance, and any efforts he might make would only cause his son to sink.

Just at that moment of realization, the father hears someone call to him to "Smile!" Mechanically he turns and smiles, and a flashbulb pops in his eyes. The next morning, the picture of the "smiling father in the pool" appears in the newspaper.

The irony in this story is stinging. Kojima relentlessly examines the emotional warping that has rendered this father incapable of expressing honest emotions; everything is a fake, a fraud, like the hypocritical smile he gives the camera. The father's smile is revealing, reverberating as it does off the enigmatic smile his son always gives in response to questions. When the father's grinning face is captured by the photographer, it becomes permanent evidence of the thin masks worn by both of these characters. Their smiles conceal their humiliation, their confusion, their inability to interact on the social level, while still retaining their earnest desire to form some kind of communicative link with those around them. The boy's smile may simply be pathetic; the father's is tinged with both ineptitude and guilt. Absent when his first son was born, he has not been taught how to behave as a father. And it would seem that, coming back to the moral uncertainties of the postwar climate, he is unable to learn parental skills on his own. In a broader sense, he has lost the ability to relate to anyone, so tormented is he by his inner sense of collapse. Like so many other Kojima characters, this father has lost his grasp on the basic tools needed to repair his life, and he does not know where to look for new ones.

IF I were to attempt to isolate a single element common to Kojima's writings that seems to me to be his most expressive motif, it would be the element of "structures." In many cases, these are actual, physical buildings—the military barracks, a prostitute's house, a teacher's dormitory, the American school, a new home for the family. Occasionally it is an enclosure that serves, for all intents and purposes, as a dwelling-place—here I am thinking of the confining, all-encompassing train car in "On the Train." At other times the structure is more metaphoric, such as the scaffolding of stars that George Sugihara builds for himself.

In virtually every instance, Kojima's characters are engaged in some act of "building." Very often, as in *Embracing Family* or "Uma" (The Horse, 1954) this is an actual physical process of creating a structure. At times it is more an attempt at accommodating oneself to one's surroundings, as in the war stories or "On the Train." But Kojima's fiction conforms closely to the structuralist's theoretical idea—that every act of construction is simultaneously an act of deconstruction. For even as we watch his characters braving the elements to build (Sano dangling from the train step; Shunsuke in *Embracing Family* erecting a Western-style house), the discourse overlaying the storyline enables us to witness a simultaneous, painful collapse taking place within the characters and their personal relationships. Thus, even as Sano finally pulls himself onto the train car and establishes a miniature domicile for himself and his wife, his insecurities and fecklessness are eating away at his ego, transforming him into a "veritable nothing." He is left with a home, of sorts, on the train, but no self to inhabit it—a fate congruent with those of Shimao's solitary wanderers and Abe Kōbō's urban vagrants.[19] Similarly, George in "Stars" stakes his own sense of identity upon his burgeoning faith in the structure of social hierarchies which he has erected for himself, but it is a system destined for collapse, like a tower of precariously stacked dominoes. Often, in fact, the struggles of these characters to build protective structures in the face of overwhelming destructive forces appears as ludicrous as the construction efforts of the Three Little Pigs.

The varied and subtle shadings of this structure-building are brought together with skill, humor, and humiliation in Kojima's best-known story, "The American School" of 1954. This is a masterfully ironic tale of an entire nation struggling to "rebuild" itself in the wake of gross humiliation, realizing only vaguely at best that the reconstruction effort too is embarrasingly inept. Kojima here draws on his personal experiences as a teacher of English to create vivid portraits of the less than confident members of a conquered race. By so doing, he has set down on paper the frustrations of the postwar Japanese populace. Blending humor and humiliation in a delicate balance, Kojima crawls alongside his characters as they grovel upon the ground, subservient but determined to preserve a vestige of dignity.

The builders of the new nation are many and varied in their sense of structure. The character in "The American School" with the closest kinship to his creator is Isa, a "shy but spirited little man"[20] who has chosen English instruction as his life's work, and who would rather die than have to utter a single word of English in conversation with native speakers of the language. Only in Kojima's satirical world would such a man become part of a group of Japanese English teachers who are selected to demonstrate their pedagogical skills at the paradisiacal American School in Japan. Isa's blueprint for construction is simple—run and hide; avoid all but the most vital contacts with the Americans.

In sharp contrast to Isa is the vigorous, samurai-spirited Yamada, whose greatest concern is to impress the Americans and prove that the Japanese, defeated but undaunted, can excel at English or anything else they set their minds to—that they can, in fact, build a better nation by copying the Western model. In many ways Yamada is reminiscent of Captain Inoma in "Stars" or the bogus spiritualist in "On the Train." He is a man always on the lookout for the new currents in society so that he may be first to ride them. He brags that during the war he had lopped off the heads of over twenty foreign prisoners of war. Yet now, after the defeat, he has quickly sought out a new way of life, and has latched on to the inevitable swelling interest in spoken English. Kojima cynically draws the character of Yamada, yet he seems a bit envious of those who can adapt themselves to shifts in the social tides. Isa is not so flexible; in the changing currents he paddles frantically to keep from going under, but he cannot easily follow the mainstream, not even when it is the only sensible path to take. There is surely profit to be had during the Occupation for those who can communicate in English; but Isa is not confident enough of his talents or sure enough just what kind of person he should be to take advantage of the opportunity. He is a traveler without guidebook on the long road that leads from the prefectural office to the American School, and he stumbles and complains of shoes too tight all along the way. His journey is in every sense a metaphorical one, the pilgrimage of a lost soul who has turned his back on one discredited blueprint for social behavior and who now travels toward—but has not yet reached—a new, imported series of construction codes that have yet to be tested. Kojima's characters are all travelers away from home who have yet to reach their longed-for destination. The road to modernity lacks those comfortable inns where the weary sojourner can rest his head.

Michiko, a female English teacher who makes the pilgrimage to the American School with the group, is something of an uneasy compromise between the two extremes of Isa and Yamada. This is most clearly indicated by the shoes they wear. Isa's are Western-style shoes, borrowed, forced upon him against his will, actually; and they torture his feet. He cannot easily accommodate the new ways, and the road he must travel toward the American School is therefore very painful. And though Kojima does not specifically tell us the kind of footgear Yamada is wearing, it is not difficult to imagine him in American army boots—just the sort of thing Inoma traded for his insignia at the end of "Stars." Michiko is the compromise: she wears high heels as part of her official uniform, but when it comes to making the trek on foot to the school, she has brought along a pair of comfortable walking shoes. Yet in her eagerness to borrow Isa's humble chopsticks at the end of the story, she stumbles on her high heels and creates a scene that leads to the banishment of Japanese teachers from the school. She thus stands—and falls—midway between Isa and Yamada, a middle ground unusual in Kojima's fiction.

Isa takes a trip he did not want to take so that he can speak a language he does not want to speak. At one point he cries, "It's a disgrace to speak a foreign language perfectly. And it's a disgrace to speak it imperfectly, too!"[21] Clearly there is no escaping disgrace. When he finally stumbles his way to the American School, wearing borrowed shoes that crimp his feet, he is forced to give a demonstration of spoken English that he does not want to give. Only a fiercely stubborn determination to keep doing something that he does not want to do keeps Isa going. These contradictions in his character make Isa a ridiculous figure, but they also make him believably human.

The physical description of the American School to which the Japanese teachers finally struggle is expressed in appropriate hyperbole:

> At the center of a large tract of land traversed by neat rows of houses stood the long-awaited school, an almost solid wall of glass on the side facing south. The fields that once occupied the site had been leveled away without a trace. An American observer would not have found the compound remarkable, much less luxurious. But the solid houses planted sparsely over the landscape, the spacious bedrooms illuminated by lamps even in broad daylight, the young Japanese maids attending to the needs of American babies—all of this was clearly revealed at a glance, and impressed the weary visitors as a vignette of some heavenly dwelling place.[22]

This is a landscape quite unlike those normally described in the literature of the Third Generation. The immensity of the compound, the "neat rows of houses" and "solid wall of glass," the "solid houses" with "spacious bedrooms" all connote an ideal, a "heavenly dwelling place" which these road-weary, dust-covered Japanese can never hope to qualify to enter. The problem, however, lies not with the economic extravagance of the Americans but with the emotional and physical impoverishment of the populace.

"The American School" is in many respects the story of all Japanese after the war. It is a tale of a people put into a situation not of their own choosing, of a nation forced to act out an embarrassing, farcical role under the careful scrutiny of a more powerful, more wealthy foreign supervisor. The story will likely remain the most significant statement of the humiliated but determine Japanese psyche following the Second World War.

The dual acts of temporal building and moral dismantling are carried out in viciously amusing detail in "The Horse," published the same year as "The American School." In this story of a man driven literally and figuratively by his wife to build the house of her dreams, Kojima not only emasculates but ultimately even dehumanizes his male protagonist. In its portrayal of moral castration and eventual dehumanization, the work may initially seem misogynistic. It strikes me, however, that the wife, Tokiko, is really only a neutral agent in this entire process. Kojima's focus is entirely upon the breakdown of the husband; he surrenders his prerogatives rather than having them snatched from him. Tokiko is no more at fault for the dismantling of her husband than America is to blame for the degraded moral sensitivities of the English teachers in "The American School."

"The Horse" effortlessly floats between reality and hallucination; everything is fluid, particularly the relationships between husband and wife and the roles they adopt. Tokiko, the dominant, self-confident wife, is pictured as the individual in control of the family. That is a result not of her thirst for power but of her husband's abrogation of his responsibilities.

On the one hand, the narrative path of the story traces the progress of the house-building, from the day when the husband arrives home late at night and stumbles over some building materials stacked outside their door—his first indication that a rebuilding is to take place—until the splendid new structure is complete. At the same time, the discourse subtly delineates the dismantling of the husband piece by piece.

When we first meet the husband-narrator, he has just tripped over the stacks of wood. It is, perhaps, no accident that we first view him stumbling; images of Michiko staggering uneasily between new-style high heels and old-fashioned chopsticks come to mind. But he proceeds to introduce himself to us as "I, who am the master of this house" (shujin de aru boku). There is a disjuncture here, and we cannot help wondering why the "master" is unaware of the plans to remodel. One additional irony, subtle though it may be, is the sustained use of "boku" (an informal male colloquial pronoun) for the otherwise nameless narrator. There is a linguistic deconstruction here as well as a moral one. "Shujin de aru boku" is, in a sense, a contradiction of terms from the outset. While in modern usage "boku" carries no overtones beyond the male "I," in origin it refers to a servant, giving us "the servant who is a master." Kojima suggests in this manner that his narrator is not anywhere near the master of his destiny that he might consider himself.

The process of transforming master into true servant begins when "boku" begins to doubt that he is in charge of the house construction.

> When I woke up the following morning, Tokiko had gotten up before me. That was unusual, and I heard a faint clamor coming from the yard, so I peered out a hole in the rain shutters. Several workmen were standing in my yard. Their backs and necks looked strong and manly. The way they encircled Tokiko to receive their instructions reminded me of the wartime. I doubted my eyes, wondering if I had turned into Tokiko, and if the person standing outside was in fact a man—me. But I knew that I was myself by looking at the note by my pillow—"Have breakfast and hurry to work . . . Tokiko."[23]

Just as the orders for construction are issued by Tokiko (who is called "danna"—another term normally reserved for the male head of the household—by the workmen), so "boku's" orders for his daily regimen are issued by his wife. Again, it is his own inability to formulate and follow through with plans that draws her into the void. He is operating his own life without blueprints, and it is up to Tokiko to provide some. But he balks at the idea of having anyone take over responsibility for his actions. This produces his ambivalence and his accompanying moral paralysis.

When Tokiko tells him that he will have a room of his own on the second floor of the new structure, he ponders:

> So I suppose I will end up sitting on the second floor of this house. But thanks to the house, I'll have to work so hard for the next several years that I won't have the time to even sit down there. I imagine that so long as I am alive, and Tokiko is alive, and as long as there is open space on this lot, that she will come up with a third and fourth plan for reconstruction. So what does that make me? And just what is this house that keeps growing larger and larger? [p. 244]

It seems clear that "boku" feels left out, superfluous because he has assumed himself the rightful master of the house without ever determining how to behave as such. His definition of "master" derives exclusively from the fact that a house exists; there is nothing within himself that defines who he is or how he is to conduct himself. He is constantly asking Tokiko absurd questions such as "Who is building this house?" to which she responds, "Why you are, silly!" "Ah, yes," he will reply, as though he has been reconfirmed as the one in control.

His status as master continues to deteriorate; late in the story, after Tokiko has announced that the grandest room in the house is going to be used as a stable for a friend's prize horse, "boku" comes to the realization that he himself is inferior to the incoming animal. The evidence for that has accumulated over the course of the story. Tokiko, he recalls, has "worked [him] like a horse" and "cracked the whip" over him for over three and a half years; during that time he has not been able to "look her in the face." He has "trotted around" trying to make enough money to keep up with her demands. Now he discovers that it is not his income at all, but the rental they will receive for lodging the horse that is actually going to pay for the addition to their house. "Boku" has become completely superfluous; indeed, he doesn't even have a name in the story, while the horse is called by the grandly masculine name of Gorō.

As Gorō moves in and takes over the house and Tokiko's love and attention, "boku" declines in status. He has descended from being "shujin de aru boku" (I who am the master) to "boku to iu yatsu" (the thing known as I [p. 266]); from there he concludes that "I am a somehow ridiculous animal" (Boku wa nanika orokana dōbutsu to iu tokoro da [p. 271]).

A second role reversal has taken place. The "man of the house" has been shifted first to a subordinate role, deferring to his wife, and then to a position roughly equivalent—or inferior—to a domesticated animal. In fact, it is clear by the end that the "horse" referred to in the story's title is not Gorō but Tokiko's confused and pathetic spouse. "Boku" takes Gorō out for a ride, hoping to display his superiority to the animal.

> I was overcome by the bizarre feeling that I had become the horse, and that I was racing along carrying Gorō on my back. . . .

> I gritted my teeth, but in an instant I was flying through the air. My eyes began to swim, and I went hurtling into a pond. [p. 273]

Gorō, the new "master" of the home, later chases away an intruder, while "boku" wonders if he should check back into the asylum until Tokiko's second-stage plans for the house are completed. The intricate interweaving of construction and dismantling in the story is, on the surface, a biting critique of the "mai-hōmu shugi" (homeownership ethic) that swept over Japan during the economic recovery. More important, however, it is a chillingly satirical evaluation of the status of the Japanese patriarchal order. The nation may be rebuilding itself economically, Kojima observes, but there is a concomitant dismantling of the moral structure of the people that renders the entire undertaking hollow and pathetic. Perhaps the most unsettling aspect of the situation is the fact that the breakdown has occurred at the most critical level—in the relationship between husband and wife. "The Horse" is a precursor to the more profoundly disturbing *Embracing Family,* but it stands on its own as a uniquely original consideration of the shifts in postwar Japanese society.

Clearly each of Kojima's early stories treats one aspect of the frustration and ambivalence of characters in modern Japan. "On the Train" is the story of a man weary of life, yet unable to release his hold upon it. A similar character appears in "Smile"—a man who lives with almost unendurable shame, unable to love even those closest to him (perhaps because he cannot love himself), but still smiling for all around him to see. Isa of "The American School" leads a life that is distasteful, but he is determined to go on living it on his own terms. "The Horse" documents the dehumanization of an utterly superfluous husband.

Consistently Kojima has written of the socially handicapped, attempting thereby to comment on the personal dislocations that have accompanied the rapid, painful transformations in postwar Japanese society. There can be little doubt that Japan has undergone at least two major traumas in the last century or so. The first, of course, occurred in the wake of the Meiji Restoration of 1868, when the feudal society that had existed since the beginning of the seventeenth century was rapidly overturned, and Japan was opened up to new ideas and technology from the West. As unsettling as this political and industrial upheaval might have been, most disturbing in the lives of the people was the uncertainty ushered in by the rejection of prevailing moral codes and a hesitant search for new guidelines.

The first major work of fiction to deal with this widespread anxiety over the modernization process—and, in fact, the work that has earned the title of "Japan's first modern novel"—was *Ukigumo* (The Drifting Clouds), written between 1887 and 1889 by Futabatei Shimei.[24] Futabatei was a taciturn intellectual and a translator more intimately familiar with Russian literature than any of his contemporaries in Meiji Japan. Though his *Ukigumo* is stylistically uneven, it represents the first serious attempt in modern Japanese literature to confront the questions raised by the nation's fast-paced, essentially uncritical importation of Western "things." All the characters in the novel "drift" in one way or another, but perhaps the most confused and indecisive is Bunzō, a young man trained in the outmoded Confucian moral literature who finds himself in a society haphazardly shifting away from the traditional moral codes. Bunzō finds himself in several situations that require decisions, but his insecurity in the new environment renders him totally incapable of choosing a proper course of action. His personal ambivalence—particularly in contrast with the ambitious, enterprising nature of his friend Noboru (literally, "the Climber")—is emblematic of the frustrations that beset Japanese society in the early Meiji period.

If *Ukigumo* is the novel that best represents the anxiety that accompanied the first overturn of traditional Japanese morality with the coming of the Western "barbarians," the work which most vividly captures the unsettled mood of the "second opening of the country" during the American Occupation years is Kojima's 1966 novel, *Hōyō kazoku* (Embracing Family). The parallels between the two novels are numerous. Both detail the inability of a central character to cope with the situations that most intimately concern him; in each instance, this stagnation is the result of the undigested assimilation of foreign ideas that jar against the deeply rooted traditional moral values. Both novels are written in a strikingly immediate colloquial language—Futabatei's work the result of a conscious attempt to produce a new literary style, Kojima's a constriction of descriptive passages aimed at placing the reader's entire focus on the dialogue. And each novel ends on a disconcertingly—but completely appropriate—inconclusive note, with the protagonists unable to make up their minds at crucial junctures in their lives.

There are, in fact, some remarkable similarities in temperament between Futabatei and Kojima. A contemporary wrote of Futabatei:

> He was extraordinarily pensive (what psychoanalysts would call introverted). He was scrupulous, unsparing, and critical of everything, and would never decide an issue easily. He was generally argumentative and cautious, to the point of being irritating, yet there was a strange kind of charm in his stubbornness.[25]

Kojima's reputation in Japanese literary circles closely mirrors that of Futabatei's; his rather forbidding melancholia and his habit of verbally lacerating even his closest associates left him a loner, and he has admitted some days to feeling "rather like a telephone answering service."[26]

More important than the private similarities between the two novelists, however, is the congruity displayed in their novels. Both *Ukigumo* and *Embracing Family* are harrowing chronicles of the Japanese reaction to the social turmoil initiated by Western visitors. There is no criticism of the foreign element as such; Kojima and Futabatei have their eyes firmly riveted on their own countrymen, and on the response to the new morality that threatens to be no guide to conduct whatsoever.

In *Embracing Family,* Kojima carries his view of postwar Japan to its logical conclusion, reducing the pathetic struggle for survival to its lowest common denominator and stripping human relationships down to the most basic of levels. That common denominator is the home itself. Kojima's eyes are fastened upon a single family in this novel, and not once does he allow himself to be distracted. *Embracing Family* concerns itself more relentlessly with interpersonal relationships than virtually any other Japanese novel of the postwar period, prompting the critic Etō Jun to label it one of the few truly "anthropocentric" novels by a modern Japanese author.[27] As in Albee's *Who's Afraid of Virginia Woolf?* human interaction takes precedence over setting; descriptive passages have been pared to the essentials, and on the rare occasions when the scene actually shifts to outside the house, it is only to follow its occupants on their tentative, brief, and generally unsuccessful ventures into the outside world. Dialogue lies at the core of the novel; it has more conversational passages than any other recent Japanese work of fiction.[28] The extensive use of dialogue effectively draws the reader's attention to the characters and their interaction by eliminating extraneous distractions.

Kojima is not the first Japanese novelist to allow minimal diversions from his study of the home. Shimazaki Tōson attempted a similar examination in his semiautobiographical novel *Ie* (Family, 1911; trans. 1977). But Tōson had nothing of the satirist about him, and Kojima's ability to laugh at the predicament of his protagonist sets him apart from the somber, confessional approach Tōson used. In any case, this almost fanatical focus on the home does not narrow the significance of *Embracing Family;* on the contrary, by shining light into each dark corner, Kojima has unearthed revelations about the family that have universal significance.

In simplest terms, *Embracing Family* is a story of destruction, and of unsuccessful attempts to prevent it. The aroma of decay issues forth from the protagonist's home, and the feeble struggles of the "head" of that home to hold it together provide both the humor and the pathos. Kojima makes it clear in this novel that the frustrations of modern individuals are not simple products of the physical state of things; the crisis extends beyond the humiliation of having to urinate on a crowded train or of speaking a foreign language with less than native proficiency. The feckless indecisiveness of contemporary men and women threatens to erode the foundations of the home, according to Kojima. When that rotting force advances too far, the most rudimentary of human associations fall to pieces. It is no accident that the questions asked in *Embracing Family* are of the simplest variety: what is a husband? A father? A man and wife? What are they supposed to be to one another? Kojima's response to all these questions, horrifying as it may be, is the equally unadorned: I don't know.

The nonhero of *Embracing Family,* Miwa Shunsuke, is Kojima's most effectively conceived ineffectual character. Shunsuke is a man of education, of reason—a university professor. He is the contemporary incarnation of Bunzō, the equally cultured, equally confused antihero of Futabatei's *Ukigumo.* Because he has translated some foreign works into Japanese, Shunsuke is considered communicant with the most recent, "enlightened" ideas to come to Japan from the West.

There are multiple levels of irony in the name which Kojima has selected for his protagonist. The family name, Miwa, literally means "three circles," a possible intimation of the adultery which incites the action of the novel. At first glance, the three circles would seem to have no correlation with the members of the Miwa family, since there are two parents and two children. Yet later in the novel, when Shunsuke's wife is dead, he counts the survivors and comes up with only two; then he realizes he has forgotten to include himself.[29] Shunsuke identifies so completely with his wife, and derives so much of his direction from her, that one could well argue that there are only three individuals within this family. And, of course, there is also the potential that Kojima intended the name to conjure up humorous images of the "three-ring" circus which the Miwa household seems at times to resemble.

"Shunsuke" is an appropriately old-fashioned-sounding name for a pedant. The "Shun" element means a person of "uncommon talent," even a genius. Though Shunsuke considers himself to be impeccably up to date, in contrast to the stodginess of his name, it is only on the superficial level of the intellect that he has truly come to terms with modern society. Just as his native Japan has on occasion borrowed foreign institutions and material technology but chosen to ignore their philosophical and moral underpinnings, Shunsuke has made Western-style learning his life's work without making the requisite internal emotional adjustments. In his perceptions, in the deepest recesses of his sensibilities, Shunsuke is still "old-fashioned." Though he longs to be a part of the modern, "liberated" society that the Occupation has introduced, inwardly he is no better prepared to cope with the traumatic "second opening of Japan" than Bunzō was to deal with the first. He is scissored between the old ways of thinking and the new way of behaving, and therefore effectively cut off from both. His inability to be totally traditional or exclusively modern robs him of the ability to act. He has no footing in either realm, no justification for the decisions he knows he should be making at critical junctures in his life. He handles problems with simple stop-gap tactics, treating the symptoms but not the disease eating away at him and his family.

Clearly the "genius" is intended sardonically; yet I suspect an even more ruthless implication to the name. The predominant usage of the "Shun" character in Japanese is in compounds that refer to some kind of intellectual or moral prowess. But a second significant semantic usage is in combinations that specifically involve horses—*shunsoku* is a swift horse, while *shumme* or *shumba* denote a horse of superior quality. Given the prominent role which horses play in many of Kojima's works (from the opening passages of "On the Train" to the middle section of *Wakareru riyū* [Reasons for Parting]), I cannot believe that this is a coincidental echo. Although no horses actually make an appearance in *Embracing Family* to challenge Shunsuke's authority in the home, he feels just as subhuman as "boku" in "The Horse." Or perhaps it would be more accurate to say that George, the American marine who stays at the Miwa house and invades their bedroom, serves the same metaphorical function as the horse in the earlier story.

As I have suggested in my discussions of the shorter works, Kojima's central concerns seem to be largely architectural. But the literary act for Kojima entails labors both of creation and of demolition. There is a central physical structure in *Embracing Family*—the house which belongs to the Miwa family. It is a dominating structure throughout the novel, the focus of each family member's dreams, frustrations, and plans. The house at times seems to govern even the syntax of the narrative—when Shunsuke makes reference to his dog, the discourse never describes the animal as "Shunsuke's dog." It is invariably "the dog which belongs to his house." Perhaps it is inaccurate to refer to this, as Etō Jun has done, as an "anthropocentric novel"—to a large extent, the house itself has taken over the position of protagonist vacated by Shunsuke. In any case, the constructive elements of the novel center upon the family's attempts to rebuild their house; at one point they tear one house to the ground and begin erecting a new structure on a different plot of land.

As in "The Horse," the actual planning and building of houses comprises a large portion of the narrative concern in *Embracing Family*. Of equal significance in the novel is the act of "housecleaning." Underscoring the attempts of the Miwas to resolve family crises by tinkering with their external environment, both Tokiko and Shunsuke are preoccupied with dust, as though attention paid to removing dirt from their house will somehow cleanse their spirits. Much of their time is spent agonizing over the difficulty of acquiring good cleaning women. In fact, the main housekeeper in the novel, Michiyo, is the syntactic focus in the opening passages of four out of the five sections that comprise the novel, and she is again brought out in sharp relief at the book's conclusion. She underscores the Miwas' disproportionate, ironic interest in surface cleanliness even as their home is collapsing internally.

Already in the opening sentence of *Embracing Family,* Kojima creates a subtle yet vital correlation between Shunsuke's house as a physical structure and its metaphorical identity as his spiritual refuge; simultaneously, he warns of the fall to come:

> Miwa Shunsuke thought, as he often had before, that his house had gotten dirtier since the housekeeper Michiyo had started coming over. [p. 5]

Regarding himself as an authority on contemporary familial relations—an ironic assumption that Kojima blasts apart early in the novel—Shunsuke has reasonably concluded that, amid all the turmoil of modern society, his home is the one sacrosanct place where he can be safe, where he can rely upon the intimacy of his relationships with his wife and two children, where he can be free of the dust of the chaotic world.

But in his opening sentence, Kojima lays bare two elements that threaten Shunsuke's dream of security. One is the befouling of his temporal home by a very real dust, which soon will be emblematic of a more profound profanation of all that Shunsuke holds sacred. The second is the intrusion of an "outsider," someone external to the family who has nonetheless become an accepted part of his home. Michiyo, the individual entrusted with the cleaning of the house—yet the one who has dirtied it in Shunsuke's eyes—is responsible for introducing yet another alien element into the Miwa home: she arranges for the family to meet George, a 23-year-old American soldier who soon becomes a frequent visitor in the home. George serves as something of a catalyst, calling attention to the shaky foundations of the Miwa abode.

Kojima swiftly moves to the crux of his story. While Shunsuke is out on a lecture junket, preaching about enlightened family relations in the modern era, his wife Tokiko hops into bed with George. Shunsuke learns about the affair from none other than the "cleaning" woman, Michiyo. Though by virtue of his learning he should be able to react in a calm, rational manner, in fact his response comes directly from the pit of his emotions. He has been wounded in his most vulnerable spot, and all thoughts of intellectual rationalization are swept away.

> Shunsuke went outside and waited for Tokiko to return. As she came around the corner, her eyes on the ground, Shunsuke ap-

> proached her and said, "Go into the house!" He wanted to get her inside the house as quickly as possible. Shunsuke followed Tokiko into the house and pushed her from behind, shoving her onto the sofa.
>
> "What have you done?" he asked.
>
> "What do you mean?" Tokiko said, getting up to her feet.
>
> . . . Now what should he say? What should he do? The answers to these questions had not appeared in any book he had read, and no one had ever taught them to him. [pp. 12–13]

Shunsuke is morally unequipped to deal with this frontal assault on the dignity and sanctity of his home. The only countermeasure that occurs to him is to get Tokiko inside the house as quickly as possible. He seems to think, as Shimao's husbands often imagine, that the home itself is some sort of protection against the outer world. Once he has gotten Tokiko inside, however, Shunsuke still has to deal with the problem. Since his old-fashioned code of ethics has been trampled underfoot by the new enlightenment, all he can fall back on is his book learning. But he has not read how to deal with an adulterous wife, particularly one who responds to his accusations with an abrupt, indignant, "You really mustn't scream at times like this" (p. 13). His inability to cope leaves him drained, and he is at Tokiko's mercy. He is so unsure of himself—of his rights and duties as patriarch, or simply as a human being—that Tokiko deftly turns all his accusations back against him, until he almost feels like the guilty party. Tokiko is obviously the dominant figure in this relationship; she has stepped in to fill the power vacuum when Shunsuke has found himself unable to take hold of the reins of family control.

The retreat of Shunsuke from the role of patriarch connects with the most intriguing feature of the discourse in *Embracing Family*. Much of the agony, frustration, and confusion that await the reader of this novel can be traced to the style of narration which Kojima has consciously adopted. Although we remain largely at Shunsuke's side throughout, there is an extraordinary degree of discursive reticence on the part of the narrator. We are fed primarily facts and thoughts, not impressions or feelings. We are bombarded with information but given no narratorial evaluation. And most tellingly, we are pelted with direct, vital questions of "meaning," but we are never provided with answers. Let me give one example:

> Why hadn't he ignored what was going on between Tokiko and George and allowed them to continue the affair? Since they'd slept together once, what difference did it make if they continued? What would have happened if they had gone on together? She probably would have grown more and more distant from her husband, as she had said herself. And what would each separate assignation with George have been like? Undoubtedly, as she had also said, she would have derived sheer pleasure from each of them. Ah, he should have let her be fully satisfied, instead of having her remain in a relationship with her tongue-tied, ill-natured husband.
>
> The shelves and desk in his room, the cushion, the bedding spread sloppily on the floor, and the splash-pattern kimono he was wearing—what did all these things mean to him in reality? When he had made the shelves, Tokiko had interjected her opinion. They had bought the desk from a salesman who showed up at their doorstep one day with a desk strapped on his back. He had come in through the garden, just like the man who came selling flowers. The flowers had been planted without Shunsuke's knowledge, and continued to blossom there. That must have been early in the spring. And then the desk salesman had come. Shunsuke had arrived on the scene just as the salesman was cutting the price for Tokiko. And the bedding—one day Tokiko had decided to restuff the futons, and a man from the futon shop came with a large bundle of cotton tied to his bicycle. [p. 49]

Shunsuke has no difficulty conjuring up questions about himself and his relationship with Tokiko, but he cannot find answers within himself, and he does not know any other sources to tap for guidance. Virtually all the tasks of his life up to this point have been handled by Tokiko—from the building of shelves to the purchasing of furniture and the stuffing of futons. Now that her adultery has disqualified her in his eyes as a source of values and judgments, he has nowhere else to turn. And there is no narrative voice to provide answers.

We are left, then, in very much the same situation as Shunsuke. Kojima has provided us with a nescient narrator, a dethroned god of discourse who has nothing to tell us. Kojima's hesitant storyteller no longer has the courage to believe in anything—not the characters, not the external facts, and certainly not himself. Thus he can only line up events in their proper chronological order, providing us with the kinds of external information given in the passage above but not deriving any sort of conclusion from it. Just as Shunsuke has been stripped of his prerogatives as a husband, so the narrator has been robbed of his traditional authority.

This leaves the reader with an enormous void in the discourse, which must either be ignored or be filled from private resources. The latter process entails a tremendous emotional investment in a novel. It is the sort of investment required by a stage play, but perhaps even more demanding, since a theatrical production is "built upon an ironic structure of spectation in which disparities of word and deed are quickly observed, so that what is enacted is privileged over what is recounted, 'appearance' over 'explanation.' The spectators are . . . active interpreters of a dynamic process."[30] Kojima certainly provides the sort of dramatic "appearances" that one encounters on the stage, and the structure of the novel and the mode of discourse expose these same gaps between word and deed—or, in Shunsuke's case, between word and nondeed. Unlike dramatic performances, however, the novel form does not allow any active interpretive interplay; the reader assumes all responsibility for interpretation.

In *Embracing Family,* Kojima places the entire burden of his story upon the external, rational level of fact and event—a process which is, I would suggest, an implicit condemnation of his characters who have attempted to "order" their lives through the creation of superficial structures. ("What I'm trying to say is that Westerners are logical," one young man in the novel insists. "Compared to them, Japanese are temperamental, imprecise, and prone to temporizing." To which Shunsuke replies, "The things we have learned from the West give rise to a wealth of contradictions. The ripples from those waves spill over into our homes" [p. 139]) Reliance upon those structures can only lead to disappointment and collapse.

The ironic gap separating reader from character is clear in the differing expectations which are formed around the various acts of construction. Tokiko, for instance, has cosmetic surgery several times in an attempt to beautify her body, but the procedures have produced the opposite effect:

> As he laughed, Shunsuke remembered that Tokiko had had plastic surgery done on her face several times. The last had been

about three weeks before his departure to the United States; she underwent the procedure in order to get rid of the deep creases in her cheeks so that she could see him off at the dock. When she returned home from the doctor's office, she removed the mask and showed her face to Shunsuke. In place of the creases, her cheeks were now ludicrously swollen from the injections.

Later, she had her teeth fixed. Because the treatment failed, her mouth came to look like that of a different person altogether. [pp. 44–45]

Because of these warnings over minor reconstructions which Tokiko instigates, we anticipate larger failures when more massive building projects are undertaken by this family. Thus we are several steps ahead of the Miwas in realizing that their new, Western-style home will not provide the sorts of comforts, physical or emotional, that they anticipate. It comes as a significant shock to Shunsuke and Tokiko when their house, which resembles "a country villa in the highlands of California" (p. 69), is a leaking, disaster-plagued architectural nightmare, but we have already anticipated this outcome. Such ironic foreknowledge makes it doubly painful to encounter passages of the following nature:

At some point, Shunsuke had come to envision a paradise in this new house.

Husband and wife swim and frolic together in the pool. Locked in each other's arms, they tumble onto the lawn. They lie there for some time. Each layer of fat on her flesh seems to be pressed against his own, but in his fantasy, both Shunsuke and his wife have slimmed down and appear incredibly fresh and young. . . . Then the bedroom—he wants to pick her up and carry her like a child. Even though she must weigh as much as he does. Everything seems ten times rosier than when they were twenty years old. I'll mutter sweet nothings in her ear. Nothing boisterous for me—just quiet chatter. Talk of the future is too cheerless. We'll talk about the distant past, before we even met each other, or gossip about how badly things are going in someone else's household. That would be fun! [pp. 53–54]

The silence of the narrator is deafening at this point, as throughout the novel. However unworthy of respect Shunsuke may seem for his indecisiveness, the purity and simplicity of his yearnings for unity and a family which he can "embrace" are touching. The scrupulously nonjudgmental discourse compels us to make radical shifts in our attitudes; in the above passage, the patent absurdity of Shunsuke's fantasies and his reliance upon a pool to resolve conflicts in his marriage invites our scorn. But the stern refusal of the narrator to label Shunsuke a fool lures us into a position of ambivalence—in one sense, replicating Shunsuke's wavering judgments. By withdrawing his narrator—and withholding his authority as author—Kojima has placed his readers in a position remarkably, and painfully, similar to that of Shunsuke.

Thus, in *Embracing Family* Kojima has expanded the private catastrophe represented by the adultery in the novel. Tokiko's infidelity nullifies the contract established between herself and Shunsuke at marriage, and the breaking of that bond renders Shunsuke unable to function in his traditional position of authority. Because he has depended upon Tokiko as the source of his values and identified himself with her so utterly, the loss of that voice of authority in his life virtually emasculates him. In similar fashion, the contract that has traditionally united reader with author in the novel genre—a contract in which ultimate decision-making power was deeded to the author—is rent asunder by the nescience of Kojima's narrator. As readers we are left to our own devices, to stumble at times, either to assume authority for the discourse ourselves or to join Shunsuke in his pathetic attempts at meaningful activity. I would suggest that the difficulty which some readers have had appreciating the quality of Kojima's work lies in their lack of preparation as participants in literary discourse to assume so much responsibility on their own. In any case, our response to the discursive reticence of *Embracing Family*'s narrator will likely resemble Tokiko's challenge to Shunsuke: "You said you'd be giving the orders from now on, that we should just do what you said. But there's no listening to the kind of orders you give. You wrote me a letter and said that when you came back from America, you might be a little different, but that was a lie. Now again you're telling me to do what you say, but that's totally beyond your capability. You make cheap promises, but I won't be deceived by them anymore" (p. 43).

Kojima carries the dismantling of Shunsuke's individuality to an extreme unprecedented in Japanese fiction. In stark contrast to the burgeoning ego within Joyce's work, which "spread[s] out to include the 'inanimate' rivers, rocks, and trees of Dublin and the world,"[31] the ego in Kojima's writing, embodied here by Shunsuke, shrinks into virtual nonexistence (as it had with Sano at the end of "On the Train"). Shunsuke, after his emotional/moral severence from Tokiko, becomes so completely isolated from his environment that he trades places with the "inanimate" objects of nature. The rocks and trees in Shunsuke's garden are given life, imbued with human-like qualities, and sent forth in this new act of creation to multiply and replenish the earth. But Shunsuke, the "creator" of this new world, must retreat into a position of inanimacy and watch the ecstasies of nature from a jealous distance.

In a scene which Kojima has described as the crux of *Embracing Family,* the slender threads that have tied Shunsuke to the other members of his family are finally severed, and he is cast adrift to wander in complete isolation. No longer certain where he stands in relation to anyone, he has lost the ability to judge how he should act toward anyone. The labels "husband" and "wife" and "father" and "mother" lose all meaning—people are reduced to neutral "men" and "women" who have no connection with one another. Shunsuke witnesses this final collapse of human bonds when he awakens the morning after his limp confrontation with Tokiko and steps out into his garden.

> Why did he peer into the garden at such times, when it held no interest for him? Why did he gaze at it when he was bewildered, as if it would offer him some assistance? In this garden were Himalayan cedars, Indian lilacs, plum trees, azaleas, horse chestnut and persimmons. There were crimson flowers on the Indian lilac.
>
> For some reason beyond his comprehension, Shunsuke lacked any interest in his own possessions. That time he had driven Tokiko to say, "I'm not your belonging!"—had she meant that he had never shown interest in any of his belongings?
>
> But now Shunsuke's interest was aroused by something different. The Indian lilac has blossomed, he realized. Three, then four swallows alighted in the garden, and pecked away assiduously at the ground. The time was ripe for the water lilies in the bowl to open their blossoms. Two dogs were sniffing about on the opposite

> side of the hedge; one of them belonged to his house. The surrounding houses seemed to lie one atop another, as though he were seeing them through a telescopic lens. Did flowers experience some sort of ecstasy when they were pollinated? Did they feel the same sensations as a man and woman locked in a tight embrace? Certainly they must, Shunsuke thought with envy.
>
> Why, even clods of earth and stones must enjoy the fulfillment of ecstasy. If that is the case, then what of the faithless Tokiko and me—what manner of creatures are we? In point of fact, what am I myself?
>
> There was water in the bowl. Why did he feel anxious about this water? Why was the insignificant water there in the bowl—or rather, why did he think it was there? [pp. 21–22]

Shunsuke's plaintive question, "In point of fact, what am I myself?" is never answered. Kojima does not pretend to be a prophet; in the relativistic fictional world he creates, such answers are not to be unearthed. That gaping, empty spot is the source of great frustration and unhappiness for the residents of his world. Shunsuke can only look on with envy at the ecstasy that pervades the dumb realm of nature. The plants in his garden, the birds, even the stones themselves seem to be capable of forming and sustaining emotionally charged relationships with one another. Shunsuke, though, is reduced to peeping voyeuristically at this coupling, jealous that he is denied the same ecstasy. But perhaps this is because the beasts and the inanimate "creatures" of the world do not have to struggle with questions of identity and moral principle; they merely *exist,* and do not have to probe for self-understanding. Shunsuke can wonder but never know why he is denied an equal measure of simple joy merely because he is a human being. The consolation that communion with Nature brought to earlier generations of Japanese writers has been taken from Kojima and his contemporaries. Their task has been to find a suitable replacement, or to conclude that none is ever to be located.

All Shunsuke's attempts at action end inconclusively, and he is reduced to total ridiculousness. What he longs for is to be able to look up and see someone in the judgment seat, some being who can pronounce final sentence upon Tokiko for what she has done, and thereby release Shunsuke from the agonizing position of wanting to judge her but lacking the capability to do so. Previous generations gazed up and pronounced that judgment seat empty; but Shunsuke cannot even muster the self-assurance to lift his eyes above his own dehumanized level. There is no more tragedy in the world, Tokiko assures him; if modern literature has taught us anything, it is that all these seeming crises are merely pratfalls in a human comedy (p. 37).

The essence of this comedy, as I have mentioned, lies in the paradox of house-building countered by the internal collapse of the family. That moral deconstruction is mirrored on the narrative level by Tokiko's development of breast cancer. In fact, not long after they take up residence in their farce of a home, Tokiko dies. The ordinary novel would end at this point,[32] but Shunsuke still has the remains of a home to look after, two children who must be cared for. The collapse moves forward at breathtaking speed. While Shunsuke's friends are trying to line him up with new marriage prospects, his son Ryōichi is preparing to move out of the house. Shunsuke has been so busy thinking up new temporary repair stratagems that he has not noticed that his home has already crumbled. Or perhaps he never really had a home. True, a house has been built, and some attempts have been made to bring about harmony. But there never seems to have been any point of emotional convergence between the members of the Miwa family from the very beginning. Shunsuke has not had the strength or the understanding to create a family unit that could withstand the assaults from a new society. He has tried to become a part of the modern world only superficially, wanting all its advantages but prepared to cope with none of its weightier challenges. He has tried mightily to draw his wife and children to him in a "family embrace," but his arms have not been sure enough or secure enough to hold them there for long. By losing sight of himself, this "modern" man has lost everything of value—except, of course, for his garish, unmanageable Western-style house.

The novel ends without Shunsuke realizing that he holds only thin air within the comforting embrace of his arms. Michiyo comes into Shunsuke's bedroom in the middle of the night to announce that Ryōichi has left home.

> "Left?"
>
> "I heard noises at the front door, and when I went to see what was going on, I found this letter from him. But I think it's better for him to leave home and see what life is like."

Shunsuke pushed Michiyo out of his way and went to Ryōichi's room.

Then he peered through the window at the dark, spacious veranda that he had scarcely ever set foot on. His heart began to pound furiously. He went down the stairs and put on his shoes, preparing to go outside. As he started out, he ran into the large glass door at the entrance. Many guests had made this mistake, but it was the first time Shunsuke had done so.

"Maybe Noriko will be next. . . ." But he doubted that Noriko would leave home; still. . . . When he went outside, Shunsuke ran down the slope. The dog began to bark. "I'll throw Yamagishi out of the house. No, first Michiyo. . . ." [p. 147]

This ending, with Shunsuke's mind racing from one useless plan to another, eerily echoes, in both style and syntax, Tokiko's aimless manner of planning the rebuilding of the Miwa house.[33] The juxtaposition painfully demonstrates the hopelessness of relying upon another human being for standards of judgment but also underscores Shunsuke's desperate need to do so when all other values have been eliminated.

Reading *Embracing Family* is a desolating experience. Because Kojima has so relentlessly maintained his focus, the repeated hammer blows against the Miwa house begin to echo within the reader's own head. Perhaps this is because it is so easy to identify with Shunsuke, and to recognize that the growing pains of modernization are not monopolized by the Japanese. But their case does perhaps provide a sample of rapid, total change as it came with the defeat and the American Occupation. It is inevitable that George will be identified with the Occupation forces, Tokiko with the rising women's consciousness, and Shunsuke with the decline of paternal authority. Certainly Kojima intended for such parallels to be drawn.

But *Embracing Family* is most moving if it is read as a personal chronicle of one man's home, and of the decay that sets in when his feeble plans for his family are buffeted by the winds of change that blow against it. Likewise it is a tale of what happens to a man who cannot commit himself to a specific course of action, when decisions will inevitably mean the survival or death of his home. Miwa Shunsuke is trapped in the middle of modernization by his own ambivalence. He has rejected the traditional Japanese lifestyle that betrayed him during the war; his education has taught him that it was faulty.

He has surrounded himself with the outer trappings of modern society, but he has not made all the necessary readjustments in thinking that accompany their adoption. He is trapped between the two poles, and when catastrophe strikes, he can neither revert to his old way of life nor welcome the new. He is lost, a blindfolded boxer swinging wildly in the dark, never landing a blow on his unseen—perhaps nonexistent—opponent.

Through all his fiction, Kojima has focused sharply on his characters' tenuous grips on life. He has often exaggerated the portraits of his struggling, handicapped protagonists, stretching their imperfections out of shape with caustic, satirical glee. But however feebly his characters may attempt to hold onto the ruins of their lives and their personal relationships, there can be no question that their creator is in firm control of his medium. No contemporary writer in Japan has as boldly twisted and molded the novel form to suit his personal needs. Kojima, for all his claims that he is a crippled individual, has demonstrated in his writing a healthy grasp of literary technique. His style may, in fact, be the last handhold he can cling to.

VI

Salvation of the Weak: Endō Shūsaku

Endō Shūsaku, a recent photograph

. . . The foolishness of God is wiser than men; and the weakness of God is stronger than men. . . . But God hath chosen the foolish things of the world to confound the wise; and God hath chosen the weak things of the world to confound the things which are mighty.

—1 Corinthians 1:25, 27

THE ROLE of the Christian writer in Japan has always been rather anomalous. Japan is widely recognized as a buffer zone between Eastern and Western civilizations, a conglomerate society that has joined the industrialized powers of Europe and America but retained a decidedly Asian suspicion of an organized, exclusivistic religion like Christianity. Though the Japanese acknowledge that a great deal of benefit has accrued to their nation from the presence of hard-working Christian missionaries, a faintly foreign "smell" (which they identify with cheese and butter, somehow) continues to hover over the religion itself. Christianity, like English literature, is one of those diversions that schoolgirls may be permitted to dally with like dolls while they are young. But once they have matured, they are expected to leave all such things behind. Questioned about their reaction to Christianity, typical Japanese are likely to say that they feel a good deal of "distance" from it.[1]

The Japanese author who has most keenly experienced that distance himself and devoted the greater part of his literary output to the examination of what it means to be a Japanese Christian is Endō Shūsaku. If he qualifies for membership in a generation of Japanese authors who have largely concentrated on the losses of the modern period, it is on the basis of his struggle to accommodate himself to the conflicting demands of his national origins and his adopted religion. Endō has never been completely at home either as a full-fledged Japanese or as a card-carrying Catholic. Unlike some of his countrymen, who have chosen to ignore the conflicts between the two, Endō has recognized that Christianity is weighted down with a burden of cultural associations derived from European tradition, and that he has been expected to bow down to these associations just as if to God. But Endō has been a Christian unable to accept the narrow strictures of Western-style Catholicism, and at the same time a Japanese equally incapable of living with the absence of a sense of sin and guilt in his native society.

Endō's tastes in literature as a child give some indication of these personal conflicts. One book which he read as a youth, continued to pore over during the war years when others were turning to propaganda writings, and still carries with him when he travels abroad is the early nineteenth-century picaresque novel, *Tōkaidōchū Hizakurige* (Travels on Foot on the Tōkai Highway, 1802–1822; trans. as *Hizakurige,* 1929). Authored by Jippensha Ikku, *Hizakurige* is a sprawling, ribald travel adventure of two ne'er-do-wells, Kita and Yaji, who pass from one rollicking episode to another in their journey along the highway. The humor in the novel is slapstick and slightly coarse—not unlike much of the humor in Endō's own writings—but the main characters are endearing.

Endō's observations about the novel are worth noting:

> Here we have two men unable to live in the provinces, yet unable to settle in Edo either. Yaji and Kita are men without roots, no matter where they travel. That is why they had to set out on their journey. . . . Those of us who, even though we are Japanese, cannot bring ourselves to plant our roots firmly into the soil of modern-day Japan, and yet who are not total strangers to the place, cannot help but think of our own plight as we watch Yaji and Kita plod along through the rain down the Kiso Highway. In the broadest sense, these two men who cannot live either in the provinces or in Edo, may indeed be us ourselves.[2]

It is no coincidence that many of Endō's characters find themselves in the same predicament as Kita and Yaji, caught between tradition and modernity, East and West. Nor would it be an exaggeration to say that Endō himself feels like something of a hybrid, trying to find soil in his native land that will nurture the buds of Christianity which he has imported from abroad.

A typical member of the war generation, Endō has felt trapped in the "middle" of social change in Japan, but in ways totally unlike Kojima or Yasuoka. Kojima, scissored between duty to country and a pedagogical devotion to the "enemy" language, emerged from the war with a pessimism since leavened only by a grudging admiration for those who continue to struggle in the face of overwhelming absurdity. For Yasuoka, the battle was between his native indolence and clumsiness on the one hand, and social demands for vigorous action on the other. The literature that grew out of his experience pitted the solitary clod against every form of social oppression, with the sluggard inevitably doomed to failure. Unlike his two comrades, however, Endō never served in the Japanese army; the language he was assigned to study in his school days was German, an allied tongue; and despite his own disclaimers to the contrary,[3] Endō never experienced the continual humiliation that Yasuoka underwent for his inability to do anything correctly.

Endō's conflicts were waged in a more abstract arena, where he found himself caught in the middle of a struggle that he never sought to engage in. He no more intended to do battle with the spiritual foundation of Western civilization than Kojima expected to stare into the vortex of human absurdity when he began his study of English. Endō was an unlikely warrior in this battle. A self-styled weakling, his temperament is more that of a prankster than a priest, his inclinations more gaudy than godly, his humor more indebted to Yaji and Kita than to the Passion plays. However uncomfortable he may have felt personally with the unwanted albatross of Christianity strung about his neck, though, he pursued the contradictions in his life with unflagging energy. While Kojima grappled with the relative "I" and found him elusive, and while Yasuoka and Shimao kept their eyes riveted upon the unpredictable "them," Endō's focus was on the eternal "He," a superior being who observes the acts of men with sorrowful eyes. Endō's struggle, in a sense, led to the creation of a Japanese *Pilgrim's Progress,* a travel journal in which his own spiritual searching provided the materials for his fiction. There is a long and rich tradition of travel diaries in Japanese literature, but Endō has been among the first of modern writers to map out a spiritual course of progress.

Endō has created a "drama" within the novel form, a central

conflict resulting from the clash between man as God expects him to be and man as he really is. The conflict can be seen in the early story "Iya na yatsu" (Despicable Bastard, 1959; trans. 1984).

The story revolves around the ambivalent cowardice of a character familiar in Endō's literature—the diffident sort who knows for certain that he will abandon all principle if he is ever subjected to physical torture. This dread of pain is almost unique to Endō in his generation; those who actually served in the army developed a near-immunity to beatings and physical discomfort. But Endō, always poised on the brink of pain but never plunged into it during the war, developed a fear of physical torture that runs through all his fiction. Not until he actually experienced intense personal agony resulting from his long bout with lung disease did his fear give way to compassionate concern for those too weak to stand up for what they believe.

Egi, the "despicable bastard" of the title, is one of a handful of non-Christian students at a Catholic dormitory in Tokyo during the war years. Forced against his will to participate in a charitable visit to a leper hospital at Gotemba, Egi is subjected to further torment when someone suggests that the students play a game of baseball with the patients.

> "Egi, you're up to bat next," someone called. From the corner of his eyes, Egi saw a thin derisive smile appear on the lips of Iijima, who was watching the game just off to one side.
>
> When Egi picked up his bat and started for the plate, Iijima walked up beside him, as though he were going to suggest a batting strategy.
>
> "Hey, Egi," Iijima whispered perversely, his breath smelling foul. "You're afraid, aren't you? You're going to get infected!"
>
> Egi resolutely swung his bat. It connected firmly, and the white ball went sailing into the distance. "Run!" someone shouted. Frantically, Egi rounded first base and continued running, but the first baseman had already caught the ball from the third and had started after Egi. Caught between two bases, Egi suddenly realized that the hand that would touch him with the ball belonged to a leper. He stopped dead in his tracks. "Keep going!" he told himself, and sprinted off again. The first baseman threw the ball to the second baseman. When he got a close-up view of the second baseman's receding hairline and gnarled lips, Egi's body was no longer willing

to respond to the promptings of his conscience. He stopped, hoping to be able to dodge his opponent, and looked up nervously at the approaching patient.

In the patient's eyes Egi saw a plaintive flicker, like the look in the eyes of an abused animal.

"Go ahead. I won't touch you," the patient said softly.

Egi felt like crying when he was finally by himself. He stared vacantly at the infirmary, which now looked somehow like a livestock shed, and at the silver fields beneath the overcast sky. And he thought, "Thanks to my fear of physical pain, I'll probably go on betraying my own soul, betraying love, betraying others. I'm a good-for-nothing, a wretch . . . a base, cowardly, vile, despicable bastard."[4]

Many of the fundamental elements of the drama which Endō has pursued throughout his career make an appearance in this passage. The story itself is spare and simple. Plot is a means rather than an end, a sturdily constructed scaffolding upon which Endō hangs the more ephemeral concerns of his writing. There is a familiar, even popular tinge to virtually all Endō's stories; by rooting his narratives in common soil, he is able to attract the attention of readers who might have little interest in his metaphysical concerns. Plot functions rather like the New Testament parables, relying upon the elements of the earth in order to convey insights into the essences of heaven.

In his recognition that plot can offer its own intrinsic rewards while serving higher purposes, Endō has much in common with the finest narrative craftsmen. As Robert Scholes has observed, "the proper way for narrative artists to provide for their audiences an experience richer than submissive stupefaction is not to deny them the satisfactions of story but to generate for them stories that reward the most energetic and rigorous kinds of narrativity. It is possible, as Shakespeare knew, to provide some plain satisfactions for the simple or the weary, while also rewarding those who are ready to give a narrative the fullest attention of their mental and emotional powers."[5]

It is no accident, and no misinterpretation, that Endō is widely regarded as a "popular," even middle-brow writer by many Japanese readers. He offers "plain satisfactions" through his stories in a manner that few of his contemporaries have been able to rival. In stories as direct as "Despicable Bastard," dime-novel plots as easygoing and predictable as *Kuchibue o fuku toki* (When I Whistle, 1974; trans. 1979), and travel adventures as rousing as *Samurai* (The Samurai, 1980; trans. 1982), Endō is able to placate not only the weary but also the wary, the simple as well as the skeptical. If in fact the art of storytelling hinges upon the ability to draw the reader into a narrative with the bait of familiarity and then lead the way to a higher plane of understanding in the realm of the new and unfamiliar, Endō qualifies as a master storyteller.

In "Despicable Bastard," Egi finds, as do so many Endō characters, that he is caught between the earnest desires of the soul and the wretched weakness of the flesh. Caught between bases—a perfect metaphor of his inner dilemma—his physical paralysis mirrors his emotional palsy. One part of him—the "narrative," earthly part—seeks only to run, to get away from this frightening situation. But another part—the "discursive," transcendent aspect of his nature—agonizes over the pain he is causing the leper and, finally, his own conscience. Egi does not have within himself the power to resolve this conflict, and so he must remain in a middle ground where only some extraordinary, unexpected act of compassion can resolve his dilemma. The words of the leper at second base, "Go ahead. I won't touch you," reverberate off Jesus's words to Judas: "That thou doest, do quickly." In a later story, Endō suggests that Christ, knowing "all the desperate acts of men," could no longer endure the torment Judas was going through, and "was overwhelmed with compassion" (p. 79) as he spoke to his betrayer.[6]

The guilt that accompanies such an act of compassion implies that Egi's pain is not assuaged by unwarranted forgiveness, merely transmuted. There is no escape from the middle ground for him, and he must always endure the taunts of those, like Iijima, who hound him with "derisive smiles" and mock him with their foul-smelling breath. These jeering figures wind through Endō's fiction, serving as constant reminders of the lure of the secular world, the seductiveness of moral cowardice. The chief torment for characters like Egi is that they have seen a fleeting image of a better life, even if it is constrained within the rotting body of a leper. Egi inveighs against himself with a stream of curses, perhaps, because he recognizes that he is an inversion of the leper's soul—his own putrefaction lies within, concealed by a body that appears whole.

While on the one hand this story transforms into literature some of the moral crises Endō faced personally as a Catholic during the war years, in a broader sense the story captures much of the sense of bewilderment, ambivalence, and loss that his generation confronted. They were presented with alternatives that seemed equally repugnant, and they remained unable to commit themselves to any specific course of action. Unlike the story, however, when the call to arms came for most, there was no one to look on sympathetically and say, "Go on ahead. I won't touch you." They were all touched by the war, wounded emotionally by it. For Endō those wounds were only intensified by his feelings of cowardice and his lukewarm adherence to the enemy religion.

To summarize, then, Endō entraps his characters in a neutral zone between the concerns of the flesh and those of the spirit, and there he impels them to battle. The clash, as in "Despicable Bastard" or *Chimmoku* (Silence, 1966; trans. 1968), may be between moral principles and physical cowardice. Or it may be between East and West, dogmatism and materialism, as in *The Samurai*. In any case, the struggle on this middle ground produces few if any clear-cut victories. What it does provide is the sole opportunity most of these characters will have to receive communications of the spirit, to hear the voice of God. Only at the point where body and spirit seem about the tear apart from one another does God break his silence. This I will deal with in more detail in my discussions of *Silence* and *The Samurai*.

This spiritual battleground is reflected in the inherent duality of the mode of narration as well. The plots are secular, the discourse celestial. It is a literary approach which Endō has fashioned both from his personal encounter with Christianity, in which he has found himself in the midst of a cultural and religious conflict with his heritage, and from his experiences of the war years as a member of the "senchū-ha," the generation caught "in the middle."

Ironically, the polarization of the war years drove Endō to embrace Christianity more fully than he had in his youth. Under the influence of a Catholic philosopher, Yoshimitsu Yoshihiko, who was his dorm master at Keiō University, Endō decided to study French Catholic literature as a means to understand foreign attitudes and to comprehend what Christianity meant in his own life. The influence of Mauriac, Bernanos, and Julien Greene is evident in his own fiction, as well as the distinctive mark of Graham Greene.

Endō was given the opportunity to pursue his studies firsthand in 1950, when he and three comrades were selected in the first group of Japanese to go abroad for study after World War II. The four Japanese were loaded into the cargo hold of a French passenger ship along with a score of armed black African soldiers. In Manila and Saigon, where the Japanese were still considered war criminals, the "exchange students" were interrogated at gunpoint. After docking in Marseilles, Endō was taken off for questioning by customs officials who believed he was Filipino trying to get into France on a false passport; only when a French teacher of Japanese was called in and Endō demonstrated his ability to read a textbook in elementary-school Japanese was he allowed to enter the country.

It was yet another experience in isolation; he began to sense the presence of vast "walls" separating him from the mysteries of European Christian culture.[7] Moreover, as he pursued his studies, he became increasingly cognizant of gaps between himself and the writers he was examining:

> I could not shake the gnawing feeling that a great gulf lay between them and myself. Each time I read their accounts of their religious conversions, I got the impression that they felt they had "returned home" when they accepted Christianity.
>
> Being Japanese, though, I could not feel inside myself that embracing Christianity was any kind of homecoming. And none of the writers I studied had anything to say about the agony endured by the stranger to Christianity.
>
> The more I studied Christian literature, the wider the gap between me and these writers grew. It was not simply a feeling of distance from Christianity, but a distance from the entire culture of a foreign country. . . .
>
> I was able to make friends with many of the French people, but no matter how long I remained there, my studies seemed to run into a massive wall, and gradually I lost the desire to go to the classroom.
>
> From that time, I gave thought to becoming a writer. For I felt that I had run across a theme that I would need to pursue my entire life.[8]

That theme, of course, was the "agony of the stranger," the vast gulfs that separate the Japanese and those brought up in a Western culture steeped in centuries of Christian tradition. During his time in France, Endō gradually came to feel culturally inferior to the Westerners he met. The symbol of that inferiority was his own yellow skin, which he concluded was dirty, less pure than the gleaming skins of the Europeans. In his early fiction, white represents a clearly formed religious philosophy, a distinct commitment to Christianity, and an implicit rejection of less exclusive religious philosophies. Yellow is a murkier, less clearly defined color representing the pantheistic tendencies of the Japanese, their willingness to live by situational ethics rather than unflinching moral standards, and their lack (as Endō sees it) of guilt feelings.

Endō's best-known early works, in fact, set up this contrast very clearly. He received the Akutagawa Prize in 1955 for *Shiroi hito* (White Men), a rather graphic tale of betrayal and faith in the French Resistance during the German Occupation. In this short novel, the demarcation lines between right and wrong are clear-cut, and those characters who choose to collaborate with the Germans do so with full knowledge of the moral weightiness of their actions.

The companion work to *White Men,* however, is set in Japan, and here these distinct lines of acceptable behavior are blurred. *Kiiroi hito* (Yellow Men, 1955) is set in a world that is, according to its author, "without God" and therefore "devoid of drama."[9] Wartime Japan provides the backdrop for Endō's tale, which is full of contrasts between guilt and apathy, faith and agnosticism, West and East—all these contrasts represented in literary terms by the distinctions between the white skins of the French priests laboring in Japan and the yellow skins of the Japanese parishioners.

A young apostate Japanese Christian, Chiba, feels a sense of affinity with a French priest, Durand, who has been expelled from the church after an affair with a Japanese woman. Chiba had been baptized as a child, and had obediently tried to ally himself with the faithful flock; in his youth he had even joined in and thrown pine cones at the apostate Durand. But as he grows up and gives in to the impulses that tear him away from the church, Chiba comes to see a link between himself and Durand. Both have turned their backs on God and indulged their fleshly lusts.

What Chiba does not understand until after Durand has died and he acquires the Frenchman's diary, however, is that the two men have responded very differently to the path their lives have shared.

Chiba, like Kimiko, the nonbelieving Japanese woman who sleeps with Durand, has committed his "sins" without a trace of compunction; his conscience is as unruffled as Kimiko's face, which Endō describes as "small, flat . . . with no shadows, no depth. No sadness, no hatred, no emotion whatsoever appeared there."[10] Chiba's sense of guilt is equally flat, equally devoid of ripples. He writes to his former parish priest: "For a yellow man like me, your high-flown concepts of guilt and nihilism and the like simply don't exist. . . . All that I feel is fatigue, only a profound weariness."[11]

Durand, on the other hand, though he longs for nothing more fervently than to be able to share the yellow men's apathy toward God, cannot stifle the eruptions of his moral conscience. His daydreams are filled with visions of the plagues poured out on sinners in the book of Revelation, and in agony he cries out: "Though I have betrayed God, I cannot deny His existence." Durand comes to understand the clouded eyes of the Japanese, numb to the concept of sin and unmoved by the prospects of punishment after death. But he cannot share their complacent, oblivious peace, and after he tries unsuccessfully to drown out the cries of his conscience by betraying the parish priest to the Japanese military police, Durand commits suicide.

The apostate—particularly the apostate foreign priest—plays a central role in Endō's fiction. These characters are, in a sense, assigned the function of mediators. One of their tasks is to bring the lofty, "distant" doctrines of Christianity down to a level that can communicate to the Japanese—in a sense, to break down the walls that surround the neutral field of battle. They stand midway between the harsh brightness and clarity of Western Christianity and the muddied, shadowy impreciseness of the Japanese ethical code as viewed from Endō's perspective. Fallen priests like Durand are, then, in much the same spiritual position that Endō has found himself—a partaker of the Christian grace, but one who doesn't quite fit into the mold designed for Western Catholic laymen, a literary heir to the whiskey priest in Graham Greene's *The Power and the Glory.* They are characters with both feet stuck in the "mud swamp" of Japanese ethics as Endō has described in it *Silence,* but their spirits continue to yearn for the Christian heaven. Driven to apostasy by their encounter with Japanese spiritual apathy, these foreign priests end up the mirror-image of how Endō has described himself—a

Japanese forced to dress up in an ill-fitting suit of Western-style clothing. Durand (along with Rodrigues in *Silence*) is a foreigner dressed up in a kimono with skirts too short to cover his mud-stained legs.

Perhaps the most painful experience with near-separation in his life came for Endō when he contracted a serious case of tuberculosis on a trip to Europe in late 1959. He was there to further his research into the career and works of the Marquis de Sade, a figure who has continued to fascinate Endō because of the passion ignited in his rebellion against Christianity. It is such passion, such human "drama" that Endō insists is missing in Japanese society because it lacks a concept of God. But during his studies in France and several other European nations, Endō fell ill and was hospitalized shortly after his return to Japan. It was the second time he had had to leave the West because of a life-threatening illness. In the last novel to center around the conflicts between East and West, *Ryūgaku* (Foreign Studies, 1965; trans. 1989), Endō writes of a Japanese scholar who tries to penetrate the thick wall of Western culture but instead returns to Japan a disheartened, sick man. He has struggled to understand the red blotches on the walls of the Marquis de Sade's ruined castle, but ultimately he has not been able to comprehend the fervor—both positive and destructive—that Christianity has aroused among the peoples of the West, and the quest defeats him.

The attitudes of this weary scholar perhaps best characterize the literary struggles the Endō was undergoing at this point in his career. He had undertaken a precise—perhaps too precise—description of the insurmountable walls separating Japan from the Christian world, and his characters came to seem trapped within their isolated state of limbo beyond the reach of literary grace. His own long stay in the hospital, however, wrought a number of changes in Endō's attitudes toward literature. Prompted perhaps by thoughts of the proximity of death that would be the final separation between himself and his family and work, Endō's thoughts turned from the static depiction of walls to the more clearly dramatic demolition of them. By 1963, after three major operations had excised one of his lungs, Endō's own writing turned to the removal of barriers separating his characters from salvation, or at least resolution between body and spirit. There is a new compassion, a new search for ways in which the apostate can be accepted.

Perhaps the first critic to recognize this change in Endō was Saeki Shōichi, who wrote in 1973:

> [Endō's early writings] are if anything a little too clear-cut, too coherent. They lack the dull resiliency of human flesh, the weightiness of a less-than-transparent human nature. His characters responded too readily to the author's commands, and seemed at times like cleverly manipulated marionettes. . . . [Endō] was more concerned with his themes than in the creation of believable human beings in his novels. His characters had to howl and suffer submissively as they writhed beneath the burden of theme that had been foisted upon them. . . .
>
> But Endō is a perceptive critic, and he recognized these faults in his own work. . . . He had clearly matured as a writer after his two and a half years in the hospital.[12]

Endō in these later works continues to describe the agony of those wrenched from their heritage and unable to cope. His novels are still populated with apostate priests, weak-willed martyrs who wish they had been born in an age free of persecution, the ugly and the ludicrous and the pathetic who are trampled on by the world. But now Endō begins to suggest that the very act of suffering, of enduring the calumnies and assaults of the world, is a sufficient act of penance, and that there is a redemption for the weak who cannot be banner-carriers for Christianity or for any other creed. A new and consistent image appears in Endō's stories after 1963—the sad, compassionate eyes of birds and dogs that wordlessly observe human activities of every variety. Clearly these eyes are a prototype of a divine gaze which sees all the external failings of men but mercifully penetrates to the purity of intent in the hearts of those too spiritually feeble to save themselves. In "Watakushi no mono" (My Belongings, 1964; trans. 1984), the middle-aged novelist Suguro[13] responds to his bored son's request for a story with:

> "One day some children were playing baseball near that grove of trees. The ball went into the trees, and the kids peered into the grove as they scrambled through the grass looking for it. . . . And then they found a man, about your father's age, hanging by his neck from one of the trees. His two unwashed legs dangled down

> from his faded nightshirt. . . . Why did he hang himself? This man, who was so much like your father, hadn't done anything particularly bad. He hadn't failed in his business. He hadn't fought with his wife. So nobody knew why he hanged himself. But there was a dog that peered into the grove of trees with mournful eyes. . . . The End."
>
> . . . Suguro hugged his knees. I'll never leave this wife and child of mine, he thought. His own parents had grown to hate each other and were divorced; but in all likelihood he would spend his entire life beside this woman with the fat body and the exhausted face. He had this feeling primarily because her look of weariness sometimes overlapped in his mind with the face of "that Man." I suppose I will never abandon Him, either. Just as I will not desert my wife, I will not desert that Man, whose eyes have a look as sorrowful as those of the dog that peered into the forest. [pp. 43–44][14]

The juxtaposition and ultimate synthesis of images exemplify the simultaneously contrastive and integrative activities under way in Endō's narrative technique. Carefree children are brought into a confrontation with the swinging corpse of a middle-aged man who has succumbed to despair. The motives for the man's suicide are murky, much like the reasons for Suguro's vague dissatisfaction with his own life. There is no clear distinction made between Suguro and the dead man—in fact, they are consciously compared. What keeps a listless Suguro from merging with the image of the hanging man is the blended images of those around him. The fat, weary body of his wife has a look that reminds him of "that Man." Suguro cannot even bring himself to utter the name of God—the distance he feels from his wife is replicated in his alienation from deity. But the look of sorrowful, somehow compassionate understanding in the eyes of "that Man," of the dog, and of his wife combine to give Suguro the courage to continue his life amidst frustration and bouts of despair. The "walls" separating Suguro from his family, and from God, are penetrated by the doglike gazes that observe Suguro but do not condemn him.

"My Belongings" examines a man's search for inner peace, a peace that can come only if he will take responsibility for his own life—for the mistakes, the sins, the weaknesses, and the hurt he has caused others. By embracing those parts of his life that he can truly call his own, he can arrive at some sort of peace with himself, and can begin to empathize with the follies and shortcomings of others. In this story, Endō is searching from amid the many separations of his life for some kind of integrating force—for a bond between human beings that will bridge the gulf of compassionless sin.

As he reflects on his life, his career, and the marriage that has a dank, foul smell to it—like the wet laundry hanging in the hallway—Suguro discovers that he has exercised very little control over it. Decisions have been made for him by others—mostly his parents—or in defiance of them, but not out of the depths of Suguro's own aspirations. He begins to wonder if there is really anything he can call his own.

In sharp contrast are the lives of two of Suguro's closest acquaintances in the literary world—the novelists Nagao and Mita, both of whom have in their middle years chosen Christianity of their own volition.[15] The surprise announcement from Mita that he has decided to be baptized makes Suguro realize what a minor part he has played in determining the course of his own life. The foreign faith he has adopted was thrust upon him by his mother and aunt; he impulsively decided to marry a woman he really did not love so that he would not have to wed someone selected by his father. Once early in the marriage Suguro had lost control and slapped his bride, telling her "I never really wanted you."[16] An earlier Endō story might have ended on such a note of unresolved despair. But Suguro is driven by a desire to hold on to his meager possessions, even if they have been forced on him by others, even if he has abused them. He is not searching for some abstract, lonely freedom that would come to him if he abandoned the woman he did not want to marry and the Man he did not want to worship. An urge within him longs for something that is his own, for individuals and beliefs he can truly say belong to him. Perhaps the basic choices in his life have been made without his active participation (as they invariably were for the war generation). Fine—his task now is to learn to accept those choices.

As he gazes into his wife's weary, puffy face, it reminds him of another face that has lived with him and helped shape the kind of person he has become.

> Hers was the weary face common to virtually every housewife. But it was, after all, a face of Suguro's own fashioning. It was one

> of his life-works, like the clumsy stories he produced by gathering and blending his materials and impatiently committing them to paper. And behind her weary face, Suguro discovered yet another face of someone he had not really wanted. He discovered the debilitated face of "that Man," a person he had cursed and despised and beaten throughout his days. . . .
>
> When Suguro cursed the Man and declared he had never really wanted Him, sad, doglike eyes peered back at him, and tears slowly trickled down those cheeks. The face was not the imposing visage that the religious artists had painted, but a face that belonged only to Suguro, that only he knew. Just as I will never leave my wife, I will never abandon you. I have tormented you the same way I have tormented my wife. I'm not at all sure that I will not go on abusing you as I do her. But I will not ever cast you off utterly.[17]

When the images of dog, wife, and God converge again at this point, Suguro recognizes the similarities in the scattered components of his life. He understands that an ultimate choice is available to him, the choice of accepting what has become of his life, of embracing the belongings that can therefore become his. He can admit that the weary look on his wife's face is of his own creation, and that the sorrowful gaze of "that Man" is motivated by his own actions. With an act of love, Suguro can lay the foundation for more meaningful contacts with both of these individuals. He can narrow the gap that has separated them for so many years.

It is no simple coincidence that the acts of integration that Suguro attempts here are compared to his work of bringing various materials together to construct his "clumsy stories." The endeavors of his art are identical to those of his religion—to bring order out of chaos, and to provide meaning where none seems available. Endō first defines the ground upon which his characters stand by enclosing it within walls of frustration, cowardice, and selfishness; from there he suggests in subtle outlines the manner in which those walls can be penetrated. He is a Christian writer by simple virtue of the manner in which he impounds and then liberates the souls of his characters, a process which is a literary type of the Christian redemption.

Suguro's struggle is, however, not mere Christianity in kimono clothing. Endō's personal experiences of loss in wartime and in the hospital add a further dimension of contemporaneity to his writings, making Suguro's story more than that of an individual's brush with religion. In his predicament—that of living on terms not of his own making—Suguro is not unlike many Japanese who lived during the war and survived its chaotic aftermath. His religious wrestling seems relevant because it is part of a larger battle to cope with all the unwanted "belongings" in his life. The equation of faith and marriage may not be a perfect one, but the acuteness of Suguro's pain is made the more immediate by the juxtaposition of the two situations. The success of "My Belongings" lies in Endō's ability to make his Christian concerns coherent and tangible for readers with no sympathies for that particular struggle.

"My Belongings" is one of several fine stories from the post hospital period which were collected into an anthology titled *Aika* (Elegies) in 1965. They represent the first step away from the uneasy pessimism of the early works and the first movement toward the redemptive vision of *Silence* and *The Samurai*. The manipulation of characters and the subjugation of psychological development to theme no longer plagues these stories. Endō is writing with assurance in this collection; he probes to the heart of a man's relationships both with his family and with his God. These stories are not essentially "religious," however; they do not attempt to defend or expound some didactic creed. Rather they are stories of men who can relate to their God only to the degree that they can subdue the demands of their own egos and communicate some form of love to those around them.

It is this quality which distinguishes the best of Endō's literary works. A fictional reflection of this quality can be found in "Sono zenjitsu" (The Day Before, 1963; trans. 1984), in which Endō proposes a remarkable affinity between carnal and sacred, a resolution made possible only by profound compassion and forgiveness. As the quasi-autobiographical narrator lies in his hospital bed awaiting what may be fatal surgery, his mind forges a correlation between the *fumie* image of Christ and the mundane pornographic talisman left him by a bedraggled peddler:

> Still vaguely in my mind were thoughts of the small, yellow-edge photographs the peddler had brought in earlier. Just as the shadowy bodies of the man and woman moaned and embraced in those pictures, the face of the copperplate Christ and the flesh of men come into contact with one another. The two strangely resem-

> ble one another. This relationship is described in the book of catechisms that children study on Sunday afternoons with nuns in the rear gardens of churches that smell of boiling jam. For many years I scoffed at those catechisms. And yet, after some thirty years, this is the only thing I can say I have learned.
>
> After [the priest] left, I snuggled down into my bed and waited for my wife to come. Occasionally the feeble sunlight shone into my room from between the grey clouds. Stream rose from a medicinal jar on an electric heater. There was a bump as something fell to the floor. I opened my eyes and looked down. It was the good-luck charm the peddler had given me. That tiny wooden doll, as grimy as life itself. [pp. 79–80]

The harsh distinctions between dogma and everyday experience are obliterated in such a passage. The experience of pain or loss—in the hospital for Endō, rather than on the battlefield—in the neutral zone of human experience leads to a transcendent understanding of the essential unity of all things. By an act of compassion or forgiveness—similar but not equal to that of Christ—the weakest human figure can break free of the prison of ego and qualify for an admirable if not heroic status in Endō's literary paradise. The comparisons in "The Day Before" are stark, yet ultimately convincing. The sacrificed body of Christ is brought into proximity with the naked grappling flesh in the pornographic photos, while the *fumie*—a sacred image defiled by the footprints of apostates—is transmogrified into a worthless wooden doll soiled from the hands of a porn peddler. And yet the world of grimy reality is distinguished by its similarities to the spiritual realm. The church gardens populated by nuns are reflected in the hospital corridors trafficked by nurses. The smell of boiling jam is replicated in the medicinal jar atop the electric heater. And the priest—the mediator between God and man—is replaced by the colorful, endearing peddler who brings the narrator as much consolation in his agony as any religious figure could provide.

The short stories in the *Elegies* collection are in a sense vignettes, *dessin*-like sketches of the weak who must bear the burden of guilt and the throbbing of their consciences. Not until his 1966 novel *Silence* did Endō give these characters a place on a larger stage, expanding their struggles to include questions of cultural assimilation and the foundations of religious faith. *Silence* is the novel in which

Endō at last forges an image of a forgiving, maternalistic Christ who accepts human frailty if—and this is crucial—it is tempered by a compassionate concern for others. This feeble charity is the saving grace for Endō, the ultimate expression of a flickering faith that has the power to forgive a multitude of sins committed by the vulnerable flesh. Likely even the coward Egi of "Despicable Bastard" could be saved through an act of love for the lepers he so fears and despises.

The story line in *Silence* is remarkably simple: Rodrigues, an early seventeenth-century Portuguese priest, learns that his former mentor, Father Ferreira, has submitted to tortures in Japan and apostatized. Unable to believe the story, Rodrigues stealthily journeys to Japan, endures many personal trials, and finally himself succumbs to the tactics of the persecutors. It is, on the surface, a tale of failure. But so, Endō would point out, is the narrative related in the four Gospels. Clearly his concerns lie deeper than the outlines of his surface plot.

Endō in this novel employs a wide variety of narrative voices in a manner that, at first inspection, seems almost haphazard. He shifts from an objective third-person narrator at the outset to letters written by Rodrigues, then back to omniscience, and finally to excerpts from the diaries of a Dutch merchant and an officer at the "Christian Residence" where Rodrigues lives out the last years of his life as a public apostate with a Japanese name and a Japanese wife.

The shifting points of view may seem disruptive at first, but by the conclusion it is clear that the focus does not rest solely upon Rodrigues' dilemma, and that we need to get both inside and outside his head and heart to comprehend what the text has to convey. Although Rodrigues stands at the center of the narrative, Endō is really more interested in Kichijirō, the cowardly apostate who reappears time and again in the novel to effect a gradual but unmistakable change in Rodrigues' heart. Kichijirō is essentially what Rodrigues becomes at the conclusion of the drama. Once again, as in the *Elegies* stories, there is a fusion between carnal and spiritual. But it takes the priest some time to recognize how much alike he and Kichijirō really are. For the reader, the central interest of the novel lies in the opportunity to observe this gradual erosion of Rodrigues' ego.

Ridrigues comes to Japan as a foreign intruder. He has a firm conviction of his mission, an image of himself as strong, a warrior forged in the express likeness of the omnipotent Christ he serves. He arrives hoping to salvage the ruins of the Catholic proselytizing effort in Japan, which has succumbed to a highly un-Western weakness. The epistolary style which comprises the major portion of the novel allows Rodrigues to speak for himself in an egocentric discourse—or sermon, even. The first person is used as the voice of self-assurance, of unshaken faith and unquestioning dedication to mission. One example will suffice to illustrate the narrative solidity of Rodrigues' letters:

> Thus far I have baptized thirty adults and children. And not only from here; for the Christians make their way through the mountains from Miyahara, Kuzushima and Harazuka. I have heard more than fifty confessions. After Sunday Mass for the first time I intoned and recited the prayers in Japanese with the people. The peasants stare at me, their eyes alive with curiosity. And as I speak there often arises in my mind the face of one who preached the Sermon on the Mount; and I imagine the people who sat or knelt fascinated by his words. As for me, perhaps I am so fascinated by his face because the Scriptures make no mention of it. Precisely because it is not mentioned, all its details are left to my imagination. From childhood I have clasped that face to my breast just like the person who romantically idealizes the countenance of one he loves. While I was still a student, studying in the seminary, if ever I had a sleepless night, his beautiful face would rise up in my heart. . . .
>
> Feelings of joy and happiness suddenly filled my breast: the feeling that my life was of value and that it was accomplishing something. I am of some use to the people of this country at the ends of the earth, I reflected. . . .[18]

Rodrigues does not hesitate to enumerate his personal accomplishments, to display to the reader of his epistles the rapid improvements in his knowledge of the Japanese language, or, most significantly, to imagine himself as very much like the "one who preached the Sermon on the Mount." His private identification with Jesus, to the point that he feels very much like a lover recalling that "beautiful face," is sustained throughout the early portions of the novel. The prolonged use of first-person voice here makes us intimately, even embarrassingly, aware of what Rodrigues regards as his own strengths.

However, the dauntless Rodrigues is escorted to Japan by Kichijirō; the same groveling excommunicate guides the priest to the villages of the hidden Christians, and is the traitor who delivers Rodrigues over to the officials in preparation for his final agony. Yet even after the betrayal, Kichijirō continues to skulk after Rodrigues from one prison to another, and he alone comes to Rodrigues after the priest's own apostasy.

This breaking-down of Rodrigues' powerfully self-confident image of himself and his God is essentially a process of "conversion." He falls from his self-constructed platform of near-Godhood to the level of helpless human being, virtually indistinguishable from Kichijirō. This is the core of concern in the novel, and the shifting points of view which Endō employs depict this gradual process of humanization (or undeification) in all its engrossing, painful detail.

In the initial stages of his mission in Japan, Rodrigues confesses nothing but contempt for the cowardice of those like Kichijirō who would defame by trampling the holy image of Christ implanted in the *fumie,* the wood and copper icons used by the officials to weed out suspected Christians. Of the craven Kichijirō he remarks:

> I told him in no uncertain terms that if he wanted to overcome this weakness of will and this cowardice that made him tremble in face of the slightest violence, the remedy was not in the *sake* he kept drinking but in a strong faith. [p, 78]

But as Rodrigues witnesses from a safe distance the torture and execution of the simple peasants who refuse to plant their feet atop the *fumie,* his faith in himself begins to waver, and the sincere compassion he feels toward the sufferers begins to eat away at his self-confidence. After two particularly devout followers of Christ are drowned in the waters of the ocean and God remains silent, Rodrigues muses:

> In this age of persecution, the strong endure as the fires rage about them and the waters rush over them. But the weak ones like Kichijirō must wander in isolation through the mountains. And me —what kind of person am I? Were I stripped of my pride and my duties as a priest, I might trample upon the *fumie* just as Kichijirō did.[19]

This is an important admission for Rodrigues. He has taken one further step down from the stairway that climbs toward a heroic martyrdom. By so doing, he has inched closer to becoming a "common," frail human being like Kichijirō. There are several more steps he must descend before he reaches the lowest level and can view Kichijirō as a total equal. The intense agony that is being suffered all around them will finally provide Rodrigues with the motivation to make his descent into the awful hell of human weakness. What ultimately sends him hurling downward is what he views as the stubborn silence of his God.

Once he has been betrayed by Kichijirō into the hands of the Japanese authorities, Rodrigues is able to move yet further away from the silent heavens he had regarded as his personal realm. This separation, a movement into the neutral zone I have discussed above, is duplicated in the shift from first-person to omniscient narration. We are transferred to a plane of objective observation, a comfortable enough vantage point for us as detached readers, but a frighteningly isolated position for Rodrigues. When he begins to sense his own frailties and to have sympathy on those who have been forced to apostatize, the narrative voice withdraws, leaving him to bear his own cross and uncover his own answers to the question "Lama sabachtani?" ("Why hast thou forsaken me?") It is clear that the experience is humbling for the priest. As he is rowed across the bay of Yokose and stares at the mute sea—one of Endō's frequent symbols for both the omnipresence of God and the multifarious deeds of mankind—Rodrigues no longer laments that others are weak; instead he murmurs, "We are not strong men like Job. . . . There are limits to the trials we can endure!"[20]

This succession of trials to which Rodrigues is subjected gradually reveals to him human weaknesses which as a priest he had never dared admit he possessed. The breakdown of layers of false pride and egotistical heroism that create walls between human beings is a prerequisite for entry into Endō's select world of weak but glowingly human characters. Throughout his literary career, Endō has sought to expose and deflate the artificial heroism and self-serving displays of strength that keep one human being from feeling empathy for another. The weak of the world are not to be pitied or looked down upon; those who cannot join them on their level, share their agonies and aid in lessening their burdens (as the Christ in Endō's *A Life of Jesus* does) are merely deluded by illusory feelings of self-importance. These condescending, uncaring strong ones are less likely to qualify for salvation than the weak who cannot stand up for what they believe, yet who bond together to comfort those equally poor in spirit. Endō has compared this paradox of salvation with the famous conundrum spoken by the Pure Land Buddhist saint Shinran: "Even the virtuous man can be saved."[21]

The second half of *Silence* essentially capsulizes all the philosophical arguments that Endō had earlier presented regarding the unsuitability of planting foreign Christian seeds in Japanese soil. More forcefully here than in any of his previous fiction, Endō places the traditions of Western Christianity in conflict with the heritage of Japanese polytheistic culture. Rodrigues' former teacher, the apostate Ferreira, claims that the God of Christianity cannot survive in Japan:

> "This country is a swamp. In time you will come to see that for yourself. This country is a more terrible swamp than you can imagine. Whenever you plant a sapling in this swamp the roots begin to rot; the leaves grow yellow and wither. And we have planted the sapling of Christianity in this swamp. . . ."
>
> "What the Japanese of that time believed in was not our God. It was their own gods. . . . .
>
> In the churches we built throughout this country the Japanese were not praying to the Christian God. They twisted God to their own way of thinking in a way we can never imagine. . . . It is like a butterfly caught in a spider's web. At first it is certainly a butterfly, but the next day only the externals, the wings and the trunk, are those of a butterfly; it has lost its true reality and has become a skeleton. In Japan our God is just like that butterfly caught in the spider's web: only the exterior form of God remains, but it has already become a skeleton." [pp. 237–38, 240]

Some readers and critics, insensitive to the subtle changes in Endō's literary techniques and attitudes, have taken this passage as evidence of a fundamental despair that Christianity can ever adapt to the Japanese climate. A study of the text itself, however, makes it evident that Rodrigues' fate is a direct refutation of Ferreira's argument. That apostate priest insists that the internal essence of Christian faith cannot exist in Japan, that only a skeletal exterior survives. Rodrigues, however, ultimately casts off the "body" of his religion by committing an act of apostasy, while within his heart gaining an even deeper understanding of the meaning of his faith. This positive action on the part of his priest can clearly be correlated with Jesus laying down his body in order to gain immortality within his soul—for that is precisely what Rodrigues does.

In this debate between Rodrigues and Ferreira over surface versus essence, the irresistible surge of a fluid, malleable culture has run into the immovable doctrines of an unbending, "universal" church. Previous Endō characters became embroiled in this struggle and broke their own lives to pieces seeking a resolution. At the conclusion of *Silence,* where he encounters the maternal Christ, Rodrigues becomes the first Endō character to gain a personal understanding of where that resolution lies.

In a sense, though, Rodrigues' private, spiritual Gethsemane precedes the Calvary of physical torture which he must endure in the pit. Worn by the debates with Ferreira, Rodrigues can no longer pass judgment on the frailties of others; he has only compassion in his heart for them. Thus, when he is paraded through the streets on a donkey (as Christ passed through Jerusalem), Rodrigues catches sight of Kichijirō once again. But all the former rancor has melted away.

> The priest looked at the faces that surrounded him, wondering if he might find some secret believer, but it was in vain. There was no face that was not stamped with hostility or hatred or curiosity. And there in the midst of them he caught sight of one who looked just like a dog that begs for pity. Unconsciously the priest stiffened. It was Kichijirō.
>
> Clad it tatters, Kichijirō stood in the front rank waiting. When his eyes met those of the priest, he cowered and quickly tried to conceal himself in the crowd. But the priest from his position on the tottering donkey knew just how far the fellow had followed after him. Amongst all these infidels this was the only man he knew.
>
> ("It's all right. It's all right! I am no longer angry with you. Our Lord is no longer displeased with you.") The priest nodded toward Kichijirō as if to give him the consolation awarded to the penitent after confession. [pp. 249–50]

Rodrigues' initial reaction, from his many years of training and experience, is to stiffen at the sight of an apostate. But now he seeks only solace and compassion amid the faces of the jeering crowd, and any face will do—even the face of a traitor. Once he had railed at

Kichijirō, ordering the Judas to "Depart!" as his own Master had once done. Now he craves only empathy, one who can understand and share the anguish that surges through his heart, the fear and the anticipation that threaten to break the strong facade he has displayed to the world. Rodrigues finds such a sympathetic party in Kichijirō. In this moment of his final passion, Rodrigues realizes that no one can better comprehend the fear in his heart, the weaknesses laid bare by trials, than can this groveling apostate. The two men are fused together at this point, joined by the torment of their mutual weakness.

It is only natural, then, that when Rodrigues faces the physical trial of the torture pit, he encounters yet another figure who had endured scorn but maintained the dignity of limitless compassion. Ferreira encourages him to stamp upon the sacred *fumie,* taunting him with the tantalizing notion that even Jesus would have apostatized in order to save the lives of all the innocent faithful who continue to endure torture. Rodrigues is inspired rather than defeated by the intimation that by trampling he will be performing an act of unconditional love, and he agrees to carry out apostasy. Though in this act of love he lowers himself to the depths of human pain and grief, it is not an act of triumph. Glory and majesty, such as the legendary saints of the past enjoyed, are not available to the fragile, drained human beings in the modern world of reality painted by Endō. There is a different reward, one filled with anguish and humiliation, that Endō's God offers to those who can strip themselves of the ego that surrounds them like a protective shield. When they abase themselves and share the burdens of another human being, God shatters His silence and speaks, using the lives of these individuals as the instrument of communication:

> The priest lifted his foot. A dull pain surged through it. This was no mere formality. He was about to trample upon that which he had regarded as the most beautiful thing in his life, that which he had believed the most holy, that which overflowed with the highest ideals and aspirations of mankind. The pain in this foot! At that moment, the Man in the copper plate spoke to the priest. "Trample!" He said. "Trample! I know better than anyone the pain in your foot. Trample! I was born into this world to be trodden upon by men. I bore my cross to share in your sufferings."

> The priest placed his foot upon the *fumie*. Dawn broke. In the distance, a cock crew.[22]

The refashioned image of Christ—as a sympathetic, forgiving deity—that lives now within Rodrigues is an affirmation, the most positive religious experience of his life. There will clearly be no public victory; the persecution that will continue to be directed at him, now from both heathen and believer, will never allow him such a victory. Inwardly, however, he is at peace, knowing that he has come into contact with Deity by ceasing to masquerade as a saint but instead joining hands with the sinner. The silence of God is broken for Rodrigues when he realizes that the essence of Christianity lies not in its organizational trappings but in the love shown by its adherents—apostle and apostate alike—a love that puts service ahead of personal convenience, that makes saints of the weakest of all men who carry the crosses of others.

Silence is a powerful novel, a private literary victory for Endō in the same way that it focuses on a personal moral victory for its protagonist. In this work Endō not only resolved the conflicts that raged in his early fiction—the search for some kind of unifying force to nullify all the separations that filled his life and his literature—but also sounded the prologue to his quest for a uniquely Japanese, uniquely forgiving brand of Christianity that forms the root of his subsequent writings.

As the Catholic playwright and critic Takadō Kaname notes:

> The paradox in Endō's literature—that a weakling can become strong despite his weaknesses—can be realized in only one way: through a meeting between a weak Jesus and these feeble human beings.[23]

If human beings qualify for salvation because of their capacity to suffer with others, yet are nevertheless burdened with weaknesses, it is only logical that an image of Jesus be fashioned along similar lines. The most effective literary expression of this image since *Silence* may be found in the 1969 story, "Haha naru mono" (Mothers; trans. 1984). Here he discovers an image of a compassionate Christ (virtually synonymous with Mary) who observes all the acts of human endeavor with sad but maternally forgiving eyes. In this discovery, which is clearly a natural extension of the imagery in "My Belongings" and other stories from *Elegies,* Endō finds the unifying force he had sought.

Endō's ability to manipulate mutilayered storylines—a rarity among modern Japanese novelists—is nowhere more evident than in "Mothers." Past and present are intermeshed, reinforcing and commenting upon one another. There is a cinematic virtuosity to the story, with Endō softening, then sharpening his focus on images, dissolving from one visual image to another, and finally producing a unified montage of incredible power.

The central visual image which Endō employs in "Mothers" is the human face. A variety of faces in different aspects appear throughout the story. Some are stern or angry, and are depicted in sharp focus—much like the clear emphasis that was achieved in *Silence* through the use of first-person narrative voice. Other faces are indistinct, muted with sorrow or soft compassion. The interplay of these faces seems random at first, but by the end of the story Endō has brought the images together in a powerful conclusion.

The face which remains hidden but is constantly felt beneath the discourse in "Mothers" is, of course, the face of Jesus that figures so centrally in *Silence.* That face, as Rodrigues noted, is never described in the New Testament. It remains the responsibility of the believer to etch in the details of that face—just as it is the task of the reader of "Mothers" to refine the final sketch that concludes the work. That task is all the more intriguing because the story is related in the first person, producing a narrator whose face is never described. We are free to draw in our private impressions of his face, perhaps including even details of our own.

"Mothers" is narrated by a novelist who has written about the Christian era in Japanese history. But he is less interested in martyrs than in the *kakure,* the "hidden" Christians descended from those in the seventeenth century who were forced to renounce their faith publicly but continued to practice it in secret. The narrator, seeking some link between himself and the weaklings of that earlier period, travels to a small island near Nagasaki to examine traces of the underground religion, which is still practiced by a handful of individuals who have doggedly refused to be reconverted to traditional Christianity.

The first faces described belong to the men of a tiny island where the *kakure* practice their hidden faith. The narrator does not know when he first sees these men whether they belong to the *kakure* sect or not. All he knows is that

> Their faces all looked the same. Their eyes seemed sunken, perhaps because of the protruding cheekbones; their faces were void of expression, as if they were afraid of something. In short, dishonesty and dread had joined together to mold the faces of these islanders. Perhaps I felt that way because of the preconceived notions I had about the island I was about to visit. Throughout the Edo period, the residents of the island had suffered through poverty, hard, grinding labor and religious persecution.[24]

We are alerted at the outset of the story that the blank landscapes of faces will be painted in with impressionistic, highly personal interpretations. The faces of the islanders are "void of expression," and yet the narrator sees something fearful within that void. The lack of expression to him denotes dishonesty and dread. While that reaction cannot be refuted at this stage of the narrative, we are clearly being guided to this island by a man who has some of these feelings within himself, whether we can read it on his face or not.

Endō reinforces this image of the cowardly island face by comparing it with an animal—"I jabbed at some of the chickens [in the cages at my feet] with the tip of my shoe. A look of fear darted across their faces. They looked just like the men from the waiting-room, and I had to smile" (p. 230). We are thus programmed to expect characters to be introduced and defined by their facial features. This holds true for most of the figures who appear in the story, and it is therefore significant to encounter those who are described in a manner that seems to be scrupulously avoiding any mention of the face.

In fact, the leaders of the Catholic parish on the island seem to be faceless. This is not a question of anonymity; rather, it seems almost as if the narrator avoids looking them directly in the face. But there is also something stern and unyielding about their demeanors that forces concentration upon other aspects of their appearance. When the narrator is met at the island dock by a representative of the parish, we are given no portrait of his face. Instead, he is described as overly deferential, somewhat detached, and decidedly stalwart:

> He bowed to me an embarrassing number of times, then tried to wrest my suitcase from my hands. No matter how often I refused,

he would not let go of it. The palms that brushed against my hand were as solid and large as the root of a tree. They were not like the soft, damp hands of the Tokyo Christians that I knew so well.

I tried to walk beside him, but he stubbornly maintained a distance of one pace behind me. I remembered that he had called me "Sensei," and I felt bewildered. If the church people persisted in addressing me in terms of respect, the locals might be put on their guard against me. [p. 231]

The faces of the Catholic converts, like the young man who greets the narrator, emanate faith and courage. As he compares the cowardly faces of the *kakure* with the assured look on the young Catholic, however, the author feels that his own appearance most resembles the sunken faces of the *kakure;* he shares in their weaknesses.

Besides the carefully detailed faces of the weak apostates and the avoidance of facial description among the faithful, the story also introduces images of stern faces. The original Catholic martyrs of the seventeenth century, for instance, are portrayed in terms of their "relentless gaze" and their "accusing eyes" (p. 256) as they observe the traitorous acts of their descendants.

The face which figures most prominently in the story, however, is that of the narrator's mother. A variety of images of this woman are presented over the course of the story, and it is the transformation of that face which lends the work its greatest interest and distinction. Some of the narrator's mental recollections of his late mother have to do with her face, and the memories are consistently discomforting: her constricted face, for instance, as she intently practiced the violin in Dairen. But often some other aspect of her body is described, and the association with the unyielding faithful of the island is evident. The narrator's focus as he recalls her violin practicing quickly shifts from her face:

With the violin under her chin, her face is hard, stone-like, and her eyes are fixed on a single point in space as she seems to be trying to isolate that one true note somewhere in the void. Unable to find the elusive note, she heaves a sigh; her irritation mounts, and she continues to scrape the bow across the strings. The brownish callouses on her chin were familiar to me. They had formed when she was still a student at the music academy and had kept her violin tucked constantly under her chin. The tips of her fingers, too, were as hard to the touch as pebbles, the result of the many thousands of times she had pressed down on the strings in her quest for that one note. [pp. 235–36]

The impressions here, like those read into the blank faces of the islanders, are primarily the interpretations of a young man overwhelmed and perhaps even intimidated by the fierce dedication of his mother. There is no overt indication that he has felt unloved or ignored because of her devotion to her music, but the unyielding tautness of her face and the hard, calloused fingers (recalling the firm hands of the island Catholic) certainly create the same sense of distance that the narrator feels from the deferential parishioners.

The connection between the dedicated mother and the devout Christians is made overt in the narrator's memories when his mother is converted to Catholicism. The same impassioned spirit that led her in a quest for the single true note now impels her in her search for the one true God; the fingers calloused from contact with the violin strings are never removed from the beads of her rosary. The description of her face as it existed in life is not elaborated any further: it has become rigid and unbending. Nor, perhaps, could the narrator bear to dwell upon it.

His apprehensions about his mother's face are, of course, related to the fact that, as a young man, he could never muster the same degree of inner strength she possessed. Little acts of betrayal smudge his own past, and each time he recalls a personal failing, he invariably sees his mother's face before him. The day his mother collapsed and died, he was at his friend's house sneaking a look at some photographs of a man and woman engaged in intercourse. The look on the woman's face in the pictures is one of pain. When the call comes informing him of his mother's collapse, he scurries home, only to arrive after she has died.

> In the back room, my mother's body was surrounded by neighbors and people from the church, sitting with stooped shoulders. No one turned to look at me; no one spoke a word to me. I knew from the stiffness of their backs that they all were condemning me.
>
> Mother's face was white as milk. A shadow of pain still lingered between her brows. Her expression reminded me of the look on

> the face of the woman in the photographs. Only then did I realize what I had done, and I wept. [pp. 251–52]

There are many elements of interest in this passage. There is, first, the back room, which will be echoed at the end of the story in the rear chamber of the *kakure* chapel where the maternal icons are kept. There is the church community, ever supportive of the mother's religious devotion, ever critical—as their stiffened backs make clear to him—of her son's wavering interest in religion. It is a community that exists in all its particulars on the distant island, where the Catholic faithful turn cold backs on the agonies of the apostate *kakure*.

And then there is mother's face. Even in death it seems to retain some of the energy that motivated her life and intimidated her son. But, as in "The Day Before," her spiritual quests are here merged with his carnal weaknesses in a scathing denunciation of his frailities and betrayals. This is the confrontation that brings the narrator into the middle ground, the purgatory where he must find some means to reconcile his fleshly weaknesses with the example of her spiritual strength.

Intimations that such a resolution is possible season the text. As the narrator is preparing to journey to the *kakure* village, he dreams of his mother, but the image that appears to him is undergoing some kind of transformation from the stern woman of his memories:

> I dreamed of my mother. In my dream I had just been brought out of the operating room, and was sprawled out on my bed like a corpse. A rubber tube connected to an oxygen tank was thrust into my nostril, and intravenous needles pierced my right arm and leg, carrying blood from the transfusion bottles dangling over my bed.
>
> Although I should have been half unconscious, through the languid weight of the anesthetic I recognized the gray shadow that held my hand. It was my mother. . . . I know little about psychoanalysis, so I have no idea exactly what this dream means. In it, I can not actually see my mother's face. Nor are her movements distinct.
>
> So far as my memory serves me, I can recollect no experience in my youth when I lay ill in bed with my mother holding my hand. Normally the image of my mother that pops into mind is the figure of a woman who lived her life fervently. [pp. 234–35]

The focus here is indistinct, the features of the face in transition. The narrator is beginning to venture beyond the realm of material experience as he commences the task of justification, hoping to resolve the conflicts between the dogmatic hardness of his mother's face and the spongy unreliability of his own moral code. That resolution must allow him to retain his love for his mother but to sense some compassion from her as well.

That compassion seems forthcoming as she clasps his hand at the bedside. Further promise is given when he makes a connection between this new image of his mother and the tiny statue of Mary that has passed into his hands from her estate:

> I superimposed on her face that of a statue of "Mater Dolorosa," the Holy Mother of Sorrows, which my mother used to own. . . . Once my mother was dead, I took those few precious things with me in a box every time I moved from one lodging-house to another. Eventually the strings on the violin snapped and cracks formed in the wood. The cover was torn off her prayer book. And the statue of Mary was burned in an air raid in the winter of 1945.
>
> The sky was a stunning blue the morning after the air raid. Charred ruins stretched from Yotsuya to Shinjuku, and all around the embers were still smouldering. I crouched down in the remains of my apartment building in Yotsuya and picked through the ashes with a stick, pulling out broken bowls and a dictionary that had only a few unburned pages remaining. Eventually I struck something hard. I reached into the still warm ashes with my hand and pulled out the broken upper half of that statue. The plaster was badly scorched, and the plain face was even uglier than before. Today, with the passage of time the facial features have grown vaguer. After I was married, my wife once dropped the statue. I repaired it with glue, with the result that the expression on the face is all the more indistinct. [p. 258]

Once again, as in so much of Endō's fiction, the moment of apotheosis combines personal experience, wartime destruction (and resurrection-like recovery), religious enlightenment, and the fusion of images that have lain in scattered chaos until this point in the narrative. It is worth noting that the resulting unity remains somewhat blurred, even hesitant. The face of the statue is as blank as the visages of the islanders that opened the story. The resolution that has come to the narrator is utterly private, and it remains for the individual reader to create a separate personal integration and interpretation of the images or to reject the notion of resolution altogether. But for this narrator, there are intimations that a compassionate understanding, if not forgiveness, of his weaknesses will become available as the dream image of his mother is superimposed with that of the Mother of Sorrows statue.

Yet there is still another layer of resolution awaiting this narrator as he visits the *kakure*. The painful memory of his mother's death, still fresh in his mind, enables him to forge links between himself and the *kakure*. They have much in common. He had rejected his mother but never truly abandoned his love for her; the *kakure* had rejected their Heavenly Father but never turned totally away from him. Because of his unfilial behavior, the boy was disdained by his friends and neighbors; for their acts of betrayal, the *kakure* must endure the mocking sternness of the strong believers on the island.

"Sometimes," the author writes, "I catch a glimpse of myself in these *kakure,* people who have had to lead lives of duplicity, lying to the world and never revealing their true feelings to anyone" [p. 252]. The cowardice and shame written upon the sunken faces of the *kakure* are the same expressions that repeated acts of weakness, or surrender to the cries of the flesh, have etched upon this writer's visage. He is a modern *kakure,* a charter member in the society of shame. He is one too weak to lead a life of open devotion, one that the strong, stern parishioners would mock if they knew the weakness within his heart. The identification between the author and the *kakure* is a powerful comparison that gives form and substance to "Mothers."

The writer, inwardly united with the hidden Christians, cannot help wondering what the consequences of their mutual cowardice might be. What path to salvation and forgiveness is available to those who cannot tread the highways to martyrdom and unwavering devotion? Is that road open solely to those who conquer their frailties and endure great hardships for the Church?

The self-appointed priest of the *kakure,* Kawahara Kikuichi, can never look anyone directly in the face. He too seems to harbor a secret shame that keeps him from direct association with those who claim to be strong. The prayers which they intone for the visiting "sensei" are supplications offered not to the stern Father, but words "of profound sorrow" that entreat the Holy Mother to intercede with God so that their frailties might be forgiven [pp. 255–56]. Driven by a concern more personal than scholarly, the author asks to be shown the image of Mary that the *kakure* have worshipped for so many generations. The image is concealed behind the Buddhist altar, to keep it from the eyes of the persecuting, mockingly strong officials.

> A drawing of the Holy Mother cradling the Christ child—no, it was a picture of a farm woman holding a nursing baby. The robes worn by the child were a pale indigo, while the mother's kimono was painted a murky yellow. It was clear from the inept brushwork and composition that the picture had been painted many years before by one of the local *kakure*. The farm woman's kimono was open, exposing her breast. Her obi was knotted at the front, adding to the impression that she was dressed in the rustic apparel of a worker in the fields. The face was like that of every woman on the island. It was the face of a woman who gives suckle to her child even as she plows the fields and mends the fishing-nets. . . .
>
> I could not take my eyes off that clumsily drawn face. These people had joined their gnarled hands together and offered up supplications for forgiveness to this portrait of a mother. Within me there welled up the feeling that their intent had been identical to mine. Many long years ago, missionaries had crossed the seas to bring the teachings of God the Father to this land. But when the missionaries had been expelled and the churches demolished, the Japanese *kakure*, over the space of many years, stripped away all those parts of the religion that they could not embrace, and the teachings of God the Father were gradually replaced by a yearning after a Mother—a yearning which lies at the heart of Japanese religion. I thought of my own mother. She stood again at my side, an ashen-colored shadow. She was not playing the violin or clutching her rosary now. Her hands were joined in front of her, and she stood gazing at me with a touch of sorrow in her eyes. [pp. 263–64]

This scene is the climax of "Mothers." Endō masterfully brings all the elements of his story together at this point. The novelist becomes one with the *kakure;* he is united with them by common weaknesses, and by an earnest desire to seek forgiveness. The stark images of his mother that have been a part of his memory since youth are superimposed over images of a stern, unforgivingly paternal God who has condemned the *kakure* for the fleshly cowardice that has led them to apostatize. In the end, however, it is not a harsh Father to whom the *kakure* turn in supplication. Their prayers for forgiveness are offered up to an image of a compassionate Mother who will intervene on their behalf. Unable to gaze directly into the blinding radiance that emanates from the Father, they avert their eyes toward the subdued warmth that comes from the holy Mother; she shields them from the full force of the light that illuminates all their shortcomings. Without her mercy, they would not be able to endure the presence of God. In the clumsily painted image of a peasant woman, the author recognizes the unfamiliar face he had seen in his dreams—the accepting, mournful mother, his own personal Mother of Sorrows that he had never known in his lifetime.

"Mothers" is a controlled juxtaposition of religious and secular yearnings—on the one hand, a search for forgiveness by weak individuals who have betrayed their God; on the other, a man's lifelong quest for a mother who can understand rather than condemn his many faults. If man cannot be persuaded from his weaknesses, then there must be salvation granted in spite of folly for those who earnestly seek it. This salvation comes from the "mothers" who can love and suffer alongside even the least worthy of God's creations. The story comes very close to providing its reader with an experience of catharsis—the narrator's final perception of acceptance, a very personal spiritual experience for him, is conveyed undiluted to the reader.

One man has found a path leading to salvation in "Mothers," but the pain inherent in human contact, the damage individuals do to one another in their jostling for self-fulfillment or even salvation, the strivings of the ego, and the need to unite solitary grief with the sorrows of others—all these problems remain for this individual (be he this novelist or Rodrigues at the conclusion of *Silence*) to cope with. If he cannot share the compassion of which he has been a partaker, then his own salvation will have no meaning. Endō leaves this problem unresolved at the conclusion of "Mothers." As Jirō and Nakamura—a parishioner and a local official who are both sturdy Christians—leave the *kakure* village, they mock the holy image they have just been shown.

"How ridiculous! Sensei, it must have been a terrible disappointment to have them show you something so stupid." As we left the village, Jirō apologized to me over and over, as though he were personally responsible for the whole thing. Mr. Nakamura, who had picked up a tree branch along the way to use as a walking-stick, walked ahead of us in silence. His back was stiff. I couldn't imagine what he was thinking. [p. 264]

The rigidity in Nakamura's back recalls the rejection that the narrator had to endure from the mourners assembled around the corpse of his mother. The weak, the traitors must cope with constant rejection—the rejection that Kichijirō, Rodrigues, and a host of other Endō characters continue to endure. Thus the separation that Endō has been struggling to overcome since the outset of his literary career remains. His characters tread a lonely path—they may indeed be "wonderful" in the eyes of their creator (and their Creator), but to others they will likely be regarded as "fools."

It is, in fact, as "wonderful fools" that many of Endō's most endearing characters appear in his popular literature. To the extent that these figures are extensions of Endō's fundamental belief in the superior value of compassion over worldly attainments, there is really little distinction between his serious and his popular fiction. Endō searches out the philosophical depths of his themes in his serious novels, then gives them rich human embodiment in his works aimed at a wider reading audience. Characters like Gaston of *Obakasan* (Wonderful Fool, 1959; trans. 1973), Mitsu in *Watashi ga suteta onna* (The Girl I Left Behind, 1963), and Flatfish and Ozu of *When I Whistle* are individuals who care, who devote their lives to sharing in the sufferings of others, doing what they can—no matter how trivial in the eyes of the world—to help even the most wretched of human beings endure their trials. That is why the popular novels are populated with murderers, thieves, abortionists, lepers, and social drop-outs; they are the counterparts of the apostate priests, the weak-willed martyrs, and the ugly, pathetic "bastards" who fill the pages of the religious works.

Weaving their uncertain way among these calloused, uncaring figures are the "hidden" saints—those who are failures in the eyes of society but unqualified successes in the areas that really count for Endō: in the expressions of tenderness and concern for the pain of others. These characters are human reflections of the maternal Jesus whom Endō has described in his historical novels. The popular fictions, in fact, are best examined as inversions of the serious works. The process of salvation in Endō's entertainment novels is a mirror opposite of what transpires in *Silence* or *Elegies*. In the religious works, a self-assured, essentially self-justified individual—one who already regards himself worthy of paradise—must be thrust into the inferno (occasionally a literal pit, as Rodrigues learns) in order to confront his own weaknesses and thereby accept the intercessory mercies of Jesus. These works chronicle the transformation of a self-proclaimed saint into a true, humbled believer. The crucifixion of ego and an infusion of compassion are the sole requirements for salvation in the central purgatory through which these characters pass.

In such popular novels as *The Girl I Left Behind*, however, a character like Mitsu is portrayed as something less than commonplace, a drab, unattractive girl who has nothing but the use of her body to offer to the intelligent, ambitious student Yoshioka. No humbling of Mitsu needs to take place in this work, for Endō portrays her as already residing in a kind of hell, hardly considered worthy to go on living by Yoshioka's standards. The transformation which takes place here is an act of elevation; although he cannot understand why, by the end of the novel Yoshioka regards Mitsu as something of a saint. Thus Mitsu is exalted to a paradisiacal glory because she already possesses those very qualities which Rodrigues has to learn through agonizing experience. Mitsu and Rodrigues meet in the neutral purgatory, where both have been prepared for their ultimate celestial rewards.

Endō manipulates point-of-view in *The Girl I Left Behind* as adroitly as he does in *Silence* or *Umi to dokuyaku* (The Sea and Poison, 1958; trans. 1972). The first view we get of Mitsu is rather persuasively negative. This bias is created by using the egotistical, materialistic Yoshioka as the first-person narrator. Because his interests are all physical and earthbound, it is inevitable that the impressions which he records of his encounters with Mitsu are tinged with sarcasm and revulsion. When he first meets her on a blind date, the girl who comes walking toward him at a train station is "short and chubby, with her hair done up in three braids that hung down over her shoulders."[25] Later, after he has almost effortlessly lured Mitsu into bed with him by preying upon her sympathy, her physical plainness is almost more than he can bear:

> Her shirt was faded from countless washings. It was the kind of knit shirt a man would wear. Beneath it were her shapeless, country-girl breasts with their embarrassingly child-like nipples. Two hairs grew from her nipples. . . . The whole thing was over in an instant. In no more than an instant. Suddenly items that had not bothered me before—the brown, sunbleached tatami, the walls smeared with fingerprints and with blood from squashed mosquitos, the bedding and the water pitcher—all appeared loathsome and nauseating to me. Even Mitsu, still lying prostrate on the bed like a corpse, was disheveled and disgusting. Two or three strands of hair clung to her sweat-soaked forehead. Her misshapen snub nose. The persimmon-colored sweater. The dark-red spot near her wrist. Her masculine shirt. I had slept with this drab woman. I had planted my lips on this bedraggled woman's chest. [pp. 67–68]

There is very little indication in the first three chapters to the novel that Yoshioka's poor opinion of Mitsu is anything but deserved. Once this unfavorable portrait of Mitsu has been painted, however—and once Yoshioka has left her in favor of more tempting targets—Endō shifts to the omniscient perspective to follow Mitsu's life after she has been discarded. She has some simple, hackneyed dreams of love and happiness locked within her heart, but each time she seems to have earned a share of them, she denies herself the rewards and instead performs an act of kindness for another. She is mistakenly diagnosed as suffering from leprosy and is for a time committed to the leper hospital in Gotemba. When the benign nature of her affliction is discovered and she is allowed to leave, however, the concern she has developed for the other patients keeps her from abandoning others as she has been abandoned:

> Mitsu realized now that even if she went back, her lonely life would go on as it always had. There was that evening last New Year's, when she had sat alone like an abandoned cat, holding her numb hands over the few remaining coals in the stove. The rumble of the trains had faintly rattled the glass windows that were patched here and there with scraps of newspaper. *I hate it. I hate that life!*
>
> (But what else can you do? There's nowhere else to go.)
>
> What Mitsu really wanted was someone beside her to keep her warm. To warm more than just her body. Sometimes she wanted a

person who would be like a mother to her, a shoulder to rest her tired head upon at the end of each lonely day. Someone to listen to all her dull-witted, foolish complaints. A friend to laugh with her at an Ishikawa Akira movie. A companion to stay beside her always and never leave her. But where could she find someone to offer the warmth she craved?

. . . "The local train for Tokyo is now arriving on track number two. . . ."

The train for Tokyo. How was Tokyo any different from the hospital dormitory in the woods? The people in Shinjuku and Kawasaki would breeze busily, coldly, uncaringly past Mitsu just as those at this station were doing. . . .

(If you run now, you can make it. If you run, you can still get on the train), a voice within her urged. But in another corner of her heart, Mitsu thought of the barracks-like hospital in the woods, the buildings that shivered in the rain. She had fled the hospital ward, where right now the women patients would be at work on their embroidery. Kanō Taeko was probably sitting in her room all alone. Mitsu felt something clutch at her heart when she remembered the expressions on those women's faces as they watched her leave the hospital.

The warning bell stopped ringing. There was a moment of silence, then with a dull clatter the train began to move forward. Smoke from the engine curled about the cars as the train slid down the platform.

Mitsu picked up her trunk and left the station. She walked across the plaza toward the bus stop. . . . [pp. 230–31]

Endō in this portion of the novel is able to look into Mitsu's heart—into that part of her that Yoshioka was unwilling to seek out—and locate there tremendous stores of compassion and empathy. We discover a Mitsu that Yoshioka never knew existed. The style employed in these chapters is direct and unembellished, a product of the restrained writing techniques Endō learned from his reading of Bernanos and Mauriac. Seldom has Endō managed to mesh such a variety of styles—including a marvelously humorous range of secondary characters who flesh out the background of the novel and create a Tokyo rather like Dickens' London.[26] Through the careful balance of banality and deep human compassion, humor and tragedy, Endō is able to persuade us, as he does Yoshioka at the end of the novel, that this simple, undesirable girl was in fact something very much like a "saint."

When Mitsu struggles within herself at the train station near the leper hospital, relieved to be free yet yearning to go back, she wins a special sort of victory, emerging from her personal Gethsemane. She has successfully fought the battle between self and selflessness. With enviable ease she is able to put personal concerns behind her and shift her attention to the predicament of others. This ability to unite oneself with the torment of others is the ultimate, triumphant virtue for Endō. The weak and ugly (and apostate) of the world who can put this principle into practice are those with true spiritual strength, for they have overcome self and formed a bond of compassion with their fellow human beings. Whatever failings of plainness, ignorance, and gullibility Mitsu may have, her silent victory over personal desires qualifies her to be the "ideal woman" Yoshioka hears about at the novel's conclusion. Even a young man as ambitious and egotistical as he has to reflect on what his encounter with Mitsu meant to his life:

> I leaned against the railing on the rooftop and looked out over the city at twilight, trying to give substance to what I was feeling. Scores of buildings and houses stretch out beneath the ashen clouds. Innumerable roadways run between those structures. Buses scurry along, cars stream past, people amble about. Countless lives are being played out here. Within those many lives, what I did to Mitsu happens once to every man. I'm not alone in this. But . . . but where does this sense of desolation come from? I've got my hands on a small but steady happiness in my life now. I have no intention of giving it up for the sake of my memories of Mitsu. But what is the source of this desolation? If Mitsu taught me anything, it is that people who pass even briefly through our lives leave behind a mark that cannot be erased. Does this desolation come from such marks? And if there really is a God . . . does He speak to us through these marks? [pp. 254–55]

Yoshioka is moved but not necessarily transformed by these feelings, by the marks left upon his conscience by his encounter with Mitsu. These marks, as inexplicable as the mysterious scars on Mitsu's wrists, are one of the modes of communication which God employs once the experiences with Mitsu have given Yoshioka a glimpse into the zone of compassion. But it is unclear whether Yoshioka has sufficient resources of feeling within himself to benefit from his knowledge in the long run.[27]

Mitsu is one of Endō's most memorable character creations, and she effortlessly attracts the reader's sympathy and admiration, for in her unresolved weakness she is no different from any other human being. But in her capacity to love, she points the path to a higher plane of human communication, a greater concern for values of abiding import. She is a tiny oasis in the midst of the "desert of love" that is our modern society.[28] In characters like Mitsu, Endō finds traces of the living water still flowing sweet and clear.

Endō's uniqueness among the writers of the Third Generation lies in his belief that, however unreliable the self has become in the wake of war and defeat, there is yet hope for a private resurgence—a resurrection, as it were, of the individual. This is brought about through simple acts of selflessness, as if in atonement for the inescapable egotism of the war years. This is nothing like the muted despair of Yasuoka, the cynical sharpness of Kojima, or even the extreme self-denial of Shimao. In Endō's writings there is a positive affirmation of the human potential for improvement, a dogged optimism that casts a faint yet distinct light through the gray clouds that hover over the surface of his fictional narratives. This element of unrelenting hope in the face of the most vile of human cruelties—the tortures, the betrayals, the vivisections, the apostasies—stands as sufficient evidence that Endō is as much a Christian novelist as he is a Japanese novelist.

It is a useful exercise to read *The Girl I Left Behind* alongside *Silence,* because the former illuminates much of the religious uproar that surrounded the publication of the latter. Part of Endō's problem in *Silence* lies in the fact that he relied on symbols of East and West to present what is to him an essentially universal ("catholic" without the uppercase "C") theme—the need for human empathy. Unfortunately, *Silence* has been read by many as a rejection of Western-style Christianity and a call for a rethinking of the religion in the Japanese context. Such open-ended challenges are, of course, raised in the novel, but this interpretation suggests that Endō is more of a theologian than a novelist. Nothing could be further from the truth. It is fairer to him to propose that the concerns in the fiction are not essentially religious but rather moral. Endō is no defender of sectarian Christianity; indeed, after the publication of *Silence,* some considered him an enemy of the Catholic cause in Japan. But in his novels Endō is clearly seeking to transcend the temporal issues of dogma and probe to the roots of the human-centered ethics that support the Christian religion.

This becomes abundantly clear in the acclaimed novel *The Samurai.* When this work is read in conjunction with *Silence,* it becomes evident that Endō is less concerned about the distinctions between Hellenistic and Oriental Christianity than about the importance of suppressing selfish urges (symbolized in *The Samurai* by the clashes in Japan between Jesuits and Franciscans) and embracing the essence of Christian charity. He emphasizes this theme in *The Samurai* by tearing down the barriers between his strong, confident Spanish priest, Velasco, and his weak, unprepossessing Japanese warrior, Hasekura. Both men qualify for true martyrdom at the end of the novel, not because of any sectarian compromise, but by virtue of their recognition of their own weaknesses and their acceptance of the companionship of a sympathetic Christ.

The Samurai encompasses two different time frames. On the surface it is a faithful retelling of a 1613 trade voyage to Mexico and Europe undertaken by Hasekura Tsunenaga, a low-ranking vassal of the powerful Sendai lord Date Masamune. Hasekura's mission was guided (or, depending on one's orientation, "misguided") by the Franciscan monk Luis Sotelo (called Velasco in the novel), whose personal ambitions included appointment to the post of Bishop of Japan. Although they enjoyed audiences with King Philip III of Spain and Pope Paul V in Rome, the embassy was unable to achieve its trade-related goals and returned in defeat to Japan, where the principals of the mission—including Hasekura—were executed for accepting Catholic baptism as an expediency to further their secular goals. Sotelo too crept back into Japan after the imposition of anti-Christian edicts and was summarily burned at the stake.

In Endō's retelling of these historical events, there are many scenes of conflict, both human and in the realm of nature, as this peculiar group of envoys makes its way across the Pacific Ocean. Unaware that they are being manipulated from both sides of the water—by the materialistic forces of government in Japan (the Council of Elders, the daimyos, the shogun Ieyasu, and the entire feudal political structure) and the spiritual bureaucracy of the church (the corresponding Council of Bishops, the cardinals, Pope, and Catholic hierarchy)—the entourage suffers through many physical trials and emotional letdowns. Despite the surface dynamics of the plot, however, at the core of the novel movement takes place much more slowly. For Endō's chief concern in *The Samurai* is not with the physical migration across land and sea but with the subtle changes that take place within an individual soul. Even as events are shifting at breathtaking speed in the outer world, as Hasekura and his comrades are deceived and betrayed by both political and religious institutions, a tiny seed of faith is beginning to sprout. For he has been cast adrift in a spiritual ocean which corresponds to the numerous other neutral zones that abound in Endō's fiction.

This contrast between external and internal evolution is echoed in the narrative structure of the novel. As with *Silence,* Endō employs both first-person and omniscient narrators; here, however, the technique is more immediate and rewarding than in the earlier work, for in *The Samurai* the focus is on the contrast between two individuals —the confident, self-assured friar Velasco and the hesitant, diffident samurai. Because Velasco is so dominant—even domineering—an actor in the surface drama of the narrative, having his voice speak directly to our ears etches the sharp outlines of his personality in our minds, as the following passage clearly illustrates:

> I left the Superior's office and returned to the room which had been provided for me. There I lit a candle and bound my wrists to avoid the temptations of the flesh. I had anticipated these machinations by my enemies. I had never assumed that everything would proceed smoothly from the outset. It is true, as the Jesuits say, that the Christians in Japan are undergoing persecution, that the Naifu and the Shōgun are not pleased with the missionary work there. But that is no reason for us to retreat and abandon that nation to Satan and to heathen religions. Missionary work is like diplomacy. Indeed it resembles the conquest of a foreign land. In missionary work, as in diplomacy, one must have recourse to subterfuge and strategy, threatening at times, compromising at others —if such tactics serve to advance the spreading of God's word, I do not regard them as despicable or loathsome. At times one has to close one's eyes to certain things for the sake of sharing the gospel.

> The conqueror Cortez landed here in Nueva España in 1519, and with only a handful of soldiers he captured and killed multitudes of Indians. In light of God's teachings, no one could call such an act proper. But we must not forget that as a result of that sacrifice, today countless Indians have come into contact with the word of our Lord, and have thereby been saved from their savage ways and begun to walk in the paths of righteousness. None can lightly judge whether it would have been better to leave the Indians to their devilish ways, or to close our eyes to a degree of evil and bring them the word of God.[29]

The Machiavellian quality of Velasco's self-justification echoes the historically confident singlemindedness of the institution he serves. It is both embarrassing and infuriating to be this privy to his thoughts and feelings. We observe him plotting stratagems, pursuing personal and religious ambitions, and deftly parrying opponents, and we recognize in him a vibrant, combative human force. The surging dynamism of his character is evidenced by the constant battle he wages with his body, so intense that he has to bind his wrists before he goes to bed at night to avoid carnal temptation. Velasco is, in short, the very embodiment of aggressive Western Christianity. There is an uncritical, premodern glibness to the manner in which he excuses the crimes of both Cortez and the church, but it is a posture he must adopt if he is to achieve his own ends. By his own words he seeks to glorify himself, but by those very utterances he becomes, from our standpoint, less worthy of trust and respect.

When the samurai mounts the stage, however, the narrative voice in the novel retreats and assumes a more subdued, passive stance. This is well in keeping with his nature, and it allows us to stand back at a distance and observe the intricate accumulation of experiences that eventually causes a change of heart—a conversion, if you will—within him. As he journeys through the Western world and has his first encounters with the symbols of occidental religion, Hasekura's unspoken thoughts are essentially of puzzlement:

> The sound of the rain was still audible. The samurai sat down on his bed and looked uncomfortably about the room. It was just like all the many monastery rooms they had slept in ever since their arrival in Nueva España. A single plain bed, a single plain desk, holding a porcelain water pitcher and a wash-basin of ara-

besque design. On the bare wall an emaciated man with both hands nailed to a cross hung with drooping head.

"A man like this. . . ." Once again, the samurai experienced the same incomprehension. "Why do they worship him?"

He remembered that he had once seen a prisoner in a similar condition. Riding bareback, he had been paraded about with both his hands lashed to a pole. Like this man on the crucifix, the prisoner was ugly and filthy. His ribs protruded, and his stomach had caved in as though he had not eaten for a long while; he wore only a cloth about his loins, and he supported himself on the horse with spindly legs. The more he looked at it, the more the image on the wall reminded the samurai of that prisoner.

"What would the people in the marshland think . . . if I worshipped someone like this?"

He pictured himself worshipping this man, and an unbearable feeling of shame swept over him. He did not believe wholeheartedly in the buddhas in the way his uncle did, but when he made a pilgrimage to a temple, his head automatically wanted to bow down before the magnificent idols, and when he stood before a shrine where pure waters were flowing, he felt an urge to clap his hands in supplication. But he could detect nothing sublime or holy in a man as wretched and powerless as this. [pp. 198–99]

Like the voice of the narrative, Hasekura focuses upon the externals of his environment. His is a detached but uninformed omniscience. Endō is careful in his descriptions of the journey through Mexico to avoid exotic scenes and idle cultural curiosities. The landscapes tend to be barren deserts, the rooms blank chambers. All the samurai's attention is directed toward the crucifixes, which seem to pursue him from one outpost to the next. He seldom makes direct, forceful statements; most often his thoughts are expressed as questions, and those are seldom answered. He makes tentative excursions of the imagination, as when he tries to picture himself worshipping the figure on the cross, but he quickly retreats back to the realm of the familiar and safe—the temples and shrines of the marshland where he has spent his entire life. This reticence, so unbecoming a warrior,[30] is a crucial part of the samurai's enclosed personality. He is not prepared for conflict—neither armed nor metaphysical. This makes him all the more susceptible to Velasco's scheming.

Thus, as events surge forward on the external plane, led by Velasco's deft, diplomatic hand, the samurai and his comrades are embroiled in violent struggles against both the powers of the West and the political machinations back in Japan. (Their ambivalent position recalls Egi trapped between bases.) Eventually they are persuaded that they too must be baptized as an expediency to further the accomplishment of their mission and return to Japan with the honor demanded of a samurai.

The embassy fails dismally, however, and Endō unsparingly details the humiliation these proud Japanese feel as they are manipulated and discarded by powers greater than themselves. One of the ambassadors commits suicide rather than go back home in disgrace. When they return to Japan physically and morally exhausted after several years, they are subjected to an even greater blow to their dignity. During their absence, the tides of political expediency have dictated a ban on the practice of Christianity in Japan, and the envoys who have submitted to a spiritually meaningless baptism abroad are branded as traitors to the nation. They are forbidden to associate one with another, and slowly their privileges as samurai are stripped from them. Hasekura is increasingly isolated from all sources of sympathy and compassion. He is left without anyone who can offer him comfort.

The final indignity comes when the domain authorities conclude that the samurai's very existence is an intolerable affront to their anti-Christian policies. When Hasekura receives a summons to appear before the Council of Elders, he know he will be ordered to atone for his crime of conversion in the only manner a Japanese warrior can publicly make his apologies. Deprived now of every recourse of human empathy, Hasekura sits beside the swamp in his homeland with his retainer, Yozō, and he is reminded of images still hazily imbedded in his memory, yet considerably more meaningful to him now.

> The samurai had no idea where these birds had come from, or why they had chosen this tiny swamp as their home for the long winter. Doubtless some had weakened and died of starvation during their journey.
>
> "These birds too," the samurai muttered, blinking his eyes, "must have crossed a wide ocean and seen many countries."

Yozō was sitting with both hands clasped on his lap, staring at the water.

"It was truly . . . a long journey."

The conversation broke off there. Once he had spoken these words, the samurai felt there was nothing more he needed to say to Yozō. It was not just the journey that had been painful. The samurai wanted to say that his own past, and Yozō's past, had been a succession of similarly painful experiences.

When the wind got up and tiny ripples skidded across the surface of the sunlit swamp, the ducks and swans shifted course and moved silently away. Lowering his head, Yozō shut his eyes tightly. The samurai knew that he was struggling against a flood of emotions. The samurai was suddenly struck by the impression that his loyal servant's profile resembled that man's. That man, like Yozō, had hung his head as though enduring all things. "He is always beside us. He listens to our agony and our grief. . . ." Yozō had never abandoned his master—not now or ever in the past. He had followed the samurai like a shadow. And he had never spoken a word in the midst of his master's sufferings.

"I've always believed that I became a Christian as a mere formality. That feeling hasn't changed at all. But since I've learned something about Government, sometimes I find myself thinking about that man. I think I understand why every house in those countries has a pathetic statue of that man. I suppose that somewhere in the hearts of men, there's a yearning for someone who will be with you throughout your life, someone who will never betray you, never leave you—even if that someone is just a sick, mangy dog. That man became just such a miserable dog for the sake of mankind." The samurai repeated the words almost to himself. "Yes. That man became a dog who remains beside us. That's what that Japanese fellow at the Tecali swamp wrote. That when he was on earth, he said to his disciples that he came into the world to minister unto men."

Yozō looked up for the first time. He shifted his eyes towards the swamp as if to ponder what his master had just said.

"Do you believe in Christianity?" the samurai asked quietly.

"Yes," Yozō answered.

"Tell no one."

Yozō nodded.

> The samurai laughed, deliberately, in an attempt to change the subject. "When spring comes, the birds of passage leave this place. But we can never leave the marshland as long as we live. The marshland is our home." [pp. 310–12]

"The samurai had no idea. . . ." It is a phrase that recurs time and again in the narrative in one form or another. Like the walls of his rooms in Nueva España, Hasekura's soul is fundamentally neutral, slow to comprehend and full of doubts and questions. His conversations, when he has them, are full of ellipses and apparent non sequiturs. Particularly with his servant Yozō, he prefers to leave matters unspoken. The communication between the two of them, like his communion with the miserable deity he has come to respect, is not carried out on the level of overt, logical interchange. It is an intuitive understanding, a bond of mutual experience that enables the samurai to know that Yozō's closed eyes indicate a flood of emotions surging through him. Just as Yozō has remained with his master through all the trials of the journey, so the image on the crucifix has been a companion—and now even a source of comfort—to Hasekura.

However antidogmatic the samurai's "conversion" may seem, his final scene in the novel strongly, yet subtly, suggests that some kind of spiritual change has come over him.

> Snow creaked on the roof and slipped to the ground. The sound reminded the samurai of the creak of the halyards. In a single moment the halyards creaked, the white seagulls flew over with a shrill call, the waves beat against the hull, and the ship moved out into the great ocean—and from that moment it was decided that this would be his fate. His long journey was now bringing him to his final destination.
>
> When he looked up, outside the open door he could see his attendant Yozō sitting in the snowy garden with his head bowed. . . . [Yozō] could tell that his master and the steward had stood up to leave. . . .
>
> "From now on He will be beside you." Suddenly he heard Yozō's strained voice behind him.
>
> "From now on He will attend you."
>
> The samurai stopped, looked back, and nodded his head em-

phatically. Then he set off down the cold, glistening corridor towards the end of his journey. [pp. 333–34]

We are left with the strong impression that religious conviction faces its most formidable challenge when an individual is hovering at the brink of death. At the moment when life itself is about to be snuffed out, it is the faith which has begun to sprout at the core of his existence that sustains the samurai and transforms his miserable death into a kind of martyrdom. Though it is a sacrifice superficially unlike the agonizing death Velasco suffers at the stake, there is a unity between the two men who share the companionship of an empathetic Christ as they make the final journeys of their lives.

While it traces the footsteps of these two men around the globe, the novel also functions as something of a "spiritual autobiography" of its author. Like Hasekura, Endō spent much of his life's voyage feeling ambivalent about the Christian faith he had had forced upon him. The distance which the seventeenth-century envoy feels from a foreign religion he shares with Endō. But for both character and author, a decisive encounter with an all-suffering, all-forgiving King is the event that shapes the remainder of their lives. And it must be borne in mind that Endō's working title for the novel was *A Man Who Met a King*. *The Samurai* powerfully argues that the external trappings of religious fervor mean little unless they are shored up by true human concern. Velasco is a self-seeking, self-righteous Westerner much as Rodrigues was in the early pages of *Silence*. But he does not have to apostatize to earn his reward in *The Samurai*. Once he has cast off his pride and ambition, Endō allows him a glorious, flaming martyr's death in the finest Western tradition. Hasekura, on the other hand, is almost passive in his acceptance of the companionship of Jesus. But he too deserves Endō's respect for his devotion to his mission and to his fellow wayfarers. In essence, then, Endō's concerns in *The Samurai* are strikingly similar to those in a work like *The Girl I Left Behind*. Hasekura, as humble and unpretentious as Mitsu, is elevated to a kind of sainthood by the purity of the relationship which he forms with his new Master.

Reared in a family broken and divided, separated from his friends by an unfamiliar religion, torn from his youth by a world war, and almost wrenched away from life itself by frequent battles with disease, Endō turned for his salvation to a literature of moral idealism.

By exalting and promoting standards of behavior which he sees as the only hope for meaningful interaction between one intrinsically selfish human being and another, Endō has sought to atone for all the loss and separation and weakness in his life and to bring a message of healing compassion to his readers. In the finest sense of moral fiction, he has been successful.

AFTERWORD

An All-But-Lost Generation

IN A perceptive essay on several of the writers of the Third Generation, the Japanese critic Saeki Shōichi, a professor of comparative literature, comments on some of the marked similarities between the Japanese authors of the fifties and the American writers of the twenties who came to be known as the Lost Generation.[1] It is tempting to consider the four authors who are the focus of this book as a Japanese "lost generation," particularly in light of the strength such a line of reasoning assumes when Malcolm Cowley's comments about the American lost generation are applied to the Japanese case:

> [This generation] was lost, first of all, because it was uprooted, schooled away and almost wrenched away from its attachment to any region or tradition. It was lost because its training had prepared it for another world than existed after the war. . . . It was lost because it tried to live in exile. It was lost because it accepted no older guides to conduct. . . . The generation belonged to a period of transition from values already fixed to values that had yet to be created. . . . They were seceding from the old and yet could adhere to nothing new. . . .[2]

However remarkable the parallels in private experience, though, the grounds for comparison when it comes to the literature seem less fertile. And the important question is not whether Japanese writers in the wake of World War II have experiences in common with the Hemingway-Fitzgerald generation, but whether the transformation of literary signifiers that grows out of those experiences is similar. My reading suggests that, whatever surface similarities may exist, the predominance of the I-novel tradition in the immediate past for the Japanese writer served to dictate a very different literary response from that of the Americans who came back alive from the war.

The assaults mounted by the Third Generation on the stalwart literary self of prewar personal fiction—as if they were retaliatory strikes to compensate for the loss of their youth—are the truly significant aspect of their writing. It appears evident now that Japanese authors, after approximately a century of experience with the modern novel, will continue to employ autobiographical materials as their means of communication with their readers. The crucial question then becomes that of the perspective or ironic distance which these novelists choose to place between themselves and their materials, since that question will determine the degree of defamiliarization that can be elicited from the private materials.

The success achieved by the prewar I-novelists in creating a layer of ironic distinction between themselves and their protagonists was minimal. While there are exceptions such as Iwano Hōmei, in whom the struggle to define a realm of concern larger than that of the narratorial consciousness is evident, for the most part the standard practitioners of the genre did not question the conception of self that was accepted as a social and literary construct in the years before the war.

With the Third Generation, however, all those assumptions have been shattered. While I would not presume to use literature as some sort of sociological textbook describing how those assumptions were dismantled, clearly destruction and rebuilding of the literary "I" were taking place. What is intriguing and ultimately revealing about the Third Generation is the diversity with which they pursue fundamentally similar literary activities.

Yasuoka undertakes his assault on the "I" by splitting the narrative ego into two separate parts—the persona who experiences the collapse but does not comprehend it, and the twin figure who stands just to the side and observes, with mute bemusement and pain, the terrible acts of selfishness that trigger the breaking down of human bonds. It is an agonizing separation, because half of the narrator's consciousness cannot see what is transpiring, while the other half sees but does not comment. There is no communication between these two voices in the discourse, and thus the narrative voice itself echoes the central thesis—that the traditional ties between one human being and another have been severed. Although in recent years Yasuoka has sought some form of mediation between the halves of his literary personae by turning to his roots in the past, at the core of his fiction is a gulf of silence that has yet to be spanned convincingly.

Shimao, in his continuing battles against himself—and I emphasize the masochistic drive in each of these authors' labors—never seems to achieve a ceasefire. His male protagonist—his "Toshio"—persists in the desperate attempt to cling to some kernel of defiant independence despite the knowledge that the same core of resistance triggers the holocaustic battles with his wife. What is remarkable about Shimao's fiction, and what sets him apart from his contemporaries (even those more conspicuously described as "Christian" writers), is the sincere attempt to stifle the last protests of the central literary ego and allow that traditionally male territory to be invaded and even dominated by the separate ego of the female protagonist. Thus Shimao's attempts at subduing the demobilized literary self are conducted with the knowledge that his male characters continue to conceal some of their weapons in the vain hope that they can retain some of their past prerogatives. The urge to plunge into the void, to receive the final orders to launch and send their torpedo boats hurtling toward certain death, is largely motivated by the guilt of knowing that the literary ego demands to go on living though it deserves to die.

The echo beneath the discourses in Kojima's fiction is that of the wrecking ball. The house that is not a home in *Embracing Family* is really a model of Shunsuke himself. It has been given the trappings of Western technological advancement, just as Shunsuke in his attempt to become a modern intellectual has made Western academic learning the center of his existence. But the house, the ideal dream home of Japan in the sixties, is found to have serious structural flaws. It may look like "a country villa in the highlands of California" (just as Shunsuke can impress others with his educational credentials), but the internal workings have gone berserk. There are leaks, mechanical breakdowns, malfunctions in the internal devices that control the environment of the home. Shunsuke, Sano, and other Kojima protagonists cannot stand at the center of the narratives because they are malfunctioning themselves. They cannot control their emotional environments, taking command of their families and asserting their private wills, because their internal thermostats have ceased to operate reliably. There is no means by which the male protagonists can respond to the adulteries of their wives: their newfangled appliances have come without directions for repair.

Finally, the process of dismantling the literary ego also takes place in the fiction of Endō. It is ironic, perhaps, that the strong, self-confident egos that appear in his fiction, and which are congruous with the central narrative intelligences of the prewar I-novelists, all happen to belong to Western proselytizers. But I am persuaded that Endō has set up these solid characters as counterparts to the narrators of the traditional I-novel: initial evidence for that can be elicited from the fact that each of these figures in Endō functions as a first-person narrator until his ego is broken down. But in his best works, such as *Silence* and *The Samurai,* the unwavering voice of the I-narrator is repeatedly challenged by a separate voice in the discourse, a voice that calls into question all the assumptions of the "I" and chips slowly—sometimes ruthlessly—away at that affirmative ego. It is, ultimately, the voice of God, demanding an abasement of the individual will and a submission to divine will. Endō's religious faith postulates the likelihood of a transformation of the shattered ego into a "new man," one who is weak but finally qualified for salvation through the renunciation of pride. In sum, then, Endō crushes the prewar literary self and damns it for its lack of humility, but through Christian intercession grants a new voice to a considerably less loquacious narrator.

What ultimately matters, then, is not whether these four writers qualify for membership in some reconstituted "lost generation" on Japanese soil. It is the separate and collective ways in which they have confronted the issue of narrative personality after the close of public hostilities. Although the private battles continue to be waged in various ways in their narratives, their victories have already been achieved through the reshaping of a new literature for contemporary Japan.

Notes

1. Demobilization of the Literary Self

1. Quoted in William Sibley, *The Shiga Hero* (Chicago: University of Chicago Press, 1979), p. 31.

2. Shiga Naoya, *A Dark Night's Passing,* trans. Edwin McClellan (Tokyo: Kodansha International, 1976), p. 340.

3. Dazai Osamu, *No Longer Human,* trans. Donald Keene (New York: Grove Press, 1958), pp. 24–25, 27.

4. Dazai Osamu, *The Setting Sun,* trans. Donald Keene (New York: Grove Press, 1956), p. 173.

5. Discussed in Endō Shūsaku, *Bungaku to geijutsu,* pp. 26–27.

6. This situation occurs in Yasuoka's story "Ga" (Moth, 1953; trans. 1984). Original text in *Yasuoka Shōtarō zenshū,* 3:107–25.

7. Hattori Tatsu, "Shinsedai no sakkatachi," *Warera ni totte bi wa sonzai suru ka,* pp. 310–11.

8. Yasuoka Shōtarō, *Boku no Shōwa-shi I,* p. 75.

9. Ibid., pp. 66–67.

10. Herbert Passin, *Society and Education in Japan,* p. 154.

11. Itō Shinkichi, et al., eds., *Nihon no shiika,* 31:327.

12. Ibid., pp. 332–33.

13. Ibid., p. 327.

14. Ibid., p. 330.

15. Shimao Toshio, "Watakushi no bungaku henreki," *Shimao Toshio zenshū,* 14:142.

16. Yasuoka, *Boku no Shōwa-shi,* pp. 180–81.

17. Endō Shūsaku, "Waga Nada-Chū jidai," *Gūtara mandanshū,* p. 10.

18. Kojima Nobuo, "Guntai jidai," *Shōsetsuka no hibi,* pp. 237–38.

19. Yasuoka, "Oyaji to segare," *Yasegaman no shisō,* pp. 81–84.

20. The title of one of Yasuoka's early stories, "Warui nakama," 1953. Original in *Zenshū,* 3:165–201.

21. Yasuoka, "Boku no seishun jidai," *Yasegaman,* pp. 94–95.

22. Yasuoka, "Chiisana katasumi no bessekai," *Nankotsu no seishin,* p. 20.

23. Shimao Toshio, "Tokkōtaiin no seikatsu," *Zenshū* 14:277–78.

24. Ibid., p. 278.

25. Ibid., p. 284.

26. Endō, "Watakushi no bungaku," *Endō Shūsaku bungaku zenshū,* 10:365; and "Endō Shūsaku no hon," a publicity flier included in Endō's *Iesu no shōgai* (Tokyo: Shinchōsha, 1973).

27. Endō, "Yoshimitsu Sensei no koto," in the first monthly bulletin included in the *Zenshū,* p. 2.

28. Yasuoka, *Boku no Shōwa-shi,* p. 252.

29. Ibid., pp. 242–44.

30. Yoshiyuki Junnosuke, *Watakushi no bungaku hōrō,* pp. 26–27.

31. The *Hagakure* was a compilation of the teachings of a samurai-priest named Yamamoto Jōchō (1659–1719). In its day, it was one of many guidebooks to proper behavior of the warrior class. "*Hagakure* became available to the reading public for the first time in the Meiji Era, when its principles of loyalty were reinterpreted in terms of loyalty to the emperor and the Japanese nation. In the nationalistic fervor of the 1930s, several editions and commentaries were published, lavishly extolling Jōchō's teachings as *yamato-damashii,* the 'unique spirit of the Japanese.' During the Second World War, editions proliferated and sold in staggering numbers. 'I found that the Way of the Samurai is death,' became a slogan used to spur young Kamikaze pilots to their deaths." Kathryn Sparling, "Translator's Note," in *The Way of the Samurai: Yukio Mishima on "Hagakure" in Modern Life* (New York: Basic Books, 1977), viii.

32. When Kojima was asked in 1981 by *Yomiuri Shimbun* to write a series of articles for serialization under the title "The Japanese Classics and Myself," the work he chose for discussion was *Mon.*

33. The leading popular writer of romance novels in the late Edo period, Tamenaga Shunsui (1790–1843) published a work, *Shunshoku umegoyomi* (Colors of Spring: The Plum Calendar), between 1832 and 1833 which is considered the finest work of fiction of the early nineteenth century in Japan. For a discussion of Shunsui and his work, see Donald Keene, *World Within Walls* (New York: Holt, Rinehart, and Winston, 1976), pp. 417–23.

34. Kawabata's wartime literary models included *Genji* and *Ise monogatari;* Kafū read Edo *gesaku* literature and wrote a scholarly study of Tamenaga Shunsui; Dazai rewrote medieval fairy tales and some of Ihara Saikaku's stories into modern Japanese.

35. For instance, Endō's remark about a gathering of new critics he attended was: "I couldn't understand a word of what they said." See Endō Shūsaku and Kita Morio, *Korian vs. Mambō,* p. 90.

36. Yasuoka, *Boku no Shōwa-shi,* pp. 148–49. Hotta Yoshie (b. 1918) studied French literature and was heavily influenced by symbolism in his own poetry. His short work "Hiroba no kodoku" (Solitude in the Plaza, 1951) established him as an important member of the Sengoha group with its focus on the crisis of intellectualism in postwar Japan.

37. Yasuoka, "Watakushi-shōsetsu to shisō," *Shisō onchi no shisō,* pp. 126–27.

38. F. Scott Fitzgerald, *Babylon Revisited and Other Stories* (New York: Scribner's, 1960), p. 229.

39. Yasuoka, "Shippai to tsumazuki," *Bushō no akuma,* p. 11.

40. Quoted in the chronology appended to Yasuoka, *Hashire Tomahōku,* p. 216.

41. Kojima, "Waga uchi o tateru ki," *Shōsetsuka,* p. 156.

42. Endō, "Shussesaku no koro," *Bungaku to geijutsu,* p. 81.

43. Shimao, "Hachi-gatsu jūgo-nichi," *Zenshū,* 14:251.

2. Collapse of the Literary Group

1. Katō Shūichi, *A History of Japanese Literature,* p. 172.

2. Shindō Junkō, *Bundan shiki,* p. 36.

3. Kuwabara Takeo is the critic who denigrated haiku in his "Daini geijutsuron," which has been translated in Kuwabara, *Japan and Western Civilization,* pp. 187–202; Usui Yoshimi questioned the foundations of Japanese poetry.

4. Hirano Ken, quoted in Matsubara Shin'ichi, Isoda Kōichi, and Akiyama Shun, *Sengo Nihon bungaku shi, nempyō,* pp. 154–55.

5. Yamamoto Kenkichi, "Daisan no shinjin," p. 86.

6. Yoshiyuki, *Bungaku hōrō,* p. 103.

7. Yamamoto's list included eight writers: Nishino Tatsukichi, Inoue Mitsuharu, Hasegawa Shirō, Hanawa Hideo, Takeda Shigetarō, Itō Keiichi, Sawano Hisao, and Yoshiyuki.

8. Yoshiyuki, *Bungaku hōrō,* pp. 74–75.

9. Yoshiyuki maintains it was "probably" on March 12, 1953; ibid., p. 76. Shindō is uncertain whether it was February or March; Shindō, *Shiki,* p. 12. Kojima, the most meticulous of the three, asserts that it was on February 12;

Kojima, "Watakushi no gurūpu: Akutagawa Shō kōho sakkatachi," *Shōsetsuka,* p. 245.

10. Yoshiyuki, *Bungaku hōrō,* p. 76.

11. Kojima, "Watakushi no gurūpu," *Shōsetsuka,* p. 249.

12. Shindō, *Shiki,* p. 39.

13. See Yoshiyuki, *Bungaku hōrō,* p. 68, and Yasuoka, *Ryōyū, akuyū,* pp. 15–16.

14. The first of the Third Generation to be nominated for the prize was Shimao Toshio, for "Shukusadame" in 1949. Yasuoka followed as a nominee in 1951 for "Garasu no kutsu," and Yoshiyuki's name was first mentioned for "Genshoku no machi" in the latter half of that same year. In the first part of 1952, Yasuoka, Yoshiyuki, and Miura were all nominees, and four from the One-Two Association received some support in the second half of the year—Yasuoka, Yoshiyuki, Kondō Keitarō, and Kojima.

15. Kojima, "Watakushi no gurūpu," *Shōsetsuka,* p. 250.

16. Kojima, ibid., and Shindō, *Shiki,* p. 20.

17. See Kojima, "Bunrui—'Daisan no shinjin' to yobarete," pp. 389–90.

18. See Shindō, *Shiki,* pp. 41, 45; and Kojima, "Ichigaya Eki fukin," *Shōsetsuka,* p. 260.

19. Or, if Yoshiyuki's chronology is accepted, five meetings.

20. Hirano Ken, *Bungei jihyō,* 1:106.

21. Hasegawa Izumi, ed., *Akutagawa Shō jiten,* p. 109.

22. Yamamoto Kenkichi, in a review of contemporary literature published in December 1954. Quoted in Shindō, *Shiki,* p. 74.

23. Shindō, *Shiki,* p. 70.

24. The "White Birch" group of the late Meiji and early Taishō periods, including Shiga Naoya, Mushakōji Saneatsu, and Arishima Takeo.

25. Shindō, *Shiki,* p. 161.

26. Yasuoka, *Ryōyū, akuyū,* pp. 40–43.

27. Both Hattori and Endō worked briefly on this magazine.

28. Yoshiyuki, *Bungaku hōrō,* p. 103.

29. In 1956, there were televisions in 165,000 households; by 1958 the number had reached 1,560,000. See Shindō, *Shiki,* p. 164.

30. Hasegawa Izumi and Takeda Katsuhiko, eds., *Gendai shimbun shōsetsu jiten,* pp. 108–40.

31. A quotation from the hero of Ishihara's Akutagawa Prize novel, *Taiyō no kisetsu* (Season of Violence; trans. 1966).

32. The title of one of Togaeri's books, *Bundan no hōkai,* 1956.

33. Shindō, *Shiki,* pp. 16, 120.

34. Endō Shūsaku, "Kōsō no kai no koto," in the fourth monthly bulletin included in *Kojima Nobuo zenshū* pp. 7–8.

35. Yoshiyuki, *Bungaku hōrō,* p. 102. Yoshiyuki speculates that the comment about being "swallowed up" was probably made by Usui Yoshimi; see p. 103.

36. Shindō suggests this in *Shiki,* p. 133.

37. American figures somewhat more importantly in Shōno Junzō's fiction and Yasuoka's essays.

38. Yoshiyuki, *Bungaku hōrō,* p. 102.

39. Ibid., p. 104.

40. Quoted in Shindō, *Shiki,* p. 203.

41. Yoshiyuki, *Bungaku hōrō,* p. 102. In Japanese, "Daisan kantai wa chimbotsu shikakatteru!"

42. The title of one of Endō's essay collections, *Boku wa kōkishin no katamari* (Tokyo: Shinchōsha, 1976).

43. Shindō, *Shiki,* p. 112.

44. Ibid., pp. 109–11.

45. Ibid., pp. 109, 116.

46. The novel received both the fifth Shinchōsha Literary Prize and the twelfth Mainichi Shuppan Cultural Prize, an unusual distinction for a work of fiction.

47. See Shindō, *Shiki,* p. 175.

48. Yoshiyuki, *Bungaku hōrō,* p. 103; Shindō, *Shiki,* p. 203.

49. Yoshiyuki, *Bungaku hōrō,* p. 105.

50. Shindō, *Shiki,* p. 212.

51. Abe Akira, in a symposium with Ueda Miyoji and Akiyama Shun, titled "Daisan no shinjin no kōzai," *Mita Bungaku* (January 1972), p. 6.

52. Hattori concentrated on ten: Agawa Hiroyuki, Maeda Yoshitaka, Shimao, Yasuoka, Yoshiyuki, Hasegawa Shirō, Hanawa Hideo, Koyama Kiyoshi, Takeda Shigetarō, and Miura.

53. Hattori, "Shinsedai no sakkatachi," *Bi wa sonzai suru ka,* pp. 300–7.

54. "Bieder" means plain or unpretentious; "Meier" is a common surname. "Papa Biedermeier" was a popular cartoon figure who emblemized the values of the Viennese middle class. See *New York Times,* November 28, 1985, p. 15.

55. See Takeda Tomoju's discussion of novel length in *Endō Shūsaku no bungaku,* p. 171.

56. Yasuoka, *Nankotsu no seishin,* pp. 16–17; see also "*Kindai Bungaku* no kōzai," in *Mita Bungaku* (March 1954), 9:22.

57. An interesting discussion of this paradox is found in Torii Kunio, "Sengo bungaku ni okeru 'Daisan no shinjin' no ichi," pp. 55–66.

58. Miura Shumon married Sono in 1953.

59. Hattori,"Rettōsei," *Bi wa sonzai suru ka,* pp. 348–49, 364.

60. See Fukuda Kōnen, "Sengo bungaku ron oboegaki."

61. In his introduction to a translation of Tayama Katai's *Futon* (The Quilt), Kenneth G. Henshall attributes considerably more of a sense of objectivity and ironic distance to Katai's narrator than I would allow. See Tayama, *The Quilt and Other Stories by Tayama Katai,* trans. Henshall (Tokyo: University of Tokyo Press, 1981). I am more inclined to sympathize with the attitudes expressed in

Fukuda Tsuneari's "Kaisetsu" (Commentary), found in Tayama, *Futon, Jūemon no saigo* (Tokyo: Shinchōsha, Shinchō Bunko, 1952), pp. 174–81, in which Fukuda expresses the view that Katai was really no more than a literary adolescent *(bungaku seinen)* who had no real artistic or intellectual perspective on his subject matter.

62. Two persuasive and enlightening studies on the prewar *shishōsetsu,* with conclusions that differ from my own, are Irmela Hijiya-Kirschnereit's *Selbstentblossungsrituale* (Wiesbaden: Steiner, 1981) and Edward Fowler's *The Rhetoric of Confession.*

63. My discussion of the role of the I-novel in pre- and postwar Japan owes much to a symposium featuring Aeba Takao, Saeki Shōichi, Ueda Miyoji, and Isoda Kōichi, titled "Watakushi-shōsetsu," in *Bungakkai* (February 1980), 34:2:148–75.

64. The other two works examined are Yoshiyuki Junnosuke's *Tsuki to hoshi wa ten no ana* (Tokyo: Kōdansha, 1966) and Shōno Junzō's *Yube no kumo* (Tokyo: Kōdansha, 1965).

65. See Natsume Sōseki, "Watakushi no kojin-shugi," *Sōseki zenshū,* 17 vols. (Tokyo: Iwanami Shoten, 1974–76), 11:431–63; a translation and critical study by Jay Rubin, "Sōseki on Individualism: 'Watakushi no Kojinshugi,' " appeared in *Monumenta Nipponica* (Spring 1979), 34:21–48.

66. See Yamamoto Kenkichi, "Kaisetsu," p. 511.

67. Yet another distinctive feature indicative of the newness of the Third Generation's fiction is this frequent use of the colloquial "boku" for the first-person male narrator, rather than the strong and confident "jibun" employed by Shiga Naoya in the prewar period.

68. Few of these authors have been translated extensively into English despite the importance of their work.

Kōno Taeko (b. 1926), richly influenced by her reading of Tanizaki, depicts contemporary women who lead placid, everyday lives as middle-class wives but whose minds are filled with dreams of perverted sexuality, sadomasochism, and violent death; her collection, *Saigo no toki* (The Last Time, 1967; title story trans. 1982), is representative, while her novella, *Fui no koe* (An Unexpected Voice, 1968), perhaps best exemplifies the layer of violent, erotic frustration that lies just beneath the surface of her female characters' consciousness.

Ōba Minako (b. 1930), who joined Kōno Taeko in 1987 as the first two women to serve on the selection committee for the Akutagawa Prize, has been called by some a "female Kojima Nobuo" for the walls of icy distance that separate the male and female characters in works such as "Sambiki no kani" (The Three Crabs, 1968; trans. 1982) and *Katachimonaku* (Without Shape, 1982), a novel which received the Tanizaki Prize.

Takahashi Takako (b. 1932) has mounted perhaps the most aggressive assaults on the concept of a literary ego in contemporary Japanese fiction. In stories such as "Ningyō-ai" (Doll Love, 1976; trans. 1982) and the novella (*Tōku, kutsū no tani o aruite iru toki* (As I Walk Through the Endless Valley of Torment, 1983), Takahashi dissolves the individuality of her characters into a kind of subterranean pool; most recently, as a result of her religious training at a Catholic convent in Paris, Takahashi has come to see this ego-demolition as a merging with God.

Tsushima Yūko (b. 1947), the daughter of Dazai Osamu, most often depicts women who are single parents and have to barter with those around them in order to cope with everyday reality; that is seen most clearly in "Danmari ichi" (The Silent Traders, 1984; trans. 1985). Her recent novel *Yoru no hikari ni owarete* (Driven by the Light of the Night, 1986) is a sensitive communication of the loss of her own son addressed to the woman author of an eleventh-century tale.

Inoue Hisashi (b. 1934) is a vibrant satirist who works extensively in drama and the novel; he is best known for his long pastiche of contemporary Japanese society, *Kirikirijin* (The People of Kirikiri, 1981), a linguistic tour-de-force.

Maruya Saiichi (b. 1925), a Joyce scholar who has also translated Graham Greene's entertainment novels into Japanese, has persuasively satirized the Japanese "businessman" ethic in *Tatta hitori no hanran* (Singular Rebellion, 1972; trans. 1986), for which he won the Tanizaki Prize.

Miura Shumon (b. 1926) and his wife Sono Ayako (b. 1931) are generally classified as members of the Third Generation. Miura began his career as a stylist who was compared to Akutagawa; his *Hakoniwa* (Miniature Garden, 1967) is considered one of the prototypes of the Third Generation "domestic novels" describing the collapse of the Japanese family. Sono's writing, as represented by the novel *Mumeihi* (Nameless Monument, 1969), places characters in conflicts that have no easy resolution, despite her clear expressions of religious faith.

Sakata Hiroo (b. 1925), a poet and lyricist for popular children's songs in Japan, established himself as a writer of fiction with a sensitive study of the death of his mother, "Tsuchi no utsuwa" (The Earthen Vessel, 1974), which also became the literary affirmation of his own Christian faith.

Yashiro Seiichi (b. 1927) is a playwright who, under the influence of Giraudoux and Anouilh, has brought poetic sensitivity to the depiction of some of the eccentrics of Edo Japan, as exemplied by his *Hokusai manga* (Hokusai Sketchbooks, 1973; trans. 1979).

Mori Reiko (b. 1928) is a playwright, novelist, and the author of numerous radio scripts; "Tanin no chi" (The Blood of Another, 1971) is her best-known work.

Ōhara Tomie (b. 1912) received both the Mainichi Cultural Prize and the Noma Prize for her *En to iu onna* (A Woman Called En, 1960; trans. 1986), a contemporary reading of the meaning of imprisonment and liberation to a woman of the Edo period.

3. The Loss of Home: Yasuoka Shōtarō

1. Yasuoka Shōtarō, *Jijōden ryokō,* pp. 5–6.
2. Yasuoka, *Ryūritan,* 1:3.
3. Yasuoka, "Kokyō," *Yasuoka Shōtarō zenshū,* 4:120.
4. Yasuoka, "Utsukushii hitomi," *Zenshū,* 5:7–8.
5. Yasuoka, "Shōnen jidai," *Yasegaman,* p. 79.
6. Yasuoka, "Kokyō," *Zenshū,* 4:122.
7. Yasuoka, "Shukudai," *Zenshū,* 3:54–55.
8. Ibid., p. 87.
9. The title of Etō's critical work on the "Third Generation," *Seijuku to sōshitsu: "haha" no hōkai,* discussed in chapter 2.
10. Yasuoka Shōtarō, *A View by the Sea,* trans. Kāren Wigen Lewis (New York: Columbia University Press, 1984), p. 31. Further page references are given in the text.
11. Lewis has been somewhat free in her translation of this passage. The sentence which she has rendered as "Since when do you think you're going to be an officer in the Imperial Navy with a thing like that?" is, in the original: "Kisama, sonna koto de Teikoku kaigun no shōkō toshite, kokka no o-yaku ni tateru to omou ka?" Taken quite literally, the sentence means, "You bastard, do you think you'll be of any value to your country as an officer in the Imperial Navy *with behavior like that?"* (emphasis mine). The navy doctor would appear to be berating a young man for standing in his loincloth with his hands covering his private parts. The "koto" thus becomes the young man's "posture" or "behavior" rather than specifically referring to his "thing," but in either case, the result for Juntarō is the same, so I have stayed with Lewis' translation here.
12. Ivan Morris, trans., *The Pillow Book of Sei Shōnagon* (Middlesex: Penguin Books, 1971), p. 21.
13. Translation by Ivan Morris, *The Nobility of Failure,* pp. 131–32. The Japanese text may be found in Itō Shinkichi, et al., eds., *Nihon no shiika,* 31:78.
14. For a brief description of this scene in English, see George Sansom, *A History of Japan, 1334–1615* (Tokyo: Tuttle, 1974), pp. 125–26. The original text is in the *Taiheiki,* Nihon Koten Bungaku Taikei (Tokyo: Iwanami Shoten, 1961), 35:169–71.
15. A significant name, in that it was the name of the protagonist in Yasuoka's first (lost) story, and reoccurs as the name of his ancestor in *Ryūritan.*
16. Hino Keizō, "Kaisetsu: Tanin o miru me," p. 224.
17. Yasuoka, *Tonsō, Zenshū,* 2:199–201. Further page references are given in the text.
18. One of Kasuke's tasks at one hospital is to chip away the ice that has frozen all the fecal matter in a drop toilet.
19. Kojima Nobuo, " 'Daisan no shinjin' to Amerika bungaku."

20. Hirano Ken, for one, considered it superior to the more widely praised "Aigan" (Prized Possessions; trans. 1977); see Hirano, *Bungei jihyō,* 1:80.

21. Yasuoka, "Kembu," *Zenshū,* 3:205.

22. See Etō, *Seijuku,* p. 17.

23. Paralepsis, or "paralepse," is described by Scholes as the art "of conveying to the reader more information than the code required by [the narrator's] perspective 'ought' to convey." Robert Scholes, *Semiotics and Interpretation,* p. 98.

24. The nine days may be significant, representing the nine months of pregnancy. Lewis has an unpublished essay on the novel, "A Translator's Postscript," which makes this point.

25. My trans.; Yasuoka, *Kaihen no kōkei, Zenshū,* 1:357.

26. Ibid., 1:427–29.

27. Yasuoka, *Maku ga orite kara, Zenshū,* 1:295–96.

28. It is no coincidence that this is also the name of the main character in *Flight.*

4. The Eternal War: Shimao Toshio

1. For a description of the torpedo boats, see Shimao Toshio and Yoshida Mitsuru, *Tokkō taiken to sengo,* pp. 10–11 ff.; in English, see Ivan Morris, *The Nobility of Failure,* ch. 10.

2. Shimao, "Tokkōtaiin no seikatsu," *Zenshū,* 14:275–87.

3. Knowing that a draft notice would arrive soon after he graduated from Kyushu University, and unable to bear the thought that he would be forced into a "group" training situation if he were placed in the army, Shimao volunteered for the navy, hoping to become a solitary pilot. But he lacked the qualifications for flight school, and he was sent off to basic, "group" training. See Shimao, "Kyarameru jiken—Waga guntai seikatsu," *Zenshū,* 14:102–5.

4. Shimao, "Tokkōtaiin no seikatsu," *Zenshū,* 14:285–86.

5. Shimao, "Shuppatsu wa tsui ni otozurezu," in *Shuppatsu wa tsui ni otozurezu,* pp. 297–98.

6. See the *nempu* in Shimao, *Shi no toge,* p. 373.

7. Morris, *Nobility of Failure,* p. 290. Morris discusses various levels of ambiguity surrounding these pilots, but my interest here is in the expectations that were thrust upon them.

8. Shimao Miho, "Tokkōtaichō no koro," in her *Umibe no sei to shi* (Tokyo: Sōjusha, 1974), pp. 143–47. Translation by Kathryn Sparling in Shimao Toshio, *"The Sting of Death" and Other Stories,* pp. 180–81.

9. Shimao, "Haishi," *Shuppatsu,* p. 232.

10. The title of one of Shimao's domestic stories.

11. Shimao, "Tandoku ryokōsha," *Shuppatsu,* pp. 75–76. Further page references are given in the text.

12. Shimao has described his realistic stories as those written with his "eyes open," and the surrealist works as those composed with his "eyes closed." See "Waga shōsėtsu," *Zenshū,* 14:73–75.

13. I place "novelist" in quotation marks because in the original Shimao purposely avoids the use of the familiar Japanese "shōsetsuka" and instead uses the term "noberisuto." The foreign ring to the term has an effect similar to that of the Western-style hotel where "Solitary Traveler" is set.

14. Sparling, *"The Sting of Death,"* p. 154. Further page references are given in the text.

15. Comment made by Ōe Kenzaburō to an informal gathering of students at the University of California, Berkeley on November 18, 1983.

16. See Donald Keene, *World Within Walls* (New York: Holt, Rinehart, and Winston, 1976), pp. 136–37 for a discussion of the aesthetic principles of *fueki* and *ryūkō* in Bashō's poetry.

17. Sparling's very interesting critical comments on this story provide a Jung-Neumann psychoanalytical approach to the work.

18. "Kisōsha" literally means "one who returns to the nest," a reference to the homing instinct in birds.

19. Shimao, "Kisōsha no yūutsu," *Shuppatsu,* p. 190.

20. See, for instance, the stories in this category by Yokomitsu Riichi and Kambayashi Akatsuki; there is a comparison of the "byōsai-mono" of these two writers in Dennis Keene, *Yokomitsu Riichi: Modernist* (New York: Columbia University Press, 1980), ch. 5.

21. For a discussion of this "therapeutic" element in Shimao's fiction, see Iwaya Seishō, *Shimao Toshio ron,* pp. 9–46.

22. Shimao Toshio, "With Maya," my trans., adapted from Van C. Gessel and Tomone Matsumoto, eds., *The Shōwa Anthology,* 1:197. Further page references are given in the text. The original is in *Shuppatsu,* pp. 251–81.

23. In a few English sources, the title is translated as *The Thorns of Death,* and confusion over its derivation is also evident in Japan; see Yamamoto Kenkichi's "kaisetsu" in Shimao, *Shi no toge,* pp. 506–14. However, there is no doubt which Japanese translation of the Bible Shimao knew, nor that the language corresponds exactly.

24. Shimao, *Shi no toge,* p. 5. Further page references are given in the text.

25. The title of the first chapter of the novel is *Ridatsu* (Separation).

26. See, for instance, my comments in the discussion of "Thick the New Leaves" in chapter 3.

27. Noriko Mizuta Lippit makes this claim about the I-novel in her review of Dennis Keene's *Yokomitsu Riichi: Modernist,* published in *Journal of Asian Studies* (November 1981), 41:138.

5. Human Handicapped: Kojima Nobuo

1. Kojima, *Zenshū,* 6:330–31.

2. Gogol's decision is cited in the translator's "Introduction," Gogol, *Diary of a Madman and Other Stories,* trans. Ronald Wilks (London: Penguin Books, 1972), p. 7. Kojima's similar declaration is found in *Zenshū,* 6:359.

3. Wilks, "Introduction," *Madman,* pp. 14–15.

4. Kojima, *Bungaku danshō,* p. 29.

5. Kojima was interested enough in Saroyan to do a translation of his *The Human Comedy* in 1957.

6. Kojima, "Atogaki," *Zenshū,* 4:329.

7. Kojima was one of the first Japanese authors to write about the war in a pervasively satirical vein. It is interesting to see an American writer use essentially the same image of the ambivalent soldier as Kojima employed more than thirty years earlier in "Stars"—see Richard Wiley's 1986 novel, *Soldiers in Hiding* (Boston: Atlantic Monthly Press, 1986).

8. Kojima, "Stars," my trans. from Gessel and Matsumoto, eds., *The Shōwa Anthology,* 1:101–2. Further page references are given in the text. The original is in Kojima, *Zenshū,* 4:137–61.

9. Excerpt translated in Donald Keene, ed., *Modern Japanese Literature* (New York: Grove Press, 1956).

10. Kojima, *Bohimei, Zenshū,* 2:287–88.

11. Kojima, "Kisha no naka," *Amerikan sukūru,* p. 8. Further page references are given in the text.

12. See Isoda Kōichi, "Kaisetsu," p. 242.

13. Kojima, "Gifu-shi no ninjō," *Shōsetsuka,* pp. 223–24.

14. Sone Hiroyoshi, "Kojima Nobuo to warai: 'Kisha no naka' o chūshin ni," *Kokubungaku Kaishaku to Kanshō* (February 1972), 37:43.

15. The essay is in *Shōsetsuka,* p. 289 ff.

16. Kojima, *Zenshū,* 6:331; this remark was made in 1954, before Kojima wrote *Hōyō kazoku.*

17. Kojima, "Bishō," *Zenshū,* 4:175. Further page references are given in the text.

18. This values inversion is discussed by Torii Kunio in "Sengo bungaku ni okeru 'Daisan no shinjin' no ichi."

19. See, in particular, Abe's "Akai mayu" (The Red Cocoon, 1950; trans. 1972) and "Mahō no chōku" (The Magic Chalk, 1950; trans. 1982).

20. Kojima, "American School," trans. William F. Sibley in Howard Hibbett, ed., *Contemporary Japanese Literature,* p. 129.

21. Kojima, "Amerikan sukūru," *Zenshū,* 4:233 (my trans.).

22. Sibley, trans., "American School," in Hibbett, ed., *Contemporary Japanese Literature,* p. 136.

23. Kojima, "Uma," *Amerikan sukūru,* p. 236. Further page references are given in the text.

24. Futabatei, *Ukigumo,* trans. as *Japan's First Modern Novel* by Marleigh Grayer Ryan (New York: Columbia University Press, 1967).

25. Tsubouchi Shōyō, "Futabatei no koto," trans. by Ryan in *First Modern Novel,* p. 75.

26. Interview with Kojima, Tokyo, February 6, 1978.

27. Etō, *Seijuku,* p. 125.

28. Kawashima Itaru, *"Hōyō kazoku," Kokubungaku Kaishaku to Kanshō* (February 1972), 37:120. The relative ease with which the novel was adapted to the stage in 1971 is further evidence of this point.

29. Kojima, *Hōyō kazoku, Zenshū* 3:105. Further page references are given in the text.

30. Scholes, *Semiotics and Interpretation,* p. 184.

31. Scholes, *Structuralism in Literature,* p. 184.

32. Isoda, "Kaisetsu," p. 257.

33. See, for instance, Tokiko's rambling thought processes at *Zenshū* 3:50.

6. Salvation of the Weak: Endō Shūsaku

1. A subjective view, no doubt, but one confirmed by my reading of Endō's work and my experience as a missionary in Japan in 1970–1971. In a survey of Japanese religious attitudes conducted by the Agency for Cultural Affairs, the following conclusion is drawn: "The status of Christianity in Japan is remarkably similar to that of Marxism. Both have been taken up to a certain extent, particularly among intellectuals, but most people find it difficult to relate to either one. Both are held at arms' length by the establishment." See *Japanese Religion: A Survey by the Agency for Cultural Affairs,* pp. 72–73.

2. Endō, "Watakushi no *Hizakurige,"* p. 1.

3. Fujitsuna Ryōzō suggests in "Rettōsei no tensai" that Endō has overemphasized his own failures; see the fifth monthly bulletin in the first volume of the *Endō Shūsaku bungaku zenshū,* pp. 4–6.

4. Endō, "Iya na yatsu," *Zenshū,* 3:199–200; my trans. from *Stained Glass Elegies: Stories by Shusaku Endo,* trans. Van C. Gessel, pp. 41–42. Further page references to the translations in *Stained Glass Elegies* are given in the text.

5. Scholes, *Semiotics and Interpretation,* p. 65.

6. From "Sono zenjitsu" (1963), *Zenshū,* 4:49.

7. The "wall" image is used extensively in Endō's 1965 novel *Ryūgaku;* text in the fifth volume of the *Zenshū.*

8. Endō, "Ihōjin no kunō," *Bessatsu Shimpyō: Endō Shūsaku no sekai* (Winter 1973), 6:57.

9. From Endō's Akutagawa Prize acceptance speech; see Hasegawa, *Akutagawa Shō jiten,* p. 198.

10. Endō, *Kiiroi hito,* p. 113.

11. Ibid., p. 87.

12. Saeki Shōichi, " 'Kanashii me' no sōzōryoku," pp. 58–59.

13. A peculiar name which Endō has used for his protagonists in *The Sea and Poison,* several short stories, and *Scandal* (1986).

14. Endō, "Watakushi no mono," *Zenshū,* 4:205–6.

15. Nagao is clearly modeled after Shimao Toshio, Mita after Miura Shumon.

16. Endō, "Watakushi no mono," *Zenshū,* 4:220.

17. Ibid., p. 221.

18. Quoted, with minor revisions in some passages, from Endō, *Silence,* trans. William Johnston, pp. 79, 82. Further page references are given in the text. Original in *Zenshū,* 6:51, 53.

19. Endō, *Chimmoku, Zenshū,* 6:92–93 (my trans.)

20. Ibid., 6:114.

21. See Endō and Miyoshi Yukio, "Bungaku–Jakusha no ronri," p. 26.

22. Endō, *Chimmoku, Zenshū,* 6:199–200.

23. Takadō Kaname, "Endō Shūsaku ni okeru jakusha no ronri," *Kokubungaku Kaishaku to Kanshō* (June 1975), 50:82.

24. Endō, "Haha naru mono," *Zenshū,* 6:230; my trans., modified from Gessel, *Stained Glass Elegies,* p. 108. Further page references to the *Zenshū* are given in the text.

25. Endō, *Watashi ga suteta onna,* p. 29. Further page references are given in the text.

26. Francis Mathy makes this comparison in the introduction to his translation of Endō's *Wonderful Fool,* p. 10.

27. Like many of his predecessors, Endō has often toyed with the names of his characters, playing upon names of his personal friends and suggesting certain personality traits with his choices of names. (With intentional irony, the murderer in *Wonderful Fool* is named Endō. In *Onna no isshō—Kiku no baai,* the villain is named Hondō Shuntarō, a humorous jab at Endō's publisher friend at Shōgakkan, Hondō Shun.) I cannot shake the impression that Endō is making a good-humored, if rather telling, swipe at the rampant antimetaphysical leanings of the postwar Japanese literary world in his selection of the name Yoshioka. Even among his close friends in the Third Generation, Endō has had to deal with a marked lack of interest in his religious literary quests. And certainly two of the most materialist of the authors in Endō's generation have been Yoshiyuki Junnosuke and Yasuoka Shōtarō. The fact that a merging of their names produces "Yoshioka" may be mere coincidence; but the proliferation of characters in their fiction who have no interest in anything they cannot comprehend with

their five senses suggests to me that the subtext of his novel reflects Endō's preoccupation with "metaphysical criticism"; along with Hattori Tatsu and Muramatsu Takeshi, Endō published a series of "Metafijikku hyōron" essays in *Bungakkai* in 1955.

28. Referring, of course, to Mauriac's novel of that title, which Endō translated into Japanese.

29. Endō, *Samurai,* pp. 113–14. Further page references are given in the text.

30. This discursive reticence on Hasekura's part suggests a warrior who has never ventured into the battlefield; it is interesting to note that one of the few changes Endō made in the historical facts surrounding the life of Hasekura was to state in the novel that the samurai had never seen battle.

Afterword

1. Saeki Shōichi, "Kaisetsu."
2. Malcolm Cowley, *Exile's Return,* p. 9.

Bibliography

Works in Japanese

All Japanese-language works were published in Tokyo, unless otherwise indicated.

Abe Akira. "Haigo ni wadakamaru mono." In Yasuoka Shōtarō, *Kaihen no kōkei,* pp. 254–68. Kōdansha, Kōdansha Bunko, 1971.

Aeba Takao. "Katorikku to Nihon bungaku." *Kokubungaku Kaishaku to Kanshō* (June 1967), 32:24–28.

Aeba Takao, Isoda Kōichi, Saeki Shōichi, and Ueda Miyoji. "Watakushi shōsetsu." *Bungakkai* (February 1980), 34:148–75.

Bessatsu Shimpyō: Endō Shūsaku no sekai. Special issue on Endō (Winter 1973), vol. 6.

An entire issue devoted to Endō, both as a literary figure and as a media personality. Over three dozen pieces, ranging from humorous reminiscences to serious critical considerations of Endō's work by such people as Hirano Ken, Etō Jun, Nakamura Mitsuo, Takeda Tomoju, and others. Includes the most detailed "self-chronology" Endō has written.

Endō Shūsaku. *Bungaku to geijutsu.* Kōdansha, Endō Shūsaku Bunko, 1977.

—— *Endō Shūsaku bungaku zenshū.* 11 vols. Shinchōsha, 1975.

Though limited to Endō's serious ("literary") works, this collection will likely remain the most convenient for readers for some time. There are informative articles in each of the monthly bulletins.

—— *Gūtara mandanshū.* Kadokawa Shoten, Kadokawa Bunko, 1978.

—— *Hechimakun.* Kōdansha, Endō Shūsaku Bunko, 1975.

Endō Shūsaku. *Jūichi no iro garasu.* Shinchōsha, 1979.

—— "Kaisetsu." In Yasuoka Shōtarō, *Maku ga orite kara,* pp. 271–82. Kōdansha, Kōdansha Bunko, 1971.

—— *Kiiroi hito.* Shinchōsha, Shinchō Bunko, 1960.

—— *Kuchibue o fuku toki.* Kōdansha, 1974.

—— *Ningen no naka no X.* Chūō Kōron Sha, 1978.

—— *Obakasan.* Chūō Kōron Sha, 1971.

—— *Samurai.* Shinchōsha, 1980.

—— *Sekai kikō.* Kōdansha, Endō Shūsaku Bunko, 1975.

—— *Sukyandaru.* Shinchōsha, 1986.

—— *Taihen daa.* Shinchōsha, Shinchō Bunko, 1973.

—— *Waga seishun ni kui ari.* Kadokawa Shoten, Kadokawa Bunko, 1974.

—— "Watakushi no *Hizakurige.*" In monthly bulletin of *Tōkaidōchū hizakurige.* Nihon Koten Bungaku Zenshū 49. Shōgakkan, 1970–76.

—— *Watashi ga suteta onna.* Kōdansha, Kōdansha Bunko, 1972.

—— *Yūmoa shōsetsu shū.* Kōdansha, Kōdansha Bunko, 1973.

Endō Shūsaku and Kita Morio. *Korian vs. Mambō.* Kōdansha, 1974.

Endō Shūsaku, Kojima Nobuo, Shōno Junzō, Yasuoka Shōtarō, and Yoshiyuki Junnosuke. "Bungaku to shishitsu." *Bungei* (July 1965), 4:124–52.

Endō Shūsaku and Miyoshi Yukio. "Bungaku—Jakusha no ronri." *Kokubungaku* (February 1973), 10–29.

Endō Shūsaku, Okuno Takeo, Muramatsu Takeshi, Hattori Tatsu, Yasuoka Shōtarō, Shimao Toshio, Kojima Nobuo, and Katsura Yoshihisa."*Kindai Bungaku* no kōzai." *Mita Bungaku* (March 1954), 9:6–23.

Etō Jun. *Etō Jun zentaiwa.* 4 vols. Ozawa Shoten, 1974. Vol. 1: *Bungaku no nagare no naka de.*

—— "Kaisetsu." *Endō Shūsaku, Kojima Nobuo shū.* Shin Nihon Bungaku Zenshū 9. Shūeisha, 1964.

—— *Seijuku to sōshitsu: "Haha" no hōkai.* Kawade Shobō Shinsha, Kawade Bungei Sensho, 1975.

Fukuda Kōnen. "Sengo bungaku ron oboegaki: Daisan no shinjin no ichizuke." *Bungakkai* (November 1966), 20:135–44.

Gendai Nihon Kirisuto kyō bungaku zenshū. 18 vols. Kyōbunkan, 1974.

Contains fiction and critical writings by Endō, Shimao, and many other modern Christian authors.

Hasegawa Izumi, ed. *Akutagawa Shō jiten. Kokubungaku Kaishaku to Kanshō* 42 (January 1977).

Hasegawa Izumi and Takeda Katsuhiko, eds. *Gendai shimbun shōsetsu jiten. Kokubungaku Kaishaku to Kanshō* 42 (December 1977).

Hattori Tatsu. *Warera ni totte bi wa sonzai suru ka.* Yasuoka Shōtarō, Endō Shūsaku, and Muramatsu Takeshi, eds., Shimbisha, 1968.

Hino Keizō. "Kaisetsu: Tanin o miru me." In Yasuoka Shōtarō, *Tonsō,* pp. 215–29. Ōbunsha, Ōbunsha Bunko, 1976.

Hirano Ken. *Bungei jihyō.* 2 vols. Kawade Shobō Shinsha, Kawade Bungei Sensho, 1978.

—— "Kaisetsu." In Endō Shūsaku, *Umi to dokuyaku,* pp. 159–64. Kadokawa Shoten, Kadokawa Bunko, 1960.

Hiroishi Renji. *Endō Shūsaku no subete.* Kōdansha, Endō Shūsaku Bunko, 1976.

Hisamatsu Sen'ichi, Teruoka Yasutaka, Yoshida Seiichi, Nishio Minoru, and Hosaka Hiroshi, eds. *Hennentai Nihon kindai bungaku shi. Kokubungaku* (February 1976), vol. 21.

Isoda Kōichi. "Kaisetsu." In Kojima Nobuo, *Hōyō kazoku,* pp. 241–58. Kōdansha, Kōdansha Bunko, 1971.

Itō Shinkichi et al., eds. *Nihon no shiika.* 31 vols. Chūō Kōron Sha, Chūkō Bunko, 1974.

Iwaya Seishō. *Shimao Toshio ron.* Kindai Bungei Sha, 1982.

Kikan Sōzō. Special issue on Endō Shūsaku. (April 1977), vol. 3.

Five critical articles on Endō, written by Inoue Yōji, Suzuki Hideko, Rizawa Yukio, and others.

Kikan Sōzō. Special issue on Shimao Toshio. (July 1977), vol. 4.

This issue contains five critical articles on Shimao, written by Matsubara Shin'ichi, Okuno Takeo, and others.

Kiyooka Takayuki. "Kaisetsu: Shūsai no kimyō na taida." In Yasuoka Shōtarō, *Aoba shigereru,* pp. 261–75. Ōbunsha, Ōbunsha Bunko, 1976.

Kojima Nobuo. *Amerikan sukūru.* Shinchōsha, Shinchō Bunko, 1967.

—— *Bungaku danshō.* Tōjusha, 1972.

—— "Bunrui—'Daisan no shinjin' to yobarete." In *Shimao Toshio, Yasuoka Shōtarō, Kojima Nobuo, Yoshiyuki Junnosuke shū.* Gendai Nihon Bungaku Taikei 90. Chikuma Shobō, 1972.

—— " 'Daisan no shinjin' to Amerika bungaku." *Bungei* (July 1965), 4:115–23.

—— *Happinesu.* Kōdansha, Kōdansha Bunko, 1977.

The commentary at the end of this volume is translated from a Ph.D. dissertation by Yukiko Tanaka: "Fiction of Kojima Nobuo: A Study of Its Development in the Historical Perspective of Modern Japanese Prose Narrative" (UCLA, 1977). Tanaka makes comparisons between Kojima and Saul Bellow.

—— *Ikyō no dōkeshi.* Mikasa Shobō, 1970.

—— *Jōheki/Hoshi.* Tōjusha, 1974.

—— "Kaisetsu." In Yasuoka Shōtarō, *Shichiya no nyōbō,* pp. 248–54. Shinchōsha, Shinchō Bunko, 1966.

—— *Kōen/Sotsugyō-shiki.* Tōjusha, 1974.

—— *Kojima Nobuo zenshū.* 6 vols. Kōdansha, 1971.

Though some of Kojima's better early stories (including "Kisha no naka") are inexplicably missing from this collection, Kojima's essays at the end of each volume are valuable, and the monthly bulletins include useful information by others.

Kojima Nobuso. *Shōsetsuka no hibi*. Tōjusha, 1971.

—— *Wakareru riyū*. 3 vols. Kōdansha, 1982.

Kokubungaku. Special issue on Yasuoka Shōtarō (August 1977), vol. 22.

Includes a dialogue between Yasuoka and Endō Shūsaku, and fifteen critical articles by Kiyooka Takayuki, Abe Akira, Hino Keizō, Okuno Takeo, Torii Kunio, and others.

Kokubungaku Kaishaku to Kanshō. Special issue on Yasuoka Shōtarō and Kojima Nobuo (February 1972), vol. 37.

Contains fourteen critical articles on Yasuoka by Ōkubo Tsuneo, Matsubara Shin'ichi, Isogai Hideo, and others; fourteen articles on Kojima, by critics such as Rizawa Yukio, Morikawa Tatsuya, Kawashima Itaru, and others.

Kokubungaku Kaishaku to Kanshō. Special issue on Endō Shūsaku (June 1975), vol. 40.

Twenty-five essays on Endō's work, by critics such as Muramatsu Takeshi, Rizawa Yukio, Sako Jun'ichirō, and others.

Kossori Endō Shūsaku. Special issue of *Omoshirohambun* on Endō Shūsaku. Vol. 16, no. 2 (January 1980).

Another three dozen essays, both casual and critical, as well as several previously unpublished short pieces by Endō.

Matsubara Shin'ichi. "Kaisetsu." In *Gendai Nihon Kirisuto kyō bungaku zenshū*. 18 vols. Kyōbunkan, 1974. Vol. 11: *Nichijō to katei*, pp. 267–93.

Matsubara Shin'ichi, Isoda Kōichi, and Akiyama Shun. *Sengo Nihon bungaku shi, nempyō*. Kōdansha, 1978.

Miyoshi Yukio, ed. *Nihon kindai bungaku kenkyū hikkei*. Gakutōsha, 1977.

Nihon Bungaku Kenkyū Shiryō Kankō Kai, eds., *Yasuoka Shōtarō, Yoshiyuki Junnosuke*. Yūseido, 1983.

A highly valuable collection of essays on these two writers, spanning most of their careers.

Ōe Kenzaburō. "Shimao Toshio: 'Kuzure' ni tsuite." In *Dōjidai toshite no sengo*. Kōdansha, 1973.

Ōhashi Kenzaburō, et al, eds. *Kojima Nobuo o meguru bungaku no genzai*. Fukutake Shoten, 1985.

Okuno Takeo. "Shimao Toshio no bungaku to yume." In *Shimao Toshio, Yasuoka Shōtarō, Kojima Nobuo, Yoshiyuki Junnosuke shū*. Gendai Nihon Bungaku Taikei 90. Chikuma Shobō, 1972.

Rizawa Yukio. "Kyūshinsei no soko ni aru mono: Kojima Nobuo ron." *Gunzō* (March 1969), 24:198–215.

Saeki Shōichi, ed. *Hihyō: '58–'70 bungaku-teki kessan*. Banchō Shobō, 1970.

—— "Kaisetsu." In *Yasuoka Shōtarō, Yoshiyuki Junnosuke, Sono Ayako shū*, pp. 492–507. Warera no Bungaku 12. Kōdansha, 1967.

—— " 'Kanashii me' no sōzōryoku." *Kokubungaku* (February 1973), 18:52–62.

Shimao Toshio. *Shima no hate*. Shūeisha, Shūeisha Bunko, 1978.

—— *Shi no toge, Shuppatsu wa tsui ni otozurezu*. Shinchō Gendai Bungaku 36. Shinchōsha, 1979.

—— *Shimao Toshio zenshū*. 17 vols. Shōbunsha, 1981.

—— *Shuppatsu wa tsui ni otozurezu*. Shinchōsha, Shinchō Bunko, 1973.

—— *Ware fukaki fuchi yori*. Shūeisha, Shūeisha Bunko, 1977.

—— *Yume no naka de no nichijō*. Shūeisha, Shūeisha Bunko, 1979.

Shimao Toshio and Yoshida Mitsuru. *Tokkō taiken to sengo*. Chūō Kōron Sha, Chūkō Bunko, 1981.

Shimaoka Akira et al., eds. *Sengoshi taikei*. 4 vols. San'ichi Shobō, 1970–71.

Shindō Junkō. *Bundan shiki*. Shūeisha, 1977.

Takahashi Takako. "Endō Shūsaku ron." *Hihyō* (August 1966), pp. 100–11.

Takeda Tomoju. *Endō Shūsaku no bungaku*. Seibunsha, 1975.

—— *Endō Shūsaku no sekai*. Kōdansha, 1971.

Torii Kunio. "Sengo bungaku ni okeru 'Daisan no shinjin' no ichi." *Nihon Kindai Bungaku* (October 1968), pp. 55–66.

Ueda Miyoji, Akiyama Shun, and Abe Akira. "Daisan no shinjin no kōzai." *Mita Bungaku* (January 1972), pp. 5–24.

Yamamoto Kenkichi. "Daisan no shinjin." *Bungakkai* (January 1953), 7:86–89.

—— "Kaisetsu." In Shimao Toshio, *Shi no toge,* pp. 506–14. Shinchōsha, Shinchō Bunko, 1981.

—— Hirano Ken, Usui Yoshimi, Sasaki Kiichi, and Takeuchi Yoshimi. "Daisan no shinjin, sengo bungaku, heiwa ron." *Kaizō* (February 1955), 36:158–68.

Yasuoka Shōtarō. *Boku no Shōwa-shi I*. Kōdansha, 1984.

—— *Bushō no akuma*. Kadokawa Shoten, Kadokawa Bunko, 1973.

—— *Garasu no kutsu*. Kadokawa Shoten, Kadokawa Bunko, 1974.

—— *Hashire Tomahōku*. Kōdansha, Kōdansha Bunko, 1977.

—— *Jijōden ryokō*. Kadokawa Shoten, Kadokawa Bunko, 1977.

—— *Mogura no kotoba*. Kōdansha, Kōdansha Bunko, 1973.

—— *Mogura no tebukuro*. Kadokawa Shoten, Kadokawa Bunko, 1977.

—— *Namakemono no shisō*. Kadokawa Shoten, Kadokawa Bunko, 1973.

—— *Nankotsu no seishin*. Kōdansha, Kōdansha Bunko, 1973.

—— *Ryōyū, akuyū*. Shinchōsha,Shinchō Bunko, 1973.

—— *Ryūritan*. 2 vols. Shinchōsha, 1981.

—— *Shisō onchi no shisō*. Kadokawa Shoten, Kadokawa Bunko, 1974.

—— *Tsuki wa higashi ni*. Shinchōsha, 1972.

—— *Yasegaman no shisō*. Kadokawa Shoten, Kadokawa Bunko, 1973.

—— *Yasuoka Shōtarō zenshū*. 7 vols. Kōdansha, 1971.

Yoshiyuki Junnosuke. *Watakushi no bungaku hōrō*. Kōdansha, Kōdansha Bunko, 1976.

Bibliography

Works in English

Brower, Robert H. and Earl Miner. *Japanese Court Poetry*. Stanford: Stanford University Press, 1961.

Cowley, Malcolm. *Exile's Return*. New York: Viking Press, 1951.

—— *A Second Flowering: Works and Days of the Lost Generation*. New York: Penguin, 1980.

Endō Shūsaku. "Fuda no Tsuji." Translated by Frank Hoff and James Kirkup. *Japan P.E.N. News* (January 1965), 14:1–9.

—— *The Golden Country*. Translated by Francis Mathy. Tokyo: Tuttle, 1970.

—— *A Life of Jesus*. Translated by Richard A. Schuchert. New York: Paulist Press, 1978.

—— "Mine." Translated by Peter W. Schumacher. *Japan Christian Quarterly* (1974), 40:205–13.

—— "Mothers." Translated by Francis Mathy. *Japan Christian Quarterly* (1974), 40:186–204.

—— *The Samurai*. Translated by Van C. Gessel. London: Peter Owen, 1982; New York: Harper and Row and Kodansha, 1983.

—— *Scandal*. Translated by Van C. Gessel. London: Peter Owen; New York: Dodd, Mead, 1988.

—— *The Sea and Poison*. Translated by Michael Gallagher. London: Peter Owen, 1972: Paperback, Tokyo: Tuttle, 1973.

—— "Shadow of a Man." Translated by Shoichi Ono and Sanford Goldstein. *Bulletin of the College of Biomedical Technology, Niigata University* (1983), 1:80–94.

—— *Silence*. Translated by William Johnston. Paperback. Tokyo: Sophia University and Tuttle, 1969.

—— *Stained Glass Elegies*. Translated by Van C. Gessel. London: Peter Owen, 1984; and New York: Dodd, Mead, 1985.

Contains translations of "Yonjussai no otoko," "Sono zenjitsu," "Fuda-no-Tsuji," "Unzen," "Watakushi no mono," "Iya na yatsu," "Hatsuharu yume no takarabune," "Osanajimitachi," "Ushirosugata," "Haha naru mono" and "Senchū-ha."

—— *Volcano*. Translated by Richard Schuchert. London: Peter Owen, 1978.

—— *When I Whistle*. Translated by Van C. Gessel. London: Peter Owen, 1979; New York: Taplinger, 1980.

—— *Wonderful Fool*. Translated by Francis Mathy. London: Peter Owen, 1974; New York: Harper and Row and Kodansha, 1984.

Fowler, Edward. *The Rhetoric of Confession: Shishōsetsu in Early Twentieth-Century Japanese Fiction*. Berkeley: University of California Press, 1988.

Gessel, Van C. "Endō Shūsaku: The Faces of a Modern Japanese Author." Unpublished essay, New York, 1975.

—— "War and Postwar in the Writings of Kojima Nobuo, Yasuoka Shōtarō, and Endō Shūsaku." *Transactions of the International Conference of Orientalists in Japan* (1978), 23:145–61.

—— "Voices in the Wilderness: Japanese Christian Authors." *Monumenta Nipponica* (Winter 1982), 37(4):437–57.

Gessel, Van C. and Tomone Matsumoto, eds. *The Shōwa Anthology: Modern Japanese Short Stories.* 2 vols. Tokyo: Kodansha International, 1985.

Includes translations of Kojima's "Hoshi," Shimao's "Maya to issho ni," Endō's "Sono zenjitsu," and Yasuoka's "Warui nakama."

Hall, Robert K., ed. *Kokutai no hongi.* Translated by John Owen Gauntlett. Cambridge: Harvard University Press, 1949.

Hibbett, Howard, ed. *Contemporary Japanese Literature.* New York: Knopf, 1977.

Includes translations of Yasuoka's "Aigan" by Edwin McClellan and Kojima's "Amerikan sukūru" by William F. Sibley.

Japanese Religion: A Survey by the Agency for Cultural Affairs. Tokyo: Kodansha International, 1972.

Katō, Shūichi. *A History of Japanese Literature.* 3 vols. Tokyo: Kodansha International, 1979–1983.

Kojima Nobuo. "Happiness." Translated by Yukiko Tanaka, with Elizabeth Hanson Warren. *Japan Quarterly* (October–December 1981), 28:533–48.

—— "Shōjū." Translated by Elizabeth Baldwin. In Robert Detweiler and Glenn Meeter, eds., *Faith and Fiction: The Modern Short Story.* Grand Rapids, MI: Eerdmans, 1979.

Kuwabara, Takeo. *Japan and Western Civilization: Essays on Comparative Culture.* Edited by Kato Hidetoshi; translated by Kano Tsutomu and Patricia Murphy. Tokyo: University of Tokyo Press, 1983.

Miner, Earl. *Japanese Linked Poetry.* Princeton: Princeton University Press, 1979.

Morris, Ivan. *The Nobility of Failure.* New York: New American Library, Meridian Books, 1975.

Passi, Herbert. *Society and Education in Japan.* New York: Teacher's College Press, 1965.

Scholes, Robert. *Semiotics and Interpretation.* New Haven: Yale University Press, 1982.

—— *Structuralism in Literature.* New Haven: Yale University Press, 1974.

Shimao Toshio. *"The Sting of Death" and Other Stories.* Translated, with an introduction and interpretive comments, by Kathryn Sparling. Michigan Papers in Japanese Studies, no. 12. Ann Arbor: University of Michigan Center for Japanese Studies, 1985.

Includes translations and critical comments on "Shi no toge," "Ware fukaki fuchi yori," "Nogare yuku kokoro," "Shima no hate," "Yume no naka de no nichijō," and "Sono natsu no ima wa."

Turnbull, Andrew, ed. *The Letters of F. Scott Fitzgerald.* New York: Dell, 1963.

Wills, Garry. "Embers of Guilt." *New York Review of Books,* February 19, 1981.

Yasuoka Shōtarō. "Circus Horse." Translated by Leon Zolbrod. *The East* (1965), 1:50–51.

—— "The Glass Slipper." Translated by Edward Seidensticker. *Japan Quarterly* (1961), 8:195–206.

—— "The Pawnbroker's Wife." Translated by Edward Seidensticker. In Yukio Mishima and Geoffrey Bownas, eds., *New Writing in Japan*. Penguin, 1972.

—— *A View by the Sea and Other Stories*. Translated by Kären Wigen Lewis. New York: Columbia University Press, 1984.

Includes translations of *Kaihen no kōkei,* "Inki na tanoshimi," "Warui nakama," "Aoba shigereru," "Ame," and "Ga."

Index

Abe Kōbō, 46. 148, 207; "Akai mayu," 141
Agawa Hiroyuki, 42
"Aikoku kōshinkyoku" (Patriotic March), 10-11
Akiyama Shun, 50
Akutagawa Prize, 38, 45, 46, 50, 51, 55, 73, 78, 123, 241
Akutagawa Ryūnosuke, 37
Albee, Edward, *Who's Afraid of Virginia Woolf?*, 216
Anderson, Sherwood, "The Egg," 104
"Aoba shigereru" (song), 92-93
Après-guerre faction, *see* Sengoha

Bernanos, Georges, 239, 270
"Biedermeyer style," 61-62
"Bivouac Song" (Roei no uta), 11-12
Bungakkai, 41, 47, 52
Byōsaimono (stories about an ailing wife), 151-152

Christianity, Japanese attitudes toward, 233-234, 302*n*1
Christian writers, Japanese, 74
Conceptions (journal), *see Kōsō*
Conceptions Society, (Kōsō no kai), 48*ff*, 53, 151
Coterie literary magazines *(dōnin zasshi)*, 37
Cowley, Malcolm, 285

Daisan no shinjin (Third Generation of New Writers), 5, 41, 102; breakdown of group, 53; differences between Sengoha and, 62-63; distance from Sengoha, 25; as eternal newcomers, 59-60; "exile" and, 54*ff*; Hattori Tatsu's defini tion of group characteristics, 61*ff*; 1960 Ampo riots and, 58; "Shinjin sakka bungaku o kataru," 42; "Shinsedai no sakkatachi," 60; *shi-shōsetsu* form and, 66*ff*
Dazai Osamu, 4, 25, 30, 48, 68
"Domestic novels," *see katei shōsetsu*
Dōnin zasshi (coterie literary magazines), 37
Dostoevsky, Fyodor, 25, 186; *Crime and Punishment,* 179; *Notes from Underground,* 136, 137

Endō Shūsaku: being Catholic during wartime, 19-20; Bernanos and, 239,

Endō Shūsaku (*continued*)
270; corporal punishment in schools, 14; Graham Greene and, 239; *Hizakurige* and, 234; hospitalized, 58; influence on Japanese Christian writers, 74; invited by Yasuoka to join Kōsō no kai, 50; Julien Greene and, 239; Marquis de Sade and, 243; Mauriac and, 239, 270; meetings of Kōsō no kai, 52-53, 55; mother figures in, 72; newspaper novels and, 51; novel length and, 62; postwar study abroad, 29; pranks and, 55-56; receives Akutagawa Prize, 51; relationship between man and God, 184; *senchū-ha* and, 239; submission of ego in fiction of, 288; Yoshimitsu Yoshihiko and, 239
——works: "Aden made," 50; *Aika,* 248, 249, 250, 258, 268; *Chimmoku,* 69, 72, 239, 242, 243, 248, 249-257, 258, 266, 268, 272, 273, 274, 280, 288; *Furansu no daigakusei,* 49; "Haha naru mono," 72, 257-267; *Iesu no shōgai,* 253; "Iya na yatsu," 236-239; *Kiiroi hito,* 241-242; *Kuchibue o fuku toki,* 238, 267; *Obakasan,* 72, 267; *Ryūgaku,* 243; *Samurai,* 238, 239, 248, 273-280, 288; *Shiroi hito,* 50, 241; "Sono zenjitsu," 248, 262; *Umi to dokuyaku,* 57, 268; "Watakushi no mono," 244-248, 257-258; *Watashi ga suteta onna,* 72, 267-272, 280
Erikson, Erik H., 69
Etō Jun, 50, 69, 210, 219; *Seijuku to sōshitsu,* 69-70

Faust (Goethe), 179
Fitzgerald, F. Scott, "Babylon Revisited," 27; *Tender is the Night,* 164
Fukuda Tsuneari, 296*n*61
Futabatei Shimei, *Ukigumo,* 35, 36, 193, 215, 216, 217

Geijutsu Senshō, 57
Gendai Hyōron, 50
Genji monogatari, 24, 35
Gilbert, William S., 97
Gogol, Nikolai, 24, 185-186
Gomi Yasusuke, 43, 45
Greene, Graham, 239; *The Power and the Glory,* 242
Greene, Julien, 239

Hagakure, 24, 292*n*31
Haley, Alex, *Roots,* 123
Haniya Yutaka, *Shirei,* 40
Hattori Tatsu, 7, 60-66
Henshall, Kenneth G., 295*n*61
Hino Keizō, 50
Hirano Ken, 47
Hitomaro, 36
Hotta Yoshie, 25

Ichi-ni-kai (One-Two Association), 44*ff*
Inoue Hisashi, 74, 183
Ishihara Shintarō, 51, 54
Ishikawa Tatsuzō, 47
Itō Keiichi, 42
Iwano Hōmei, 286

Japanese Literature Patriotic Association, (Nihon Bungaku Hōkokukai), 37
Jippensha Ikku, *Tōkaidōchū Hizakurige,* 234
Joyce, James, 226

Kafka, Franz, 186
Kaikō, Ken, 55
kakure (hidden Christians), 258-266 *passim*
Kambayashi Akatsuki, 68
Kanagaki Robun, *Aguranabe,* 193
Kasai Zenzō, 67
katei shōsetsu ("domestic novels"), 31, 58, 60, 70
Kawabata Yasunari, 6, 25, 37, 49; *Yama no oto,* 38
Keene, Dennis, 300*n*20
Kenne, Donald, 300*n*16
Kenyūsha, 37
Kindai Bungaku, 39, 44, 47, 48-49, 51, 52, 60
Kitahara Takeo, 55
Kojima Nobuo: "classical Japanese literature" and, 24; cynicism in fiction of, 272; discussion topics at Ichi-ni-kai, 44; Dostoevsky and, 186; English language and, 15-16; family tragedies and fiction, 148; fictional settings in wartime brothels, 64; Futabatei and, 193, 215, 216, 217; *Gendai Hyōron* critics and, 50; Gogol and, 24, 185-186; Hattori's list and, 65; influence of American experience on writings of, 55; influence on later writ-

ers, 73, 74; Kafka and, 186; *katei shōsetsu* and, 58; leaves for America, 54; malfunctioning protagonists in fiction of, 287; military training, 15-16; novel length and, 62; pessimism from war experience, 235; postwar and, 28-29; Saroyan and, 186-187; satire and, 30, 74, 183; selected as member of Ichi-ni-kai, 43; Thackeray and, 185; uniqueness in Ichi-ni kai, 45
——works: "American sukūru," 71, 187, 204, 208-211, 214; "Bishō," 202-207, 214; *Bohimei,* 188, 194-195; "Hoshi," 183, 188-195, 208, 209; *Hōyō kazoku,* 69, 71, 108, 207, 214, 215-230, 287; "Kisha no naka," 183, 186, 187, 196-202, 207, 208, 214, 219, 226; "Nikutai to seishin," 202; "Uma," 207, 211-214, 219; *Wakareru riyū,* 219
Kokka sōdōinhō (National General Mobilization Law), 12
Kokutai no hongi, 9
Kondō Keitarō, 44, 46
Kōno Taeko, 73
Kōsō (Conceptions), 49, 52
Kōsō no kai (Conceptions Society), 48*ff,* 53, 151
Kusunoki Masashige, 92-94
Kusunoki Masatsura, 92-94

Lippit, Noriko Mizuta, 300*n*27
Literary groups, prewar, 35*ff*
"Lost Generation," 285

Man'yōshū, 25
Maruya Saiichi, 74
Marxism, 23
Matsuo Bashō, 147
Mauriac, Francois, 239, 270
Medea (Euripides), 179
Miller, Arthur, 174; *After the Fall,* 164-165
Mishima Yukio, 30, 46, 48
Miura Shumon, 42, 43, 44, 56, 58, 65, 74
Miyamoto Yuriko, 39
Morals education (Shūshin), 9
Mori Ōgai, 36
Mori Reiko, 74
Mother, in Third Generation fiction, 70
Mouloudji, Marcel, 123
Muramatsu Takeshi, 48, 50
Murasaki Shikibu, 35

Nagai Kafū, 6, 25, 37, 49
Nakamura Shin'ichirō, 39
National General Mobilization Law (Kokka sōdōinhō), 12
Natsume Sōseki, 71; *Kokoro,* 137, 158; *Mon,* 24
Naturalism, 37, 39, 67
Neoaesthetics, 37
Neosensationalists, 37
Newspaper novels, 51
Nihon Bungaku Hōkokukai (Japanese Literature Patriotic Association), 37
Noma Hiroshi, 48, 62, 64; *Shinkū chitai,* 40
Noma Prize, 57

Ōba Minako, 73
Ochiai Naobumi, 92
Ōe Kenzaburō, 55, 66, 73, 148, 300*n*15; "Sora no kaibutsu Aguii," 158
Ōhara Tomie, 74
Okuno Takeo, 48, 50
One-Two Association (Ichi-ni kai), 44*ff*
Ōoka Shōhei, 48, 57, 64; *Nobi,* 40
Ozaki Kōyō, 58

Passin, Herbert, 9
Patriotic songs, 10-12
"Patriotic March," ("Aikoku kōshinkyoku"), 10-11
Pilgrim's Progress (Bunyan), 235
Proletarian literature, 37, 38, 49

Renga (linked verse), 36
Rensaku (linked prose), 62
Romanticism, 37
Rōnin, 94

Sade, Marquis de (Comte Donatien Alphonse François de Sade), 243
Saeki Shōichi, 244, 285
Sakaguchi Ango, "Hakuchi," 198
Sakata Hiroo, 74
Saroyan, William, 186-187
Scholes, Robert, 237, 299*n*23
Sei Shōnagon, 91

Senchū-ha (war generation), 4, 23, 239
Sengoha (après-guerre faction), 23, 25-26, 39, 62-63
Shiga Naoya, 31, 58, 67, 143, 178; *An'ya kōro,* 3; "Han no hanzai," 184; "Kozō no kamisama," 184
Shiina Rinzō, 48
Shimao Toshio: anomaly in Ichi-ni-kai, 45-46; battle of the literary ego in fiction of, 287; baptized a Catholic, 30; Conceptions Society friends, 151; death, missed appointments with, 20-21, 129; defection from Kōsō no kai, 53-54; deification of wife characters, 71; *Gendai Hyōron* critics and, 50; influence on later writers, 73; *katei shōsetsu* and, 58; physical infirmity as metaphor, 205; postwar confusion, 29-30; relationship between man and God, 184; *rensaku* and, 62; selected for Ichi-ni-kai, 43; self-denial in fiction of, 272; solitary wanderers in fiction of, 207; suicide squadrons, 19; "them" as the enemy, 235; volunteerism in wartime, 18-19; wartime censorship, 12-13; wife's insanity, 30; works on magazine *Kōki* with Mishima, 46
——works: "Haishi," 132-134; "Kisōsha no yūutsu," 148-151; "Maya to issho ni," 136, 152-158; *Shi no toge,* 71, 158-179; "Shuppatsu wa tsui ni otozurezu," 128-129, 177; "Tandoku ryokōsha," 135-141, 142, 144; "Tsuma e no inori," 152; "Ware fukaki fuchi yori," 151-152; "Yume no naka de no nichijō," 141-148, 155
Shimao Miho, 71, 130-131
Shimazaki Tōson, 58, 67, 178; *Ie,* 217
Shinchō, 47, 55
Shindō-Junkō, 39, 44, 48, 56
Shinran, 254
Shinyō (torpedo boats), 127
Shirakaba-ha, 37, 49
Shi-shōsetsu ("I-novel"), ix, 3, 5, 39-40, 61, 66-69, 73, 74, 80, 109, 112, 124, 143, 151, 177, 185, 286, 288
Shōno Junzō, 46, 47, 54, 55, 58, 65, 295*n*37, 296*n*64
Shūshin (morals education), 9
Sono Ayako, 65, 74
Sparling, Kathryn, 292*n*31
Suzuki Susumu, 43

Taiheiki, 94
Takadō Kaname, 257
Takahashi Takako, 74
Takeda Shigetarō, 42, 43
Takeda Taijun, 39, 45, 48
Takeda Tomoju, 295*n*55
Tamenaga Shunsui, 25
Tanizaki Jun'ichirō, 6, 37, 64; *Sasameyuki,* 25, 38
Tayama Katai, 67
Thackeray, William, 185
Third Generation of New Writers, *see* Daisan no shinjin
Third Man, The (film), 41
Togaeri Hajime, 51
Tokutomi Roka, 58
Tsushima Yūko, 74

uchi/soto, 134-135, 149
Ueda Miyoji, 50
Usui Yoshimi, 41, 294*n*35

Wife, in Third Generation fiction, 71
Wiley, Richard, 301*n*7

Yamamoto Kenkichi, 41, 44, 47-48, 61
Yashiro Seiichi, 74
Yasuoka Shōtarō: absurdity of military life, 188; birthdate, 77; co-translates *Roots,* 123; differences between Third Generation and Sengoha, 25-26; end of war, 21-22; Endō's pranks and, 56; entrance exams and Hitler, 7-8; failures in the fiction of, 235; family tragedies and fiction, 143, 148; father's profession, 16; fictional settings in military latrines, 64; Fūten Club, 17; Gomi Yasusuke and, 45; "Grand Illusion" banned, 8-9; Hattori's list and, 65; intestinal problems as literary metaphor, 64, 141; invites Endō to join Conceptions Society, 50; Kojima Nobuo on, 104; learning Edo style chanting, 17; learning French, 13-14; leaves for Nashville, 58; loss of home, 6; meetings of Kōsō no kai, 55; mother figures in fiction of, 70; muted despair

in fiction of, 272; newcomer to Ichi-ni-kai, 44; newspaper novels, 51; Ōe Kenzaburō and, 73; parents, 78; postwar idleness, 28; receives Akutagawa Prize, 46, 78; repatriation, 22-23; selection of Ichi-ni-kai members, 43; "Shinjin sakka bungaku o kataru" symposium, 42; *shishōsetsu* and, 80; short stories and, 62; splitting of narrative ego in fiction of, 286-287; translates Mouloudj, 123; use of *kana,* 172; war experience, 17-18; Yoshioka character in Endō's *Watashi ga suteta onna* and, 303*n*27

——works: "Aigan," 105; "Aoba shigeru," 85-95; "Inki na tanoshimi," 46, 78; *Kaihen no kōkei,* 57, 64, 69, 70, 78, 104, 108-120, 121-122; "Katei," 95; "Kembu," 104-107; "Kokyō," 79; *Maku ga orite kara,* 120-121, 123; "Mogura no tebukuro," 108; *Ryūritan,* 123-124; "Sābisu daitai yōin," 47; *Shita dashi tenshi,* 57; "Shukudai," 80-84, 108; *Tonsō,* 95-104; *Tsuki wa higashi ni,* 120, 122-123; "Utsukushii hitomi," 79; "Warui nakama," 46

Yosa Buson, 122

Yoshimitsu Yoshihiko, 20, 239

Yoshiyuki Junnosuke, 23-24, 41, 42, 43, 50, 55, 56, 58-59, 62, 65; "Shūu," 47, 296*n*64, 303*n*27

OTHER WORKS IN THE COLUMBIA ASIAN STUDIES SERIES

Modern Asian Literature Series

Modern Japanese Drama: An Anthology, ed. and tr. Ted Takaya. Also in paperback ed. 1979

Mask and Sword: Two Plays for the Contemporary Japanese Theater, by Yamazaki Masakazu, tr. J. Thomas Rimer 1980

Yokomitsu Riichi, Modernist, by Dennis Keene 1980

Nepali Visions, Nepali Dreams: The Poetry of Laxmiprasad Devkota, tr. David Rubin 1980

Literature of the Hundred Flowers, vol. 1: *Criticism and Polemics*, ed. Hualing Nieh 1981

Literature of the Hundred Flowers, vol. 2: *Poetry and Fiction*, ed. Hualing Nieh 1981

Modern Chinese Stories and Novellas, 1919–1949, ed. Joseph S. M. Lau, C. T. Hsia, and Leo Ou-fan Lee. Also in paperback ed. 1984

A View by the Sea, by Yasuoka Shōtarō, tr. Kären Wigen Lewis 1984

Other Worlds: Arishima Takeo and the Bounds of Modern Japanese Fiction, by Paul Anderer 1984

Selected Poems of Sŏ Chŏngju, tr. with intro. by David R. McCann 1989

The Sting of Life: Four Contemporary Japanese Novelists, by Van C. Gessel 1989

Translations from the Oriental Classics

Major Plays of Chikamatsu, tr. Donald Keene. Also in paperback ed.

Four Major Plays of Chikamatsu, tr. Donald Keene. Paperback text edition

Records of the Grand Historian of China, translated from the Shih chi of Ssu-ma Ch'ien, tr. Burton Watson, 2 vols.

Instructions for Practical Living and Other Neo-Confucian Writings by Wang Yang-ming, tr. Wing-tsit Chan

Chuang Tzu: Basic Writings, tr. Burton Watson, paperback ed. only

The Mahābhārata, tr. Chakravarthi V. Narasimhan. Also in paperback ed.

The Manyōshū, Nippon Gakujutsu Shinkōkai edition

Su Tung-p'o: Selections from a Sung Dynasty Poet, tr. Burton Watson. Also in paperback ed.

Bhartrihari: Poems, tr. Barbara Stoler Miller. Also in paperback ed.

Basic Writings of Mo Tzu, Hsün Tzu, and Han Fei Tzu, tr. Burton Watson. Also in separate paperback eds.

The Awakening of Faith, Attributed to Aśvaghosha, tr. Yoshito S. Hakeda. Also in paperback ed.

Reflections on Things at Hand: The Neo-Confucian Anthology, comp. Chu Hsi and Lü Tsu-Ch'ien, tr. Wing-tsit Chan

The Platform Sutra of the Sixth Patriarch, tr. Philip B. Yampolsky. Also in paperback ed.

Essays in Idleness: The Tsurezuregusa of Kenkō, tr. Donald Keene. Also in paperback ed.

The Pillow Book of Sei Shōnagon, tr. Ivan Morris, 2 vols.

Two Plays of Ancient India: The Little Clay Cart and the Minister's Seal, tr. J. A. B. van Buitenen

The Complete Works of Chuang Tzu, tr. Burton Watson

The Romance of the Western Chamber (Hsi Hsiang chi), tr. S. I. Hsiung. Also in paperback ed.

The Manyōshū, Nippon Gakujutsu Shinkōkai edition. Paperback text edition

Records of the Historian: Chapters from the Shih chi of Ssu-ma Ch'ien. Paperback text edition, tr. Burton Watson

Cold Mountain: 100 Poems by the T'ang Poet Han-shan, tr. Burton Watson. Also in paperback ed.

Twenty Plays of the Nō Theatre, ed. Donald Keene. Also in paperback ed.

Chūshingura: The Treasury of Loyal Retainers, tr. Donald Keene. Also in paperback ed.

The Zen Master Hakuin: Selected Writings, tr. Philip B. Yampolsky 1971
Chinese Rhyme-Prose: Poems in the Fu Form from the Han and Six Dynasties Periods, tr. Burton Watson. Also in paperback ed. 1971
Kūkai: Major Works, tr. Yoshito S. Hakeda. Also in paperback ed. 1972
The Old Man Who Does as He Pleases: Selections from the Poetry and Prose of Lu Yu, tr. Burton Watson 1973
The Lion's Roar of Queen Śrīmālā, tr. Alex and Hideko Wayman 1974
Courtier and Commoner in Ancient China: Selections from the History of the Former Han by Pan Ku, tr. Burton Watson. Also in paperback ed. 1974
Japanese Literature in Chinese, vol. 1: *Poetry and Prose in Chinese by Japanese Writers of the Early Period,* tr. Burton Watson 1975
Japanese Literature in Chinese, vol. 2: *Poetry and Prose in Chinese by Japanese Writers of the Later Period,* tr. Burton Watson 1976
Scripture of the Lotus Blossom of the Fine Dharma, tr. Leon Hurvitz. Also in paperback ed. 1976
Love Song of the Dark Lord: Jayaveda's Gītagovinda, tr. Barbara Stoler Miller. Also in paperback ed. Cloth ed. includes critical text of the Sanskrit. 1977
Ryōkan: Zen Monk-Poet of Japan, tr. Burton Watson 1977
Calming the Mind and Discerning the Real: From the Lam rim chen mo of Tsoṅ-kha-pa, tr. Alex Wayman 1978
The Hermit and the Love-Thief: Sanskrit Poems of Bhartrihari and Bilhaṇa, tr. Barbara Stoler Miller 1978
The Lute: Kao Ming's P'i-p'a chi, tr. Jean Mulligan. Also in paperback ed. 1980
A Chronicle of Gods and Sovereigns: Jinnō Shōtōki of Kitakabe Chikafusa, tr. H. Paul Varley 1980
Among the Flowers: The Hua-chien chi, tr. Lois Fusek 1982
Grass Hill: Poems and Prose by the Japanese Monk Gensei, tr. Burton Watson 1983
Doctors, Diviners, and Magicians of Ancient China: Biographies of Fang-shih, tr. Kenneth J. DeWoskin. Also in paperback ed. 1983
Theater of Memory: The Plays of Kālidāsa, ed. Barbara Stoler Miller. Also in paperback ed. 1984
The Columbia Book of Chinese Poetry: From Early Times to the Thirteenth Century, ed. and tr. Burton Watson. Also in paperback ed. 1984
Poems of Love and War: From the Eight Anthologies and the Ten Songs of Classical Tamil, tr. A. K. Ramanujan. Also in paperback ed. 1985
The Columbia Book of Later Chinese Poetry, ed. and tr. Jonathan Chaves. Also in paperback ed. 1986

Companions to Asian Studies

Approaches to the Oriental Classics, ed. Wm. Theodore de Bary 1959
Early Chinese Literature, by Burton Watson. Also in paperback ed. 1962
Approaches to Asian Civilization, ed. Wm. Theodore de Bary and Ainslie T. Embree 1964
The Classic Chinese Novel: A Critical Introduction, by C. T. Hsia. Also in paperback ed. 1968
Chinese Lyricism: Shih Poetry from the Second to the Twelfth Century, tr. Burton Watson. Also in paperback ed. 1971
A Syllabus of Indian Civilization, by Leonard A. Gordon and Barbara Stoler Miller 1971
Twentieth-Century Chinese Stories, ed. C. T. Hsia and Joseph S. M. Lau. Also in paperback ed. 1971
A Syllabus of Chinese Civilization, by J. Mason Gentzler, 2d ed. 1972
A Syllabus of Japanese Civilization, by H. Paul Varley, 2d ed. 1972
An Introduction to Chinese Civilization, ed. John Meskill, with the assistance of J. Mason Gentzler 1973
An Introduction to Japanese Civilization, ed. Arthur E. Tiedemann 1974
Ukifune: Love in the Tale of Genji, ed. Andrew Pekarik 1982
The Pleasures of Japanese Literature, by Donald Keene 1988
A Guide to Oriental Classics, ed. Wm. Theodore de Bary and Ainslie T. Embree; third edition ed. Amy Vladek Heinrich 1989

Neo-Confucian Studies

Instructions for Practical Living and Other Neo-Confucian Writings by Wang Yang-ming, tr. Wing-tsit Chan 1963
Reflections on Things at Hand: The Neo-Confucian Anthology, comp. Chu Hsi and Lü Tsu-ch'ien, tr. Wing-tsit Chan 1967
Self and Society in Ming Thought, by Wm. Theodore de Bary and the Conference on Ming Thought. Also in paperback ed. 1970
The Unfolding of Neo-Confucianism, by Wm. Theodore de Bary and the Conference on Seventeenth-Century Chinese Thought. Also in paperback ed. 1975
Principle and Practicality: Essays in Neo-Confucianism and Practical Learning, ed. Wm. Theodore de Bary and Irene Bloom. Also in paperback ed. 1979
The Syncretic Religion of Lin Chao-en, by Judith A. Berling 1980
The Renewal of Buddhism in China: Chu-hung and the Late Ming Synthesis, by Chun-fang Yu 1981

Neo-Confucian Orthodoxy and the Learning of the Mind-and-Heart, by Wm. Theodore de Bary 1981
Yüan Thought: Chinese Thought and Religion Under the Mongols, ed. Hok-lam Chan and Wm. Theodore de Bary 1982
The Liberal Tradition in China, by Wm. Theodore de Bary 1983
The Development and Decline of Chinese Cosmology, by John B. Henderson 1984
The Rise of Neo-Confucianism in Korea, by Wm. Theodore de Bary and JaHyun Kim Haboush 1985
Chiao Hung and the Restructuring of Neo-Confucianism in the Late Ming, by Edward T. Ch'ien 1985
Neo-Confucian Terms Explained: Pei-hsi tzu-i, by Ch'en Ch'un, ed. and trans. Wing-tsit Chan 1986
Knowledge Painfully Acquired: K'un-chih chi, by Lo Ch'in-shun, ed. and trans. Irene Bloom 1987
To Become a Sage: The Ten Diagrams on Sage Learning, by Yi T'oegye, ed. and trans. Michael C. Kalton 1988
The Message of the Mind in Neo-Confucianism, by Wm. Theodore de Bary 1989

Studies in Oriental Culture

1. *The Ōnin War: History of Its Origins and Background, with a Selective Translation of the Chronicle of Ōnin,* by H. Paul Varley 1967
2. *Chinese Government in Ming Times: Seven Studies,* ed. Charles O. Hucker 1969
3. *The Actors' Analects (Yakusha Rongo),* ed. and tr. by Charles J. Dunn and Bungō Torigoe 1969
4. *Self and Society in Ming Thought,* by Wm. Theodore de Bary and the Conference on Ming Thought. Also in paperback ed. 1970
5. *A History of Islamic Philosophy,* by Majid Fakhry, 2d ed. 1983
6. *Phantasies of a Love Thief: The Caurapañcāśikā Attributed to Bilhaṇa,* by Barbara Stoler Miller 1971
7. *Iqbal: Poet-Philosopher of Pakistan,* ed. Hafeez Malik 1971
8. *The Golden Tradition: An Anthology of Urdu Poetry,* by Ahmed Ali. Also in paperback ed. 1973
9. *Conquerors and Confucians: Aspects of Political Change in the Late Yuan China,* by John W. Dardess 1973
10. *The Unfolding of Neo-Confucianism,* by Wm. Theodore de Bary and the Conference on Seventeenth-Century Chinese Thought. Also in paperback ed. 1975
11. *To Acquire Wisdom: The Way of Wang Yang-ming,* by Julia Ching 1976

12. *Gods, Priests, and Warriors: The Bhṛgus of the Mahābhārata*, by Robert P. Goldman 1977
13. *Mei Yao-ch'en and the Development of Early Sung Poetry*, by Jonathan Chaves 1976
14. *The Legend of Semimaru, Blind Musician of Japan*, by Susan Matisoff 1977
15. *Sir Sayyid Ahmad Khan and Muslim Modernization in India and Pakistan*, by Hafeez Malik 1980
16. *The Khilafat Movement: Religious Symbolism and Political Mobilization in India*, by Gail Minault 1980
17. *The World of K'ung Shang-jen: A Man of Letters in Early Ch'ing China*, by Richard Strassberg 1983
18. *The Lotus Boat: The Origins of Chinese Tz'u Poetry in T'ang Popular Culture*, by Marsha L. Wagner 1984
19. *Expressions of Self in Chinese Culture*, ed. Robert E. Hegel and Richard C. Hessney 1985
20. *Songs for the Bride: Women's Voices and Wedding Rites of Rural India*, by W. G. Archer, ed. Barbara Stoler Miller and Mildred Archer 1986
21. *A Heritage of Kings: One Man's Monarchy in the Confucian World*, by JaHyun Kim Haboush 1988

Introduction to Oriental Civilizations
Wm. Theodore de Bary, Editor

Sources of Japanese Tradition 1958; paperback ed., 2 vols., 1964
Sources of Indian Tradition 1958; paperback ed., 2 vols., 1964; second edition, 1988
Sources of Chinese Tradition 1960; paperback ed., 2 vols., 1964